MICROSOFT® OFFICE BUSINESS SIMULATION BASICS

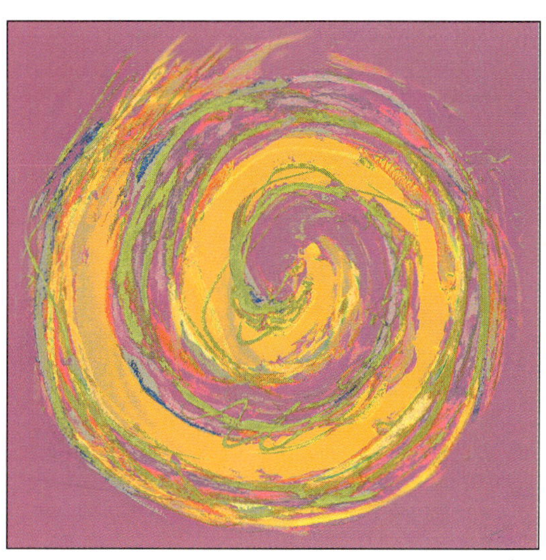

H. Albert Napier

Phillip J. Judd

THOMSON

COURSE TECHNOLOGY

Australia • Canada • Mexico • Singapore • Spain • United Kingdom • United States

Microsoft® Office Business Simulation BASICS

By H. Albert Napier and Phillip J. Judd

Senior Vice President
Chris Elkhill

Managing Editor
Chris Katsaropoulos

Senior Product Manager
Dave Lafferty

Product Marketing Manager
Kim Ryttel

Associate Product Manager
Jodi Dreissig

Development Editor
Anne Chimenti
Custom Editorial Productions, Inc.

Production Editor
Jean Findley
Custom Editorial Productions, Inc.

Compositor
GEX Publishing Services

Printer
Banta—Menasha

Get Back to the Basics...
With these *exciting new products*

Our exciting new series of short concepts and application suite books will provide everything needed to learn this software.

NEW! Microsoft Office Business Simulation BASICS, by Napier and Judd
20+ hours of instruction for capstone projects

0-619-18287-3   Textbook, Soft Bound Cover
0-619-18288-1   Instructor Resource CD-ROM
0-619-18293-8   Review Pack (Data CD)

NEW! Computer Concepts BASICS, by Wells and Ambrose
35+ hours of instruction for additional projects on computer concepts

0-619-05578-2   Textbook, Hard Spiral Bound Cover
0-619-18295-4   Textbook, Soft Perfect Bound Cover
0-619-05581-2   Activities Workbook
0-619-05579-0   Instructor Resource CD-ROM
0-619-05580-4   Review Pack (Data CD)

Computer Projects BASICS, by Korb
35+ hours of instruction for additional projects on all software applications

0-619-05987-7   Textbook, Soft Spiral Bound Cover
0-619-05988-5   Instructor Resource CD-ROM

Internet BASICS, by Barksdale, Rutter, & Teeter
35+ hours of instruction for beginning through intermediate features

0-619-05905-2   Textbook, Soft Spiral Bound Cover
0-619-05906-0   Instructor Resource CD-ROM
0-619-05907-9   Review Pack (Data CD)

Microsoft OfficeXP BASICS, by Morrison
35+ hours of instruction for beginning through intermediate features

0-619-05908-7   Textbook, Hard Spiral Bound Cover
0-619-05906-0   Instructor Resource CD-ROM
0-619-05909-5   Activities Workbook
0-619-05911-7   Review Pack (Data CD)

How to Use This Book

What makes a good computer instructional text? Sound pedagogy and the most current, complete materials. Not only will you find an inviting layout, but also many features to enhance learning.

Objectives— Objectives are listed at the beginning of each lesson, along with a suggested time for completion of the lesson. This allows you to look ahead to what you will be learning and to pace your work.

Step-by-Step Exercises—Preceded by a short topic discussion, these exercises are the "hands-on practice" part of the lesson. Simply follow the steps, either using a data file or creating a file from scratch. Each lesson is a series of these step-by-step exercises.

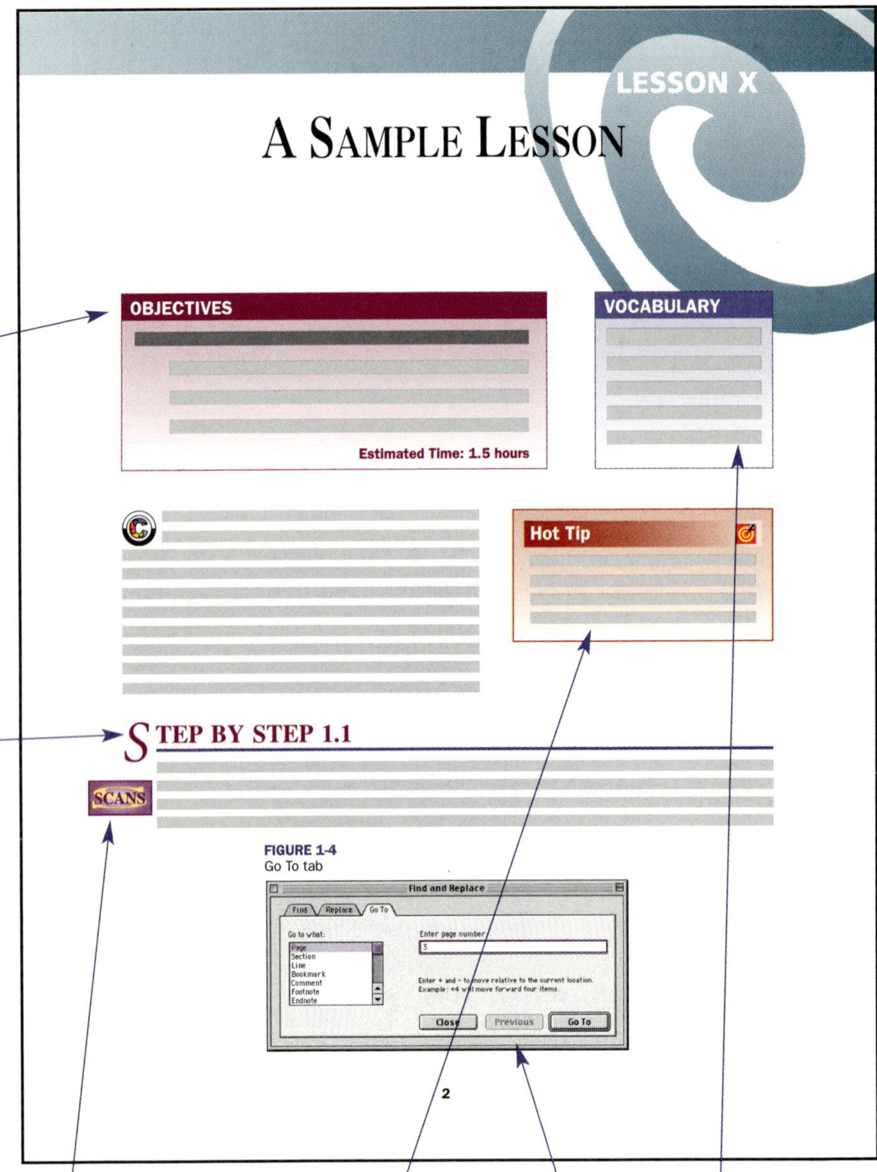

SCANS—(Secretary's Commission on Achieving Necessary Skills)—The U.S. Department of Labor has identified the school-to-careers competencies.

Marginal Boxes— These boxes provide additional information, such as Hot Tips, fun facts (Did You Know?), Computer Concepts, Internet Web sites, Extra Challenges activities, and Teamwork ideas.

Vocabulary—Terms identified in boldface throughout the lesson and summarized at the end.

Enhanced Screen Shots—Screen shots now come to life on each page with color and depth.

How to Use This Book

Summary—At the end of each lesson, you will find a summary to prepare you to complete the end-of-lesson activities.

Vocabulary/Review Questions—Review material at the end of each lesson and each unit enables you to prepare for assessment of the content presented.

Lesson Projects—End-of-lesson hands-on application of what has been learned in the lesson allows you to actually apply the techniques covered.

Critical Thinking Activities—Each lesson gives you an opportunity to apply creative analysis and use various resources to solve problems.

End-of-Unit Projects—End-of-unit hands-on application of concepts learned in the unit provides opportunity for a comprehensive review.

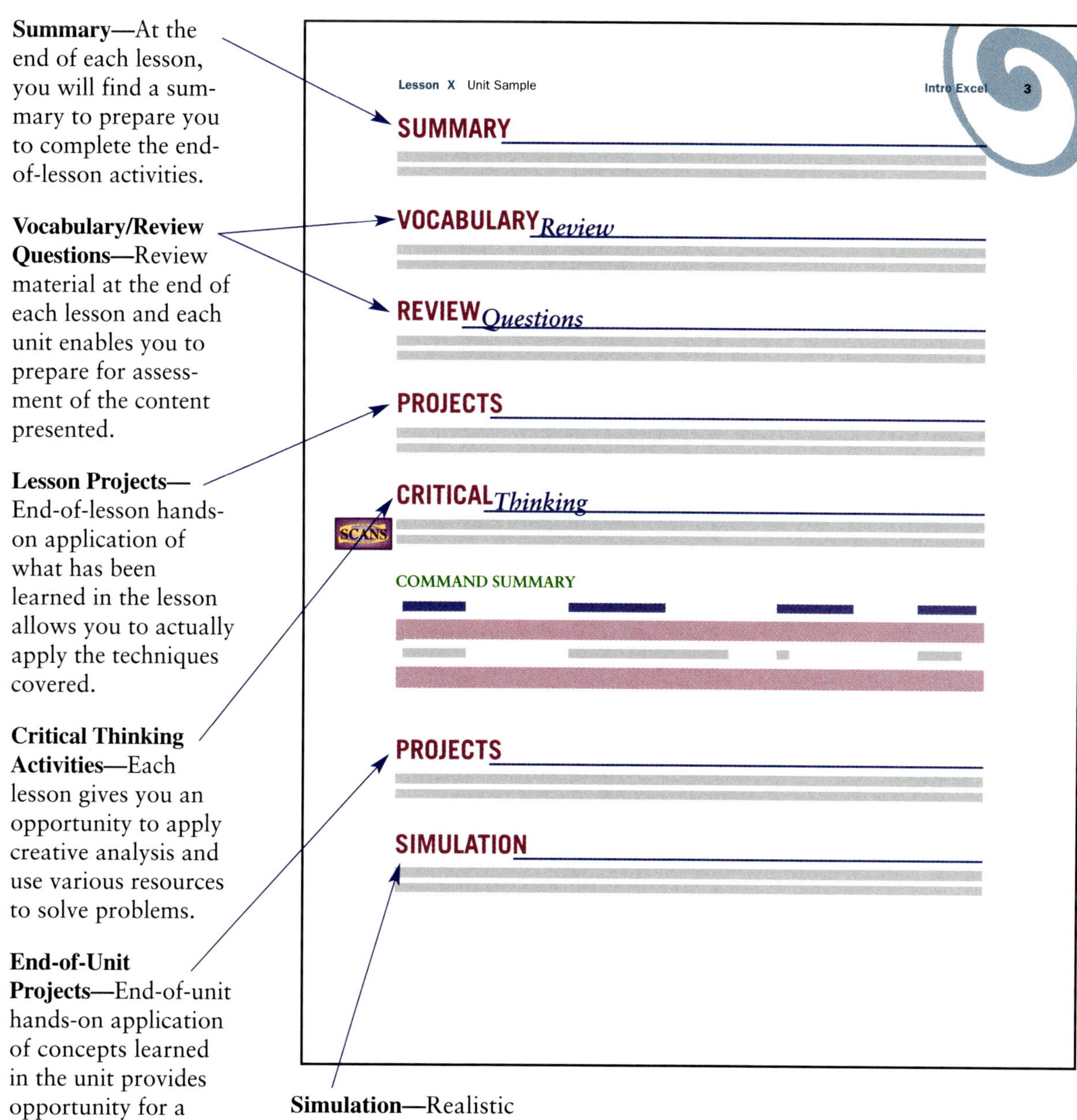

Simulation—Realistic simulation jobs are provided at the end of each unit, reinforcing the material covered in the unit.

PREFACE

One of the most common questions learners may ask themselves and their instructor is: "How does what I'm learning relate to what I'll be doing in a real job?" In a course designed to teach such practical skills as how to create documents with a word-processing application or how to perform calculations in a worksheet application, the answer seems obvious. But this answer doesn't go far enough. It addresses specific technical skills, but not necessarily how these skills are actually applied on the job.

Microsoft Office Business Simulation BASICS is designed not only to test the learner's mastery of the core Office XP or Office 2000 technical skills, but also to challenge the learner to use those skills in a hypothetical work setting. As the administrative assistant to the president of Wilderness Treks, Inc., a company that sells backcountry and adventure travel packages, the learner completes 20+ hours of assignments (not including the Advanced Challenge assignment or the additional end-of-job and end-of-unit activities) spread out over four business weeks leading up to an important annual marketing conference. These assignments draw on the Office XP or 2000 core skills the learner has already developed. Because the learner is expected to complete tasks similar to those that may be assigned in the workplace, there is more to do than execute a series of steps on the computer. For example, the learner will be asked to go beyond the confines of the information supplied in this text and the files on the learner data disk to complete business-related Internet and critical thinking assignments.

Perhaps the most important resource available to the learner as he or she works through the assignments for each week is imagination. In some cases, the course of action the learner should take is obvious. But in others, where the learner is asked to solve a problem, do research, or initiate a project, he or she must imagine situations as they might occur in the workplace and think the issues through independently.

Use, Organization, and Features

Because this text is a business simulation, the authors assume that learners are currently taking or have already taken a basic Microsoft Office XP or Office 2000 course. It is also assumed that learners are already familiar with the basic features of the Word, Excel, PowerPoint, Access, and Outlook applications and how to create basic documents, worksheets, presentations, and databases. *Microsoft Office Business Simulation BASICS* is appropriate as a supplemental text or an end-of-course project as part of a basic Microsoft Office XP or Office 2000 course. It is also appropriate for use in a computer lab or as a Word, Excel, PowerPoint, or Access Microsoft Office Specialist (MOS) core certification review course.

Microsoft Office Business Simulation BASICS is organized into four units, each unit representing one business week of assignments in the learner's job as administrative assistant. Each business week consists of six independent jobs, and each job consists of activities related to the preparation for the Wilderness Treks, Inc., annual marketing conference.

Unit 1 Business Week 1: Correspondence, Memos, and Reports

In this unit, the Wilderness Treks, Inc., organizational structure and its products and services are introduced. The responsibilities assigned to an administrative assistant for a top-level executive are identified. In Jobs 1–6, the learner completes letters, envelopes, mailing labels, memorandums, and a monthly sales report using core Word and Excel features.

Unit 2 Business Week 2: Appointments, Contacts, Newsletters, and Presentations

In Jobs 7–12, the learner updates an Outlook calendar with appointments, maintains an Outlook contact list, and sends and receives e-mail. Then he or she uses Word core features to create a monthly newsletter containing text, graphics, diagrams, and charts. Next, Word character and paragraph formatting, tabs, styles, tables, and other core features are used to formalize memos and reports. Finally, a PowerPoint presentation is created from a Word outline.

Unit 3 Business Week 3: Worksheets and Presentations

In Jobs 13–18, the learner uses Excel core features to create and format a budget report complete with charts. Next, the learner uses PowerPoint features to update a presentation by editing and formatting slides, linking Excel data to a slide, creating chart and table slides, adding animations and transitions, and creating speaker notes and handouts.

Unit 4 Business Week 4: Databases

In Jobs 19–24, the learner uses Access core features to create and manage databases including creating tables, queries, forms, and reports. Next, the learner imports data into a database, exports data from a database, and creates a data access page.

Review Pack and Instructor's Resource CD-ROMs

The *Review Pack* CD-ROM contains all the data files needed to complete the exercises. The *Instructor's Resource* CD-ROM contains a wealth of instructional material you can use to prepare for teaching this course. The CD-ROM stores the following information:

- Data and solution files. Data and solution files in Microsoft Word, Excel, PowerPoint, and Access 2002 formats and HTML formats are provided.

- ExamView® tests for each lesson. ExamView is a powerful testing software package that allows instructors to create and administer printed, computer (LAN-based), and Internet exams. ExamView includes hundreds of questions that correspond to the topics covered in this text, enabling learners to generate detailed study guides that include page references for further review. The computer-based and Internet testing components allow learners to take exams at their computers, and also save the instructor time by grading each exam automatically.

- Electronic *Instructor Manual* that includes lecture notes for each lesson, lesson plans, Quick Quizzes, and troubleshooting tips.

- Answers to the lesson and unit review questions, and suggested/sample solutions for Step-by-Step exercises, end-of-lesson activities, and Unit Review projects.

- Copies of the figures that appear in the text, which can be used to prepare transparencies.

- Suggested schedules for teaching the lessons in this course.

- Tables of MOS correlations and job filenames and descriptions.

- PowerPoint presentations that illustrate objectives for each lesson in the text.

SCANS

The Secretary's Commission on Achieving Necessary Skills (SCANS) from the U.S. Department of Labor was asked to examine the demands of the workplace and whether new learners are capable of meeting those demands. Specifically, the Commission was directed to advise the Secretary on the level of skills required to enter employment.

SCANS workplace competencies and foundation skills have been integrated into *Microsoft Office Business Simulation BASICS*. The workplace competencies are identified as 1) ability to use resources, 2) interpersonal skills, 3) ability to work with information, 4) understanding of systems, and 5) knowledge and understanding of technology. The foundation skills are identified as 1) basic communication skills, 2) thinking skills, and 3) personal qualities.

Exercises in which learners must use a number of these SCANS competencies and foundation skills are marked in the text with the SCANS icon.

Certification and Assessment

Microsoft Office Specialist Program

This business simulation covers most of the Microsoft Office Specialist (MOS) Core skills for Word, Excel, PowerPoint, and Access. To learn more about the Microsoft Office Specialist certification, visit www.microsoft.com/traincert/mcp/officespecialist/requirements.asp.

Acknowledgements

Thanks to Anne Chimenti and her colleagues at Custom Editorial Productions for their fine work and valuable support throughout the writing and publishing of this book. We are also very appreciative of the personnel at Napier & Judd, Inc. who helped to prepare this book. We acknowledge, with great appreciation, the assistance provided by Ollie Rivers and Nancy Onarheim in preparing and checking the material in this book and the Instructor's Resource CD-ROM.

About the Authors

H. Albert Napier, Ph.D., is the Director of the Center on the Management of Information Technology and Professor in the Jesse H. Jones Graduate School of Management at Rice University. Philip J. Judd is a former instructor in the Management Department and the Director of the Research and Instructional Computing Service at the University of Houston. Phil now dedicates himself to consulting as a principal of Napier & Judd, Inc.

START-UP CHECKLIST

HARDWARE

Minimum Configuration

✓ PC with Pentium 133 MHz or higher processor. Pentium III or higher recommended.

✓ RAM requirements:

- ✓ Windows 98 and Windows 98 Second Edition – 24 MB of RAM plus 8 MB for each application running simultaneously.

- ✓ Windows ME, Windows NT Workstation 4.0, or Windows NT Server 4.0 – 32 MB of RAM plus 8 MB for each application running simultaneously.

- ✓ Windows 2000 Professional – 64 MB of RAM (128 MB RAM recommended) plus 8 MB for each application running simultaneously.

- ✓ Windows XP Professional - 128 MB of RAM plus an additional 8 MB of RAM for each application running simultaneously.

✓ Hard disk with 245 MB free for typical installation

✓ CD-ROM Drive

✓ Super VGA monitor with video adapter, 800 × 600 or higher resolution. 256 colors or more required.

✓ Microsoft Mouse, IntelliMouse, or compatible pointing device

✓ 14,000 or higher baud modem

✓ Printer

Recommended Configuration

✓ Pentium III or higher with 128 MB RAM or higher

✓ 56,000 baud modem

✓ Multimedia capability: Accelerated video card and audio output device

✓ For e-mail: Microsoft Mail, Internet SMTP/POP3, or other MAPI-compliant messaging software

SOFTWARE

✓ Windows 98, Me, NT Workstation 4.0 with Service Pack 6.0 installed, Windows 2000, or Windows XP

✓ For Web access, Internet Explorer 5.0 or higher browser.

System Requirements

Concepts in this book are illustrated using screen captures from Microsoft Word, Excel, PowerPoint, Access, and Outlook 2002. However, the concepts and exercises in this book are designed to be compatible with both Office XP and Office 2000 applications.

Computer systems that support these programs include PCs running Microsoft Windows. In order to complete some of the step-by-step activities and projects in this book you should have access to the Internet via a modem or a direct connection.

TABLE OF CONTENTS

UNIT 3 BUSINESS WEEK THREE: WORKSHEETS AND PRESENTATIONS

UNIT 4   BUSINESS WEEK FOUR: DATABASES

Business Week One: Correspondence, Memos, and Reports

Unit 1

Job 1 .5 hr.
Introducing Wilderness Treks, Inc. and Creating Custom AutoText

Job 2 1 hr.
Creating Letters and Envelopes

Job 3 .5 hr.
Preparing Labels

Job 4 .5 hr.
Creating an Interoffice Memorandum

Job 5 .5 hr.
Preparing a Monthly Sales Report

Job 6 .5 hr.
Creating a Memo with Embedded Excel Data

 **Estimated Time for Unit 1: 3.5 hours**

INTRODUCING WILDERNESS TREKS, INC. AND CREATING CUSTOM AUTOTEXT

OBJECTIVES

Upon completion of this job, you should be able to:

- Describe Wilderness Treks, Inc.
- Identify the skills required and duties performed by an administrative assistant.
- Key and format text for AutoText.
- Create and save custom AutoText.
- Insert custom AutoText.

Estimated Time: 0.5 hour

VOCABULARY

Administrative assistant

AutoText

Complimentary closing

Preparer's initials

Writer's name

Writer's title

Describe Wilderness Treks, Inc.

Wilderness Treks, Inc. is an international adventure travel company with headquarters in Austin, Texas, and branch offices in London, England; Calgary, Canada; and Sydney, Australia; as shown in Figure 1-1.

FIGURE 1-1

Austin, Texas

London, England

Calgary, Canada

Sydney, Australia

The company creates and sells wilderness adventure travel packages through its branch offices, affiliated travel agencies, and travel-related Web sites. A modestly sized organization with about 200 worldwide employees and gross sales of about $300 million annually, Wilderness Treks packages travel adventures including guides and itineraries. Figure 1-2 illustrates some of the different adventure travel packages sold by Wilderness Treks, Inc.

FIGURE 1-2
Wilderness Treks, Inc. travel adventures

Scuba diving in
the Caribbean

Photo safari
in Africa

Backpacking in
the Swiss Alps

Ballooning in
New Zealand

Dog sledding in Alaska

Sailing in the
Mediterranean

Recently, Wilderness Treks' management decided to sell a line of wilderness and backcountry-travel equipment from a new Web site. The organization has also recently moved into new corporate offices in Suite 500 of the Travis Building in Austin's Riverside Plaza. The organization chart in Figure 1-3 identifies the Wilderness Treks, Inc. management team.

FIGURE 1-3
Wilderness Treks, Inc. management team

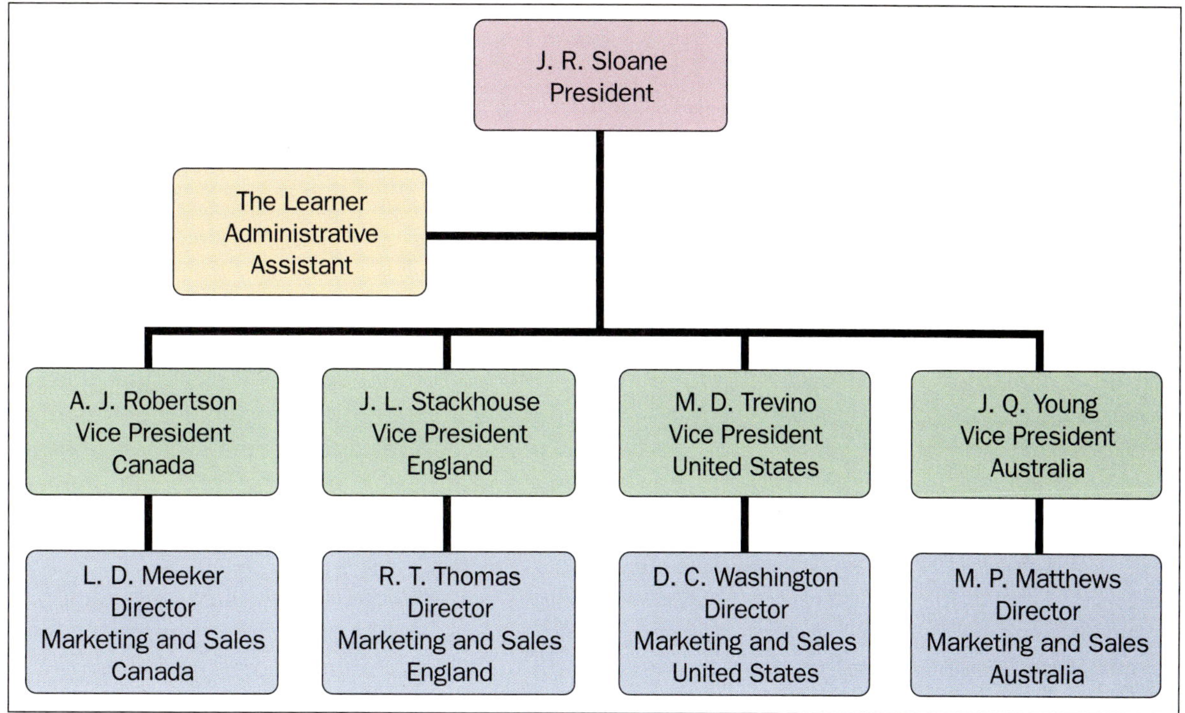

Identify Administrative Assistant Skills and Duties

An *administrative assistant* generally supports a top-level executive in charge of a major department or business division in an organization. It is an important position, and the person holding it is responsible for critical tasks, often acting for and on behalf of his or her manager. An administrative assistant must have strong reading, writing, and calculating skills as well as good listening and verbal communication skills. Skills in critical thinking, problem solving, decision making, mental visualization, and reasoning are also very important.

An administrative assistant must be able to assume responsibility, have a high level of self-esteem, be friendly and empathetic, and adapt well to new situations. Personal integrity and honesty are critical qualities, and the ability to exercise self-management is essential. On a daily basis, an administrative assistant must demonstrate the ability to manage resources (time, material, people, and so forth); exercise good interpersonal skills; acquire, evaluate, and process information; and display top-notch technological skills using computers for word processing, spreadsheet, presentation, database, e-mail, and Internet activities.

You began working at Wilderness Treks, Inc. several months ago as administrative assistant to the president, J. R. Sloane. As the administrative assistant to J. R. Sloane at Wilderness Treks, your responsibilities include the following:

- Preparing, proofing, editing, and transmitting correspondence
- Sending and responding to e-mail correspondence
- Setting and preparing meeting agenda
- Preparing and distributing all sales and marketing data
- Maintaining business partner and vendor data and correspondence
- Representing Sloane in meetings when Sloane cannot attend
- Making all travel arrangements for Sloane
- Acting on behalf of Sloane when Sloane is out of the office
- Completing other tasks as determined by Sloane

Wilderness Treks is sponsoring a marketing conference to be held in July in Calgary, Canada. Attendees will include Wilderness Treks management team, administrative assistants, clerical support personnel, invited business partners, and potential clients. The purpose of the conference is to introduce Wilderness Treks' new season of travel adventures and its new Web site. During the next four business weeks, you work with Sloane and other Wilderness Treks employees to prepare for the conference. You meet with Sloane at 8:30 a.m. each Monday to identify individual assignments for the week.

Several important topics were discussed at today's morning meeting with Sloane, including the need to notify business partners of the new Wilderness Treks corporate address and other contact information, reminding the vice presidents of their luncheon meeting with Sloane to discuss the upcoming marketing conference, and preparing the annual sales report.

Computer Ethics

An administrative assistant holds a position of trust and responsibility. It is quite common for the activities and tasks performed by an administrative assistant to involve highly sensitive or confidential information; therefore, an administrative assistant must be careful to protect the information to which he or she has access by not casually sharing information with other employees.

This information protection extends to the administrative assistant's computer and electronic files. It is important that an administrative assistant follow all company policies regarding network and electronic file security.

Key and Format Text for AutoText

Before you begin to tackle the assignments made at this morning's meeting, you decide it would save time to use the Word AutoText feature to create and insert a standard closing in all of Sloane's letters. *AutoText* is saved text that you insert in your Word documents. Word provides standard AutoText entries such as the phrases "Sincerely yours," or "Attention:". Additionally, you can create custom AutoText entries containing your own preformatted text.

Using custom AutoText to insert frequently keyed text saves time by eliminating the need to re-key the same text over and over. For example, one way to use custom AutoText is to insert a standard letter closing that contains *complimentary closing* text, three blank lines, the *writer's name*, the *writer's title* followed by a blank line, and the *preparer's initials*.

You want to create a custom AutoText entry to add the identical closing text to all of J. R. Sloane's letters. To create custom AutoText, you begin with a new blank document and then you key and format the text to be used as AutoText. All of Sloane's letter text is formatted with the Times New Roman, 12-point font.

Hot Tip

You can insert standard AutoText with the AutoText command on the Insert menu. Unless you specify another template, a custom AutoText entry is saved with the Normal template and is available for all documents created using the Normal template.

Note

The Step-by-Step activities in this business simulation assume you are familiar with Windows operating systems. It is also assumed that you are familiar with the basic features of the Office XP or Office 2000 applications (Word, Excel, PowerPoint, Access, and Outlook), such as opening and closing documents, using menus and toolbars, moving the insertion point in a document, and various selection techniques.

S TEP-BY-STEP 1.1

1. Start the Word application, if necessary. If you are using Word 2002, click the **Close** button on the New Document task pane to close the task pane. 

2. If the Word application is already open, click the **New Blank Document** button on the Standard toolbar, if necessary, to create a new blank document. 

3. Click the **Print Layout View** button, if necessary, in the lower-left corner of the Word window to switch to Print Layout view. 

STEP-BY-STEP 1.1 Continued

4. Verify that the insertion point is at the top of the document and key the text illustrated in Figure 1-4. Insert three blank lines between the complimentary closing and the writer's name. Follow the writer's title with one blank line and key your initials instead of *xx*. (Do not press the Enter key after your initials.)

FIGURE 1-4
J. R. Sloane letter closing

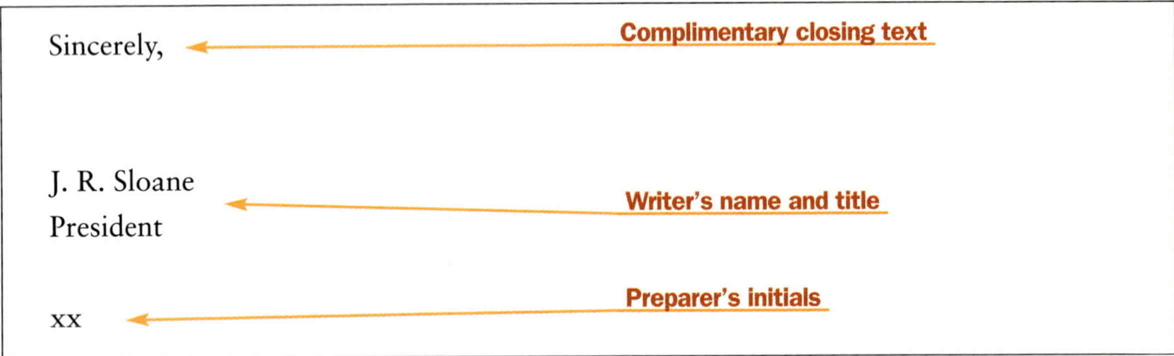

5. Select all the text, beginning with the complimentary closing *Sincerely,* and ending with your initials. Click the **Font** button on the Formatting toolbar and click Times New Roman, if necessary. 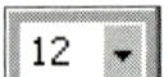

6. Click the **Font Size** button on the Formatting toolbar and click 12, if necessary.

7. Leave the document containing the selected and formatted closing text open just as it is for the next Step-by-Step.

Create and Save Custom AutoText

Each custom AutoText entry must have a unique name. AutoText names are not case sensitive. If you name AutoText with uppercase letters, you can insert the entry in the document using lowercase letters. Because AutoText entries are shortcuts you use to save time when creating documents, you should give an AutoText entry a short but easy-to-remember name.

STEP-BY-STEP 1.2

1. Select the letter closing text you keyed and formatted in Step-by-Step 1.1, if necessary.

2. Click the **Insert** menu, point to AutoText, and click **AutoText** to open the AutoText tab in the AutoCorrect dialog box.

STEP-BY-STEP 1.2 Continued

3. Observe that Word automatically uses *Sincerely,* (the first several characters of the selected text) as the AutoText entry name in the Enter AutoText entries here text box. You want to use a name that contains many fewer characters. Select the text *Sincerely,* in the Enter AutoText entries here text box and key the characters *Cl*. Your dialog box should look similar to Figure 1-5.

FIGURE 1-5
AutoText Tab in the AutoCorrect dialog box

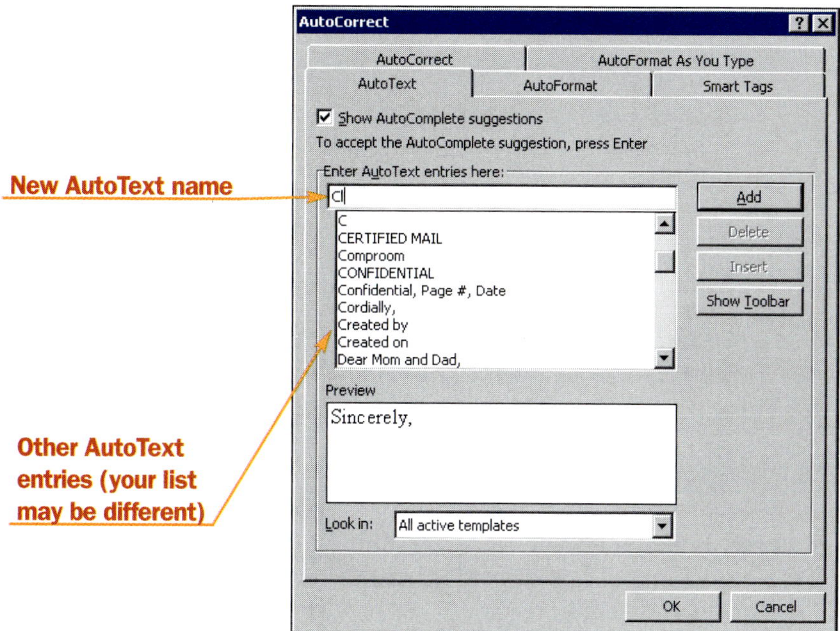

4. Click **Add** to save the *Cl* custom AutoText.

5. If custom AutoText already exists with the same name, a confirmation dialog box appears asking whether or not you want to redefine the AutoText entry. Click **Yes**, if asked.

6. Delete the selected text you used to create the AutoText entry, leaving a blank document open for the next Step-by-Step.

Insert Custom AutoText

You can insert custom AutoText by viewing the AutoText tab in the AutoCorrect dialog box, selecting the AutoText name in the list of available AutoText, and clicking Insert. A faster way to insert custom AutoText is by keying the name of the AutoText and pressing the F3 key. To test your custom AutoText, you open an existing letter and insert the new *Cl* custom AutoText as the letter closing.

Hot Tip

You can also key just enough characters for the Word AutoComplete feature to identify an AutoText unique name and display an AutoComplete tip, then press the **F3** key or the **Enter** key.

STEP-BY-STEP 1.3

1. Open **Step1-3** from the data files.

2. Save the document as **Wentworth Letter**.

3. Press **Ctrl + End** to move the insertion point to the bottom of the document.

4. Key **cl**.

5. Press the **F3** key to insert the custom AutoText letter closing.

6. Observe the change to the document and then spell check, print, save, and close it.

SUMMARY

In this job, you learned:

- Wilderness Treks, Inc. is an adventure travel company headquartered in Austin, Texas, with branch offices in Calgary, Canada; London, England; and Sydney, Australia.

- Skills needed by an administrative assistant include strong fundamental reading, writing, calculating, listening, and verbal skills. Other important skills include critical thinking, problem solving, decision making, mental visualization, and reasoning skills.

- You perform a variety of duties as the administrative assistant to J. R. Sloane including preparing correspondence, sending and receiving e-mail, preparing and distributing marketing reports, and making travel arrangements.

- Standard and custom AutoText is used to insert preformatted text into Word documents.

- You first key and format text prior to creating custom AutoText.

- You create custom AutoText by selecting the appropriate text, opening the AutoCorrect dialog box and viewing the AutoText tab, keying a unique name for the AutoText, and adding the new AutoText to the list.

- You insert a custom AutoText entry into a document by first positioning the insertion point, opening the AutoCorrect dialog box and viewing the AutoText tab, selecting the AutoText by name, and clicking Insert. A faster way to insert custom AutoText is to key the AutoText name and then press the F3 key.

VOCABULARY *Review*

Define the following terms:		
Administrative assistant	Complimentary closing	Writer's name
AutoText	Preparer's initials	Writer's title

REVIEW *Questions*

TRUE / FALSE

Circle T if the statement is true or F if the statement is false.

T   F   **1.** It is not important for an administrative assistant to be able to adapt well to new situations.

T   F   **2.** The preparer's initials immediately follow the writer's title in a letter closing.

T   F   **3.** Standard AutoText can be selected from a list by using the AutoText command on the Insert menu.

T   F   **4.** Unless you specify otherwise in the AutoText tab of the AutoCorrect dialog box, custom AutoText is saved with the Normal template and is available for all documents created with the Normal template.

T   F   **5.** Before you create custom AutoText you must first key and format the text you will use to create the AutoText.

FILL IN THE BLANK

Complete the following sentences by writing the correct word or words in the blanks provided.

1. You can insert custom AutoText by keying the AutoText name and pressing the __________ key.

2. A(n) __________ generally supports a top-level executive in charge of a major department or business.

3. __________ is saved text you can insert in your Word documents.

4. When creating a letter closing, the writer's title is generally followed by __________ blank line(s).

5. Each custom AutoText entry must have a unique __________.

PROJECTS

PROJECT 1-1

1. Open **Project 1-1** from the data files.

2. Save the document as **Richardson Letter**.

3. Insert the *Cl* letter closing at the bottom of the document.

4. Observe the changes to the document and then spell check, save, print, and close it.

5. Leave the Word application open until you complete Project 1-2.

PROJECT 1-2

As the administrative assistant to Sloane, you sometimes must act on Sloane's behalf. This may require creating letters with your own signature instead of Sloane's signature. You also want to have an AutoText letter closing for those letters you create for your own signature. Create a new blank document and create a new custom AutoText letter closing for your own letters using *Yours truly,* as the complimentary closing, your name as the writer's name, *Administrative Assistant* as the writer's title, and your initials as the preparer's initials. Format the closing text with the Times New Roman, 12-point font. Save the AutoText as *MyCl*. Open **Step1-3** from the data files and save it as **My Wentworth Letter**. Then insert the *MyCl* letter closing at the bottom of the document. Finally, save, print, and close the document. Close the Word application without saving the document that contains your AutoText.

WEB PROJECT

Sloane wants you to review the Web sites for other travel adventure companies. Use the search feature in your Web browser or a search tool such as Google (*www.google.com)* to locate adventure travel business Web sites. Print the home pages for at least four Web sites.

TEAMWORK PROJECT

Create a new blank document and then key a list of the skills required and duties performed by an administrative assistant. Save and print the document. Then, using your document as your guide, discuss with your classmates the skills required of an administrative assistant and the duties generally performed by an administrative assistant. At the end of the discussion, each discussion participant should answer the following question: Do you think you would enjoy working as an administrative assistant? Why or why not?

CRITICAL *Thinking*

 ACTIVITY 1-1

After you create custom AutoText, you must sometimes edit or delete it. Use the Word online Help to research creating, editing, inserting, and deleting AutoText and then discuss your findings with your classmates.

CREATING LETTERS AND ENVELOPES

OBJECTIVES

Upon completion of this job, you should be able to:

- Open and edit an existing Word document.
- Insert a date field and AutoText.
- Save a Word document as a custom template.
- Create a letter using a custom template.
- Create an envelope and save it with the accompanying letter.

Estimated Time: 1 hour

VOCABULARY

Body

Boilerplate text

Date field

Delivery address

Letter address

Letterhead

Letterhead paper

Return address

Salutation

Template

Open and Edit an Existing Word Document

Many of the tasks you are assigned for the current week involve preparing, proofing, editing, and transmitting Sloane's correspondence. Before you begin creating and editing Sloane's correspondence, you decide you could save time by using a custom letter template to create Sloane's letters. A custom letter *template* is a model document that already contains pre-keyed and pre-formatted letter text, sometimes called *boilerplate text*, such as company information, a date field, and the letter closing. When you create a new letter based on a letter template, you simply key in the variable text (the text that changes) such as the *letter address*, the *salutation* Dear *[individual's name]*, and the *body* text.

Hot Tip

Word also contains many standard templates that you can use to create new documents. You can choose one of these standard templates by clicking the General Templates command on the New Document task pane (Word 2002) or by opening the New dialog box and clicking a template tab (Word 2000).

Some companies print their letters on special paper called *letterhead paper* or simply *letterhead* that contains preprinted company information at the top of each sheet. Because of its recent move to new offices, Wilderness Treks, Inc. has not yet purchased preprinted letterhead for its letters. You begin creating a custom letter template for Sloane's letters by first opening an existing Word document that already contains the company name as part of the letterhead text and then you modify the document so that the letterhead contains the new corporate address, phone number, and the Web site address.

Warning

Word automatically formats the address of a Web page (called its URL) such as *www.microsoft.com* or an e-mail address such as *Sloane@wildernesstreks.biz* as a hyperlink whenever you key them and then press the Enter key or the Spacebar. In either version of Word you can click the Undo button on the Standard toolbar to remove the hyperlink formatting.

S TEP-BY-STEP 2.1

1. Start the Word application, if necessary. If you are using Word 2002, click the **Close** button on the New Document task pane to close the task pane. 

2. Open **Step2-1** from the data files.

3. Save the document as **My Working Document**.

4. Key the company address, phone number, and Web site address as shown in Figure 2-1 at the left margin immediately below the Wilderness Treks, Inc. letterhead text.

FIGURE 2-1
New Corporate address, phone number, and Web site address

Travis Building, Suite 500

Riverside Plaza

Austin, Texas 77301-0500

512-555-8979

www.wildernesstreks.biz

5. Select all the text beginning with Travis Building, and ending with www.wildernesstreks.biz. Click the **Center** button on the Formatting toolbar to center the selected text below the Wilderness Treks, Inc. letterhead. 

6. Press **Ctrl + End** to move the insertion point to the bottom of the document.

7. Save the document and leave it open for the next Step-by-Step.

Insert a Date Field and AutoText

You can insert the current date in a Word document as text or as a set of codes called a *date field*. When you insert a date field, Word automatically updates the date field to contain the current date each time you open the document. Using a date field to automatically insert the current date saves time when creating letters based on a letter template because you do not have to key the date for each letter. After you insert a date field, you complete the boilerplate text by inserting the Sloane AutoText letter closing you created in Job 1.

S TEP-BY-STEP 2.2

1. Press **Enter** four times to insert four blank lines.

2. Click the **Insert** menu and click **Date and Time** to open the Date and Time dialog box.

3. Click the **third** date option in the Available formats: list.

4. Click the **Update Automatically** check box to insert a check mark, if necessary. Your dialog box should look similar to Figure 2-2.

FIGURE 2-2
Date and Time dialog box

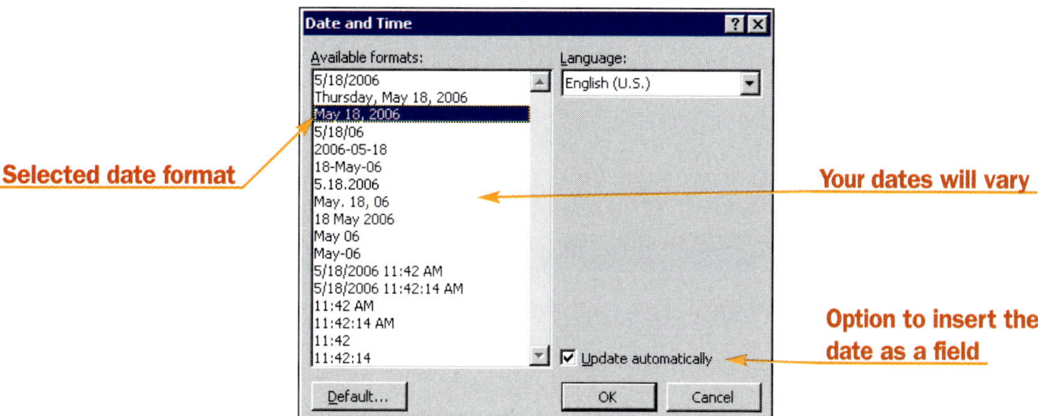

Selected date format

Your dates will vary

Option to insert the date as a field

5. Click **OK**.

6. Press **Enter** ten times to insert ten blank lines.

7. Key **cl** and press the **F3** key.

8. Observe the changes to the document, save it, and leave it open for the next Step-by-Step.

Save a Word Document As a Custom Template

Every document you create in Word is based on a template or model document. For example, each time you click the New Blank Document button on the Standard toolbar you create a new document based on the Normal template. Word provides many built-in document templates or you can create your own custom templates. An easy way to create your own custom template is to save an existing Word document as a template. In the next Step-by-Step, you save My Working Document as a template named Sloane Letter Template.

Hot Tip

Document templates supply settings that affect only the current document and help you automatically format letters, faxes, memos, reports, manuals, brochures, newsletters, and special documents, such as Web pages. There are two types of templates: global templates and document templates. The Normal template is an example of a global template, which means its settings are available for all documents.

STEP-BY-STEP 2.3

1. Click the **File** menu and click **Save As** to open the Save As dialog box.

2. Key **Sloane Letter Template** in the File name list box.

3. Click the down arrow on the Save as type list box and click **Document Template**.

4. Observe that Word automatically switches to the Templates folder where document templates are stored. Your dialog box should look similar to Figure 2-3.

FIGURE 2-3
Save As dialog box

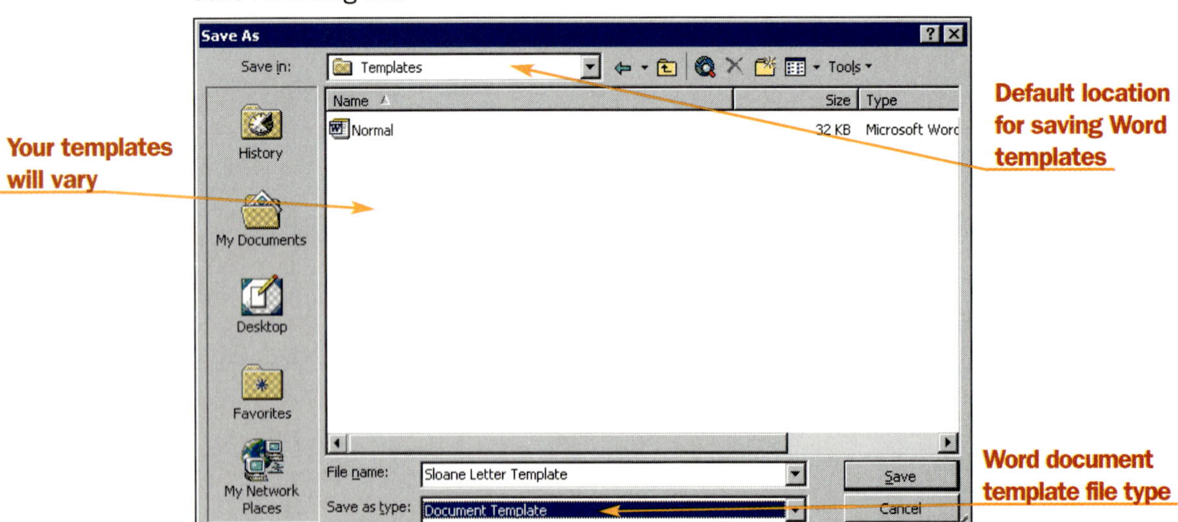

5. Click **Save** to save the Word document as a template and then close the document.

Create a Letter Using a Custom Template

Now you are ready to complete Sloane's correspondence. You need to prepare letters to several business partners advising them of the new corporate address, phone number, Web site address, and Sloane's e-mail address. You begin by creating a new document based on the Sloane Letter Template and then keying the variable text in the document. Your new letter should look like the letter in Figure 2-4 when it is completed.

Hot Tip

Wilderness Treks, Inc. uses the block style for its business letters. This means that the left and right margins are set at 1 inch and all text begins at the left margin. The date begins approximately 2 inches from the top of the page, the letter address begins on the fourth blank line below the date, the salutation begins on the second blank line below the letter address, the body of the letter begins on the second blank line below the salutation, and the letter closing begins on the second blank line below the body of the letter.

FIGURE 2-4
Completed Washington letter

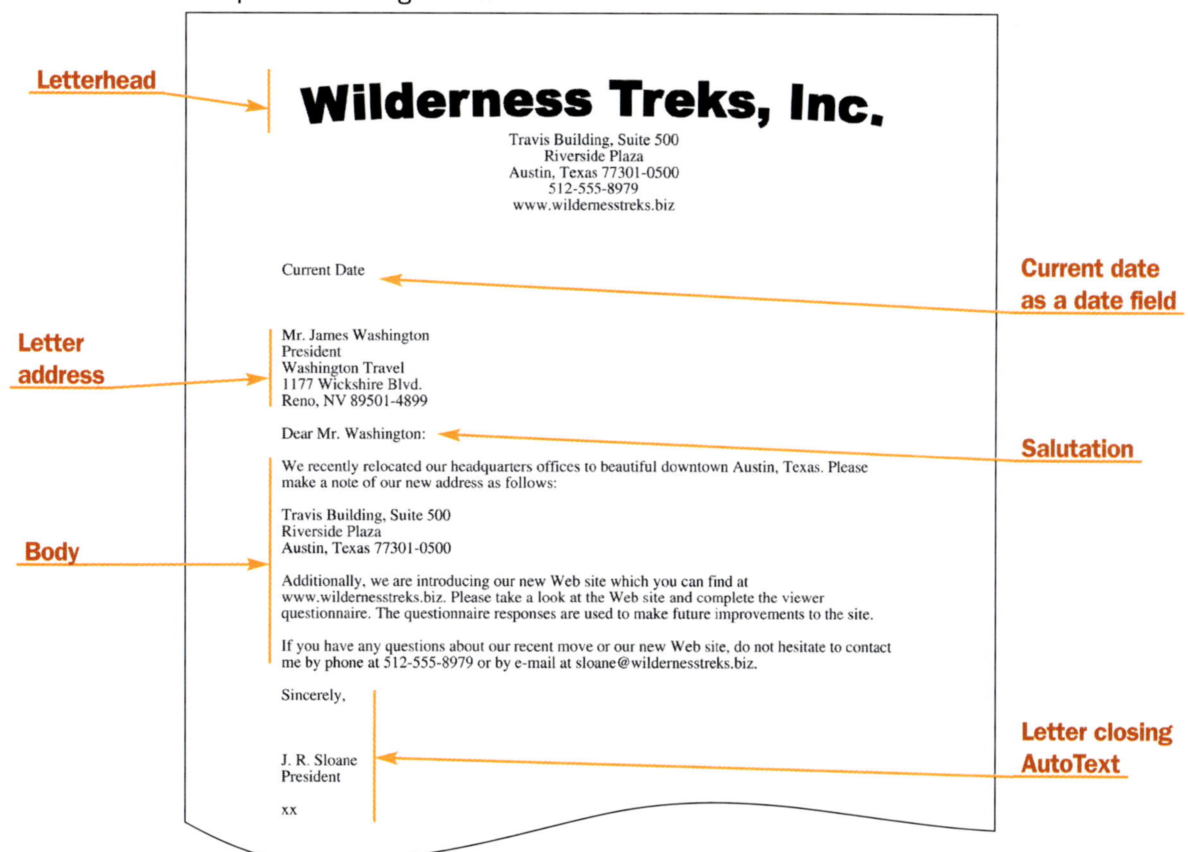

STEP-BY-STEP 2.4

1. Click the **File** menu and click **New** to view the New Document task pane. (If you are using Word 2000, click the **File** menu and click **New** to open the New dialog box. Then click the **General** tab, if necessary.)

2. Click the **General Templates** link in the New Document task pane to open the General tab in the Templates dialog box. If you are using Word 2002, your dialog box should look similar to Figure 2-5. (If you are using Word 2000 the New dialog box also looks similar to Figure 2-5.)

FIGURE 2-5
Templates dialog box

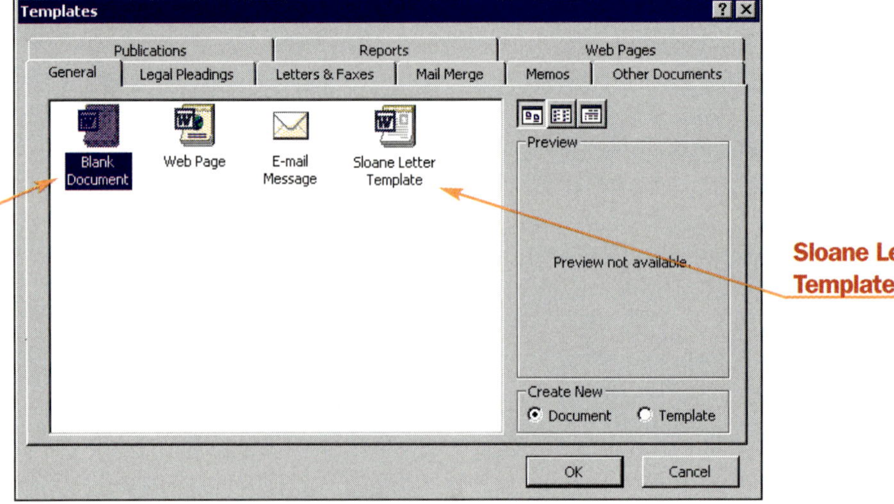

3. Double-click the **Sloane Letter Template** icon to create a new document based on the template.

4. Save the new document as **Washington Letter**.

5. Click the **Show/Hide** button on the Standard toolbar to view the paragraph marks and other nonprinting characters, if desired. 

6. Key the letter address as shown in Figure 2-6 on the fourth blank line below the current date.

FIGURE 2-6
Letter address

Mr. James Washington

President

Washington Travel

1177 Wickshire Blvd.

Reno, NV 89501-4899

STEP-BY-STEP 2.4 Continued

7. Key **Dear Mr. Washington:** as the salutation on the second blank line below the letter address.

8. Key the body of the letter as shown in Figure 2-7 beginning on the second blank line below the salutation. If Word automatically formats www.wildernesstreks.biz and Sloane@wildernesstreks.biz as hyperlinks, click the Undo button on the Standard toolbar to remove the hyperlink formatting.

FIGURE 2-7
Body

We recently relocated our headquarters offices to beautiful downtown Austin, Texas. Please make a note of our new address as follows:

Travis Building, Suite 500

Riverside Plaza

Austin, Texas 77301-0500

Additionally, we are introducing our new Web site which you can find at www.wildernesstreks.biz. Please take a look at the Web site and complete the viewer questionnaire. The questionnaire responses are used to make future improvements to the site.

If you have any questions about our recent move or our new Web site, do not hesitate to contact me by phone at 512-555-8979 or by e-mail at sloane@wildernesstreks.biz.

9. Delete any unnecessary blank lines so that the letter closing begins on the second blank line below the body of the letter.

10. Click the **Spelling and Grammar** button on the Standard toolbar to spell check the document. Make any necessary corrections.

11. Save the document and leave it open for the next Step-by-Step.

Create an Envelope and Save It with the Accompanying Letter

An envelope has two addresses: the recipient's address, called the *delivery address*, positioned in the approximate center of the envelope and the sender's address, called a *return address*, positioned in the upper-left corner of the envelope. You may key a return address for an envelope, or instead you may use envelopes that are preprinted with a return address. Envelopes are created using options in the Envelopes and Labels dialog box.

You can quickly create an envelope for a letter and then save the envelope in the same file as the letter. First you open a letter document and move the insertion point to the letter address. This allows Word to automatically select the letter address for the envelope's delivery address. Next you open the Envelope and Labels dialog box, key a return address (if desired), specify the envelope size, and add the envelope as *Page 0* to the open letter document. Note that all of Sloane's letters are mailed in Size 10 business envelopes.

Note

In the activities in this job you may use plain paper to print your envelopes, or you may use size 10 envelopes, as specified by your instructor.

Did You Know?

When you create an envelope using the Envelopes tab in the Envelopes and Labels dialog box, Word automatically formats the envelope delivery and return addresses with the Arial font preferred by the U.S. Postal Service. Using this font makes it easier for the envelope addresses to be automatically read by the Postal Service equipment.

STEP-BY-STEP 2.5

1. Verify that the **Washington Letter** is still open. Move the insertion point anywhere inside the letter address text.

2. Click the **Tools** menu, point to **Letters and Mailings**, click **Envelopes and Labels**, and click the **Envelopes** tab (if necessary) to view the envelope options in the Envelopes and Labels dialog box. (If you are using Word 2000, click the **Tools** menu and click **Envelopes and Labels**.)

STEP-BY-STEP 2.5 Continued

3. Key the Wilderness Treks, Inc. return address (see Figure 2-7) in the Return Address: text box. Your dialog box should look similar to Figure 2-8.

FIGURE 2-8
Envelopes Tab in the Envelopes and Labels dialog box

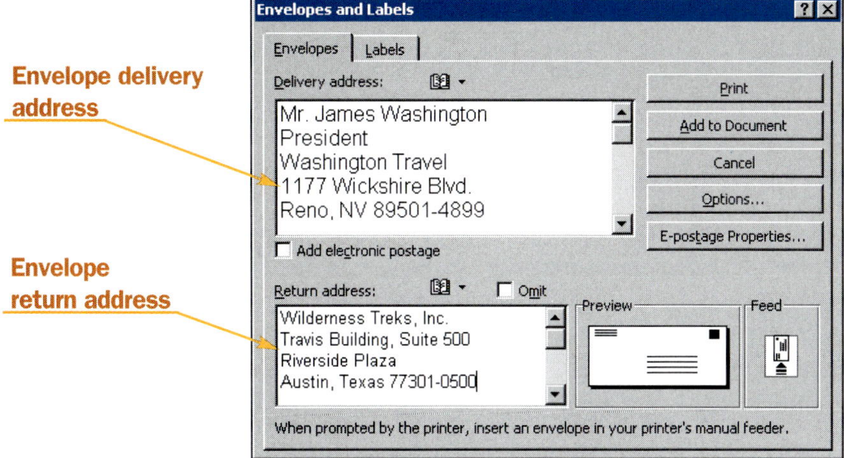

4. Click **Options** to select the envelope size and other envelope options.

5. Click the **Envelope size** list arrow and click **Size 10 (4 1/8 × 9 1/2 in)**, if necessary. Your dialog box should look similar to Figure 2-9.

FIGURE 2-9
Envelope Options dialog box

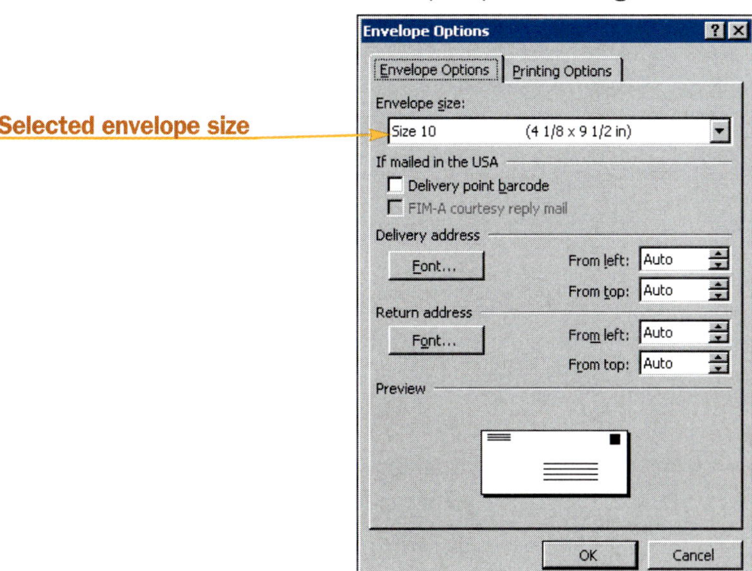

6. Click **OK** to accept the options in the Envelope Options dialog box.

STEP-BY-STEP 2.5 Continued

7. Click **Add to Document** to add the envelope as Page 0 to the Washington Letter.

8. Click **NO** when asked if you want to save the return address as the new default return address for all future envelopes.

9. Click the **Print Layout View** button to switch to Print Layout View, if necessary.

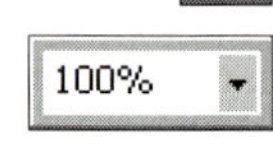

10. Click the **Zoom** button list arrow on the Standard toolbar and click **Whole Page**, if necessary, to view both the envelope and the letter. Your screen should look similar to Figure 2-10.

FIGURE 2-10
Washington Letter with envelope

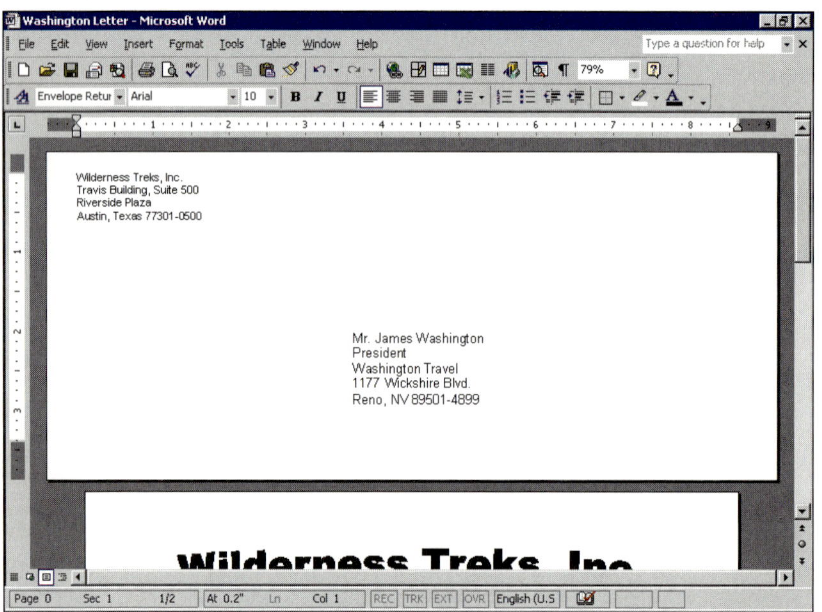

11. Save, print preview, print, and close the document.

SUMMARY

In this job, you learned:

■ A custom letter template is a model document that already contains pre-keyed and pre-formatted text called boilerplate text.

■ Examples of custom letter template boilerplate text include the letterhead text, the current date, and a standard letter closing.

■ Variable text you key in a document based on a custom letter template includes the letter address, the salutation, and the text in the body of the letter.

■ You can insert the current date as text or as an automatically updated Word date field.

- You can easily create a custom template by saving an existing Word document as a template.

- By default when you save a custom template, it is stored in the Templates folder.

- You can use a custom template icon to create a new document by opening the New Document task pane and clicking the General Templates link. (If you are using Word 2000 you find the template icons in the New dialog box.)

- You can create an envelope for an existing letter by opening the letter document, moving the insertion point to the letter address text, and opening the Envelopes tab in the Envelopes and Labels dialog box.

- When you create an envelope for an existing letter, you can add the envelope to the top of the open letter document where it becomes Page 0.

VOCABULARY *Review*

Define the following terms:		
Body	Letter address	Return address
Boilerplate text	Letterhead	Salutation
Date field	Letterhead paper	Template
Delivery address		

REVIEW *Questions*

TRUE / FALSE

Circle T if the statement is true or F if the statement is false.

T   F   **1.** A custom template usually contains boilerplate text.

T   F   **2.** When you use the Date and Time dialog box, you can insert the date only as an automatically updated date field.

T   F   **3.** An envelope document must always be saved separately from the letter document it accompanies.

T   F   **4.** Word automatically formats the delivery address in the Envelopes tab of the Envelopes and Labels dialog box with the Times New Roman font preferred by the U.S. Postal Service.

T   F   **5.** When you add an envelope to a letter document, it is added to the bottom of the document.

FILL IN THE BLANK

Complete the following sentences by writing the correct word or words in the blanks provided.

1. You can insert a date that automatically updates to the current date each time a document is opened with an option in the __________ dialog box.

2. Using a(n) __________ that contains boilerplate text and formatting enables you to prepare a document more quickly.

3. The Normal template is an example of a(n) __________ template.

4. When you add an envelope to a letter document it becomes Page __________ in the document.

5. To save an existing Word document as a template, you must first change the document file type to __________ .

PROJECTS

PROJECT 2-1

1. Open **Project 2-1** from the data files.

2. Insert the date as a date field four lines below the letterhead.

3. Insert the **MyCl** letter closing you created in Unit 1 Project 1-1 ten lines below the date field. If you have not created the **MyCl** letter closing, do so now.

4. Save the document as a template named **My Letter Template** and then close it.

5. Create a new document based on My Letter Template.

6. Save the new document as **Sample Letter** and then print preview, print, and close it. Leave the Word application open for the next project.

 ### PROJECT 2-2

    To complete Sloane's correspondence for this week, you must create two additional letters. Open **Project 2-2** from the data files and then print preview, print, and close it. Use the name and address information in the printed document together with the **Sloane Letter Template** to create two letters. Use the text shown in Figure 2-7 as the body of each letter. Create a size 10 envelope for each letter and save the envelope with the letter. Use the filenames **Gartner Letter** and **Gonzales Letter**. Print preview and print both letters and accompanying envelopes.

 ### WEB PROJECT

    Because you are responsible for preparing Sloane's correspondence, you sometimes must look up zip code information. Use the search feature in your Web browser or a search tool such as AltaVista (*www.altavista.com*) to locate Web sites that provide zip code information. Print at least two Web pages.

 **TEAMWORK PROJECT**

 As an administrative assistant, it is important that you be familiar with the Word standard templates. Using the Templates dialog box (for Word 2002) or the New dialog box (Word 2000) and Word online help, explore the standard document templates available in Word. Then create two documents: one based on the Professional Letter template and one based on the Contemporary Fax template, save the documents, and print them. Then, using your printed example documents as your guide, discuss with your classmates your experience creating documents from these templates.

CRITICAL*Thinking*

 ## ACTIVITY 2-1

Once you create a custom template, you then must sometimes modify it. Use the Word online Help to research how to modify a custom template and then discuss your findings with your classmates.

PREPARING LABELS

Create an Individual Mailing Label

A *label* is a small, adhesive-backed piece of paper on which you print text. You can print text on many different types of labels in a variety of sizes, such as mailing labels, name tags, file folder labels, and computer diskette labels. To make it easy to work with labels, manufacturers place multiple labels on an underlying page of slick paper. To print text on labels, you then place a page of labels in your printer's paper tray or manually feed a page of labels into the printer. After you print text on a label, you then peel the label away from the underlying page and stick it on the destination envelope, file folder, diskette, and so forth.

You create labels by keying the label text in the Address text box in the Labels tab in the Envelopes and Labels dialog box. You select the label size and printer options and then print the text on a specific label. You can easily create mailing labels by opening a document that contains an address (such as a letter or a list of addresses), selecting the address text, and then opening the Labels tab in the Envelopes and Labels dialog box. The selected address automatically appears in the Address text box.

Sloane calls to ask you to send a conference brochure to Steve Yang, a business partner in Indiana. The conference brochure is quite large and must be mailed in a large envelope that can't be used in your printer; therefore, you need to create a mailing label for the envelope. You begin by opening an existing Word document that contains a list of business partner addresses.

Warning 

There are specific types of labels for copiers, dot matrix printers, and inkjet and laser printers. Dot matrix printers use labels that pass through the printer by tractor feed. Laser and ink jet printers use labels on pages that enter the printer through the sheet feeder. If you are using a laser printer, be sure to use labels designed specifically for laser printers. Using labels made for a copier in a laser printer may damage your printer.

S TEP-BY-STEP 3.1

1. Start the Word application, if necessary. If you are using Word 2002, click the **Close** button on the New Document task pane to close the task pane. 

2. Open **Step3-1** from the data files.

3. Select the **Steve Yang** address. The document on your screen should look similar to Figure 3-1.

FIGURE 3-1
Selected address for mailing label

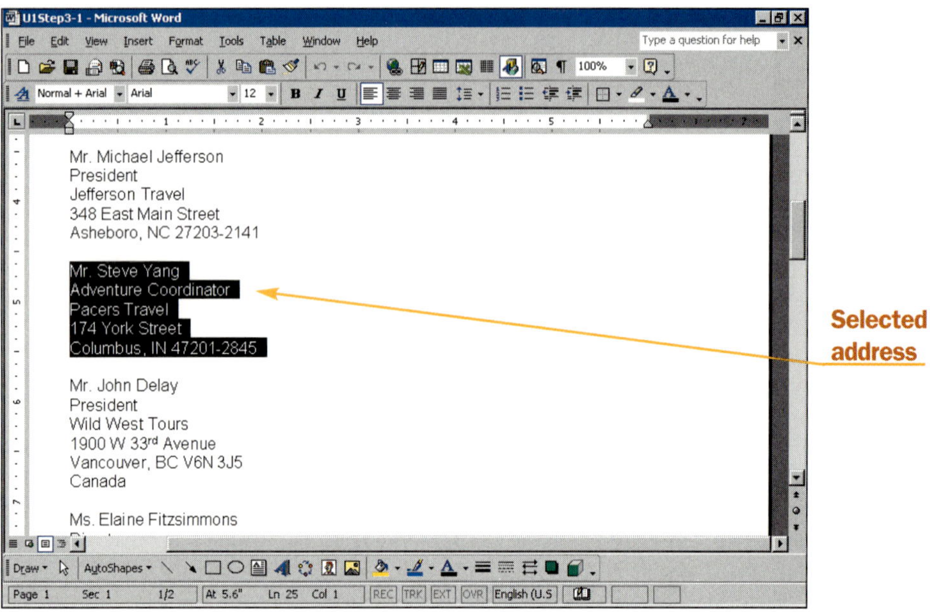

4. Leave the document open on your screen (with the Yang address selected) for the next Step-by-Step.

Select the Label Format and Printer Options

Word has built-in label formats for most types of labels. The default formats are for Avery standard labels, which are the type of labels used at Wilderness Treks, Inc. You generally use an Avery 5260 – Address label for your mailing labels. In addition to selecting the label format, you also specify if your printer is a dot matrix or laser printer and how the label page is fed into the printer. The printer you use at Wilderness Treks, Inc. is a laser printer and you use the default paper tray for your labels.

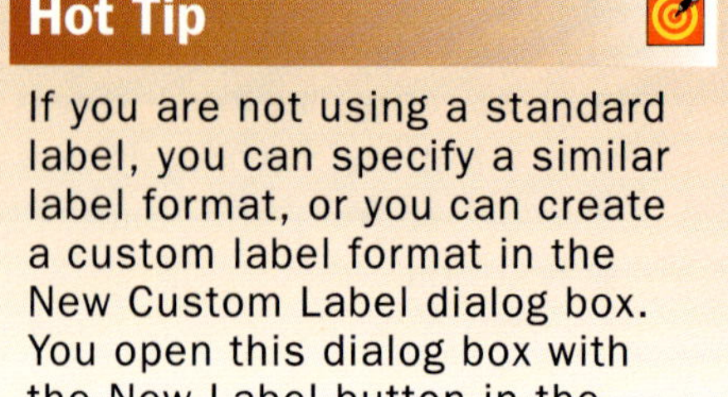

Hot Tip

If you are not using a standard label, you can specify a similar label format, or you can create a custom label format in the New Custom Label dialog box. You open this dialog box with the New Label button in the Label Options dialog box.

S TEP-BY-STEP 3.2

1. Click the **Tools** menu, point to **Letters and Mailings**, click **Envelopes and Labels**, and click the **Labels** tab to view the labels options in the Envelopes and Labels dialog box. (If you are using Word 2000, click the **Tools** menu, click **Envelopes and Labels**, and click the **Labels** tab.)

2. Click the **Options** button to open the Label Options dialog box.

3. Click the **5260 – Address** Avery label product in the **Product number** list to select it.

4. Click the **Tray** list arrow and click **Default tray (Automatically Select)**. Your dialog box should look similar to Figure 3-2.

FIGURE 3-2
Label Options dialog box

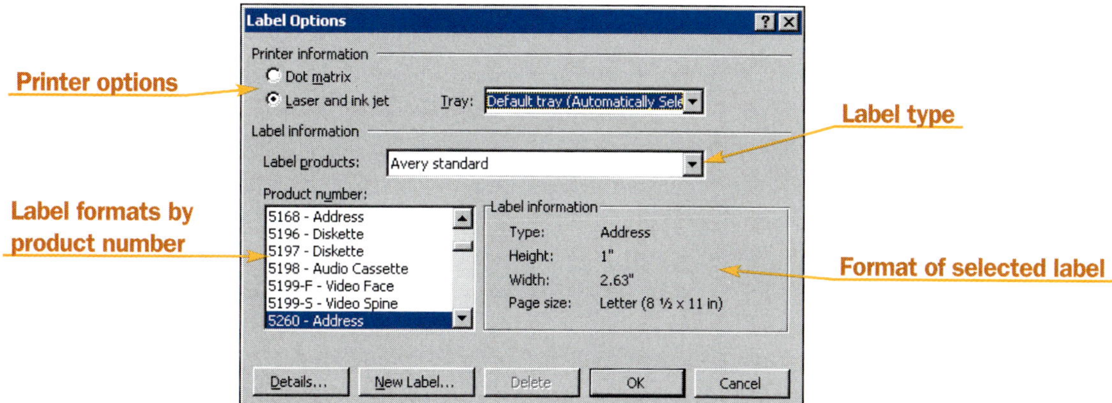

5. Click **OK**.

6. Leave the document and the Labels tab in the Envelopes and Labels dialog box open for the next Step-by-Step.

Print an Individual Mailing Label

After selecting the label format and printer options, you are ready to print Yang's mailing label. When printing an individual label, you can specify exactly which label on a page of labels you want to use by specifying the exact row and column of the label you want to use. For example, the

Avery 5260 – Address labels are positioned on an 8½" by 11" size page in ten rows containing three labels per row. Each label has a height of 1 inch and a width of 2.63 inches. Figure 3-3 illustrates a page of 5260 – Address labels in the ten-row by three-column arrangement.

FIGURE 3-3
Page of ten-row by three-column labels

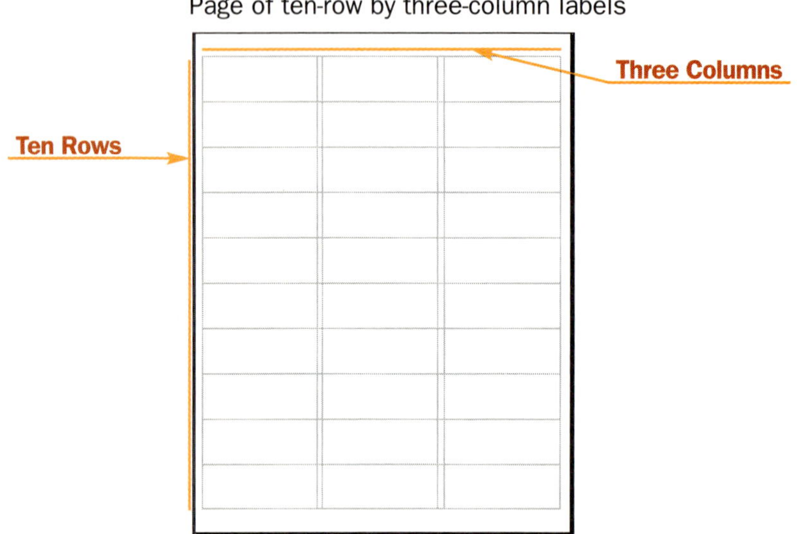

To create the Yang mailing label, you use a page of 5260 – Address labels that you have used previously and this page has only one label left in row 1, positioned in column 3. To avoid throwing away unused labels, you want to print Yang's address on this label.

S TEP-BY-STEP 3.3

1. Click the **Single label** option button to select it.

> **Hot Tip** 
>
> Word does not automatically use the Arial font for mailing label addresses as it does with envelope addresses. If you want to change the label text font to Arial, simply select the text in the Address text box, right-click the selected text, and click Font to open the Font dialog box. Then select the Arial font from the Font list box and click OK.

> **Note** 
>
> For the Step-by-Step activities in this job, you can use plain paper for printing labels or you can use actual labels as specified by your instructor.

STEP-BY-STEP 3.3 Continued

2. Key **3** in the **Column**: text box to specify that the label you want to use is in Column 3. Your dialog box should look similar to Figure 3-4.

FIGURE 3-4
Labels tab in the Envelopes and Labels dialog box

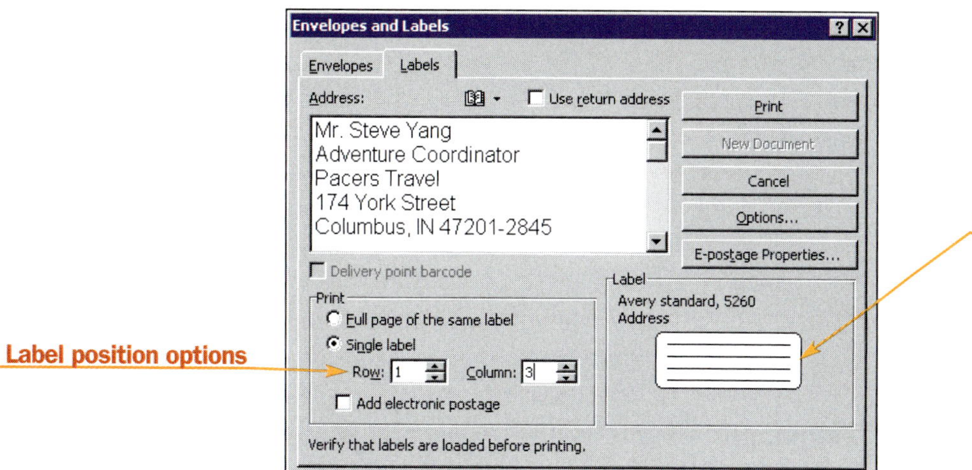

3. Click **Print**.

4. Close the **Step3-1** document without saving changes and leave Word open for the next Step-by-Step.

Create and Print a Page of Return Address Labels

You now need to add the Wilderness Treks, Inc. return address to the large envelope. You do this with a *return address label*. Because of the move to the new corporate offices, you need to create a page of return address labels with the new corporate address. You create return address labels in the same way you create individual labels except that you specify a full page of the same label in the Labels tab in the Envelopes and Labels dialog box instead of a single label.

When you create a full page of the same label, you can either print the page immediately or create a new return address label document containing the label text and the 5260 – Address label format. If you frequently use return address labels, it is a good idea to create a new return address label document. You can then open the return address label document and print new labels whenever you need them without first having to key the label text and select the label options. You use the Arial font preferred by the U.S. Postal service for the Wilderness Treks, Inc. return address labels.

S TEP-BY-STEP 3.4

1. View the **Labels** tab in the Envelopes and Labels dialog box.

STEP-BY-STEP 3.4 Continued

2. Key the Wilderness Treks, Inc. return address as shown in Figure 3-5 in the Address text box.

FIGURE 3-5
New Corporate address

Wilderness Treks, Inc.

Travis Building, Suite 500

Riverside Plaza

Austin, Texas 77301-0500

3. Select the **Wilderness Treks, Inc. return address** in the Address text box.

4. Right-click the selected address and click **Font** to open the Font dialog box.

5. Click **Arial** in the Font: list box. Your dialog box should look similar to Figure 3-6.

FIGURE 3-6
Font dialog box

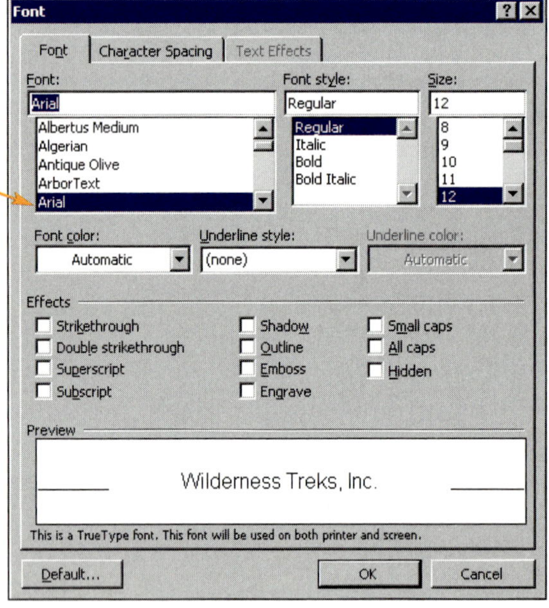

6. Click **OK**.

STEP-BY-STEP 3.4 Continued

7. Click the **Full page of same label** option button in the Labels tab in the Envelopes and Labels dialog box, if necessary, to select it. Your dialog box should look similar to Figure 3-7.

FIGURE 3-7
Labels tab in the Envelopes and Labels dialog box

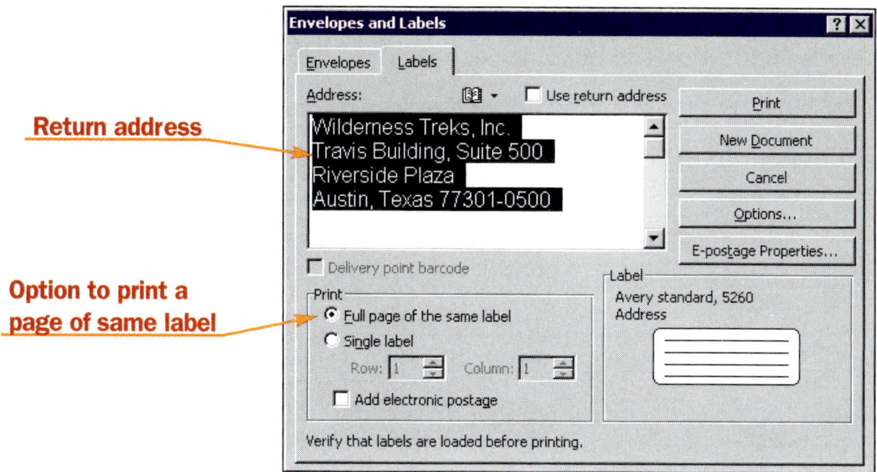

8. Click **New Document** to create a new return address label document.

9. Click the **Print Layout View** button to switch to Print Layout view, if necessary. The document on your screen should look similar to Figure 3-8.

FIGURE 3-8
Wilderness Treks, Inc. return address labels

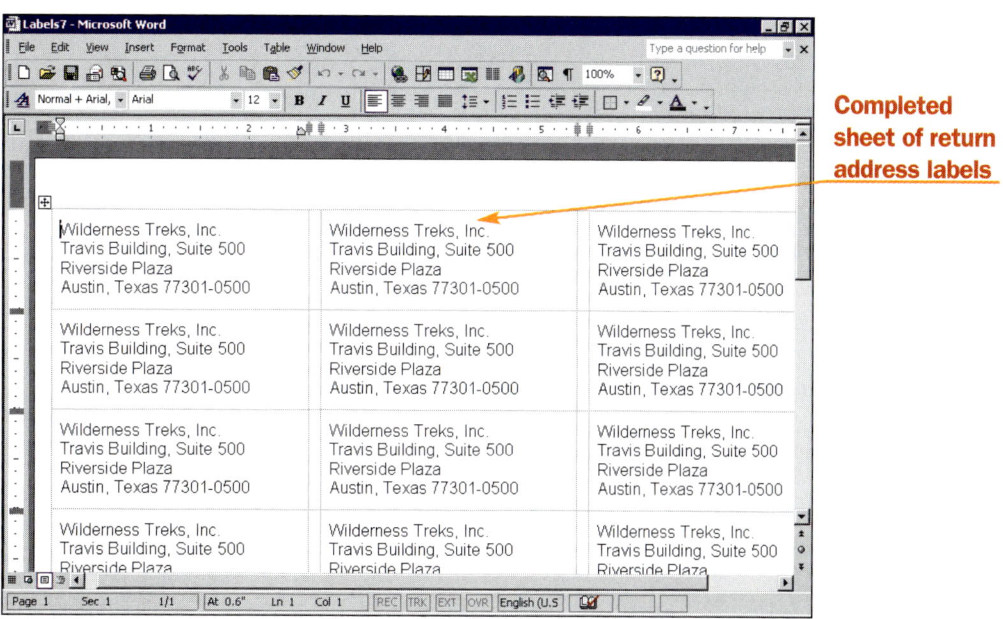

10. Save the document as **Return Address Labels**, then print preview, print, and close it.

SUMMARY

In this job, you learned:

- A label is a small, adhesive-backed piece of paper on which you print text.

- Labels come in many different types and sizes such as mailing labels, name tags, file folder labels, and computer diskette labels.

- Labels are created in the Labels tab in the Envelopes and Labels dialog box.

- You can create a mailing label by first selecting address text in a letter or other document.

- Word provides several different label type options; however, the Avery standard label type contains the default label formats.

- In addition to specifying a label format, you must also specify printer options such as the type of printer you use to print the labels and how the label page is fed into the printer.

- When you print an individual label, you can specify exactly which row and column on the label page contains the individual label you want to use.

- You can create and print a full page of the same label by specifying this option in the Labels tab in the Envelopes and Labels dialog box.

- If desired, you can create a full page of the same label as a new document which you can save and use later for printing more labels.

VOCABULARY *Review*

> **Define the following terms:**
> Label   Return address label

REVIEW *Questions*

TRUE / FALSE

Circle T if the statement is true or F if the statement is false.

T   F   1. A label is a small, adhesive-backed piece of paper on which you print text.

T   F   2. The default label type is Avery A4.

T   F   3. You should have no problem using labels designed for a copier in a laser printer.

T   F   4. It is not possible to specify an exact label on which to print.

T   F   5. Word automatically changes the font for mailing labels to Arial.

FILL IN THE BLANK

Complete the following sentences by writing the correct word or words in the blanks provided.

1. You click the __________ button in the Labels tab in the Envelopes and Labels dialog box to create a new label document.

2. To change the font of text you key in the Labels tab in the Envelopes and Labels dialog box, you use a shortcut menu to open the __________ dialog box.

3. To create a label from a letter or other document that contains an address, you can open the document and move the __________ to the address.

4. If you are not using a standard label, you can specify a similar label format or create a custom label format in the __________ dialog box.

5. You use the __________ option in the Labels tab in the Envelopes and Labels dialog box to print an individual label.

PROJECTS

PROJECT 3-1

1. Open the **Project 3-1** data file.

2. Move the insertion point to the letter address.

3. Open the Labels tab in the Envelopes and Labels dialog box.

4. Change the label address font to Arial.

5. Create a single 5260 – Address label and print it on the label in row 2, column 1 on the label page.

6. Close the document and leave Word open for the next project.

PROJECT 3-2

Sloane calls to remind you to send a conference brochure to John Delay in Vancouver and Elaine Fitzsimmons in London. The Delay and Fitzsimmons addresses are in the Step3-1 data file. Create a single label for each address. Print the labels on size 5262 - Address labels in row 4, column 2 and row 5, column 1, respectively.

WEB PROJECT

In addition to zip code information, you also frequently need to locate area code information. Use the search feature in your Web browser or a search tool such as Google (*www.google.com*) to locate Web sites that provide area code information. Print at least two Web pages.

  **TEAMWORK PROJECT**

 As an administrative assistant, you must often create different types of labels: for file folders, computer diskettes, and so forth. Using the Labels tab in the Envelopes and Labels dialog box, explore the types of labels and the different formats within each type. Print at least three examples of labels that *are not address labels*. Then, using your printed label examples as your guide, discuss with your classmates how to use different label types and formats.

CRITICAL*Thinking*

ACTIVITY 3-1

Sometimes you need to create a custom label format. Using Word online help, research how to create and save a custom label format and then discuss your findings with your classmates.

JOB 4

CREATING AN INTEROFFICE MEMORANDUM

OBJECTIVES

Upon completion of this job, you should be able to:

- Set margins for an interoffice memorandum.
- Set custom tab stops using the horizontal ruler.
- Insert a horizontal line.
- Copy and paste between Word documents.
- Create a bulleted list.

Estimated Time: 0.5 hour

VOCABULARY

Bulleted list
Horizontal line
Interoffice memorandum
Memo
Tab formatting mark
Tab stops

Set Margins for an Interoffice Memorandum

When you arrive at work this morning, you have several incoming e-mail messages that require your attention. One of the e-mail messages (illustrated in Figure 4-1) is from Sloane, who reminds you to notify the vice presidents about the luncheon on Thursday and about the conference topics to be discussed during the luncheon.

FIGURE 4-1
Sloane's e-mail message

Message From: J. R. Sloane [sloane@wildernesstreks.biz]
Sent: Monday, May 22, 2006 5:36 PM
To: adminasst@wildernesstreks.biz
Subject: Discussion topics for luncheon

Please remind the vice presidents that Thursday's luncheon discussion will cover the following topics:
Conference travel arrangements
Conference accommodations
Special conference events for guests' family members
Conference speakers

Sloane

An *interoffice memorandum* or *memo* is written communication to someone inside your organization. Memos generally follow a standard format as shown in Figure 4-2. The memo text should begin approximately two inches from the top of the page. The left and right margins should be set at one inch. There should be a blank line between each line of the heading text TO:, FROM:, DATE:, and SUBJECT: and between the heading text and the memo body. Occasionally the heading text is bolded and some memos have a horizontal line between the heading text and the body of the memo. Also, some memos include a company name or logo at the top of the page.

FIGURE 4-2
Completed memo

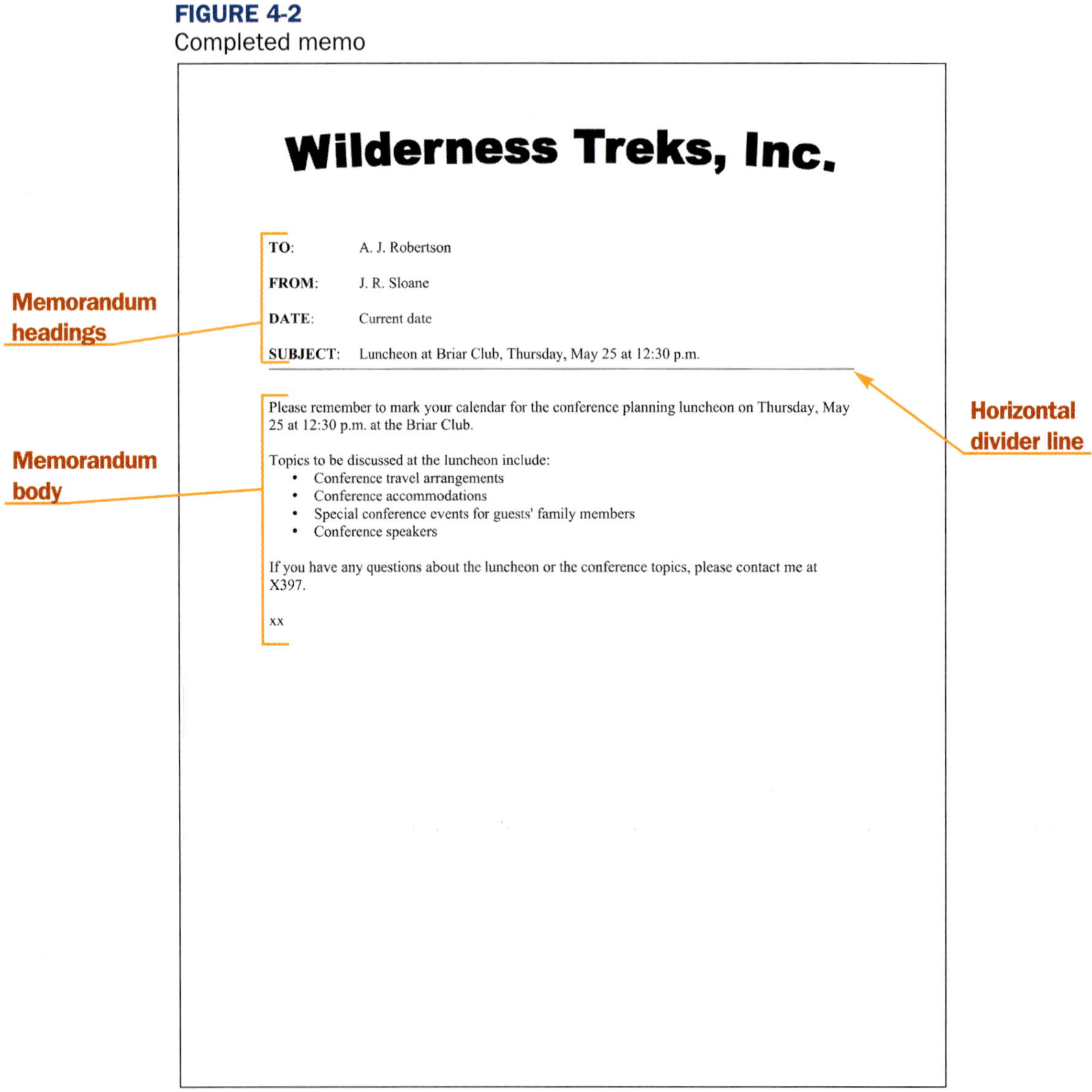

To remind the vice presidents about the luncheon, you create and send a memo to each of them: A. J. Robertson, J. L. Stackhouse, M. D. Trevino, and J. Q. Yong.

STEP-BY-STEP 4.1

1. Start the Word application, if necessary. If you are using Word 2002, close the New Document task pane.

2. Open **Step4-1** from the data files.

3. Save the document as **Robertson Memo**.

4. Switch to Print Layout view if necessary and click the **Show/Hide** button on the Formatting toolbar to view the nonprinting characters, if necessary.

5. Click the **File** menu, click **Page Setup**, and then click the **Margins** tab, if necessary, to view the margins options in the Page Setup dialog box.

6. Key **1** in the Left text box and key **1** in the Right text box to set the left and right margins to one inch. Your dialog box should look similar to Figure 4-3.

FIGURE 4-3
Margins tab in the Page Setup dialog box

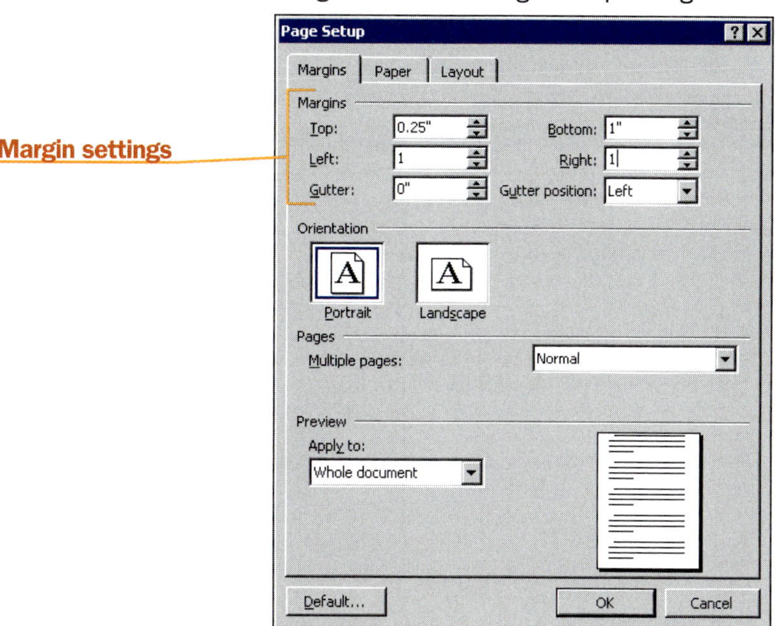

7. Click **OK**.

8. Save the document and leave it open for the next Step-by-Step.

Set Custom Tab Stops Using the Horizontal Ruler

A *tab formatting mark* is a nonprinting character you insert in your document by pressing the Tab key. Custom *tab stops* are text alignment icons you insert on the horizontal ruler to indicate where text should align. Each tab formatting mark you insert moves the text to the right of the tab formatting mark to the next tab stop position indicated on the horizontal ruler.

Word has four frequently used types of tab alignments: Left, Center, Right, and Decimal. By default, Word documents have left-aligned tab stops set at every 0.5 inch; however, you can insert left-, center-, right-, or decimal-aligned custom tab stops. Table 4-1 describes the four most frequently used tab text alignments.

TABLE 4-1
Tab alignment options

TAB	ALIGNMENT
Left	Text is left aligned at the tab
Center	Text is centered over the tab
Right	Text is right aligned at the tab
Decimal	Text is aligned at the decimal character

You can quickly set the left, center, right, and decimal tab stops by selecting the appropriate tab alignment icon on the Tab Alignment button located to the left of the horizontal ruler, and then clicking at the appropriate position on the horizontal ruler. To begin the memo, you key and format the heading text and then you use left-aligned tab stops to align the TO, FROM, DATE, and SUBJECT headings' variable text.

STEP-BY-STEP 4.2

1. Verify that the Robertson Memo document is open and then move the insertion point to the blank line below the Wilderness Treks, Inc. heading text.

2. Press **Enter** five times to insert five blank lines.

3. Key **TO:** and press **Tab** and then key **A. J. Robertson** and press **Enter** twice.

4. Key **FROM:** and press **Tab** and then key **J. R. Sloane** and press **Enter** twice.

5. Key **DATE:** and press **Tab** and then key today's date in the month/dd/yyyy format and press **Enter** twice.

6. Key **SUBJECT:** and press **Tab** and then key **Luncheon at Briar Club, Thursday, May 25 at 12:30 p.m.** and press **Enter**. Note that the variable heading text is not aligned properly. You fix this alignment in steps 9 to 11.

7. Move the insertion point to the TO: heading to select it and click the **Bold** button on the Formatting toolbar.

Did You Know?

You can set custom tab stops at any position between the left and right margins for one or more selected paragraphs or the entire document.

Tab stops are part of paragraph formatting. This means that only the selected paragraph or paragraphs are affected when you set or modify tabs stops. To set custom tab stops for individual paragraphs, you must first select the paragraphs. To select a single paragraph, simply move the insertion point into the paragraph.

To set custom tab stops that affect all the paragraphs in a new document, set the tab stops before you begin keying the first paragraph. When you press the Enter key to begin a new paragraph, the tab settings are added to the new paragraph.

STEP-BY-STEP 4.2 Continued

8. Apply the bold formatting to the FROM:, DATE:, and SUBJECT: headings.

9. Select the TO:, FROM:, DATE:, and SUBJECT: heading paragraphs (the headings and the variable text).

10. Move the mouse pointer to the **Tab Alignment** button to the left of the horizontal ruler. Click the **Tab Alignment** button until the ScreenTip indicates Left Tab. (The icon on the button looks like an L.)

11. Move the mouse pointer to the one-inch position on the horizontal ruler and click to insert a left-aligned tab stop on the ruler. Note that the all variable heading text is now left aligned at the one-inch position as indicated on the horizontal ruler.

12. Press **Ctrl + End** to move the insertion point to the end of the document (the blank line below the SUBJECT: heading paragraph).

13. Save the document and leave it open for the next Step-by-Step.

Insert a Horizontal Line

You can give a memo a professional look by inserting a *horizontal line* between the TO:, FROM:, DATE:, and SUBJECT: heading paragraphs and the body of the memo. An easy way to do this is with the Horizontal Line button on the Borders button grid on the Formatting toolbar.

S TEP-BY-STEP 4.3

1. Verify that the Robertson Memo is open and the insertion point is at the left margin on the blank line below the SUBJECT: heading paragraph.

2. Click the **Border** button list arrow on the Formatting toolbar to view the Border grid buttons. 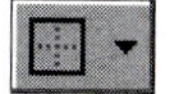

3. Click the **Horizontal Line** button on the Border button grid. Observe that the horizontal line is inserted from the left to the right margin. 

4. Press **Enter** to insert another blank line.

5. Key the text shown in Figure 4-4 beginning on the blank line below the horizontal divider line.

FIGURE 4-4
Memo body text

Please remember to mark your calendar for the conference planning luncheon on Thursday, May 25 at 12:30 p.m. at the Briar Club.

Topics to be discussed at the luncheon include:

STEP-BY-STEP 4.3 Continued

6. Press **Enter** to insert a blank line. The document on your screen should look similar to Figure 4-5. Save your changes and leave the document open for the next Step-by-Step.

FIGURE 4-5
Partially completed memo

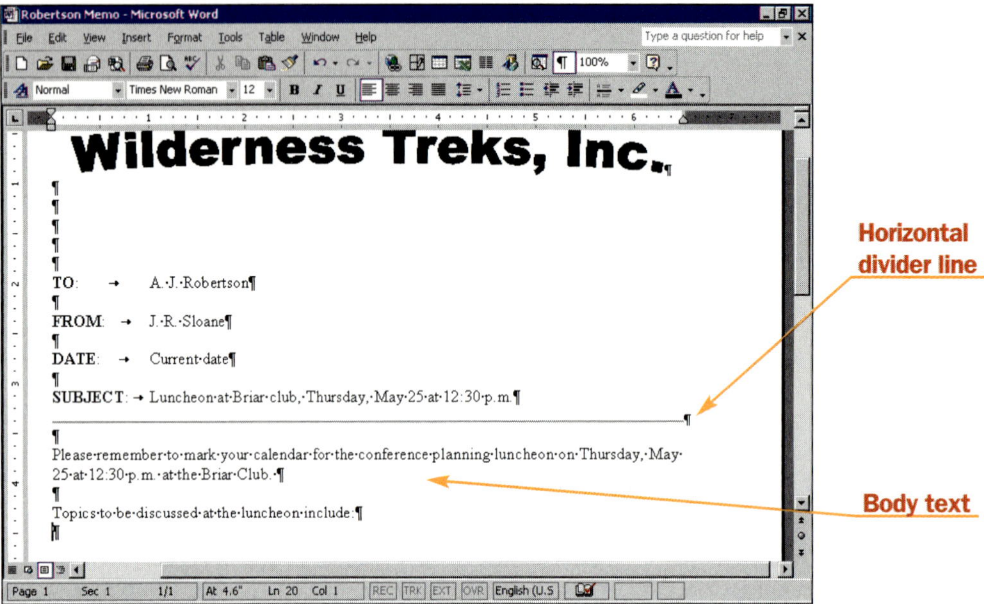

Copy and Paste Between Word Documents

You need to add the list of topics Sloane plans to discuss with the vice presidents during the luncheon. A quick way to do that is to copy the list of topics from Sloane's e-mail message (saved as a Word document) and paste the list into the memo.

Text copied from one Word document and pasted into another Word document retains its original formatting. After you paste the copied list of topics into the memo, you must reformat it to agree with the font and font size formats used in the memo. An easy way to control the formatting of pasted text in Word 2002 is to use the Paste Options smart tag button and menu to specify that the pasted text be formatted like the other text in the document. If you are using Word 2000, you can select the pasted text and reformat it with options on the Formatting toolbar or you can use the Format Painter button on the Standard toolbar to copy formats from existing text to the new pasted text.

Hot Tip

To use the Format Painter, first position the insertion point in the text that contains the formats you want to copy. Then click the **Format Painter** button on the Standard toolbar to turn on the Format Painter. Next, select the text you want to reformat. Word copies the formats from the original text to the selected text.

S TEP-BY-STEP 4.4

1. Open **Step4-4** from the data files. This is Sloane's e-mail message text saved as a Word document.

2. Select the list of conference topics beginning with *Conference travel arrangements* and ending with *Conference speakers.*

3. Click the **Copy** button on the Standard toolbar.

4. Close the **Step4-4** document.

5. Move the insertion point in the Robertson Memo document to the end of the document (the blank line below the *Topics to be discussed at the luncheon include:* paragraph), if necessary.

6. Click the **Paste** button on the Standard toolbar. Note that the pasted text is formatted with its original Courier, 10-point font instead of the Times New Roman, 12-point font used in the memo.

7. Click the **Paste Options** button list arrow near the bottom right corner of the pasted text to view the menu and then click the **Match Destination Formatting** option button to reformat the pasted text with the Times New Roman, 12-point font used in the memo that is the destination document. (If you are using Word 2000, select the pasted text and format it with the Times New Roman, 12-point font using buttons on the Formatting toolbar.)

8. Press **Enter** to insert a blank line.

9. Key the remaining sentence and your initials as shown in Figure 4-6.

FIGURE 4-6
Remaining memo body text

> If you have any questions about the luncheon or the conference topics, please contact me at X397.
>
> xx

10. Save the document and leave it open for the next Step-by-Step.

Create a Bulleted List

Adding numbers or small graphic bullets to a list of items makes the list easier to read and also adds emphasis to it. You want the vice presidents to carefully review the list of conference topics in the memo, so you draw attention to the list by formatting it as a ***bulleted list.***

STEP-BY-STEP 4.5

1. Select the list of conference topics beginning with *Conference travel arrangements* and ending with *Conference speakers*.

2. Click the **Bullets** button on the Formatting toolbar to add small graphic bullets to the selected list. 

3. Deselect the bulleted list text. The document on your screen should now look similar to Figure 4-2, the completed memo.

4. Check the spelling and grammar in the document.

5. Save the document and then print preview, print, and close it.

SUMMARY

In this lesson, you learned:

- An interoffice memorandum or memo is written communication to someone inside your organization.

- Memos generally follow a standard format with the text beginning approximately two inches from the top of the page; there should be a blank line between the TO:, FROM:, DATE:, and SUBJECT: heading paragraphs; there should be a blank line between the heading text and the body of the memo.

- A tab formatting mark is a nonprinting character you insert in your document by pressing the Tab key.

- Custom tab stops are text alignment icons you insert on the horizontal ruler to indicate where text should align in the document.

- The four most frequently used tab alignments are Left, Center, Right, and Decimal. By default, Word documents have left-aligned tab stops every 0.5 inch. You can replace the default tab stops with custom tab stops.

- You use the Tab Alignment button to the left of the horizontal ruler to specify the type of tab alignment and then you click on the horizontal ruler where you want to insert a tab stop.

- A horizontal line can be inserted in a memo between the heading paragraphs and the memo body text to give the memo a polished and professional look.

- A quick way to place a copy of existing text in a new document is to copy the text from the original document and paste it into the new document. Text copied and pasted from one Word document into another retains is original formatting; therefore, you may need to reformat pasted text.

- Adding numbers or small graphic bullets to a list of items makes the list easier to read and adds emphasis to it.

VOCABULARY *Review*

Define the following terms:

Bulleted list	Interoffice memorandum	Tab formatting mark
Horizontal line	Memo	Tab stops

REVIEW *Questions*

TRUE / FALSE

Circle T if the statement is true or F if the statement is false.

T   F   **1.** A tab formatting mark is an icon that you insert on the horizontal ruler to align document text.

T   F   **2.** Custom tab stops are considered part of paragraph formatting, which means you must select the appropriate paragraph(s) before you create custom tab stops.

T   F   **3.** You can insert a horizontal line in a Word document using the Horizontal Line button on the Bulleted List button grid.

T   F   **4.** The Format Painter button is used to copy formatting from text containing specific formatting to text that should have that same formatting.

T   F   **5.** One way to add emphasis to a list of items is to format it as a bulleted list.

FILL IN THE BLANK

Complete the following sentences by writing the correct word or words in the blanks provided.

1. Interoffice memorandums generally have __________ inch left and right __________.

2. Common interoffice memorandum headings include TO:, __________, __________, and __________.

3. You can quickly create custom tab stops using the mouse pointer, the __________ button, and the __________ ruler.

4. Text copied from one Word document and pasted into another Word document retains its original __________.

5. Adding numbers or small graphic __________ to a list of items makes the list easier to read.

PROJECTS

PROJECT 4-1

1. Open the **Project 4-1** data file.

2. Save the document as a template named **Sloane Memo Template** in the default Templates folder and then close it.

3. Create a new memo document based on the Sloane Memo Template.

4. Save the document as **Stackhouse Memo**.

5. Address the memo to **J. L. Stackhouse** and key the current date for the **DATE:** variable text.

6. Open the **Robertson Memo** and copy the **SUBJECT:** variable text and the body text and paste them into the Stackhouse Memo document in the appropriate locations. Then close the **Robertson Memo** document.

7. Save the **Stackhouse Memo** document and then print preview, print, and close it.

8. Follow steps 4 through 7 to create, save, print, and close memos for M. D. Trevino and J. Q. Yong.

9. Leave Word open for the next project.

 ### PROJECT 4-2

Sloane drops by your office and asks you to send a memo to the four marketing and sales directors asking them to turn in the most recent expense accounts no later than May 31. The marketing and sales directors' names are available in the organization chart you reviewed in Job 1. Remind the directors that their expense account information must be broken into four sections: Travel, Entertainment, Meals, and Other Expenses. Using the Sloane Memo Template, create the memos. Use the current date. Use a bulleted list to itemize the expense account breakdown. Remember to check the memos' spelling and grammar. Save each memo with its recipient's name followed by the word *Memo*. Print preview, print, and close each memo.

  ### WEB PROJECT

During lunch today, one of your coworkers mentions that she found several new Word document templates at the Microsoft Office Web site (*www.microsoft.com/office/*). You want to check out the Word templates and see if any of them could be useful. View the Microsoft Office Web site in your Web browser and search the site for the Template Gallery. Review the available Word templates and then create a Word document containing a bulleted list of at least three templates that might be useful. Save, print preview, and print the document.

  ## TEAMWORK PROJECT

 Creating memos is an important part of your job as the administrative assistant to the president. Another important part of an administrative assistant's job is the ability to work well with others. Choose a classmate to work with on this project. You and your classmate think that Word might have some useful memo templates or wizards and want to review them. If you are using Word 2002, open the Templates dialog box. (If you are using Word 2000, open the New dialog box.) Click the Memos tab and review the templates and wizards available. Create at least two memos based on a template or wizard and save and print it. Then using your printed memo examples, you and your classmate should describe to your other classmates how to use Word memo templates and memo wizards.

 # CRITICAL *Thinking*

 ## ACTIVITY 4-1

Word has several different bullet graphics you can use to create bulleted lists. Using the Bullets and Numbering command on the Format menu, explore some of these different bullet graphics. Create a document containing at least three bulleted list examples using different bullets. Then using your examples, describe to your classmates how to use different bullet graphics.

PREPARING A MONTHLY SALES REPORT

OBJECTIVES

Upon completion of this job, you should be able to:

- Enter data in a worksheet.
- Use the AutoSum feature to calculate totals.
- Format a worksheet.
- Change a Sheet tab name and color.
- Preview and print a worksheet.

Estimated Time: 0.5 hour

VOCABULARY

Cell

Columns

Footer

Formula

Function

Range

Rows

Workbook

Worksheet

Enter Data in a Worksheet

Each month, the accounting department gives you a list of the previous month's sales data reported by each branch office. One of your responsibilities is to prepare a report of this sales data for Sloane's review using the Microsoft Excel application. Monitoring sales data is very important to Sloane; therefore, you create the monthly sales report as soon as you receive the sales data from the accounting department.

You use the Microsoft Excel application to organize and analyze numerical data in a document called a *worksheet*. A set of worksheets saved together in one file is called a *workbook*. A worksheet is organized into horizontal *rows* and vertical *columns*. The intersection of a worksheet row and column is called a *cell*. A worksheet has 256 columns and 65,536 rows. A column is identified by its alphabetical column heading such as A, B, C, and so forth up to the last column, which is IV. A row is identified by its numerical row heading such as 1, 2, 3, and so forth up to the last row, which is 65,536. Because a cell is the intersection of a column and row, it is referenced by both its column heading and its row heading. For example, the cell at the intersection of column A and row 1 is always referenced as *cell A1* and the cell at the intersection of column C and row 5 is always referenced as *cell C5*. By default, a new workbook contains three blank worksheets.

Did You Know?

Two other selection techniques are also important: the Shift + Click technique and the Ctrl + Click technique. To select a large group of cells, click the upper-left cell in the group and then press the **Shift** key while you click the lower-right cell in the group. To select multiple cells that are not grouped together, click the first cell and then press the **Ctrl** key as you click additional cells. You can also use the Shift + Click and Ctrl + Click techniques to select adjacent and nonadjacent rows and columns.

The cell you select to work in is called the active cell. The active cell has a heavy black border. To activate a cell, simply click the cell with the mouse pointer. You can also press the Enter key to activate the next cell in the same column and the arrow keys to active a cell to the left, right, above, or below the currently active cell. You enter text and numbers in worksheet cells in the following three-step process:

Step 1: Activate the cell.

Step 2: Key the text or number.

Step 3: Press the Enter key or press an arrow key to enter the cell contents in the worksheet.

You can select cells, rows, and columns in several ways. To select a single cell, simply click the cell. To select a group of cells, press and hold the left mouse button while you drag across the cells. Select an entire row or an entire column by clicking the row header button or column header button. Select multiple rows or multiple columns by dragging across the row or column header buttons. Select the entire worksheet by clicking the **Select All** button (the blank button above row 1 and to the left of column A).

This morning you receive a note from the accounting manager giving you the most recent monthly sales data, shown in Table 5-1. Each monthly sales report contains the same heading, branch office, and travel package text. To make it easier to prepare the report each month, you use an existing worksheet and simply enter the new sales report data, perform the total calculations, format the worksheet, and print it. You begin by opening the partially completed worksheet and entering the sales data.

TABLE 5-1
Monthly sales data

	AUSTIN	CALGARY	LONDON	SYDNEY
Backpacking	13,000	35,000	5,750	3,500
Ballooning	23,500	15,650	10,450	16,780
Dog Sledding	3,200	17,900	4,500	5,000
Sailing	11,000	8,750	45,870	57,450
Safaris	8,350	9,000	34,750	17,500
Scuba Diving	23,750	18,300	75,850	65,250
Other	3,000	7,500	9,300	5,750

S TEP-BY-STEP 5.1

1. Start the Excel application, if necessary. If you are using Excel 2002, close the New Workbook task pane.

2. Open the **Step5-1** Excel workbook from the data files.

3. Save the workbook as **Monthly Sales Report**.

4. Click cell **B8** to make it the active cell.

5. Key **13000** and press **Enter** to enter the sales data in the cell and move the active cell indicator down to the next cell in the column. (Do not key the comma; you apply formatting to the sales numbers later in this lesson.)

6. Verify that cell **B9** is now the active cell.

7. Key **23500** and press **Enter**.

STEP-BY-STEP 5.1 Continued

8. Continue entering the sales data from Table 5-1 in the appropriate cells. After you enter the data, the partially completed worksheet should look similar to Figure 5-1.

FIGURE 5-1
Worksheet with data

	A	B	C	D	E	F
1	Wilderness Treks, Inc.					
2	Monthly Sales Report					
3						
4						
5		Austin	Calgary	London	Sydney	Pkg. Total
6						
7	Travel Packages					
8	Backpacking	13000	35000	5750	3500	
9	Ballooning	23500	15650	10450	16780	
10	Dog Sledding	3200	17900	4500	5000	
11	Sailing	11000	8750	45870	57450	
12	Safaris	8350	9000	34750	17500	
13	Scuba Diving	23750	18300	75850	65250	
14	Other	3000	7500	9300	5750	
15	Branch Total					
16						

9. Save the workbook and leave it open for the next Step-by-Step.

Use the AutoSum Feature to Calculate Totals

Next, you want to calculate the total sales for each adventure travel package and the total sales for each branch office. To do this, you must enter formulas in the cells that should contain the totals. A *formula* is a mathematical calculation. When entering a formula, you begin by keying the equal sign (=) to indicate you are creating a formula. Then you specify the cell references containing the numbers on which you are performing the calculations and the type of calculation to take place such as addition (+), subtraction (-), multiplication (*), or division (/).

Some formulas include a *function*, which is a predefined calculation. There are hundreds of functions you can use to perform many different calculations; however, the most commonly used function is the SUM function. The SUM function is used to calculate the total value of a group of cells called a *range*. For example, in the Monthly Sales Report workbook, the range B8:B14 represents the cells containing the sales data for the Austin branch office. You could use the SUM function to calculate the total sales for the Austin branch office by activating cell *B15* and entering the following formula: =SUM(B8:B14).

Hot Tip

A function consists of the function name and the cell references or other values used in the calculation placed inside a set of parentheses. A function must always have a set of parentheses even when the function calculation does not act on specific cell references. For example, the NOW function, which adds the current system date and time to a worksheet, does not act on specific cells. However, you enter the NOW function as NOW(). Also note that when a function is the first calculation in a formula, it is preceded by the equal (=) sign, but the equal (=) sign is not part of the function.

To save time you can also enter this same formula using the AutoSum button on the Standard toolbar. AutoSum automatically enters the equal (=) sign, enters the SUM function, and selects and enters the range of cells to add. You can also use AutoSum to quickly calculate row or column totals or both row and column totals at once by first selecting the appropriate range of cells, including blank cells, in which AutoSum can place the total calculations. You use AutoSum to calculate both the branch office totals and the adventure travel package totals in one step.

> **Warning** 
>
> AutoSum guesses the range of cells to add by looking at the cells above or to the left of the cell containing the SUM function. You must always carefully review any AutoSum calculation to be certain the correct range of cells is included in the calculation. If the AutoSum feature places the incorrect range of cells in the SUM function's parentheses, you can simply select the correct range of cells to replace the range inside the parentheses.

S TEP-BY-STEP 5.2

1. Verify that the Monthly Sales Report workbook is open. Select the range **B8:F15** to select the cells containing the sales data and blank cells in which to enter the total calculations.

2. Click the **AutoSum** button on the Standard toolbar. Your worksheet should look similar to Figure 5-2. 

FIGURE 5-2
Selected range with totals

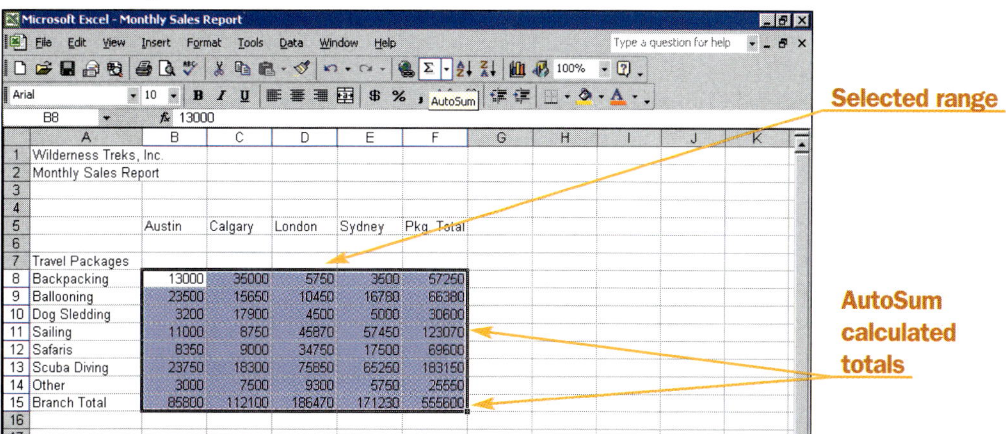

	A	B	C	D	E	F
1	Wilderness Treks, Inc.					
2	Monthly Sales Report					
3						
4						
5		Austin	Calgary	London	Sydney	Pkg. Total
6						
7	Travel Packages					
8	Backpacking	13000	35000	5750	3500	57250
9	Ballooning	23500	15650	10450	16780	66380
10	Dog Sledding	3200	17900	4500	5000	30600
11	Sailing	11000	8750	45870	57450	123070
12	Safaris	8350	9000	34750	17500	69600
13	Scuba Diving	23750	18300	75850	65250	183150
14	Other	3000	7500	9300	5750	25550
15	Branch Total	85800	112100	186470	171230	555600
16						

3. Press an arrow key or click a cell to deselect the range.

4. Save the workbook and leave it open for the next Step-by-Step.

Format a Worksheet

To give the worksheet a professional look, you format it by changing the worksheet title font size, right-aligning and bolding the column labels, indenting row labels, applying special formatting to cells containing numbers, and centering worksheet titles across a range of cells.

Changing the Font Size

It is important that all financial documents contain the date for which the financial data is relevant. Next, you add a worksheet title that adds a date to the report. To emphasize the three worksheet titles, you increase the font size. You want the company name and report name to be formatted with the 14-point font and the date to be formatted with the 12-point font. To quickly change the font size, you first select the appropriate range of cells and then use the Font Size button on the Formatting toolbar to select the new font size.

S TEP-BY-STEP 5.3

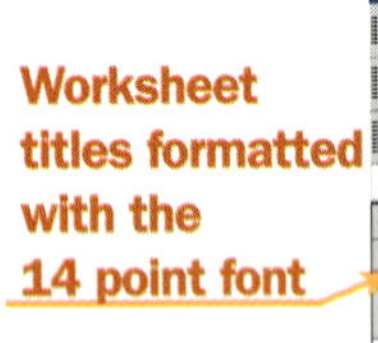

1. Verify that the Monthly Sales Report workbook is open. Activate cell **A3** and enter **4/30/yyyy** (where yyyy is the current year).

2. Select the range **A1:A2**. Although you can see the heading text overflow across cells to the right, the actual title text is in the range of cells A1:A3.

3. Click the **Font Size** button list arrow on the Formatting toolbar.

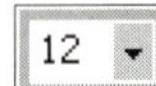

4. Click **14**.

5. Activate cell **A3** and change the font size to **12** point. The titles in your worksheet should look similar to Figure 5-3.

FIGURE 5-3
Formatted worksheet titles

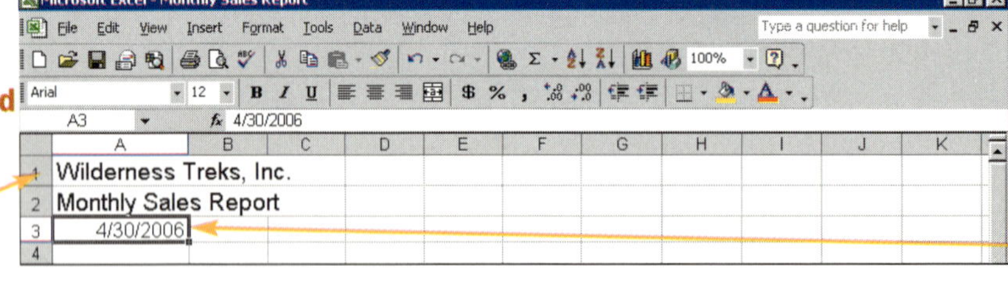

6. Save the workbook and leave it open for the next Step-by-Step.

Center the Worksheet Titles Across a Range of Cells

To center multiple rows of text across a range of cells, you must first select the cells containing the text plus the range of cells over which the text is to be centered. Then you use an option in the Alignment tab in the Font dialog box to center the text over the selected range.

> **Warning**
>
> You can also center text across a range of cells using the Merge and Center button on the Formatting toolbar; however, you can only center one row at a time using this method.

S TEP-BY-STEP 5.4

1. Verify that the Monthly Sales Report workbook is open. Select the range **A1:F3** to select both the cells that contain the text and the range over which the text is centered.

2. Click the **Format** menu, click **Cells**, and click the **Alignment tab** to view the Alignment options in the Format Cells dialog box.

3. Click the **Horizontal** list arrow and click **Center Across Selection**. The dialog box on your screen should look similar to Figure 5-4.

FIGURE 5-4
Alignment tab in the Format Cells dialog box

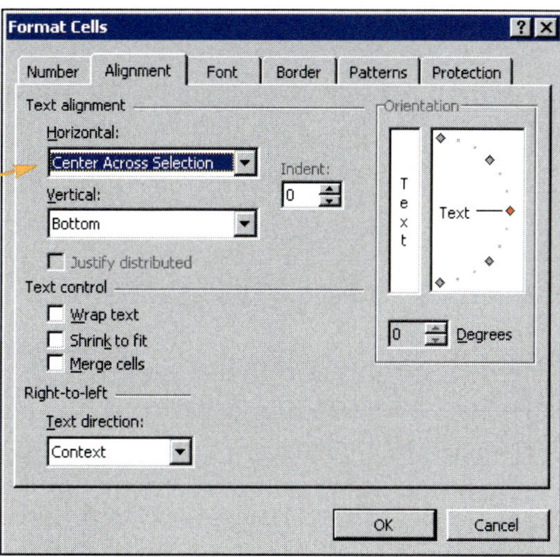

4. Click **OK**.

5. Observe that the worksheet titles are now centered across the range A1:F3.

6. Deselect the range.

7. Save the workbook and leave it open for the next Step-by-Step.

Aligning and Bolding Cell Contents

You can align cell contents to the left, right, or center within the cell. To make the column label text align more attractively with the sales data, you right-align the column label within each cell. You also add emphasis to cell contents by applying the bold, italic, or underline format. You want to apply the bold format to the column label text.

S TEP-BY-STEP 5.5

1. Verify that the Monthly Sales Report workbook is open. Select the range **B5:F5**.

2. Click the **Align Right** button on the Formatting toolbar to right align each cell's contents within the cell. 

3. Click the **Bold** button on the Formatting toolbar to apply the bold format to each cell's contents. 

4. Deselect the range and observe the new formatting applied to the column label text. Your worksheet should look similar to Figure 5-5.

FIGURE 5-5
Formatted column labels

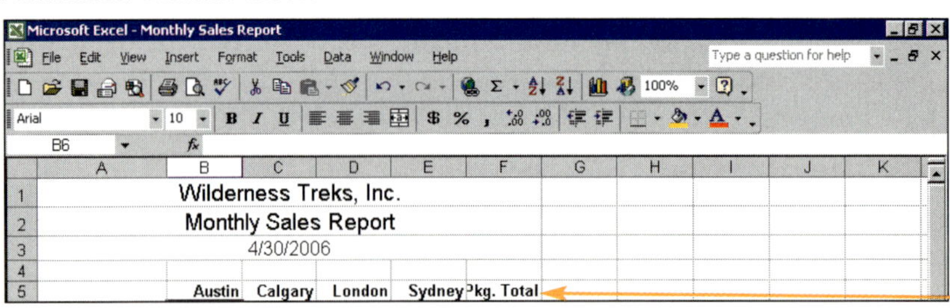

Right-aligned and bolded column labels

5. Save the workbook and leave it open for the next Step-by-Step.

Indenting Cell Contents

To make financial reports easier to read, you can indent subheading text. For example, the Monthly Sales Report is easier to read if you indent the names of the individual packages in the range A8:A14. To indent cell contents, you first select the cell or range of cells and then click the Increase Indent button on the Formatting toolbar.

Did You Know?

To indent cell contents more than one position to the right within the cell, click the **Increase Indent** button on the Formatting toolbar multiple times. You can remove the indentation formatting cell contents by first selecting the cell or range of cells and clicking the **Decrease Indent** button on the Formatting toolbar.

STEP-BY-STEP 5.6

1. Verify that the Monthly Sales Report workbook is open. Select the range **A8:A14**.

2. Click the **Increase Indent** button on the Formatting toolbar to indent the cells' contents one position to the right.

3. Deselect the range. The worksheet on your screen should look similar to Figure 5-6.

FIGURE 5-6
Indented text

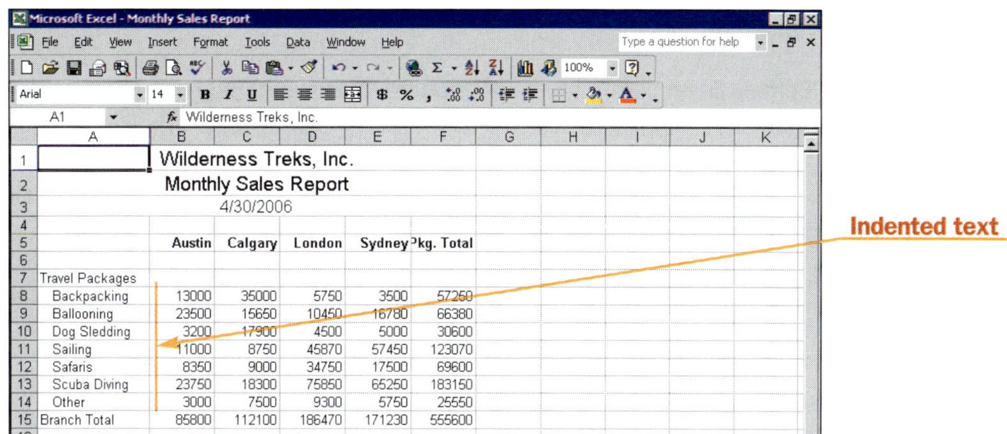

Indented text

4. Save the workbook and leave it open for the next Step-by-Step.

Formatting Numbers

When working with financial data, it is very important that the numbers be easy to read. For example, in most financial reports, dollar values are presented in whole dollars instead of dollars and cents. Additionally, dollar signs are used sparingly, usually just on the first and last rows of data. The comma is used to indicate thousands, millions, and so forth. Finally, a single underline is used before a column total and a double underline is often added below a column total.

A quick way to format numbers is with the Currency Style and Comma Style buttons on the Formatting toolbar. The Currency Style and Comma Style buttons apply a group of formats that include a comma and two decimal places. The Currency Style also adds a dollar sign. If you use the Currency Style or Comma Style buttons to format numbers that should be viewed in whole dollars, you need to decrease the number of decimal places to zero (0) with the Decrease Decimal button on the Formatting toolbar.

> **Hot Tip** 
>
> When you apply formatting to cell contents, a series of number signs (######) may appear in a cell indicating that the column is no longer wide enough to see the formatted cell contents. If you see ####### in a cell, simply widen the column with the mouse pointer or the Column command on the Format menu.

STEP-BY-STEP 5.7

1. Verify that the Monthly Sales Report workbook is open. Select the ranges **B8:F8** and **B15:F15** using the **Ctrl** key.

2. Click the **Currency Style** button on the Formatting toolbar to format the cells' contents with a dollar sign, comma, and two decimal places. 

3. Click the **Decrease Decimal** button on the Formatting toolbar twice to decrease the decimal places to zero.

4. Select the range **B9:F14**.

5. Click the **Comma Style** button on the Formatting toolbar to format the cells' contents with a comma and two decimal places.

6. Click the **Decrease Decimal** button on the Formatting toolbar twice to decrease the decimal places to zero.

7. Select the range **B14:F14** and click the **Underline** button on the Formatting toolbar to add a single underline. 

8. Select the range **B15:F15** and click the **Format** menu, click **Cells**, and click the **Font** tab to view the underline options in the Format Cells dialog box.

9. Click the **Underline** list arrow and click **Double Accounting**. The dialog box on your screen should look similar to Figure 5-7.

FIGURE 5-7
Font tab in the Format Cells dialog box

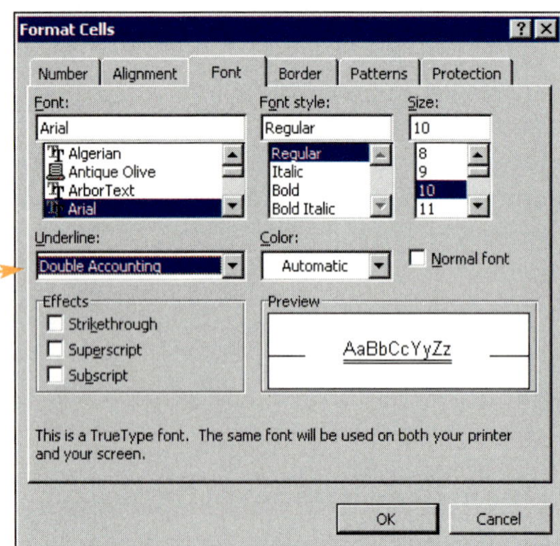

10. Click **OK**.

11. Deselect the range. Your worksheet should look similar to Figure 5-8.

FIGURE 5-8
Completed worksheet

	Austin	Calgary	London	Sydney	Pkg. Total
Travel Packages					
Backpacking	$ 13,000	$ 35,000	$ 5,750	$ 3,500	$ 57,250
Ballooning	23,500	15,650	10,450	16,780	66,380
Dog Sledding	3,200	17,900	4,500	5,000	30,600
Sailing	11,000	8,750	45,870	57,450	123,070
Safaris	8,350	9,000	34,750	17,500	69,600
Scuba Diving	23,750	18,300	75,850	65,250	183,150
Other	3,000	7,500	9,300	5,750	25,550
Branch Total	$ 85,800	$ 112,100	$ 186,470	$ 171,230	$ 555,600

12. Save the workbook and leave it open for the next Step-by-Step.

Change a Sheet Tab Name and Color

Each workbook automatically contains three worksheets and can contain up to 255 worksheets. Each worksheet has a Sheet tab that is named Sheet1, Sheet2, Sheet3, and so forth. It is a good idea to change the name on a Sheet tab to provide more information about the contents of the worksheet. For example, you change the Sheet1 name to April Sales Report to better identify the worksheet. Additionally, if you are using Excel 2002, you can change the color of a Sheet tab. This is useful when there are multiple worksheets in the same workbook and you want to color-code them. To color-code the worksheet, you change the April Sales Report Sheet tab to red.

STEP-BY-STEP 5.8

1. Verify that the Monthly Sales Report workbook is open. Right-click the **Sheet1** tab and click **Rename** to select the contents of the Sheet1 tab.

2. Key **April Sales Report** and press **Enter**.

3. Right-click the **April Sales Report** Sheet tab and click **Tab Color**. (*Note:* If you are using Excel 2000, skip Steps 3–5.)

STEP-BY-STEP 5.8 Continued

4. Click the **Red** square on the Format Tab Color grid. The Format Tab Color grid on your screen should look similar to Figure 5-9.

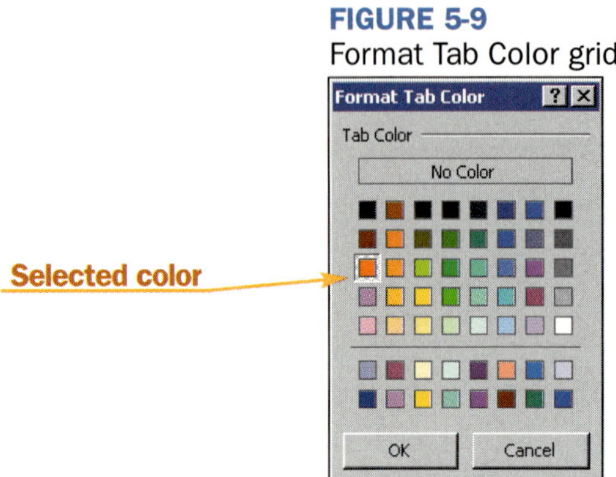

FIGURE 5-9
Format Tab Color grid

5. Click **OK**. The April Sales Report Sheet tab should look similar to Figure 5-10.

FIGURE 5-10
Formatted Sheet tab

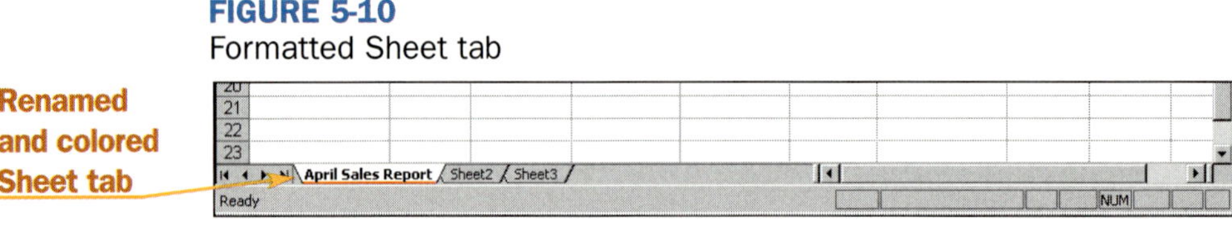

6. Save the workbook and leave it open for the next Step-by-Step.

Preview and Print a Worksheet

Now that you have finished the April Sales Report worksheet, you are ready to print it. Before you print the report, you want to add your name and the current date at the bottom of the printed worksheet. You can do this by keying the information in a special area called a *footer*. Then you print preview the worksheet to see how it looks before it is printed. This gives you the opportunity to make any additional changes to the layout of the worksheet before you print it. Finally, you print the worksheet.

STEP-BY-STEP 5.9

1. Verify that the Monthly Sales Report workbook is open. Click the **File** menu, click **Page Setup**, and click the **Header/Footer** tab to view the Header/Footer options in the Page Setup dialog box.

2. Click **Custom Footer**.

3. Key your name at the left margin in the **Left section** text box of Footer dialog box.

STEP-BY-STEP 5.9 Continued

4. Press **Tab** twice to move the insertion point to the right margin in the **Right section** text box of the Footer dialog box and click the **Date** button in the Footer dialog box to insert the current date as a code. Your Footer dialog box should look similar to Figure 5-11. 

FIGURE 5-11
Footer dialog box

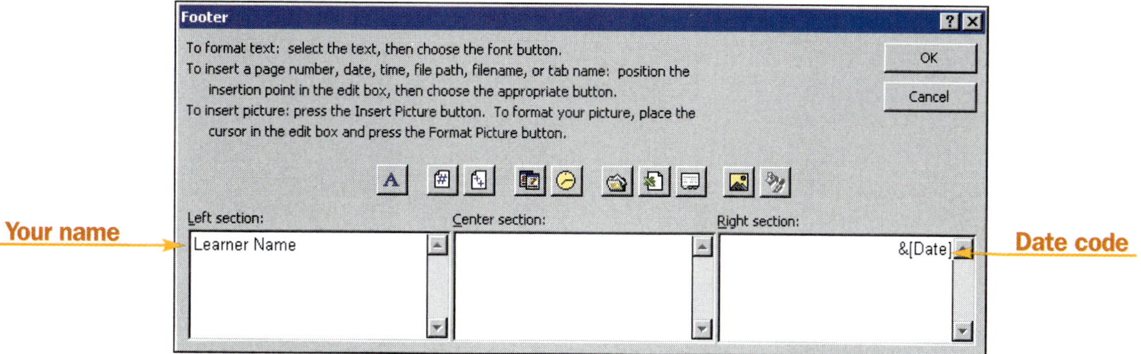

5. Click **OK** to close the Footer dialog box. Your Page Setup dialog box should look similar to Figure 5-12.

FIGURE 5-12
Page Setup dialog box

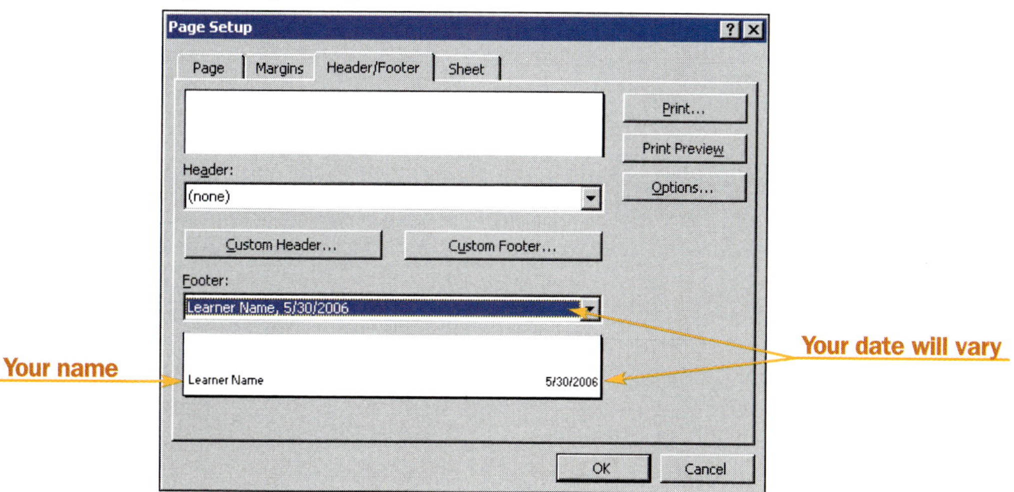

6. Click **OK**.

STEP-BY-STEP 5.9 Continued

7. Click the **Print Preview** button on the Standard toolbar. Your worksheet should look similar to Figure 5-13.

FIGURE 5-13
Print Preview

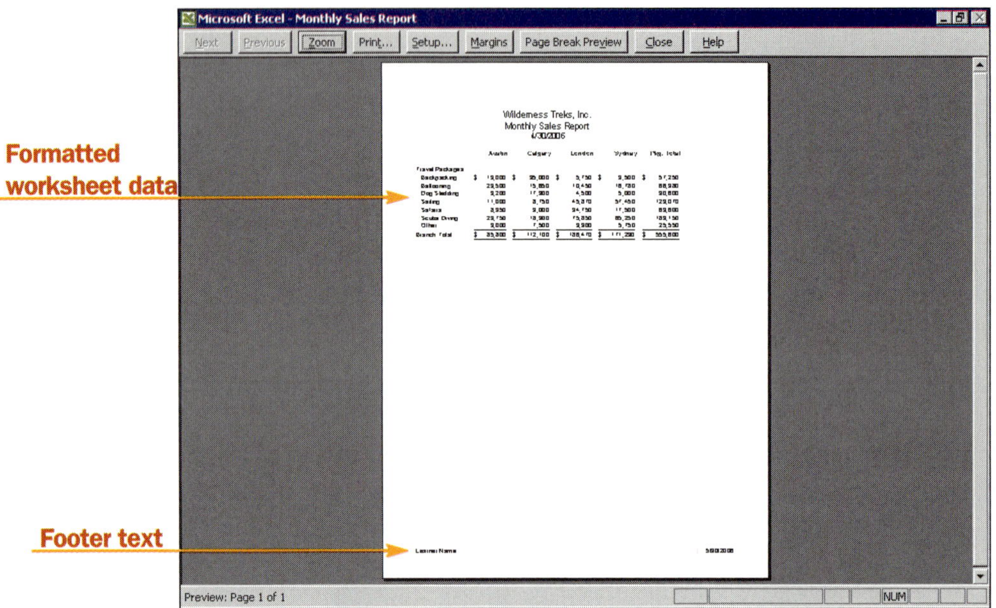

8. Print the worksheet, save the workbook, and close it.

SUMMARY

In this lesson, you learned:

- Microsoft Excel is used to analyze numerical data in a document called a worksheet.

- A worksheet is organized into 65,536 horizontal rows and 256 vertical columns.

- The intersection of a row and column is called a cell and you enter text and numbers in cells.

- A cell is always referenced by its column letter and row number. For example, the cell at the intersection of column A and row 1 is referenced as cell A1 in formulas and written instructions.

- A formula is a mathematical calculation you begin by keying an equal (=) sign. You complete a formula by keying the appropriate cell references and mathematical operators such as addition (+), subtraction (-), multiplication (*), or division (/).

- Functions are predefined calculations and the most common function is the SUM function used to add the numbers in a range of cells.

- The AutoSum button on the Standard toolbar automatically inserts the equal (=) sign, the SUM function, a set of parentheses, and within the parentheses a range of cells to be added.

- To give a worksheet a professional look, you can format the cell contents in a variety of ways: for example, you can change the font size; change the alignment; apply bold, italic, and underline formatting; indent text; and apply special formatting to numbers including dollar signs, commas, and decimal points.

- To better identify a worksheet, you can change the Sheet tab name and add a color.

- You can add additional text to a worksheet in a footer and then preview the worksheet to see how it will look before you print it.

VOCABULARY *Review*

Define the following terms:

Cell	Formula	Rows
Columns	Function	Workbook
Footer	Range	Worksheet

REVIEW *Questions*

TRUE / FALSE

Circle T if the statement is true or F if the statement is false.

T   F   **1.** A document that is organized into horizontal rows and vertical columns used for numerical analysis is called a workbook.

T   F   **2.** By default, a workbook contains five worksheets.

T   F   **3.** A function is a predefined calculation.

T   F   **4.** A group of cells is called a range.

T   F   **5.** You can center multiple rows of data across a range of cells using the Merge and Center button on the Formatting toolbar.

FILL IN THE BLANK

Complete the following sentences by writing the correct word or words in the blanks provided.

1. The Currency Style button applies a group of formats that includes a dollar sign, a comma, and _________ decimal points.

2. When you see a series of number _________ in a cell, it means the column is not wide enough to view the formatted cell contents.

3. You can add a footer to a worksheet with options in the _________ _________ dialog box.

4. The appropriate reference for the cell in column A and row 5 is ___________.

5. To use the AutoSum button to automatically total both rows and columns in one step, you must first select a range of cells that includes ___________ cells in which to store the totals.

PROJECTS

PROJECT 5-1

1. Open the **Project 5-1** Excel workbook data file.

2. Save the workbook as **Monthly Expense Report**.

3. Select the range **B8:F13** and use the **AutoSum** button on the Standard toolbar to create branch office totals and travel expense totals.

4. Activate cell **A3** and key the current date in the **mm/dd/yyyy** format.

5. Select the range **A1:A3** and format the cells with the **12**-point font, then center the cell contents over the range **A1:F3**.

6. Select the column labels in the range **B5:F5** and center them within the cells.

7. Select the row labels in the range **A8:A12** and indent the cell contents one position to the right.

8. Select the ranges **B8:F8** and **B13:F13** using the **Ctrl** key, format the cell contents with the Currency Style, and decrease the decimal places to 0.

9. Select the range **B9:F12**, format the cell contents with the Comma Style, and decrease the decimal places to 0.

10. Change the Sheet1 tab to **Monthly Expense Report** and, if you are using Excel 2002, make the tab color blue.

11. Key your name at the left margin and key the current date at the right margin in a footer on the Monthly Expense Report worksheet.

12. Save the workbook and then print preview and print the Monthly Expense Report worksheet. Finally, close the worksheet.

 PROJECT 5-2

Sloane calls and asks you to modify the Monthly Expense Report to correct some data and change the formatting. Open the **Monthly Expense Report** workbook you created in Project 5-1. If you have not yet completed Project 5-1, do so now. Save the workbook as **Revised Monthly Expense Report**. Change the London airfare expense to $3,500 and the Sydney Other expense to $350. Add a single underline before the column totals and a Double Accounting underline after the column totals. Then apply the bold format to the indented row labels and the column labels. Save, print preview, and print the worksheet.

  ## WEB PROJECT

In preparation for the conference, Sloane asks you to get sample roundtrip airfares from Austin, London, and Sydney to Calgary. Using the search tool in your Web browser or another online search tool such as Yahoo! (*www.yahoo.com*), locate at least three different Web sites you can use to find roundtrip airfare. Find at least two airfare quotes for each city and print the Web pages.

  ## TEAMWORK PROJECT

 A coworker asks for your help. She knows how to select cells by dragging across them with the mouse pointer; however, she would like to learn other selection techniques. Using online Excel Help, if necessary, practice multiple selection techniques using the mouse pointer to select adjacent cells, nonadjacent cells, rows, columns, and the entire worksheet. Then demonstrate to a classmate the various selection techniques.

 # CRITICAL *Thinking*

 ## ACTIVITY 5-1

Because the AutoSum button on the Standard toolbar saved you so much time in preparing the Monthly Sales Report and the Monthly Expense Report, you want to explore other AutoSum button functions. Using online Excel Help and the AutoSum button drop-down menu, explore the other functions available on the button menu: Average, Count, Max, and Min. Create a worksheet that contains examples of each function and then save, print preview, and print it. Then using your printed worksheet, discuss how to use these functions with your classmates. (If you are using Excel 2000, the AutoSum button only acts on the SUM function and does not contain a menu of other frequently used functions. Use online Help to review the Average, Count, Max, and Min functions.)

CREATING A MEMO WITH EMBEDDED EXCEL DATA

OBJECTIVES

Upon completion of this job, you should be able to:

- Include a distribution list with a memo.
- Embed Excel data as an object in a Word document.
- Edit an embedded Excel object in a Word document.
- Send a Word document as an e-mail message.

Estimated Time: 0.5 hour

VOCABULARY

Destination file

Distribution list

Embedded object

Object

Source file

Include a Distribution List with a Memo

Your remaining task on this week's list of assignments is to distribute the Monthly Sales Report. Sloane reminds you to send a copy of the report to all vice presidents and directors. To avoid creating eight individual memos, you decide to create one memo and send it to all recipients via e-mail. However, there are too many names to fit attractively in the TO variable text area in the memo, so you want to create a distribution list for the memo. A *distribution list* is a list of multiple TO addressees keyed on the last page of a memo. You begin by creating the memo using the Sloane Memo Template you created in Job 4. Then you create a second page and key the vice presidents' and directors' names on the page.

By default, the Automatic numbered lists option (found in the AutoFormat As You Type tab in the AutoCorrect dialog box) is turned on when either Word 2002 or Word 2000 is installed. When this option is turned on, Word attempts to create a numbered list using the "A., B., C." numbering scheme whenever you key text beginning with "A." If you are keying initials as part of a name, you should either turn off the option or stop the creation of the numbered list. To stop the creation of the numbered list in Word 2002, you can click the AutoCorrect Options smart tag action button list arrow and click Undo Automatic Numbering in the smart tag menu. If you are using Word 2000, you can select the numbered items, click the Bullets and Numbering button on the Formatting toolbar to remove the number format, and continue with the list.

> ### Hot Tip
>
> You can quickly do many frequently performed tasks by using Word keyboard shortcut keys. For example, press **Ctrl + End** to move the insertion point to the bottom of a document; press **Ctrl + Home** to move the insertion point to the top of a document; or press **Ctrl + Enter** to create a new page by inserting a page break. To review a complete list of the Word keyboard shortcut keys, search Word online Help using the search phrase "keyboard shortcuts."

STEP-BY-STEP 6.1

1. Start the Word application, if necessary. If you are using Word 2002, close the New Document task pane.

2. Create a new memo document based on the Sloane Memo Template you created in Unit 1 Project 4-1. If you have not yet completed Unit 1 Project 4-1, do so now.

3. Key the memo variable information as shown in Figure 6-1.

FIGURE 6-1
Sales Report Memo variable information

TO:	Distribution
FROM:	J. R. Sloane
DATE:	Current Date
SUBJECT:	Monthly Sales Report for April

Please review the Monthly Sales Report data as shown below. Be prepared to discuss your branch office's April sales data at the next staff meeting.

4. Press **Ctrl + End** to move the insertion point to the end of the document.

5. Press **Enter** four times to create four blank lines.

6. Press **Ctrl + Enter** to create a new, blank second page.

7. Key **Distribution:** on the first line of the page and press **Enter** twice.

8. Key the list of names as shown in Figure 6-2. If the Automatic numbered lists option is turned on in the AutoFormat As You Type tab of the AutoCorrect dialog box, use the AutoCorrect Options smart tag (in Word 2002) or the shortcut menu (in Word 2000) to stop the creation of the numbered list beginning with "A."

FIGURE 6-2
Distribution list names

A.J. Robertson
J. L. Stackhouse
M. D. Trevino
J. Q. Yong
L. D. Meeker
R. T. Thomas
D. C. Washington
M. P. Matthews

STEP-BY-STEP 6.1 Continued

9. Switch to **Print Layout view**, if necessary, click the **Zoom** button list arrow on the Standard toolbar, and click **Two Pages**. Your document should look similar to Figure 6-3.

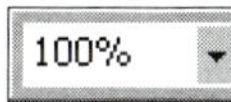

FIGURE 6-3
Two-page memo

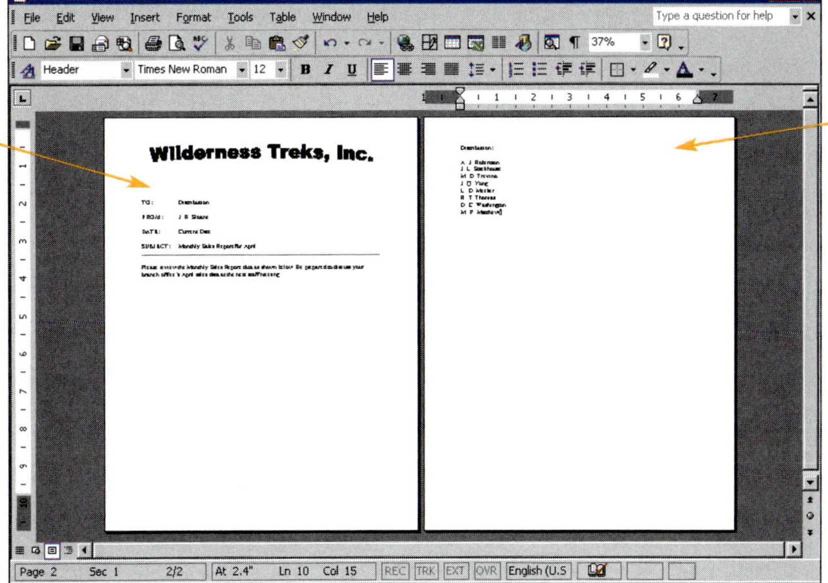

10. Press **Ctrl + Home** to move the insertion point to the top of the document and then click the **Zoom** button list arrow on the Standard toolbar and click **100%**.

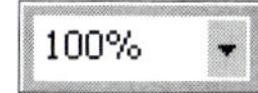

11. Click the **Spelling and Grammar** button to check the spelling and grammar in the document. Make any necessary changes.

12. Save the document as **Sales Report Memo** and leave it open for the next Step-by-Step.

Embed Excel Data As an Object in a Word Document

An *object* is information from one file called the *source file* that is placed in another file called the *destination file*. An *embedded object* is an object that must be edited with the menus, toolbars, and other features from the source application. For example, if you paste information copied from an Excel worksheet (the source file) into a Word document (the destination file) as an embedded object, the object can be edited only by using Excel menus, toolbars, and other features. Pasting Excel information into a Word document as an embedded object allows you to take advantage of the superior number formatting and calculating features of Excel while still working with a Word document.

The next step in preparing the Sales Report Memo is to include the sales report data. Instead of keying the data in the memo, you copy the report data from the Monthly Sales Report workbook and then paste it into the memo as an embedded Excel object.

Hot Tip

You can also copy Excel data and paste it into a Word document using the **Paste** command on the **Edit** menu or the **Paste** button on the Standard toolbar. However, this method pastes the Excel data into a Word table that must then be edited using Word editing features.

S TEP-BY-STEP 6.2

1. Start Excel and open the **Step6-2** Excel workbook from the data files.

2. Select the range **A1:F15**.

3. Click the **Copy** button on the Standard toolbar. 

4. Switch to the **Word** application and the **Sales Report Memo** document.

5. Move the insertion point to the second blank line below the memo body text in the Sales Report Memo document to indicate where you want to paste the Excel data.

6. Click the **Edit** menu and click **Paste Special** to open the Paste Special dialog box.

7. Click the **Paste** option button, if necessary, to select it.

Did You Know?

You can share data between different Office applications in a variety of ways. For example, you can embed or link Excel data in a PowerPoint slide, send a PowerPoint presentation to Word to create audience handouts, send a Word outline document to PowerPoint to create a presentation, use names and addresses in an Outlook Contacts list or Access database together with a Word form letter document to create multiple letters at one time, export an Access database to an Excel worksheet, and so forth. For more information on the many ways to share data between Office applications, see Word, Excel, PowerPoint, or Access online Help.

STEP-BY-STEP 6.2 Continued

8. Click **Microsoft Excel Worksheet Object** in the As list box. The dialog box on your screen should look similar to Figure 6-4.

FIGURE 6-4
Paste Special dialog box

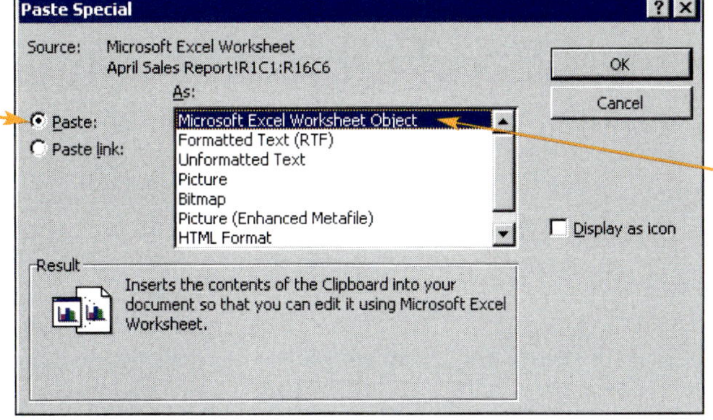

9. Click **OK**.

10. Click the embedded object to select it and then click the **Center** button on the Formatting tool-bar to center the object between the left and right margins. (*Note:* If you are using Word 2000, you cannot use the Center button to center an embedded Excel object in a Word document. You can drag the object to center it or leave it at the left margin.) 

11. Click below the embedded object at the left margin to deselect the object. Your memo with the embed-ded Excel object should look similar to Figure 6-5. (*Note:* You may not be able to see the double under-lines below the column totals at a 100% zoom or less; however, the double underlines are there and print appropriately. If you are using Word 2000, the Excel worksheet gridlines may also be visible.)

FIGURE 6-5
Memo with embedded object

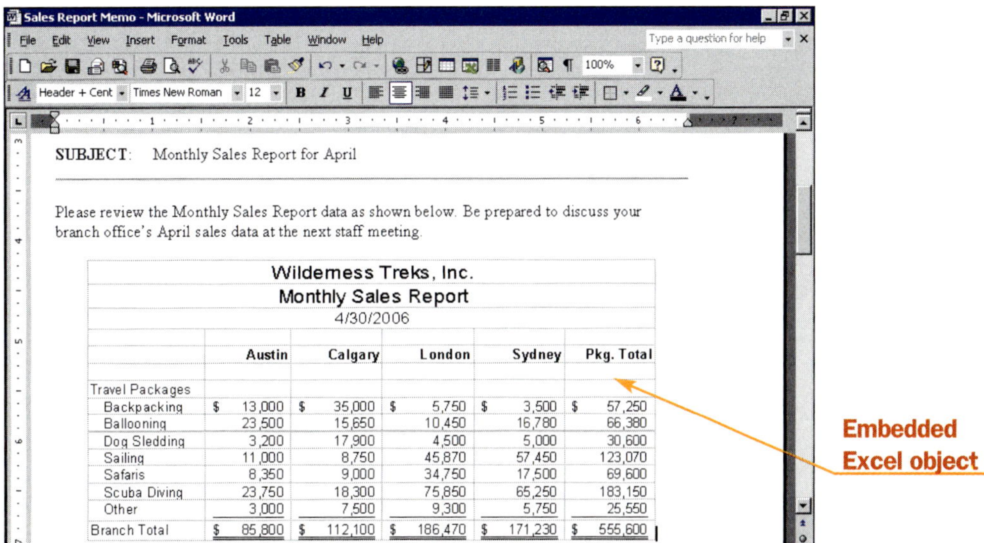

STEP-BY-STEP 6.2 Continued

12. Save the document and leave it open for the next Step-by-Step.

13. Close the Excel application and workbook. If asked whether or not you want to save the large Clipboard item, click No.

Edit an Embedded Excel Object in a Word Document

To edit an embedded Excel object in a Word document, you simply double-click the object. Double-clicking an embedded Excel object displays the Excel menu and toolbars at the top of the Word window and displays the Excel information within a small worksheet-style window. You make your changes using Excel features and then you click outside the object to deselect it when the editing is complete. Editing an embedded Excel object in a Word document *does not* change the original Excel worksheet source file. The changes only occur in the Excel object in the Word document destination file.

After reviewing the memo, you decide to reformat the worksheet heading text and the column labels in the Excel embedded object. You want to apply the italic format to add additional emphasis to the heading and column label text.

> **Did You Know?** 
>
> You can also copy Excel data and paste it into a Word document as a linked object. When you link an Excel object in a Word document, you create a reference (or link) to the original Excel worksheet. A linked Excel object must be edited in its original file. Any changes you make to the original Excel file are reflected in the Word document. In Word 2000 or Word 2002 you can use the Paste Special command on the Edit menu to paste a linked Excel object.

STEP-BY-STEP 6.3

1. Verify that the Sales Report Memo is open. Double-click the embedded Excel object to select it for editing.

STEP-BY-STEP 6.3 Continued

2. Observe the Excel menu bar, toolbars, and formula bar at the top of the Word window. Observe that the Excel information is now placed in a worksheet-style window complete with columns, rows, and other worksheet features. Observe the Word title bar above the menu bar to confirm that you are still working in the Word document.

3. Using the Ctrl key, select the ranges **A1:A3** and **B5:F5** in the embedded Excel object inside the worksheet-style window.

4. Click the **Italic** button on the Formatting toolbar to add the italic format.

5. Deselect the range and activate cell A1. Your embedded Excel object should look similar to Figure 6-6.

> **Warning**
>
> When editing an embedded Excel object in a Word document, it is a good idea to activate the upper-left cell in the embedded worksheet (usually cell A1) before you deselect the object so that you are viewing the beginning of the embedded object when it is deselected.

FIGURE 6-6
Edited embedded Excel object

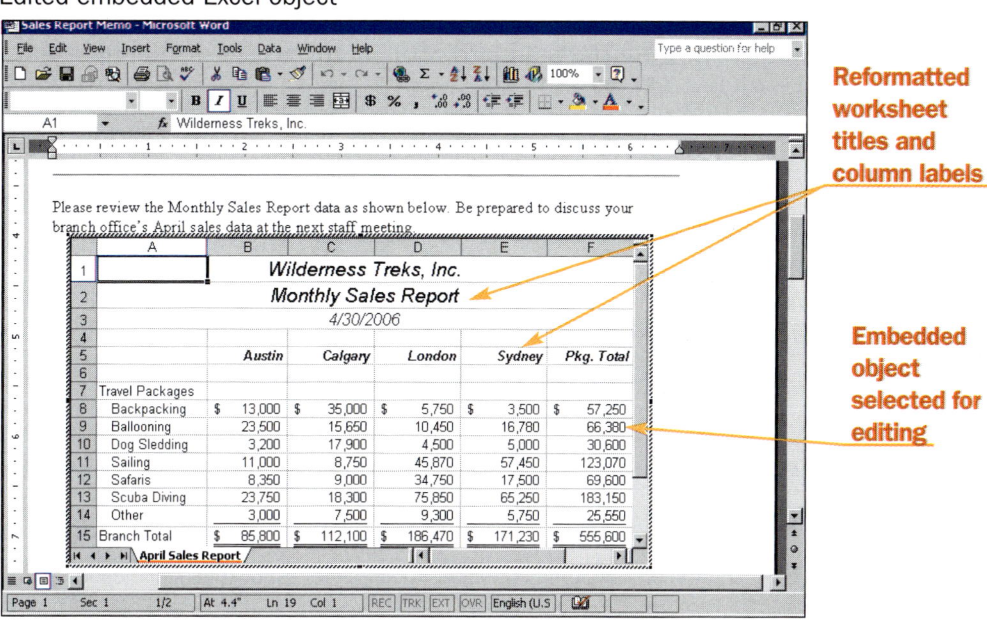

Reformatted worksheet titles and column labels

Embedded object selected for editing

STEP-BY-STEP 6.3 Continued

6. Click at the left margin below the embedded Excel object to deselect the object.

7. Save, print preview, and print the document, leaving it open for the next Step-by-Step.

Send a Word Document As an E-mail Message

Now you are ready to send the completed memo to the vice presidents and directors. One way to do that is to open your e-mail message window, create a new message addressed to the persons on the distribution list, and then attach the saved Sales Report Memo document to the message. However, you can save time by creating an e-mail message as you work in Word. You use the E-mail button on the Standard toolbar to create an e-mail message that includes the Sales Report Memo document as the body of the message.

In the following Step-by-Step 6.4, you create an e-mail message. It is assumed that Microsoft Outlook is installed on your computer. If Outlook is not installed on your computer, your instructor may provide alternate instructions. Additionally, your instructor will provide a valid e-mail address if you are to actually send the e-mail message to a classmate or to the instructor.

Did You Know?

An e-mail distribution list is especially useful when you frequently send messages to the same group of recipients. If you are using Microsoft Outlook to send your e-mail messages, you can create a distribution list of multiple e-mail addresses and then key the distribution list e-mail address in the e-mail message To text box rather than keying several e-mail addresses. Use the **Distribution List** command on the **New** button list on the Outlook Standard toolbar to create a distribution list.

Hot Tip

In Word 2002 you can also use the E-mail button in Excel to send individual worksheets as the body of an e-mail message, or you can use the E-mail button in PowerPoint to send an entire presentation as an attachment to an e-mail message.

S TEP-BY-STEP 6.4

1. Move the insertion point to the top of the document.

2. Click the **E-mail** button on the Standard toolbar to attach an e-mail message header to the document. 

3. Click in the To text box in the e-mail message header, if necessary, and key **Distribution @wildernesstreks.biz**. (*Note:* This e-mail address is not a valid address. If you are going to send this e-mail message to your instructor or to a classmate, your instructor will provide you a valid e-mail address for this step.)

4. Click in the **Subject:** text box in the e-mail message header and key **Monthly Sales Report**. (*Note:* If you are using Excel2000, the filename automatically appears in the Subject: text box. Select the filename and key Monthly Sales Report.)

STEP-BY-STEP 6.4 Continued

5. Click in the **Introduction** text box in the e-mail header and key **Here is your monthly sales report. Contact me if you have any questions.** Then key your name. (*Note:* If you are using Word 2000, you will not have an Introduction text box; skip this step.) Your e-mail message header and memo should look similar to Figure 6-7.

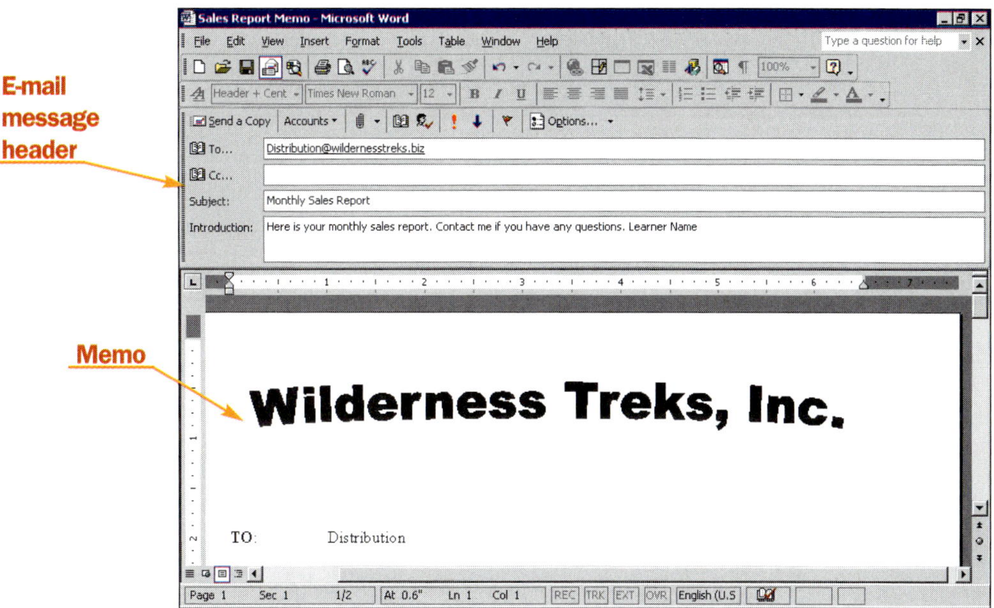

FIGURE 6-7
E-mail message header and memo

6. Save the document. (The e-mail message header information is saved with the document.)

7. Click the **Send a Copy** button in the e-mail header *only if your instructor has provided a valid e-mail address for Step 3 above.* Ignore this step if you are not actually sending the e-mail message.

8. Click the **E-mail** button on the Standard toolbar to close the e-mail header, if necessary, and close the document. Click **No** when asked whether or not you want to save the document.

SUMMARY

In this job, you learned:

- A distribution list is a list of multiple TO addressees keyed on the last page of a memo.

- An object is information from one file called the source file placed in another file called the destination file.

- An embedded object is an object that must be edited with the menus, toolbar, and other features from the source application.

■ You use the Paste Special command on the Edit menu to paste information copied from a source file into a destination file as an embedded object.

■ You can send a Word document as the body of an e-mail message while working in Word.

VOCABULARY *Review*

Define the following terms:

Destination file	Embedded object	Source file
Distribution list	Object	

REVIEW *Questions*

TRUE / FALSE

Circle T if the statement is true or F if the statement is false.

T   F   **1.** A distribution list is a list of multiple TO addressees keyed on the last page of a memo.

T   F   **2.** You can use the Ctrl + Home keys to move the insertion point to the end of a document.

T   F   **3.** An embedded object must be edited with the tools of the destination application.

T   F   **4.** Changes you make to an embedded Excel object in a Word document do not change the original Excel source file.

T   F   **5.** A distribution list is keyed on the last page of a memo.

FILL IN THE BLANK

Complete the following sentences by writing the correct word or words in the blanks provided.

1. To edit an embedded Excel object in a Word document, you must first _________ it to select it for editing.

2. A(n) _________ is information from a source file that is placed in a destination file.

3. To paste Excel information into a Word document as an embedded object you use the _________ _________ command on the Edit menu.

4. The e-mail button on the Standard toolbar adds an e-mail message _________ to an open Word document.

5. Pasting Excel information into a Word document as a(n) _________ _________ allows you to take advantage of the superior number formatting and calculating features of Excel while working in a Word document.

PROJECTS

PROJECT 6-1

1. Open the **Project 6-1** Word file from the data files.

2. Save the document as **Travel Expense Memo**.

3. Key **Distribution** as the TO variable text, key your name as the FROM variable text, and key **June 5, 20XX** (current year) as the DATE variable text.

4. Add a second page and key **Distribution** at the top of the page, press **Enter** twice, and then key the following names in the distribution list: **L. D. Meeker, R. T. Thomas, D. C. Washington**, and **M. P. Matthews**.

5. Save the document and leave it open.

6. Open the **Project 6-1A** Excel file from the data files.

7. Copy the range **A1:F14** and then switch to the **Travel Expense Memo** and paste the range as an embedded Excel object two lines below the body of the memo.

8. Center the embedded Excel object.

9. Double-click the embedded Excel object to edit it, remove the bold and italic formatting from cells A8 and A14, and deselect the object.

10. Save the document, print preview, print, and close it. Close the Excel application and workbook.

PROJECT 6-2

Because you want to distribute the Travel Expense Memo quickly, you send it to the addressees via e-mail. Open the **Travel Expense Memo** you created in Project 6-1. If you have not yet completed Project 6-1, do so now. Attach an e-mail message header to the document and key the following information: in the To text box key **Distribution**; in the Subject text box key **Travel Expenses**. Leave the Introduction text box blank. Save the document as **Travel Expcnse E-mail**, print preview, print, and close it. (You can send the e-mail to a classmate or to your instructor if your instructor provides you with a valid e-mail address.)

WEB PROJECT

Many of the conference attendees are bringing their families for a mini-vacation. Sloane asks you to create a list of family-oriented activities available in the Calgary, Canada, area. Choose a classmate to help you with this project. Using the search tool in your Web browser or another search tool such as Google (*www.google.com*), search for information about family-oriented activities in the Calgary, Canada, area. Print at least three Web pages.

  ## TEAMWORK PROJECT

As Sloane's administrative assistant, you use Excel workbooks and worksheets to create a variety of monthly reports similar to the Monthly Sales Report and the Monthly Expense Report. You think it would save time if you could use a worksheet template to create these reports in the same way you use templates to quickly create Word documents. Using Excel online Help, locate information on how to create workbook and worksheet templates and print the Help page. Then, using the Monthly Expense Report workbook as your guide, work with a classmate to create a worksheet template named **Wilderness Worksheet Template** that contains the company name in A1, but centered across the range A1:F1, and the branch office names, centered in the range B5:F5, as column labels. Save the worksheet template in the Templates folder. To test the worksheet template, create a new blank workbook, right-click any **Sheet** tab, and click **Insert**. When the Insert dialog box opens, double-click the **Wilderness Worksheet Template** icon to insert a new worksheet based on the template.

CRITICAL*Thinking*

 ## ACTIVITY 6-1

Linking Excel information in a Word document is useful when you want to be certain that the Word document always contains the most current information from the Excel file. If you are using Word 2002, use Word online Help to review how to create a linked Excel object in a Word document using the Paste Command and the Paste Options smart tag button and menu. If you are using Word 2000, use Word online Help to review how to create a linked Excel object in a Word document using the Paste Special command. Create a document describing the linking process and then use the document to explain to a classmate how to create a linked Excel object in a Word document.

BUSINESS WEEK ONE

COMMAND SUMMARY

WORD FEATURE	MENU COMMAND	KEYSTROKE	TOOLBAR BUTTON	JOB
AutoText	Insert, AutoText	F3		1
Bold	Format, Font	Ctrl + B		4
Border	Format, Borders and Shading			4
Bullets	Format, Bullets and Numbering			4
Center alignment	Format, Paragraph	Ctrl + E		2
Copy	Edit, Copy	Ctrl + C		4
Date and Time	Insert, Date and Time			2
E-mail	File, Send To, Mail Recipient			6
Envelopes and Labels	Tools, Letters and Mailings, Envelopes and Labels			2,3
Font	Format, Font	Ctrl + Shift + F	Times New Roman	1
Font Size	Format, Font	Ctrl + Shift + P	12	1
Insertion point		Ctrl + Home, Ctrl + End		1,4
New Word document	File, New	Ctrl + N		1
Page break	Insert, Break	Ctrl + Enter		6
Page Setup	File, Page Setup			4
Paste	Edit, Paste	Ctrl + V		4
Paste embedded object	Edit, Paste Special			6
Paste Options				4
Print Layout view	View, Print Layout			1
Save a document	File, Save As or Save	Ctrl + S		2
Send a copy	File, Send To, Mail Recipient		Send a Copy	6
Show/Hide			¶	2
Spelling and Grammar	Tools, Spelling and Grammar	F7		2
Task Pane	File, New; View, Task Pane			1
Zoom	View, Zoom		100%	2

EXCEL FEATURE	MENU COMMAND	KEYSTROKE	TOOLBAR BUTTON	JOB
Align Right	Format, Cells	Ctrl + I		5
AutoSum				5
Bold	Format, Cells	Ctrl + B		5
Comma Style	Format, Style			5
Currency Style	Format, Style	Ctrl + Shift + $		5
Decrease Decimal	Format, Cells			5
Font Size	Format, Cells	Ctrl + Shift + P		5
Increase Indent	Format, Cells	Ctrl + I		5
Italic	Format, Cells	Ctrl + I		6
Page Setup	File, Page Setup			5
Print Preview	File, Print Preview			5
Tab Color	Format, Sheet, Tab Color			5
Underline	Format, Cells	Ctrl + U		5

REVIEW *Questions*

TRUE/FALSE

Circle T if the statement is true or F if the statement is false.

T   F   **1.**   AutoText names must be unique and are not case sensitive.

T   F   **2.**   Many companies use special paper called letterhead that is preprinted with their company name, address, and other contact information.

T   F   **3.**   The preparer's initials immediately follow the writer's title in a letter closing.

T   F   **4.**   It is not possible to specify an exact label on which to print label text.

T   F   **5.**   In Word 2002 you can use the Paste Options smart tag button and menu to control the format of pasted text.

T   F   **6.**   Every time you click the Word New Blank Document button, you are creating a document based on a custom template.

T   F   **7.**   Pasting Excel data into a Word document using the Paste button on the Standard toolbar creates an embedded Excel object.

T   F   **8.**   A worksheet has 256 rows and 65,536 columns.

T   F   **9.**   When you create a full page of the same label, you must create and save a new label document.

T   F   **10.**   When naming AutoText, it is a good idea to use a long name containing several characters.

MATCHING

Match the correct term in Column 1 to its description in Column 2.

Column 1

____ 1. Arial

____ 2. AutoText

____ 3. Custom tab stops

____ 4. Ctrl + Enter

____ 5. Administrative assistant

____ 6. Boilerplate text

____ 7. Tab formatting mark

____ 8. Ctrl + End

____ 9. Envelopes and Labels

____ 10. Cell

Column 2

A. Employee who supports a top-level executive in charge of a major department or business division in an organization

B. A Word feature that allows you to insert saved preformatted text

C. Pre-keyed and formatted text that is part of a template

D. The dialog box that contains a list of mailing label products

E. Keyboard shortcut keys you press to move the insertion point to the end of a Word document

F. Text alignment icons you insert on the horizontal ruler with the mouse pointer

G. The font the U.S. Postal Service prefers for envelopes and mailing labels

H. The intersection of a row and column in a worksheet

I. A nonprinting character you insert in your Word document by pressing the Tab key

J. Keyboard shortcut keys you press to insert a page break

CRITICAL *Thinking*

 ## PROJECT 1

Your next task is to prepare a confirmation letter to the travel agency that is reserving a block of rooms for the conference at various hotels in Calgary. Open the **Review Project 1** Word document from the data files and save the document as **Hotel Reservations**. Open the **Review Project 1A** Excel workbook from the data files and embed the data in the range **A1:F8** as an object on the second line above the Hotel Reservations letter closing. Edit the embedded object to center the worksheet headings in the range **A1:A3** over the range **A1:F3**. Then change the worksheet titles in the range **A1:A3**

to the 12-point font size and apply bold formatting to them. Next, apply bold formatting to the column labels in the range B5:F5. Finally, calculate the total reservations for each hotel and center the contents of the cells in the range B6:F8.

Add a size 10 envelope and save it with the letter. Don't forget to include the Wilderness Treks return address (found in Job 2) on the envelope. When you are finished, save the letter and envelope and then print and close them.

PROJECT 2

Ms. Wentworth calls to tell you she needs the room reservation information immediately. She asks you to e-mail her the room reservations information Excel worksheet. Open the **Review Project 2** Excel workbook from the data files and save it as **Wentworth E-mail**. Add an e-mail message header to the open worksheet. Ms. Wentworth's e-mail address is **wentworth@international-travel.biz** (your instructor will provide a valid e-mail address if you are to send this e-mail to a classmate or to your instructor) and **July Marketing Conference Reservations** is the subject of the e-mail. Add the following note followed by your name: **Please make the following room reservations for our July marketing conference**. Save the workbook, print preview, and print the worksheet. Send the e-mail (only if your instructor has provided a valid e-mail address) and close the workbook.

ADVANCED *Challenge*

One of your frequent assignments as Sloane's administrative assistant is to send the same letter to multiple addressees just as you did in Job 2. However, instead of creating several individual letters, you can combine one letter (called a main document) with a second document containing a list of variable data including names and addressees (called a data source) to create multiple letters at one time. This process is called a mail merge. You can also use the mail merge process to create envelopes, labels, multiple e-mails, and a directory such as a telephone list. Although you always use a Word document as the main document, your data source can be another Word document, an Outlook contact list, an Excel worksheet, or an Access database table.

You can use Word to create a mail merge in two ways: by using the Mail Merge Wizard, or by using the Mail Merge toolbar. The Mail Merge Wizard is a series of six task panes that guide you through the process of identifying your main document, selecting your data source, creating your merge fields (the instructions for which variable data to insert in each letter), previewing the mail merge results, and then either sending the mail merge results to a printer or to a document file. The Mail Merge toolbar provides all the features available in the Mail Merge Wizard while allowing you to more quickly complete a mail merge process.

Sloane wants you to send a letter inviting several business partners to the marketing conference. You use the mail merge process to create both the letters and the envelopes needed to mail the letters. You already have a Word document containing the conference invitation information and another Word document containing the names and addresses needed for the letters. Now you use the Mail Merge toolbar method to quickly create the individual merged invitation letters and envelopes. (If you are using Word 2000, your instructor will provide alternative step-by-step instructions for creating mail merged letters and envelopes using the Word 2000 Mail Merge toolbar.)

MAIL MERGE LETTERS

1. Open the **Challenge 1** Word document from the data files and save the document as **Invitation Main Document**.

2. Right-click any toolbar and click **Mail Merge** to display the Mail Merge toolbar. (*Note:* Your Mail Merge toolbar may appear floating in its own window on your screen or may be anchored below the Formatting toolbar bar or in some other position on your screen.)

3. Click the **Main document setup** button on the Mail Merge toolbar to open the Main Document Type dialog box. You identify the type of mail merge in this dialog box. 

4. Click the **Letters** option button, if necessary, to select the Letters mail merge type. Your screen should look similar to Figure UR1-1.

FIGURE UR1-1
Main Document Type dialog box

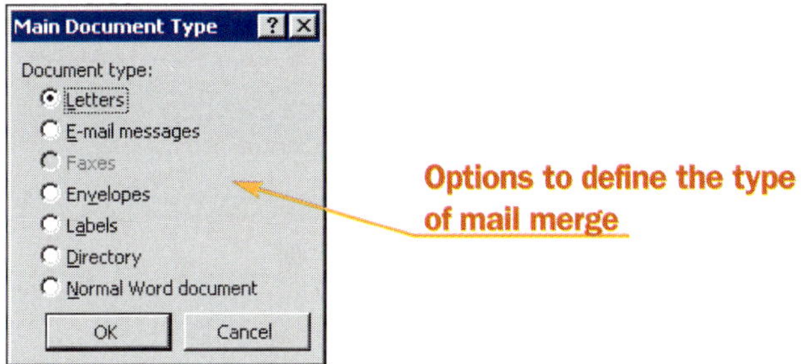

5. Click **OK**. The Invitation Main Document is now identified as a mail merge main document. Next, you select the data source file that contains the variable name and address information.

6. Click the **Open Data Source** button on the Mail Merge toolbar to open the Select Data Source dialog box. This dialog box is similar to the Open dialog box. Switch to the location and folder that contains the data files. Double-click **Challenge 1A** to select it as the data source. (You will not see the variable data from the selected data source until you complete the next step.)

7. Click the **Mail Merge Recipients** button on the Mail Merge toolbar to open the Mail Merge Recipients dialog box. The list of names and addresses contained in the Challenge1A data source file appear in the dialog box. You can sort the data in ascending or descending alphabetical order and filter (select data to be included or excluded) in this dialog box. You want to sort the variable data in ascending alphabetical order by last name and you want to exclude the Jennifer Gartner data.

8. Click the **Last** button column header in the Mail Merge Recipients dialog box to sort the variable information in ascending alphabetical order by last name and then click the check box to the left of the Gartner data to remove the Gartner data from the mail merge process. Your dialog box should look similar to Figure UR1-2.

FIGURE UR1-2
Mail Merge Recipients dialog box

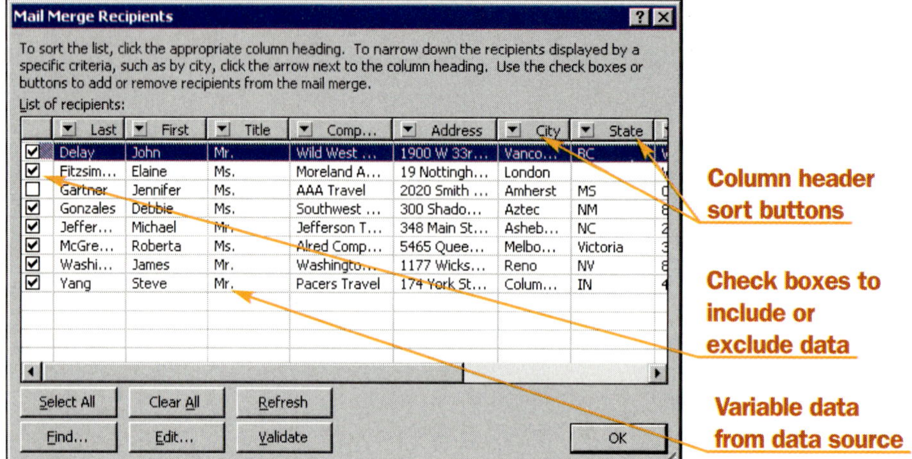

9. Click **OK**. The sorted and filtered list of variable names and addresses or recipients is now available for the merge process; however, you cannot review or edit the list unless you reopen the Mail Merge Recipients dialog box. Now you are ready to insert the merge fields, which are instructions that identify which information from the data source to include in each letter. You can insert a group of merge fields for the letter address (called the Address block) or the salutation (called the Greeting line), or you can insert individual merge fields. You insert individual merge fields in the next step.

10. Move the insertion point to the blank line above the salutation. This is where you will insert the merge fields in the Invitation Main Document.

11. Click the **Insert Merge Fields** button on the Mail Merge toolbar to open the Insert Merge Field dialog box. Each type of data in the data source file has a name called a field name. By default, this dialog box contains a list of the field names included in the selected data source file. For example, the field name *Title* represents the courtesy title *Mr., Ms.,* or *Mrs.* and the field name *Last* represents the last name.

12. Click **Title** in the Fields list in the Insert Merge Field dialog box to select it, if necessary, and then click **Insert** to insert the courtesy title merge field at the position of the insertion point. Observe that the <<Title>> merge field is inserted at the left margin above the salutation. Your screen should look similar to Figure UR1-3.

FIGURE UR1-3
Inserted <<Title>> merge field

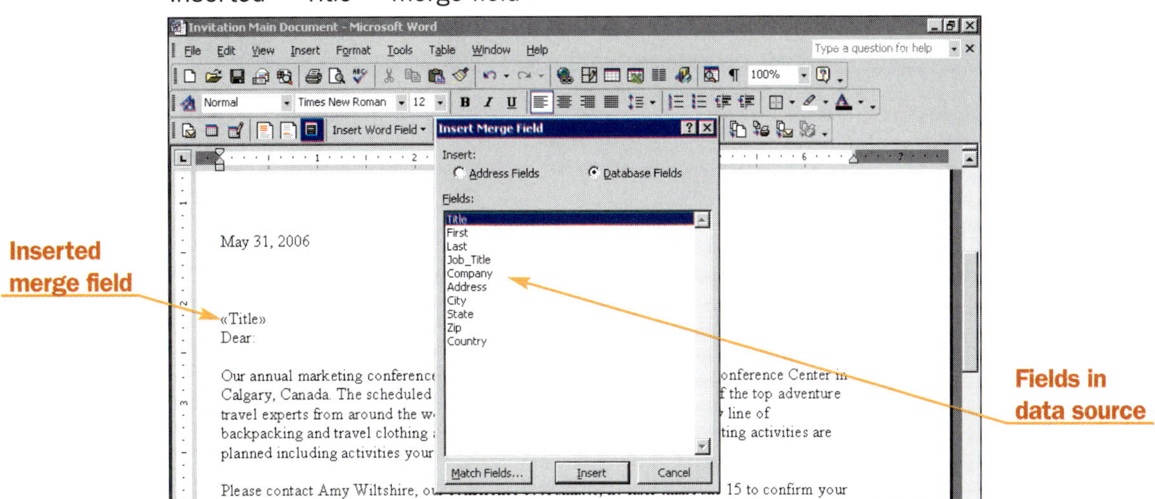

13. Click **Close** to close the dialog box. You must add the appropriate spacing and punctuation as you insert the merge fields. Press the spacebar to insert a space between the <<Title>> merge field and the merge field you insert in the next step.

14. Click the **Insert Merge Fields** button on the Mail Merge toolbar to open the Insert Merge Field dialog box. Double-click **First** to insert the first name merge field and then click **Close** to close the dialog box. Press the spacebar to insert a space between the <<First>> merge field and the merge field you insert in the next step. 

15. Click the **Insert Merge Fields** button on the Mail Merge toolbar to open the Insert Merge Field dialog box. Double-click **Last** to insert the last name merge field and then click **Close** to close the dialog box. Press **Enter** to move the insertion point to the next line.

16. Continue by inserting the Job_Title, Company, Address, City, State, Zip, and Country merge fields in the letter address and the Title and Last merge fields in the salutation, using Figure UR1-4 as your guide. Don't forget to follow the City merge field with a comma and a space and add a space between the State and Zip merge fields. Your screen should look similar to Figure UR1-4.

FIGURE UR1-4
Inserted letter address and salutation merge fields

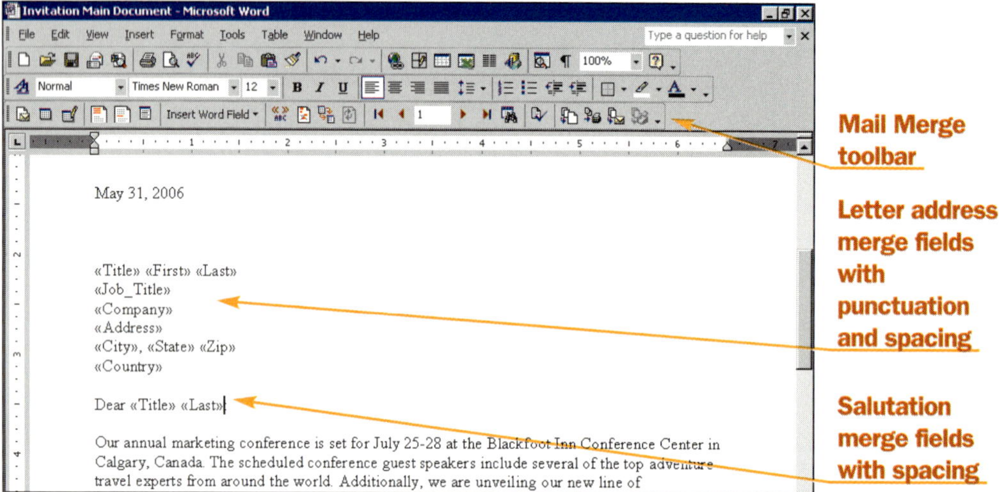

17. Save the document.

18. Click the **View Merged Data** button on the Mail Merge toolbar to preview the letters before you actually create them. Your screen should look similar to Figure UR1-5. 

FIGURE UR1-5
Previewed first letter

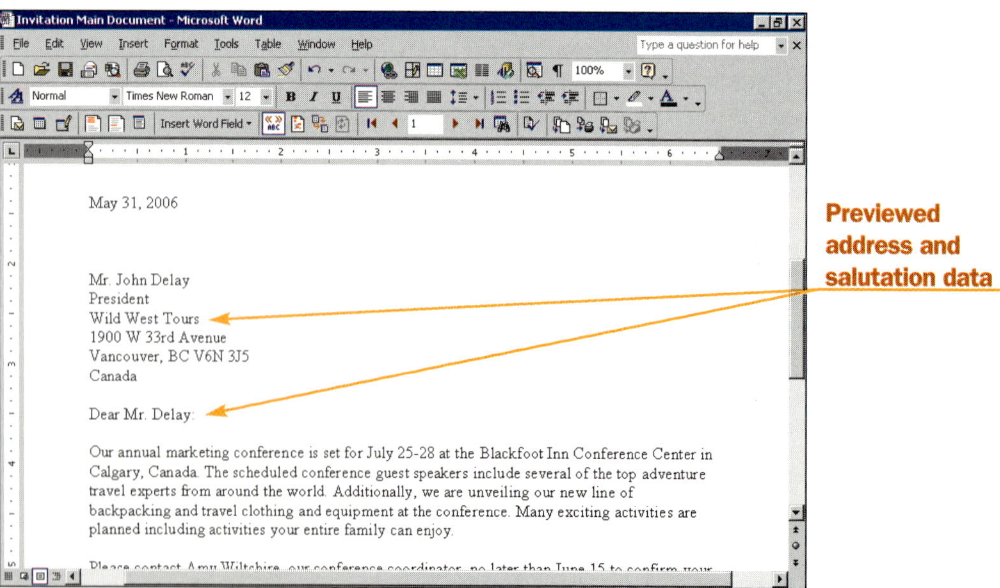

19. Click the **Next Record** button on Mail Merge toolbar to preview the second letter. Continue clicking the **Next Record** button to preview the remaining letters and then click the **View Merged Data** button to turn off the preview. After you preview the letters and make any necessary corrections (watch for missing merge fields and incorrect punctuation or spacing in the main document), you are ready to merge the main document with the data source to create the letters. You can merge directly to a printer or you can merge to a new document that contains the individual letters. In the next step you merge to a new document. 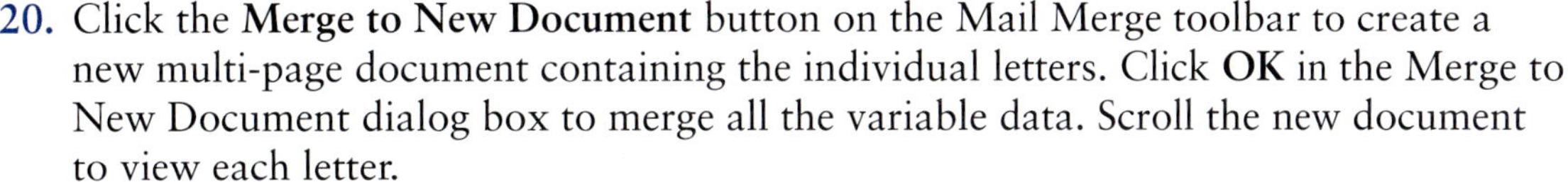 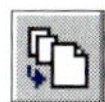

20. Click the **Merge to New Document** button on the Mail Merge toolbar to create a new multi-page document containing the individual letters. Click **OK** in the Merge to New Document dialog box to merge all the variable data. Scroll the new document to view each letter.

21. Save the new document as **Merged Invitation Letters** and print preview, print, and close it. Then save, print preview, print, and close the **Invitation Main Document**.

MAIL MERGE ENVELOPES

1. Create a new blank document.

2. Save the document as **Envelope Main Document** and display the Mail Merge toolbar, if necessary.

3. Click the **Main document setup** button on the Mail Merge toolbar to open the Main Document Type dialog box, click the **Envelopes** option button, and click **OK** to open the Envelope Options dialog box. 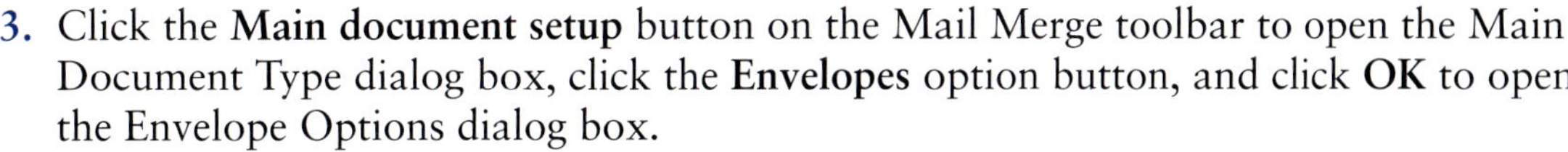 

4. Click the **Envelope size** list arrow in the Envelopes Options dialog box and click Size 10 (4 ⅛"× 9 ½"). Click OK. The document on your screen should now look like a size 10 envelope, as shown in Figure UR 1-6.

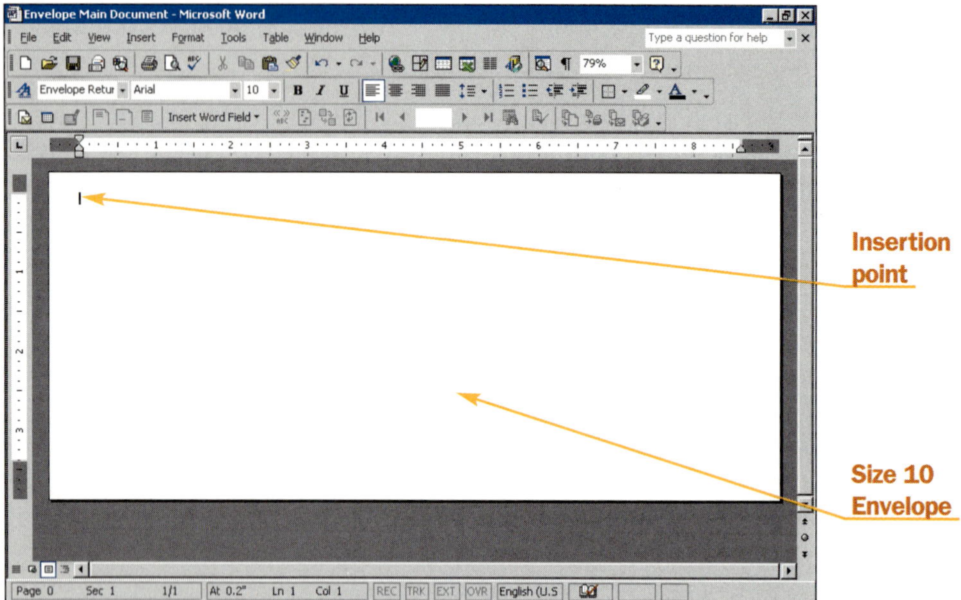

FIGURE UR1-6
Envelope Main Document

5. Click the **Open Data Source** button on the Mail Merge toolbar to open the Select Data Source dialog box. Double-click **Challenge 1A** in the data files to select it as the data source. 

6. Click the **Mail Merge Recipients** button on the Mail Merge toolbar to open the Mail Merge Recipients dialog box. As you did with the letters, you want to sort the variable data in ascending alphabetical order by last name and you want to exclude the Jennifer Gartner data. 

7. Click the **Last** button column header in the Mail Merge Recipients dialog box to sort the variable information in ascending alphabetical order by last name, click the check box to the left of the Gartner data to remove the Gartner data from the mail merge process, and click **OK**.

8. Key the Wilderness Treks, Inc. return address in the upper-left corner of the envelope. (You find the address in Job 2.)

9. Click at approximately the 2-inch horizontal and 2.25-inch vertical position near the middle of the envelope to position the insertion point inside the delivery address frame.

10. Click the **Insert Merge Fields** button on the Mail Merge toolbar to open the Insert Merge Field dialog box. Insert the address merge fields as they should appear on the envelope using Figure UR1-7 as your guide. Because the U.S. Postal Service prefers envelopes to use the open punctuation style, *do not insert a comma between the City merge field and the State merge field.*

FIGURE UR1-7
Envelope Main Document with merge fields

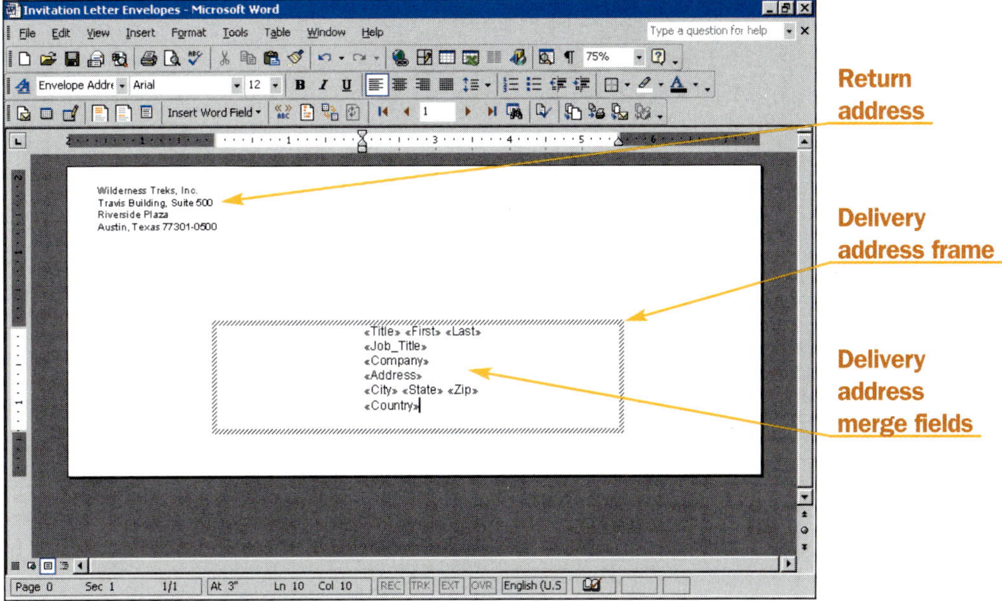

11. Click the **View Merged Data** button on the Mail Merge toolbar to preview the envelopes. Then turn off the preview and click the **Merge to New Document** button on the Mail Merge toolbar to create a new document containing the all the merged envelopes. 

12. Save the new document as **Merged Invitation Envelopes** and then print preview, print, and close it.

13. Save **Envelope Main Document** and then print preview, print, and close it.

Business Week Two: Appointments, Contacts, Newsletters, and Presentations

Unit 2

Estimated Time for Unit 2: 4.5 hours

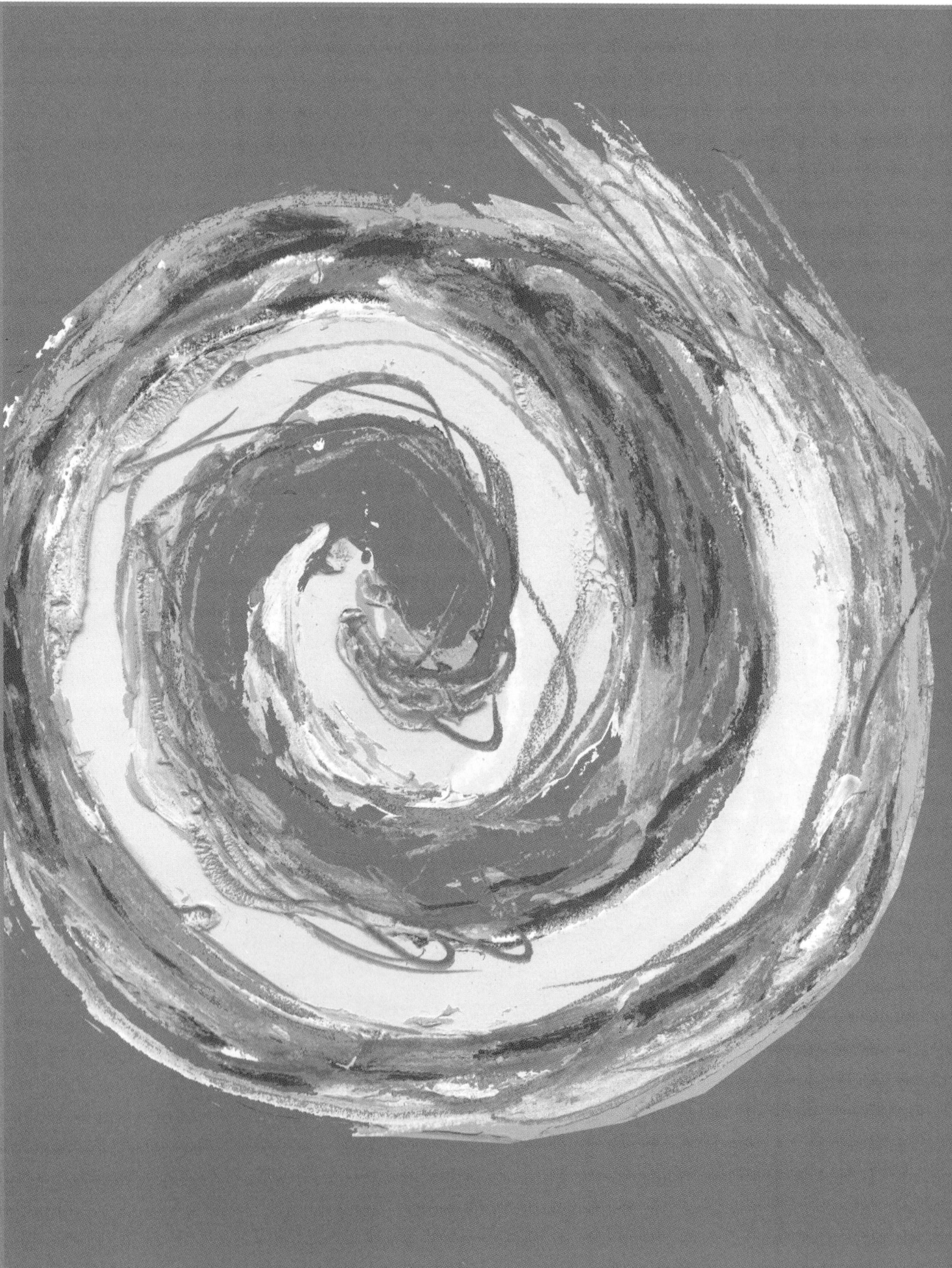

Updating an Outlook Calendar and Outlook Contacts

Add, Edit, and Delete Appointments in an Outlook Calendar

Microsoft Outlook is an information management application you use to send and receive e-mail messages. It also allows you to maintain a schedule of appointments for Sloane and information about important business or personal contacts such as clients, vendors, and your family doctor or dentist. Each e-mail message you receive or send and each appointment or contact you create using Outlook is called an Outlook *item* and each type of item is stored in a separate *Outlook folder* on your hard drive or on a network server. For example, the individual appointment items you create for Sloane are stored in the *Calendar folder*. Each Outlook folder also has several different *views* or ways to look at the folder's contents. The default view for the Calendar folder is Day view, which allows you to view or create appointments on a specific day.

> **Note**
>
> The Step-by-Step activities in this job assume you have Outlook 2000 or Outlook 2002 installed on your computer and have access to the Outlook Calendar and Outlook Contacts features. If you do not have Outlook installed, your instructor will provide alternate instructions. Also, the dates and times shown in the figures will be different from the dates and times you see on your screen.

Incoming e-mail messages are stored in the Inbox folder, copies of sent e-mail messages are stored in the Sent Items folder, and deleted items are stored in the Deleted Items folder. You can also save drafts of unsent e-mail messages in the Drafts folder. You can maintain an electronic "to do" list of items called tasks stored in the Tasks folder and brief electronic "sticky" notes stored in the Notes folder. You can also keep a log of Outlook and Office file activities in the Journal folder. Each Outlook folder (Calendar, Contacts, Inbox, Sent Items, Drafts, Deleted Items, Notes, Journal) has its own set of menu commands and toolbar buttons that are available when you open the folder.

Adding an Appointment Using the Appointment List in Day View

An *appointment* is an item you enter in the Calendar folder that is less than 24 hours in duration and has a specific starting and ending time. Examples of appointments include short meetings and business lunches. This morning you receive an e-mail message from Sloane (see Figure 7-1) reminding you to set up several new appointments for next week.

FIGURE 7-1
Sloane's e-mail message

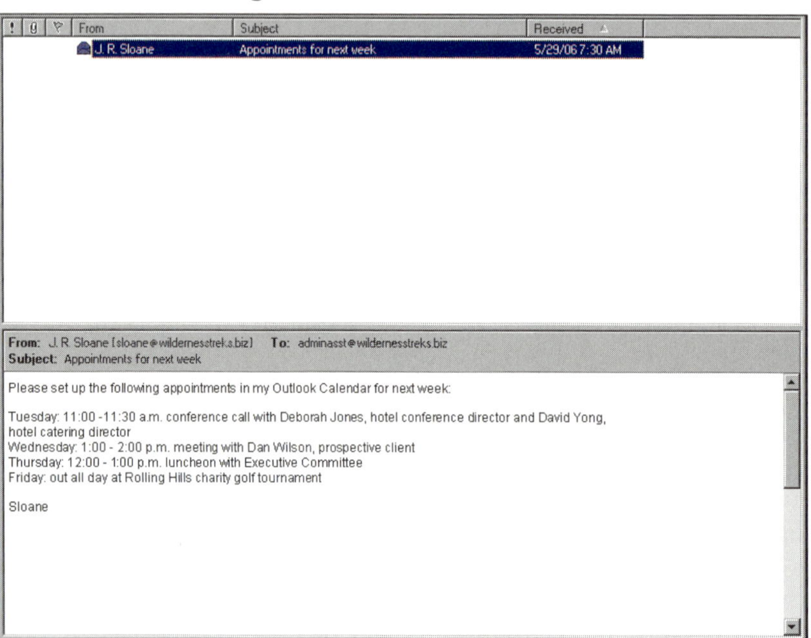

When you start Outlook, it may be configured to open with Outlook Today, a window containing summary information about e-mail messages and a list of today's appointments and tasks, as shown in Figure 7-2, or it may be configured to open with the incoming e-mail Inbox folder shown in Figure 7-3. In either case you use the Calendar shortcut button on the Outlook Bar to open the Calendar folder and add Sloane's appointments to next week's schedule.

Did You Know?

You can modify the "look and feel" of your Calendar folder by changing options such as the specific days that make up your five-day work week, the first day of the seven-day week, the start and end time for the Appointments list, and other options in the Calendar Options dialog box. You can view this dialog box by clicking **Calendar Options** in the Preferences tab of the Options dialog box. To view the Options dialog box, click **Tools** on the menu bar and then click **Options**.

FIGURE 7-2
Outlook Today

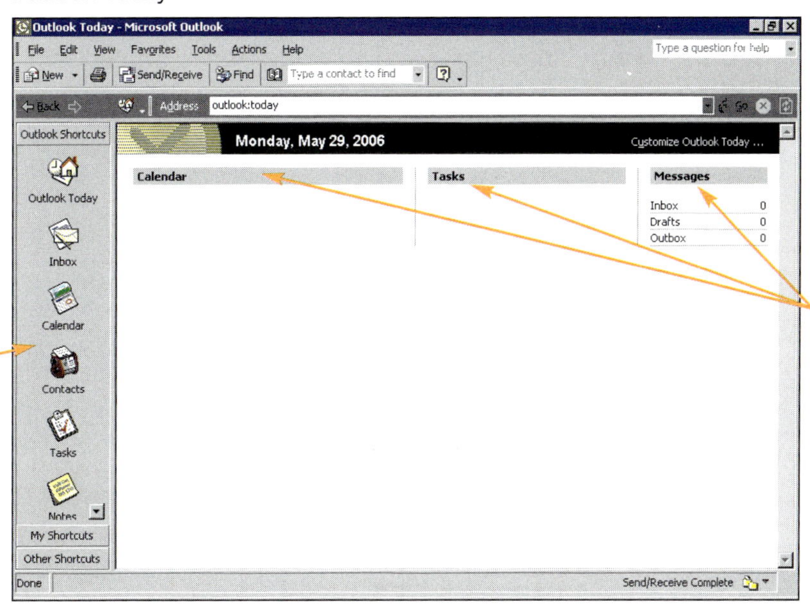

FIGURE 7-3
Inbox

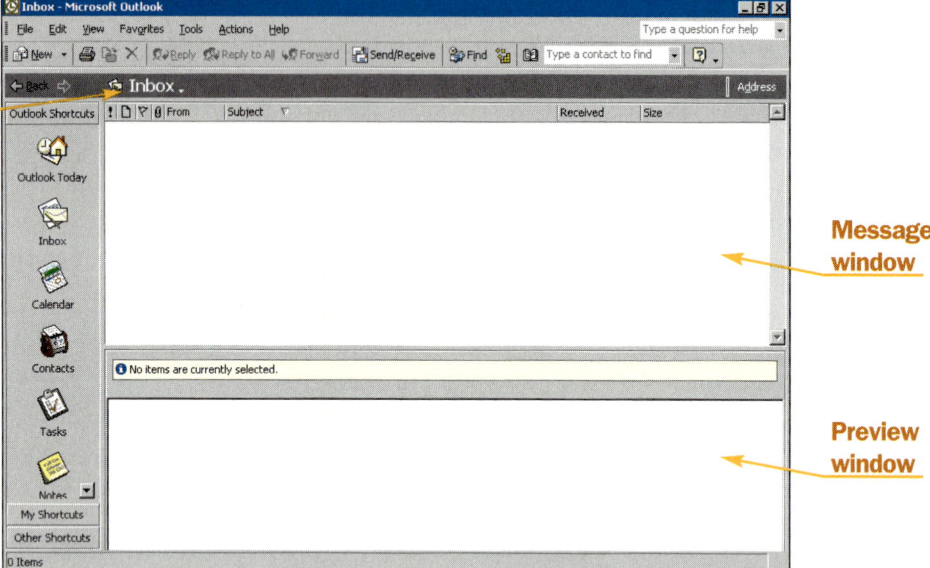

You can quickly add appointments by selecting the appointment time block in the Appointments list in the Calendar Day view and entering the appointment subject. You can also open the Appointment window to enter the appointment details. You enter the first appointment using the Appointments list in the Calendar Day view.

S TEP-BY-STEP 7.1

1. Start the Outlook application, if necessary, and click the **Calendar** button on the Outlook Bar to open the Calendar folder.

> **Did You Know?**
>
> Many Outlook users prefer to use the Folder List to navigate between Outlook folders instead of the Outlook Bar. You can turn off the Outlook Bar and turn on the Folder List with commands on the View menu. Also, because Outlook is used to receive and send e-mail messages, many business users start Outlook in the morning and leave it open throughout the day, minimizing it to a button on the taskbar when it is not being used.

STEP-BY-STEP 7.1 Continued

2. Click the **Day** button on the Calendar folder Standard toolbar to switch to Day view, if necessary. Your Calendar folder window should look similar to Figure 7-4.

FIGURE 7-4
Outlook Calendar

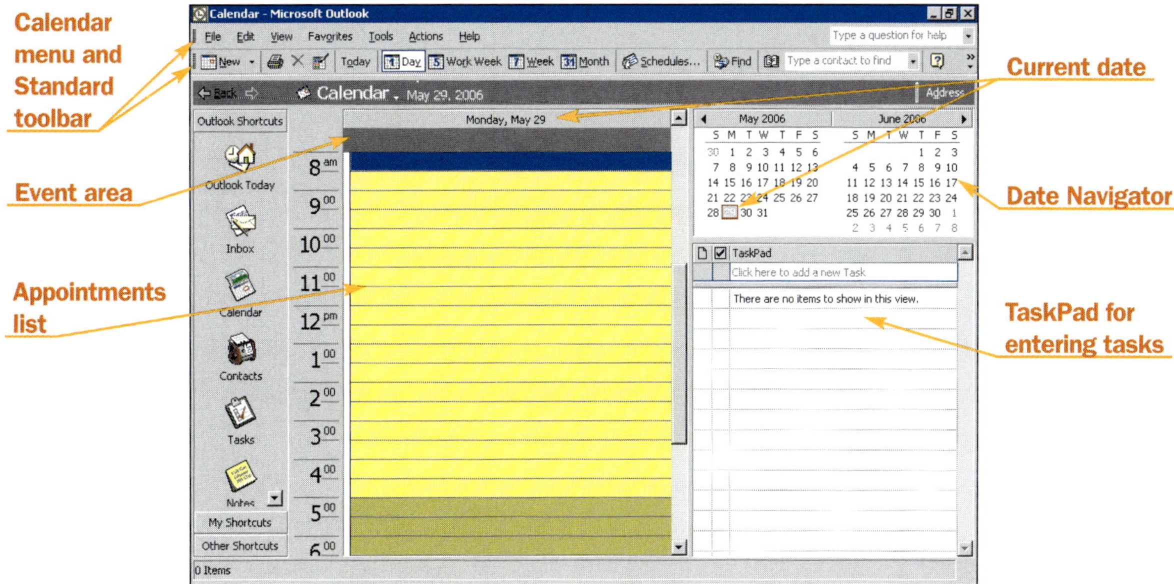

3. Click the Tuesday of next week date in the Date Navigator to switch the Appointments list from today to Tuesday of next week.

4. Click the time block beginning with 11:00 a.m. and ending with 11:30 a.m. in the Appointments list to select it.

Hot Tip 

If you are using Outlook 2002 and have a large number of appointments in your Calendar folder, you can color-code those appointments to make it easier to distinguish different types of appointments such as business or personal appointments, appointments that require travel, or appointments involving a phone call. To apply one of the 10 predefined color codes to an appointment, first select the appointment and then click the **Calendar Coloring** button on the Calendar folder Standard toolbar and click the desired color code.

STEP-BY-STEP 7.1 Continued

5. Key **Conference call with Jones and Yong** in the selected time block and press **Enter**. Your screen should look similar to Figure 7-5.

FIGURE 7-5
Jones and Yong appointment

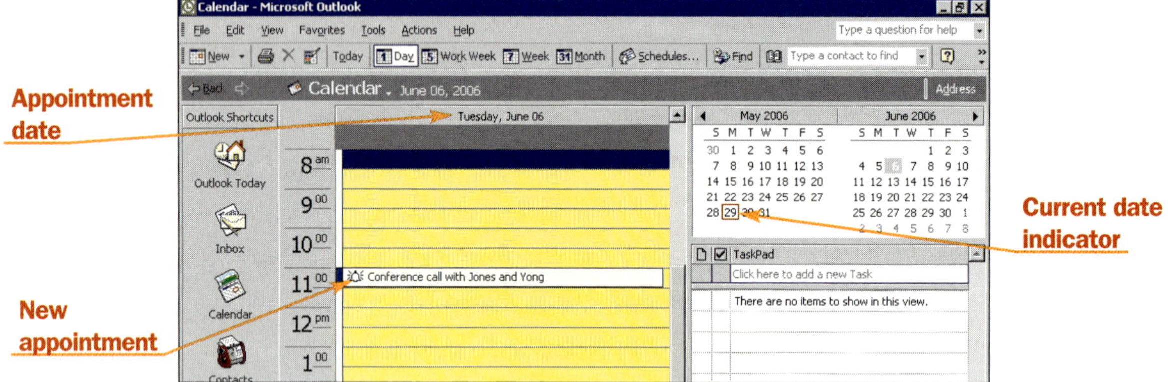

6. Click the **Go to Today** button on the Standard toolbar to return to the view of today's appointments.

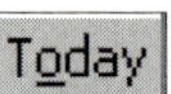

7. Keep the Calendar folder open and maximized for the next Step-by-Step.

Adding an Appointment Using the Appointment Window

You also can add an appointment item to the Calendar folder by opening the Appointment window, keying the appointment subject, specifying the date and time for the appointment, and setting various other appointment options such as specifying where the appointment will take place, turning on and off the automatic appointment reminder feature, or marking the appointment as a recurring appointment. You enter the next appointment using the Appointment window.

By default, each appointment is created with the automatic reminder feature turned on. This means that when Outlook is open, a small reminder window pops up 15 minutes before each appointment. You can turn off the automatic reminder for an individual appointment by opening the appointment in the Appointment window and removing the check mark in the Reminder check box. You can also change the default reminder time for the selected appointment with the Reminder list box in the Appointment window. You turn off the automatic reminder for all appointments or change the default reminder time in the Options dialog box, which you open by clicking the **Options** command on the **Tools** menu.

STEP-BY-STEP 7.2

1. Click the **New Appointment** button on the Standard toolbar to open the Appointment window.

2. Key **Meeting with Dan Wilson** in the Subject text box on the Appointment tab and press **Tab** three times to move the insertion point to the Start time date text box to select its contents.

3. Key **next Wednesday** and press **Tab** to enter the correct date for Wednesday of next week and move the insertion point to the Start time text box to select its contents.

Did You Know?

You can enter an appointment date and the starting and ending time for an appointment in the Appointment window by keying phrases such as "next Tuesday" or "two weeks" for the date and "11 am" or "four thirty" for the starting or ending time. For more information on how to enter text phrases for appointment dates and times, see Outlook online Help.

4. Key **1 pm** and press **Tab** twice to enter the correct starting time and move the insertion point to the End time text box to select its contents.

5. Key **2 pm**, if necessary, to change the ending appointment time to 2:00 p.m. The Appointment window on your screen should look similar to Figure 7-6.

FIGURE 7-6
Wilson appointment

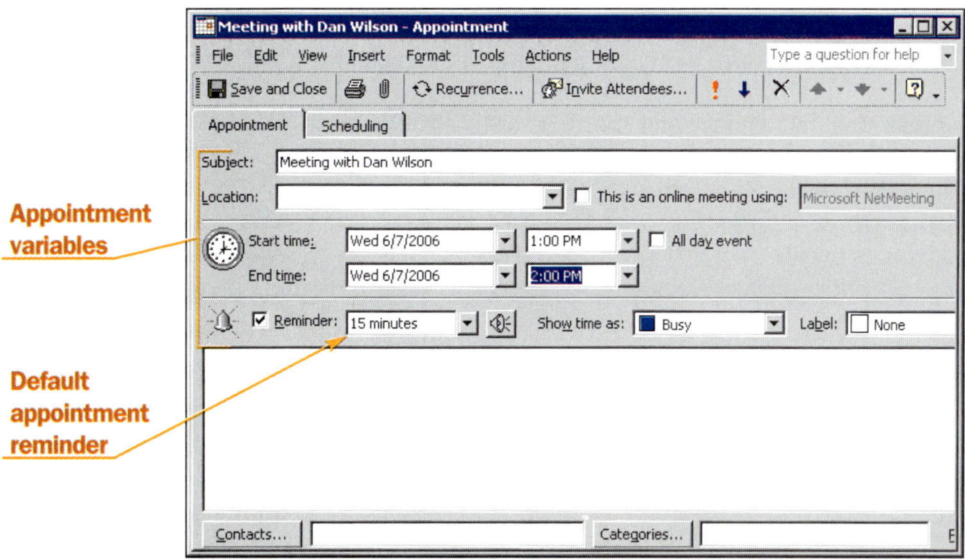

Appointment variables

Default appointment reminder

6. Click the **Save and Close** button on the Appointment window Standard toolbar to enter the appointment item in the Calendar folder and close the Appointment window.

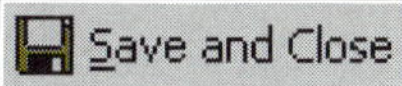

7. Click the Wednesday of next week date in the Date Navigator to view the Wilson appointment and then click the **Go to Today** button to return to today's Day view.

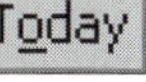

STEP-BY-STEP 7.2 Continued

8. Create an appointment for Thursday of next week from 12:00–1:00 p.m. for the Executive Committee luncheon using either the Appointments list method or the Appointment window method, whichever you prefer.

9. Click the **Go to Today** button to return to the view of today's appointments in Day view and leave the Calendar folder open and maximized for the next Step-by-Step. 

Adding an Event to the Calendar

An *event* is an activity you enter in a Calendar that lasts 24 hours or longer. Examples of events include conferences, marketing trade shows, and vacation days. The last item you enter in the Calendar folder is an event for next Friday when Sloane will be out of the office all day participating in the Rolling Hills charity golf tournament.

> **Hot Tip**
>
> You can enter an event in the Calendar either by selecting the **Event** text box at the top of the Appointments list in Day view or by opening the **Event** window with the New All Day Event command on the **Actions** menu.

STEP-BY-STEP 7.3

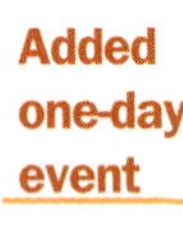

1. Click the Friday of next week date in the Date Navigator to view the Appointments list for Friday of next week.

2. Click the **Event text box** (the gray box below the date) at the top of the Appointments list to select it.

3. Key **Rolling Hills Golf Tournament** and press **Enter** to add the event to the Calendar folder. Your screen should look similar to Figure 7-7.

FIGURE 7-7
Rolling Hills event

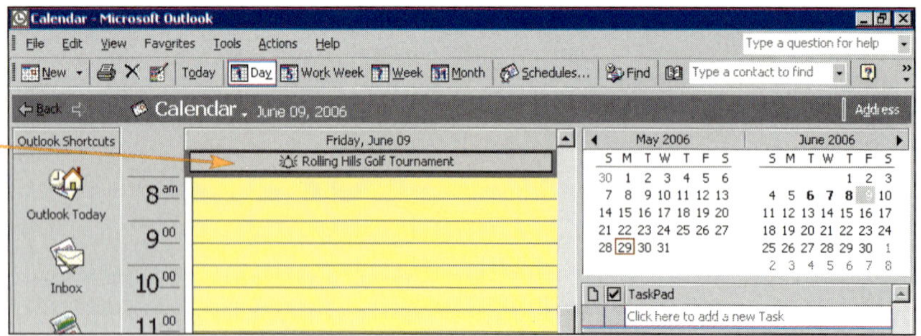

Added one-day event

4. Return to the view of today's appointments in Day view and minimize Outlook to a button on the taskbar.

Editing an Appointment

You can edit an appointment item by opening the Appointment window and making the desired changes, or by making changes to the appointment in the Appointments list in Day view. Sloane calls and asks you to change Wednesday's appointment for Wilson from 1:00–2:00 p.m. to 4:00–5:00 p.m. You can make this change quickly in the Appointments list in Day view.

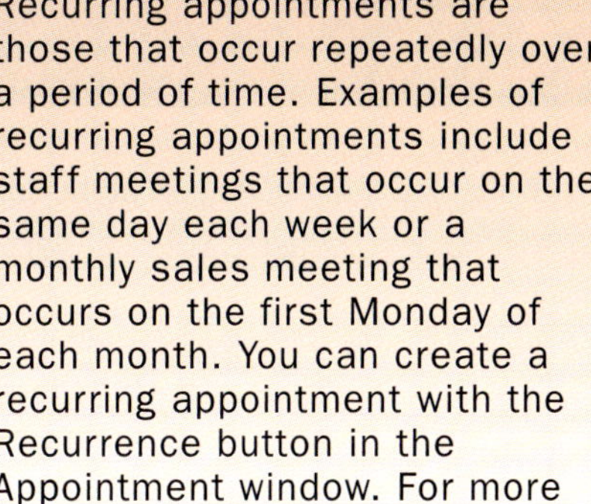

Hot Tip

Recurring appointments are those that occur repeatedly over a period of time. Examples of recurring appointments include staff meetings that occur on the same day each week or a monthly sales meeting that occurs on the first Monday of each month. You can create a recurring appointment with the Recurrence button in the Appointment window. For more information on creating recurring appointments, see Outlook online Help.

STEP-BY-STEP 7.4

1. Maximize Outlook and open the Calendar folder, if necessary.

2. Click the Wednesday of next week date in the Date Navigator to view the Wilson appointment.

3. Move the mouse pointer to the left boundary of the Wilson appointment in the 1:00–2:00 p.m. time block. The mouse pointer becomes a selection-and-move pointer when placed on the left boundary of the appointment.

4. With the move pointer on the left boundary, drag the selected appointment downward to the 4:00–5:00 p.m. time block to change the starting and ending times for the appointment. Your screen should look similar to Figure 7-8.

FIGURE 7-8
Modified appointment times

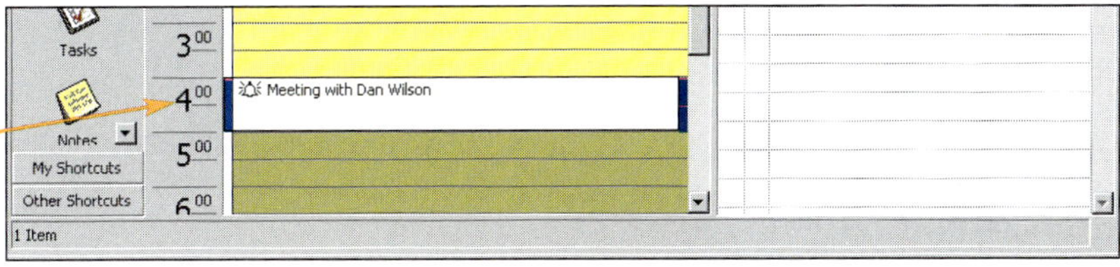

5. Switch to today's appointments in Day view and minimize Outlook.

Deleting an Appointment

You can easily delete an appointment item by selecting it in the Appointments list in Day view and then clicking the Delete button on the Calendar folder Standard toolbar, or pressing the Delete key. While you are away from your desk, Sloane leaves you a note telling you that next Tuesday's conference call has been cancelled and will be rescheduled at a later date. You now need to delete the appointment item from the Calendar folder.

STEP-BY-STEP 7.5

1. Maximize Outlook and open the Calendar folder, if necessary.

2. Click the Tuesday of next week date in the Date Navigator to view the Jones and Yong appointment.

3. Click the left boundary of the Jones and Yong appointment in the 11:00–11:30 a.m. time block to select the appointment. Note the dark blue boundary around the appointment indicating that it is selected.

4. Press the **Delete** key to delete the appointment from the Calendar.

5. Switch to today's appointments in Day view and leave the Calendar folder open and maximized for the next Step-by-Step.

Printing a Calendar

You can print a Calendar in several different ways, including daily, weekly, and monthly formats. First, you select the format and then you specify the starting and ending dates to be printed. Sloane likes to receive a printed copy of the Calendar each time you update it. You print the Calendar in the monthly format for the month that contains next week's appointments.

STEP-BY-STEP 7.6

1. Click the **Print** button on the Standard toolbar to open the Print dialog box.

2. Click **Monthly Style** in the Print style list box.

3. Click the Print range **Start** list arrow and click the first day of the month that contains next week's appointments as the starting date.

4. Click the Print range **End** list arrow and click the last day of the month that contains next week's appointments as the ending date. Your Print dialog box should look similar to Figure 7-9.

FIGURE 7-9
Print dialog box

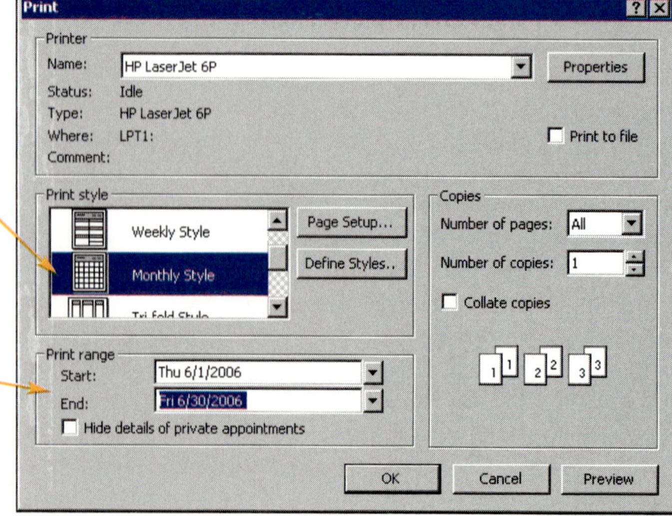

STEP-BY-STEP 7.6 Continued

5. Click **OK** to print a monthly Calendar for the selected date range and leave the Calendar folder open and maximized for the next Step-by-Step.

Customizing the Calendar Folder Views

You can view the contents of the Calendar folder in many ways, including viewing a single day's appointments or viewing appointments for five working days, seven Calendar days, and a full month. You can also customize the current view (day/week/month) to view appointments and events in a variety of ways such as listing appointments, events, or recurring appointments or events in a table-style format. You want to first review the weekly and monthly Calendar that includes next week's appointments and then view and print a list of events.

STEP-BY-STEP 7.7

1. Click the first day of the five-day work week that contains next week's appointments in the Date Navigator.

2. Click the **Work Week** button on the Standard toolbar to view all five days in the Appointments list. Your screen should look similar to Figure 7-10.

> **Did You Know?**
>
> You can view multiple days in Day view or view a specific work week or Calendar week by first selecting multiple days in the Date Navigator. You can click a single date to select it; drag across multiple days to select them; use the Shift + Click method to select multiple adjacent days; or use the Ctrl + Click method to select random (nonadjacent) days in the Date Navigator and then click the desired view button on the Standard toolbar.

FIGURE 7-10
Five-day work week view

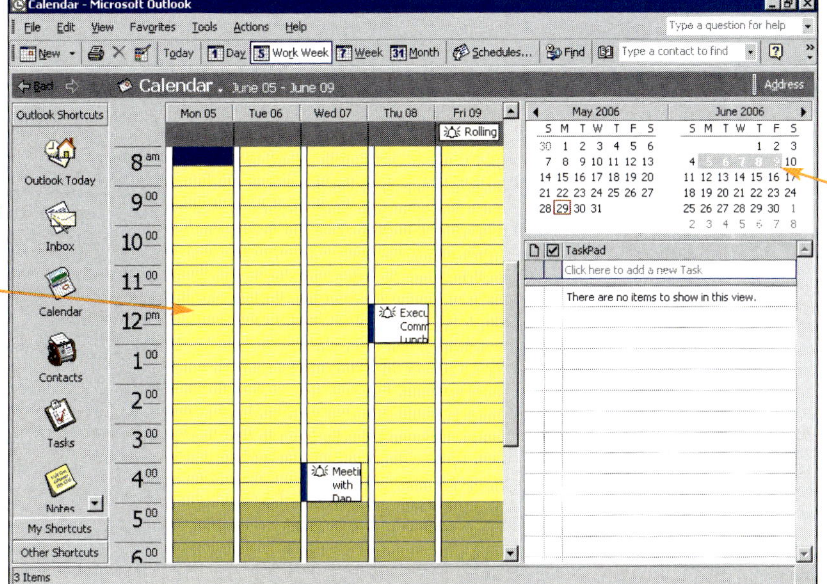

STEP-BY-STEP 7.7 Continued

3. Click the **Week** button on the Calendar folder Standard toolbar to view a seven-day week beginning with the selected date. Your screen should look similar to Figure 7-11.

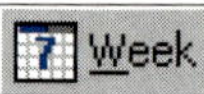

FIGURE 7-11
Seven-day week view

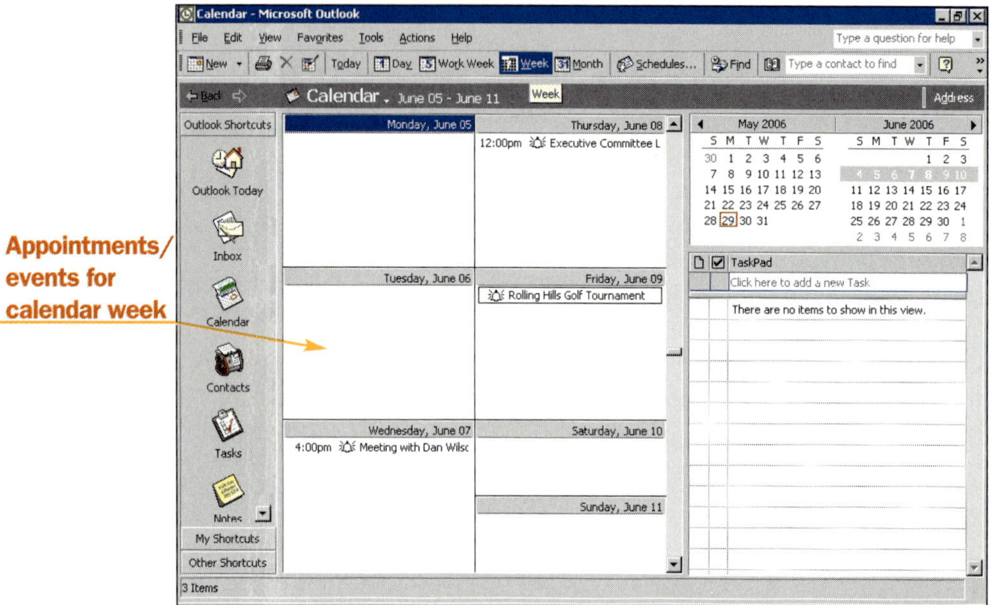

4. Click the **Month** button on the Standard toolbar to view the entire month that includes next week's appointments. Your screen should look similar to Figure 7-12.

FIGURE 7-12
Month view

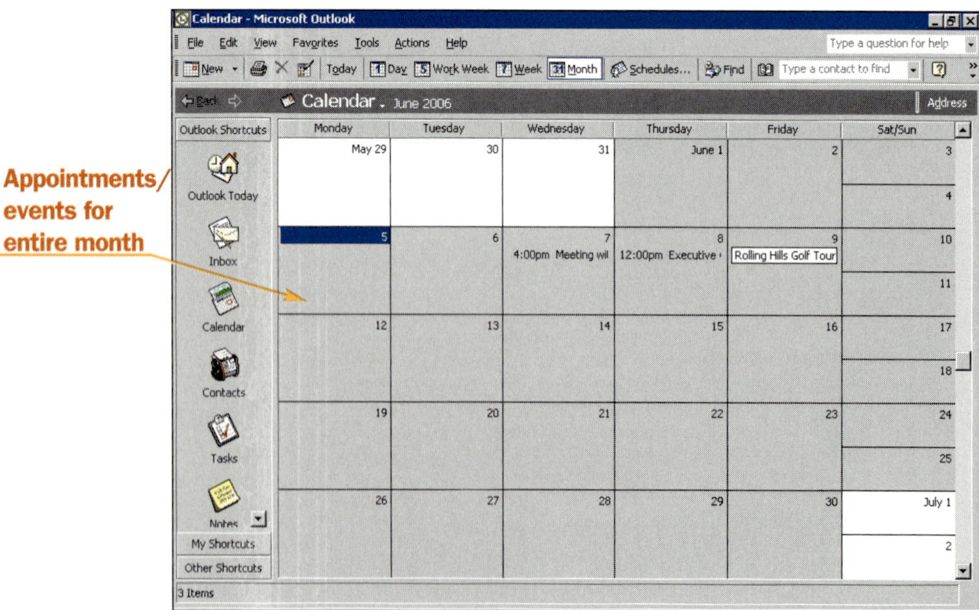

STEP-BY-STEP 7.7 Continued

5. Return to the view of today's appointments in Day view.

6. Click the **View** menu, point to Current View, and then click **Events** to view a list of events. Your screen should look similar to Figure 7-13.

FIGURE 7-13
List of events

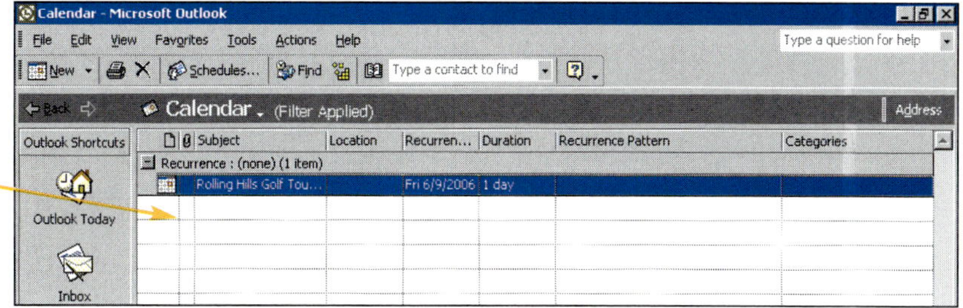

7. Click the **Print** button to open the Print dialog box and then click **OK** to print a list of events formatted in the default table format. 

8. Click the **View** menu, point to Current View, and click **Day/Week/Month** to return to the Day view of today's appointments in Day view and minimize Outlook.

Add, Edit, and Delete Outlook Contacts

A *contact* is an item that contains the name, addresses, phone numbers, e-mail addresses, Web site address (URL), and other information for an individual. Contacts are stored in the Outlook *Contacts folder*. You can use contacts to make phone calls, send e-mail, view a Web site, and together with documents created in Word, create mail merge letters, envelopes, and labels. Just like the Calendar folder, the contents of the Contacts folder can be viewed in many different ways. For example, the default view of the Contacts folder is the Address Cards view, which shows an abbreviated version of the information stored for each contact.

> **Did You Know?** 
>
> You can share Outlook folders (such as your Calendar or Contacts folders) with coworkers on the same network. You can give a coworker the authorization to open your Outlook folders and then specify whether or not the coworker can simply view the contents of the folders or actually make changes to items in the folders. For more information on sharing Outlook folders, see Outlook online Help.

Adding Contacts to the Contacts Folder

At this Monday morning's meeting, Sloane gives you a list of clients and asks you to add them to the Contacts folder. You begin by adding Sloane's new contacts, shown in Figure 7-14.

FIGURE 7-14
List of clients

Mr. Michael Jefferson	Mr. John Delay
President	President
Jefferson Travel	Wild West Tours
348 East Main Street	1900 W 33rd Avenue
Asheboro, NC 27203-2141	Vancouver, BC V6N 3J5
Business phone: 336-555-1897	Canada
E-mail address: mjefferson@jeffersontravel.biz	Business phone: 778-555-2304
URL: www.jeffersontravel.biz	E-mail address: jdelay@wildwesttours.biz
	URL: www.wildwesttours.biz
Ms. Elaine Fitzsimmons	Ms. Roberta McGregor
Director	Training Director
Moreland Adventures	Alred Company, Inc.
19 Nottingham Place	5465 Queens Road
London, W1M3FF	Melbourne, Victoria 3004
England	Australia
Business phone: 44 20 5555 3793	Business phone: 61 03 9601 5555
E-mail address: efitz@morelandadventures.biz	E-mail address: rmcg@trainingatalred.biz
URL: www.morelandadventures.biz	URL: www.trainingatalred.biz

STEP-BY-STEP 7.8

1. Maximize Outlook and click the **Contacts** button on the Outlook Bar to open the Contacts folder.

2. Click the **New Contact** button on the Standard toolbar to open the Contact window. 

3. Key **Mr. Michael Jefferson** in the Full Name text box and press **Tab** to move the insertion point to the Job title text box.

4. Key **President** in the Job title text box and press **Tab** to move the insertion point to the Company text box.

5. Key **Jefferson Travel** in the Company text box.

Hot Tip

You can create a new contact by double-clicking the **Contacts folder workspace** (the white area).

Note

The e-mail addresses and the URLs used in this job are fictitious. Your instructor will provide valid e-mail addresses and URLs if you are instructed to actually send an e-mail message to a contact or view a Web page in your Web browser using a contact.

STEP-BY-STEP 7.8 Continued

6. Click the **Address** text box to position the insertion point, key **348 East Main Street**, press **Enter**, and key **Asheboro, NC 27203-2141**.

7. Click the **Business** (phone number) text box and key **336-555-1897**.

8. Click the **E-mail** text box and key **mjefferson@jeffersontravel.biz**.

9. Click the **Web page address** text box and key **www.jeffersontravel.biz**. Your Contact window should look similar to Figure 7-15.

FIGURE 7-15
Jefferson contact

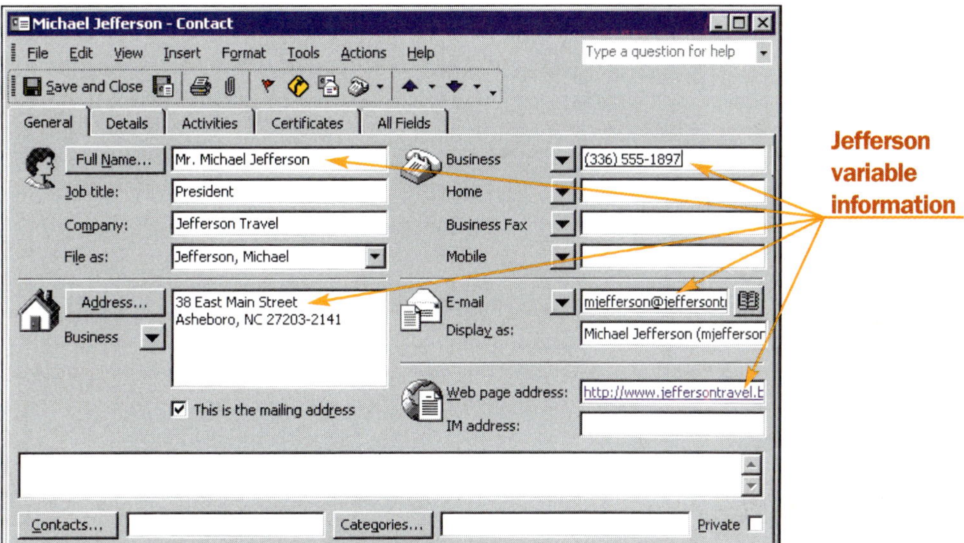

10. Click the **Save and New** button on the Contact window Standard toolbar to save the Jefferson contact and open a blank Contact window. 

STEP-BY-STEP 7.8 Continued

11. Using Figure 7-14 and the previous steps 3 through 10, create new contacts for Delay, Fitzsimmons, and McGregor. When completing the McGregor item, click the **Save and Close** button to save the item and close the Contact window. After adding the contacts, your Contact window should look similar to Figure 7-16.

FIGURE 7-16
Completed contacts

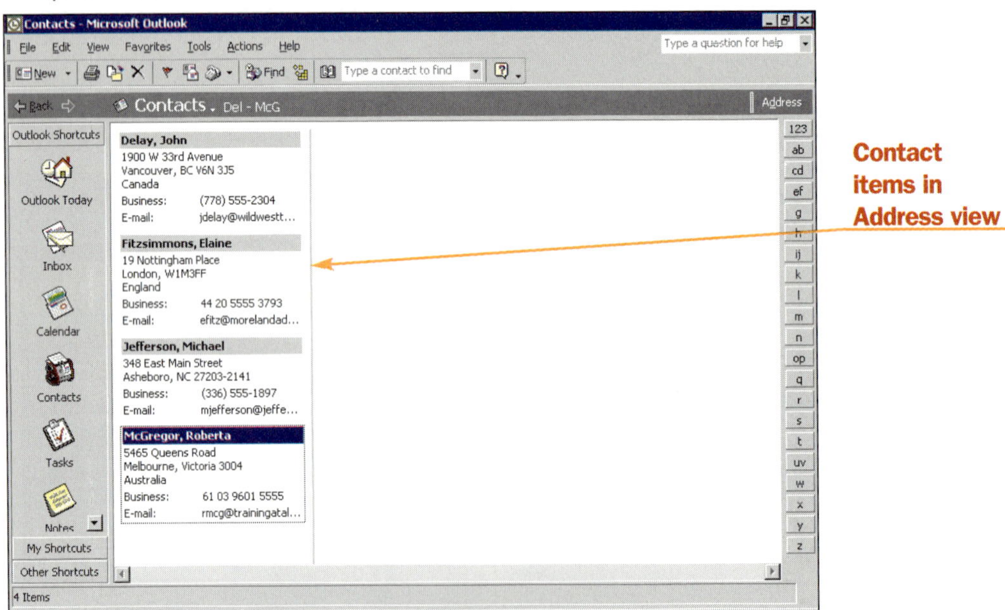

12. Minimize Outlook.

Editing a Contact

You can edit a contact by opening the Contact window and making your changes. You can also edit certain portions of a contact such as the address or phone number without first opening the contact. If you can see the information that needs to be changed, you can simply click the contact to position the insertion point in it and then make the necessary changes. As you return from lunch, the receptionist hands you a note explaining that the phone number for Michael Jefferson at Jefferson Travel has changed. You need to correct the Jefferson contact to reflect the new phone number.

STEP-BY-STEP 7.9

1. Maximize Outlook and open the Contacts folder, if necessary.

2. Click the Business (phone) number for the Michael Jefferson contact to position the insertion point in the phone number and activate the item for editing.

STEP-BY-STEP 7.9 Continued

3. Select the last two digits of the phone number (97), key **79**, and press **Enter**. Your Contact window should look similar to Figure 7-17.

FIGURE 7-17
Edited Jefferson contact

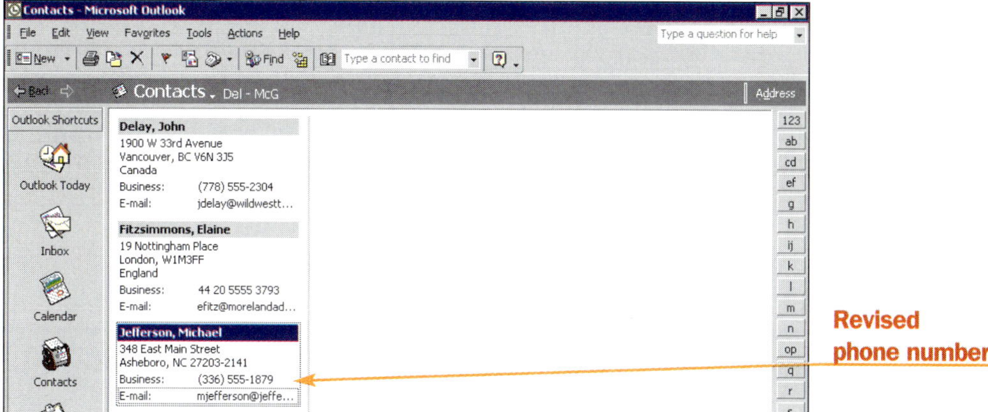

4. Minimize Outlook.

Deleting a Contact

You can easily delete a contact by first selecting it and then clicking the Delete button on the Contacts folder Standard toolbar, or by pressing the Delete key. Michelle Snowdon, the administrative assistant for M. P. Matthews, Director of Marketing and Sales for the Australia branch, calls. She tells you that Roberta McGregor is no longer employed at the Alred Company in Melbourne and reminds you to delete the McGregor contact.

S TEP-BY-STEP 7.10

1. Maximize Outlook and open the Contacts folder, if necessary.

2. Click the Roberta McGregor Contact item to select it, press the **Delete** key to delete the item, and then minimize Outlook.

Hot Tip

Each Outlook item you delete (such as an appointment, a contact, or an incoming e-mail message) is temporarily stored in the Deleted Items folder. This allows you to quickly restore a deleted item by opening the Deleted Items folder and dragging the item back to its original folder. You can empty the Deleted Items folder manually as desired, or you can have Outlook automatically empty the Deleted Items folder each time you close Outlook by turning on this option in the Other tab in the Options dialog box.

Sending an E-mail Message Using a Contact

If you are working in the Contacts folder, you can quickly send an e-mail message to a contact without first opening the Inbox folder. One way to do this is to click the New Contact button list arrow on the Contacts folder Standard toolbar and click Mail Message. Another way is to select a contact, click Actions on the menu bar, and click New Message to Contact. Finally, you can click the New Message to Contact button on the Standard toolbar. Sloane drops by your desk and asks you to send an e-mail to John Delay reminding him to return his signed copy of the Wilderness Treks, Inc. client agreement by next Thursday.

Did You Know?

You can quickly and easily use one item to create another item by dragging items between folders. For example, you can drag an incoming e-mail message to the Calendar folder to create an appointment, or drag a Contact item to the Inbox folder to create an e-mail message. For more information on using drag-and-drop to create Outlook items, see Outlook online Help.

S TEP-BY-STEP 7.11

1. Maximize Outlook and open the Contacts folder, if necessary.

2. Click the shaded John Delay name in the Delay Contact item to select the item without positioning the insertion point in the item.

3. Click the **New Message to Contact** button on the Contacts folder Standard toolbar to open  the e-mail message window containing Delay's e-mail address in the To text box.

4. Key **Client Agreement** in the Subject text box.

5. Key **Please remember to send us your signed copy of the Wilderness Treks, Inc. client agreement by next Thursday**.

6. Press **Enter** and key your name. Your e-mail message window should look similar to Figure 7-18.

FIGURE 7-18
Delay e-mail message

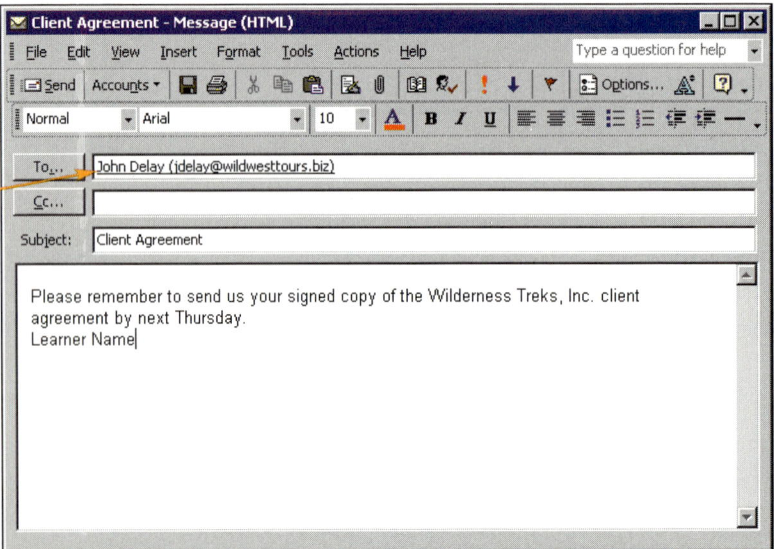

STEP-BY-STEP 7.11 Continued

7. If your instructor provides a valid e-mail address, send the message. Otherwise skip this step and go to step 8.

8. Print the message and save it as **Delay Message**. Then close the message window leaving the Contacts folder open and maximized for the next Step-by-Step.

Customizing the Contacts Folder Views

You can view the contents of the Contacts folder in many ways, including viewing more details for each item and viewing a phone list. Because you sometimes need to access your client phone numbers when away from your desk, you want a phone list you can carry with you. First, you view more details for each contact, and then you view and print a phone list.

> **Did You Know?** 
>
> There are many, many pieces of information called fields that you can use to add additional information to a contact. A large number of the available fields do not appear in the default set of fields you see in the General tab in the Contact window. To see more available fields, click the **Details** and **All Fields** tabs in the Contact window.

STEP-BY-STEP 7.12

1. Click **View** on the menu bar, point to Current View, and click **Detailed Address Cards** to see more complete information for each Contact item. Your Contact window should look similar to Figure 7-19.

FIGURE 7-19
Detailed Address Cards view

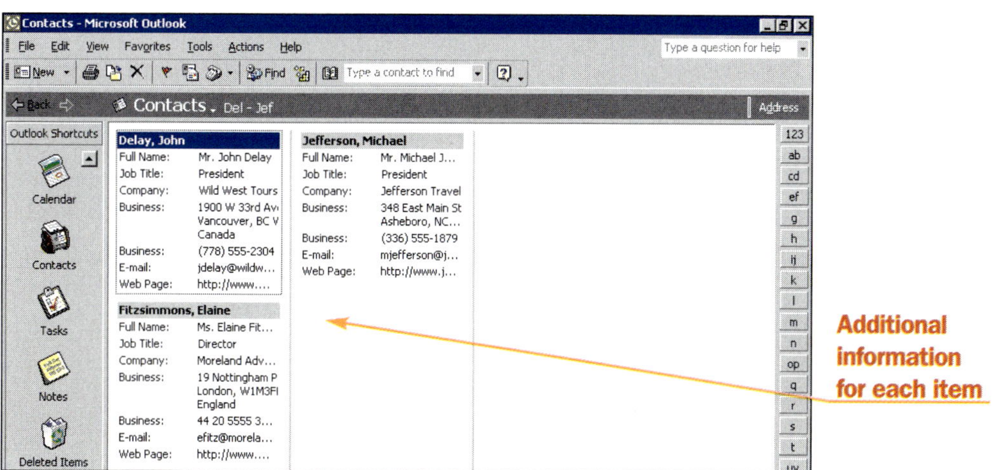

Additional information for each item

STEP-BY-STEP 7.12 Continued

2. Click **View** on the menu bar, point to Current View, and click **Phone List** to see a list of client phone numbers. Your Contact window should look similar to Figure 7-20.

FIGURE 7-20
Phone List view

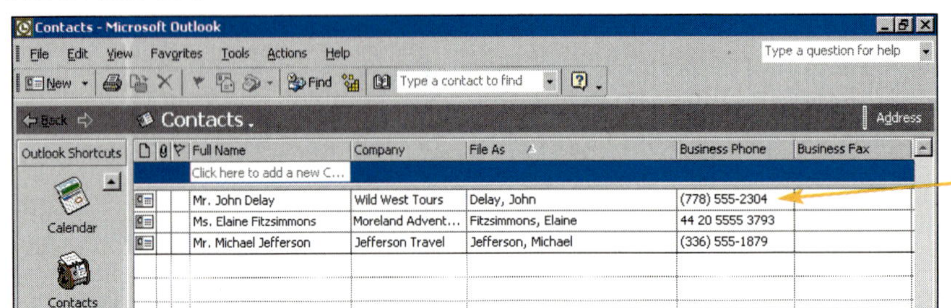

3. Print the phone list, change the view to Address Cards, and close Outlook.

SUMMARY

In this lesson, you learned:

■ Microsoft Outlook is an information management application that can be used to send and receive e-mail, maintain an appointments calendar, and maintain important information about business and personal contacts.

■ Each e-mail, appointment, or contact you create in Outlook is called an item and each type of item is stored in a separate Outlook folder such as the Calendar folder, Contacts folder, or Inbox folder on your hard drive or a network server.

■ An appointment is an item you enter in the Calendar folder that is less than 24 hours in duration and has a specific starting and ending time. You can enter an appointment in the Appointment window or in the Appointment list in the Calendar folder Day view.

■ An event is an item you enter in the Calendar folder that has a duration of 24 hours or longer.

■ You can delete an appointment item by selecting it in the Appointment list in the Calendar folder Day view and clicking the Delete button on the Calendar folder Standard toolbar or by pressing the Delete key.

■ You can print a calendar in several different ways including daily, weekly, and monthly formats.

■ You can view the contents of the Calendar folder in a variety of ways, such as viewing a single day's appointments, viewing appointments for five working days, seven calendar days, and a full month. You can also customize the Calendar folder views to see only appointments, events, or recurring appointments or events.

■ A contact is an item you enter in the Contacts folder that contains the name, address, phone numbers, e-mail addresses, Web site address, and other information for an individual.

- You can edit the information in a contact by opening the Contact window or by positioning the insertion point in the information area (field) you want to change while viewing the Contacts folder in Address Cards or Detail Address Cards view.

- You can quickly send an e-mail message to a contact with commands on the Contacts folder menu bar or Standard toolbar or by dragging a contact item to the Inbox folder.

- The contents of the Contacts folder can be viewed in several different ways including Detail Address Cards view and Phone List view.

VOCABULARY *Review*

Define the following terms:

Appointment	Contacts folder	Outlook folder
Calendar folder	Event	Views
Contact	Item	

REVIEW *Questions*

TRUE / FALSE

Circle T if the statement is true or F if the statement is false.

T   F   **1.** Each Outlook folder, such as the Contacts or Calendar folder, has several different ways to view the folder's contents.

T   F   **2.** An appointment item you enter in the Contacts folder must be longer than 24 hours.

T   F   **3.** You can use either the Appointment window or the Appointment list in Day view to enter a new appointment item.

T   F   **4.** A contact is an item that has a duration of less than 24 hours and has a specific starting and ending time.

T   F   **5.** You cannot send an e-mail message to a contact by dragging the contact item to the Inbox folder.

FILL IN THE BLANK

Complete the following sentences by writing the correct word or words in the blanks provided.

1. You can print a phone list by switching the Contacts folder to __________ view.

2. Each Outlook item you delete is temporarily stored in the __________ folder.

3. To see all your appointments scheduled during next week's working hours, you can switch the Calendar folder to the __________ view.

4. A(n) __________ is a Calendar folder item that is not bound by starting and ending times.

5. To create an appointment for Wednesday of next week, you can open the Appointment window and key __________ in the Starting time text box.

PROJECTS

PROJECT 7-1

1. Start Outlook and open the **Calendar folder**, if necessary.

2. Change the Executive Committee luncheon appointment to next Thursday from 1:00–2:00 p.m.

3. Print a monthly calendar that includes the modified appointments for next week.

4. Delete the Wilson and Executive Committee appointments and the Rolling Hills event.

5. Open the Inbox window and minimize Outlook.

PROJECT 7-2

Sloane calls and asks you to print a list of contacts and wants you to be certain that the printed list contains all the information on each contact. Maximize Outlook and open the Contacts folder. Change the view to Detailed Address Cards and print the contacts in the Card Style. Then return the Contacts folder to Address Cards view, delete the three contact records, open the Inbox, and close Outlook.

WEB PROJECT

Because of Wilderness Treks' international business activities in your London, Vancouver, and Melbourne branch offices, you often have to make international long distance phone calls. Use the search feature in your Web browser or a search tool such as Google (*www.google.com*) to locate Web sites that provide international long distance country code and city code information for England, Canada, and Australia. Print at least two Web pages.

TEAMWORK PROJECT

As an administrative assistant, one of your most important tasks is keeping track of important client and vendor information. Select a classmate to work with you on this project and then, using Outlook online Help, research how to add additional fields of information *not included in the default information fields* to Outlook contacts. Working together with your classmate, demonstrate to other classmates how to add and remove additional fields from contact items.

CRITICAL*Thinking*

 ACTIVITY 7-1

You want to know more about sharing Outlook folders with coworkers. Using Outlook online Help, research ways to share Outlook folders and then create a brief outline describing how to share Outlook folders. Use your outline to describe the folder sharing processes to your classmates.

CREATING A MONTHLY NEWSLETTER WITH COLUMNS, PICTURES, DIAGRAMS, AND CHARTS

Create and Edit Newspaper-style Columns

Each month Dave Smithy, the administrative assistant in the Human Resources Department, creates and distributes an employee newsletter. Unfortunately, Dave is ill and it appears he will be out of the office for several days. At this Monday morning's meeting, Sloane asks you to help by finishing the June newsletter that Dave drafted before he became ill. You need to format the text in newspaper-style columns, insert some attractive pictures, add an explanatory diagram, insert a chart, and add emphasis to some of the text with a bulleted list.

Most documents such as letters and reports are single column documents, meaning that the text starts at the left margin and extends to the right margin. Some documents such as newsletters use two or three columns of text instead of a single column. These multicolumn documents are created using *newspaper-style columns*, which are vertical columns of text side by side on a page. When you create newspaper-style columns, the text flows from the leftmost column to the rightmost—in the same way text flows from column to column on a newspaper page.

Word automatically inserts selected text in the number of columns you specify. It is often necessary, however, to adjust the amount of text in each column to make the layout more attractive by inserting a column break using the Break command on the Insert menu or the Ctrl + Shift + Enter shortcut key combination. You begin by opening Dave's June newsletter draft, formatting the body of the document in two newspaper-style columns, and then inserting a column break to balance the amount of text in each column.

Hot Tip

You can create newspaper-style columns by first selecting the appropriate text and then clicking the **Columns** command on the **Format** menu.

STEP-BY-STEP 8.1

1. Start the Word application, if necessary, and open the **Step8-1** document from the data files.

2. Save the document as **June Newsletter**.

3. Move the insertion point to the left margin at the text beginning Happy Birthday!

4. Press the **Ctrl + Shift + End** keys to select the text from the position of the insertion point to the end of the document.

5. Click the **Columns** button on the Standard toolbar and then click the second column from the left in the grid (2 Columns) to place the selected text in two newspaper-styled columns.

6. Click at the left margin to the left of the United We Care Contributions paragraph heading to position the insertion point.

7. Press the **Ctrl + Shift + Enter** keys to insert a column break and move the United We Care Contributions heading paragraph and following paragraph to column two. Your screen should look similar to Figure 8-1.

FIGURE 8-1
Text in newspaper columns

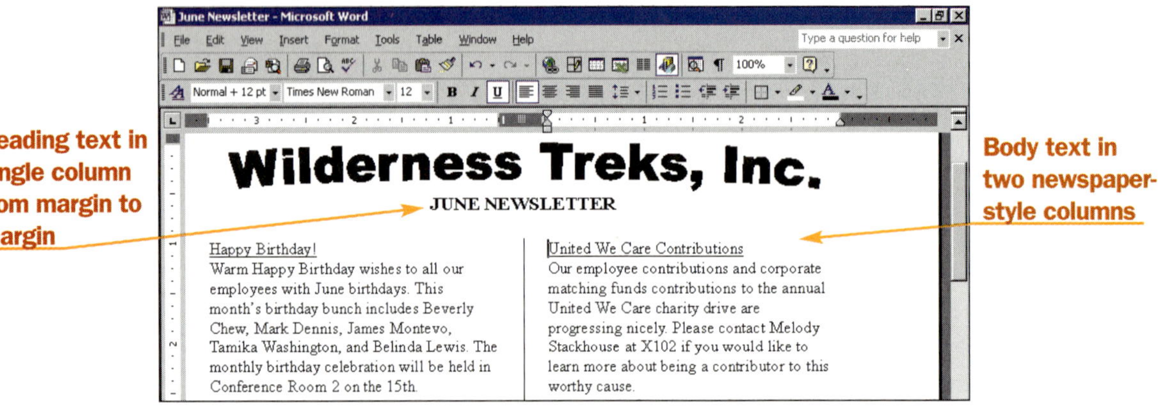

8. Save the document and keep it open for the next Step-by-Step.

Insert, Size, and Position a Picture

A *picture* is an image file you insert in an Office document (Word document, Excel worksheet, or PowerPoint presentation) to add interest and excitement to the document. You can insert pictures from the Clip Organizer or from a folder on your hard drive, network server, or diskette. You can quickly size a picture by selecting it and

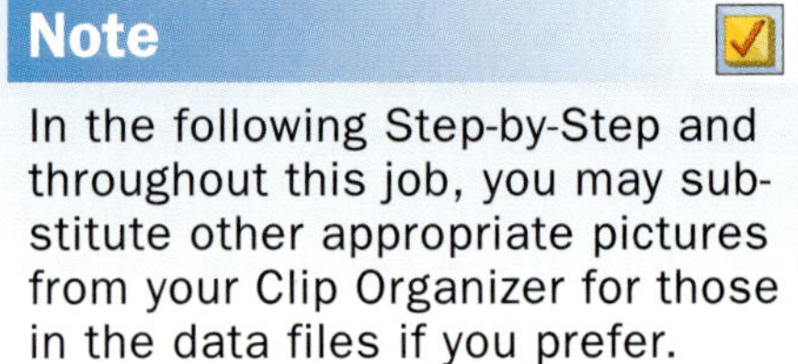

dragging a sizing handle. When you select a picture, the Picture toolbar should automatically appear. You can position a selected picture within paragraph text with the Text Wrapping button on the Picture toolbar.

In Office XP the **Clip Organizer** contains picture, sound, video, and other media files (often simply called clips) that you can insert in Office documents. These clips are organized into catalogs of similar clips. You can search for clips in the Clip Organizer with the Insert, Picture, Clip Art commands or with the Insert Clip Art button on the Drawing toolbar. You can open the Clip Organizer with the Clip Organizer link on the Insert Clip Art task pane. Note that in Office 2000, the Clip Organizer is called the Media Gallery, and you search for clips using the Insert Clip Art dialog box.

You think it would make the newsletter more interesting if you added a picture of Calgary, Canada (the conference city), to the Annual Conference topic and a birthday celebration picture to the paragraph discussing June birthdays. You begin by inserting a picture of Calgary and then sizing it and positioning it to fit attractively in the paragraph following the Annual Conference paragraph heading.

S TEP-BY-STEP 8.2

1. Verify that the June Newsletter document is open and then click the **Drawing** button on the Standard toolbar to display the Drawing toolbar. 

2. Move the insertion point to the left margin of the Annual Conference paragraph heading in column two.

3. Click the **Insert Picture** button on the Drawing toolbar to open the Insert Picture dialog box.  (*Note:* If you are using Word 2000, click **Insert** on the menu bar, point to **Picture**, and click **From File**.)

Did You Know?

A Word document has a text layer in which the text and pictures appear and additional layers that allow you to position pictures and other objects in front of or behind the text. The default is for pictures to be inserted in the same layer as the text, or in line with the text, which means that the picture is on the same line as text that appears before or after it. When a picture is in line with text, you can position it with the alignment buttons on the Formatting toolbar, just as you would text. You can size a picture object proportionally by dragging a corner sizing handle. If you want to size a picture object proportionally while maintaining its center position, press and hold the Ctrl key while you drag a corner sizing handle.

STEP-BY-STEP 8.2 Continued

4. Open the data files folder and double-click the **Calgary** image file to insert it at the position of the insertion point. Your screen should look similar to Figure 8-2.

FIGURE 8-2
Inserted Calgary picture

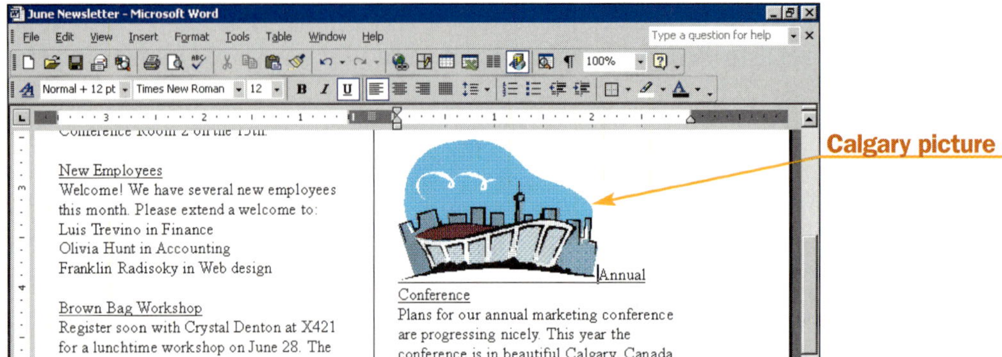

5. Click the **Calgary** picture to select it, if necessary, and then move the mouse pointer to the lower-right corner sizing handle, where it becomes a double-headed arrow sizing pointer. Your screen should look similar to Figure 8-3.

FIGURE 8-3
Selected picture and sizing pointer

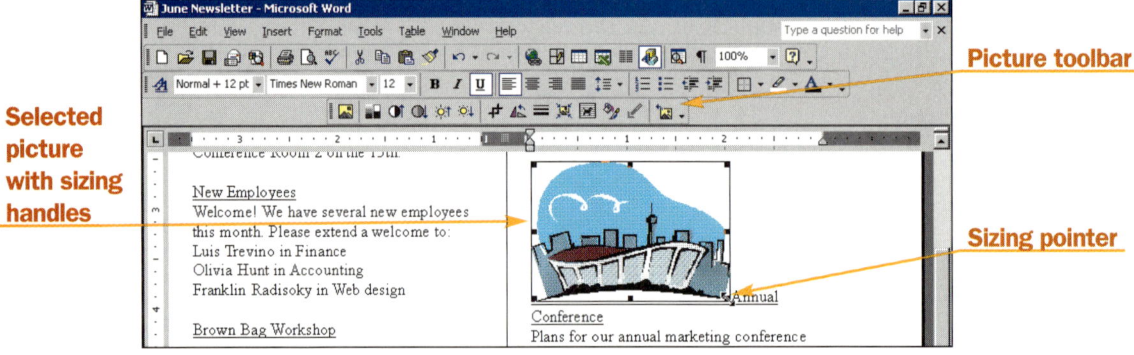

6. Press and hold the **Ctrl** key and drag the lower-right sizing handle diagonally up and to the left to size the picture proportionally approximately 1/4 its original size.

7. Click the **Text Wrapping** button on the Picture toolbar and click **Square** to place the picture in a different layer than the text. 

STEP-BY-STEP 8.2 Continued

8. Drag the selected picture downward to the left margin of the paragraph below the Annual Conference paragraph heading and then click in the document outside the picture to deselect the picture. Your screen should look similar to Figure 8-4.

FIGURE 8-4
Resized and repositioned picture

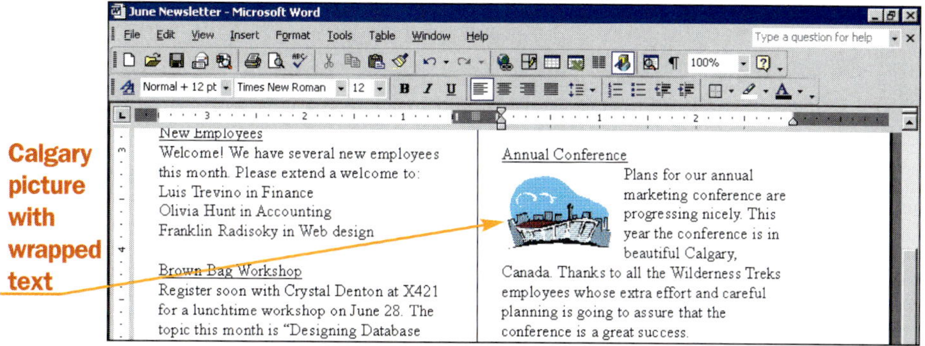

9. Move the insertion point to the left margin of the Happy Birthday! paragraph heading and insert the **Birthday** picture located in the data files at the insertion point. Size the picture proportionally to approximately 1/4 its original size, set the text wrapping to **Square**, and drag the picture to the right margin of the paragraph below the Happy Birthday! paragraph heading. Deselect the picture. Your screen should look similar to Figure 8-5.

FIGURE 8-5
Inserted, sized, and positioned Birthday picture

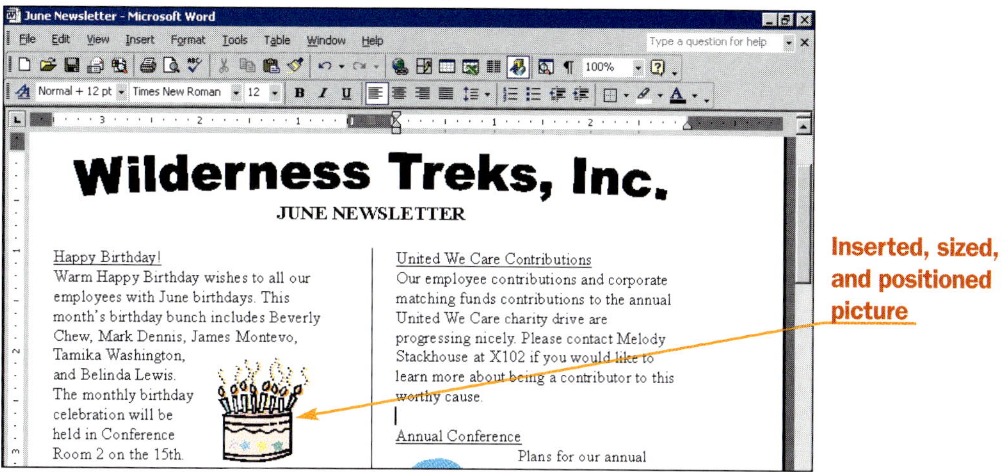

10. Save the document and leave it open for the next Step-by-Step.

Create and Format a Diagram

A *diagram* is a figure used with or instead of text to help explain complex relationships and ideas. For example, cycle diagrams show a process with a continuous cycle; radial diagrams illustrate relationships to and from central core element; pyramid diagrams show foundation-based relationships; Venn diagrams illustrate areas that overlap between elements; and a target diagram shows steps toward a goal. An organization chart illustrates hierarchical relationships between people in an organization. You can use the Insert Diagram or Organization Chart button on the Drawing toolbar to turn on the drawing canvas and insert special diagrams.

The *drawing canvas* is an area that surrounds your drawing objects and helps you keep parts of your drawing together. The drawing canvas gives you a boundary between your drawing objects and the rest of your document. Although the drawing canvas has no border or background, you can format it in the same way you format other drawing objects. To learn more about the drawing canvas, see Word online Help.

Crystal Denton, the training manager, calls and asks you to add an attractive picture or diagram to the June newsletter Brown Bag Workshop paragraph. You decide to use a Venn diagram and place it behind the text. First you insert the diagram in the drawing canvas and then you resize it, change its layout style, and position it behind the paragraph text.

In the next Step-by-Step you are instructed to position a diagram in a layer behind the text. When you do this, it may be a little difficult for you to then select the diagram for further editing. One way to do this is to click where you expect the drawing canvas boundary to be. Another way to select the diagram is by using the Special option in the Find dialog box to find all graphic images. If you use the Find dialog box method, remember to turn on the Text Boxes in Main Document highlighting feature.

Note

If you are using Word 2000, the feature that allows you to draw diagrams is not available. You can read but not complete the following Step-by-Step instructions. Your instructor will provide alternate instructions to insert a picture and position it behind the paragraph text.

Hot Tip

You can change the shape, position, size, formatting and text wrapping elements of a diagram with buttons on the Diagram toolbar.

STEP-BY-STEP 8.3

1. Verify that the June Newsletter document is open and move the insertion point to the end of the paragraph following the Brown Bag Workshop heading paragraph.

2. Click the **Insert Diagram or Organization Chart** button on the Drawing toolbar to open the Diagram Gallery dialog box. 

3. Click the Venn Diagram icon (the second icon in the second row). Your dialog box should look similar to Figure 8-6.

FIGURE 8-6
Diagram Gallery dialog box

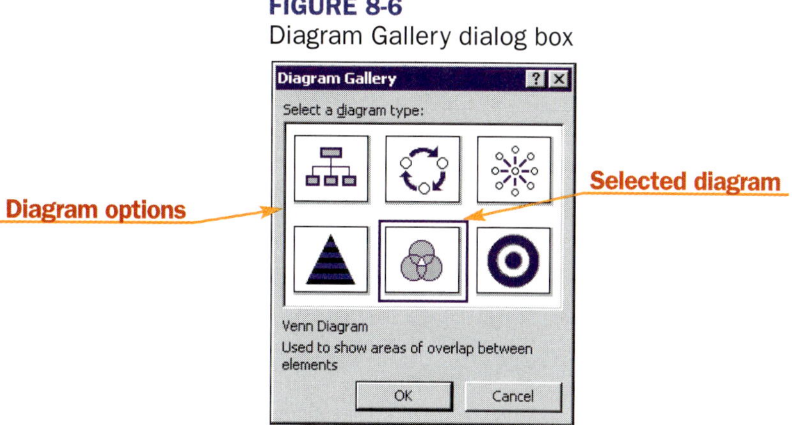

4. Click **OK** to open the drawing canvas, insert a Venn diagram, and display the Diagram toolbar. Your screen should look similar to Figure 8-7.

FIGURE 8-7
Drawing canvas and Venn diagram

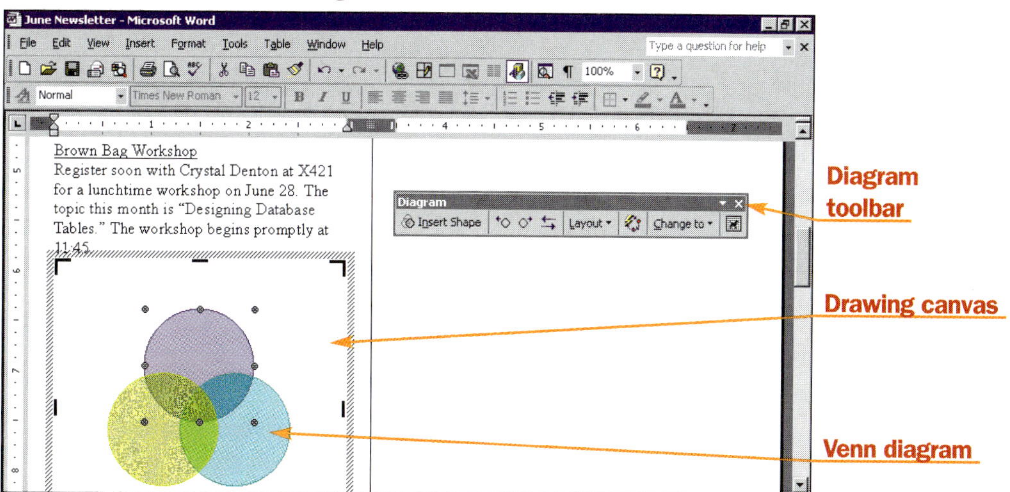

5. Click the **Layout** button on the Diagram toolbar to view the Layout menu options and then click **Scale Diagram**. Observe that the drawing canvas now has clear circle sizing handles. 

STEP-BY-STEP 8.3 Continued

6. Press and hold the **Ctrl** key and drag the lower-right sizing handle on the drawing canvas diagonally up and to the left to size the diagram approximately 1/6 its original size.

7. Click the **AutoFormat** button on the Diagram toolbar to open the Diagram Style Gallery dialog box, then click the **3-D Color** option in the Select a Diagram Style list box. Your dialog box should look similar to Figure 8-8. 

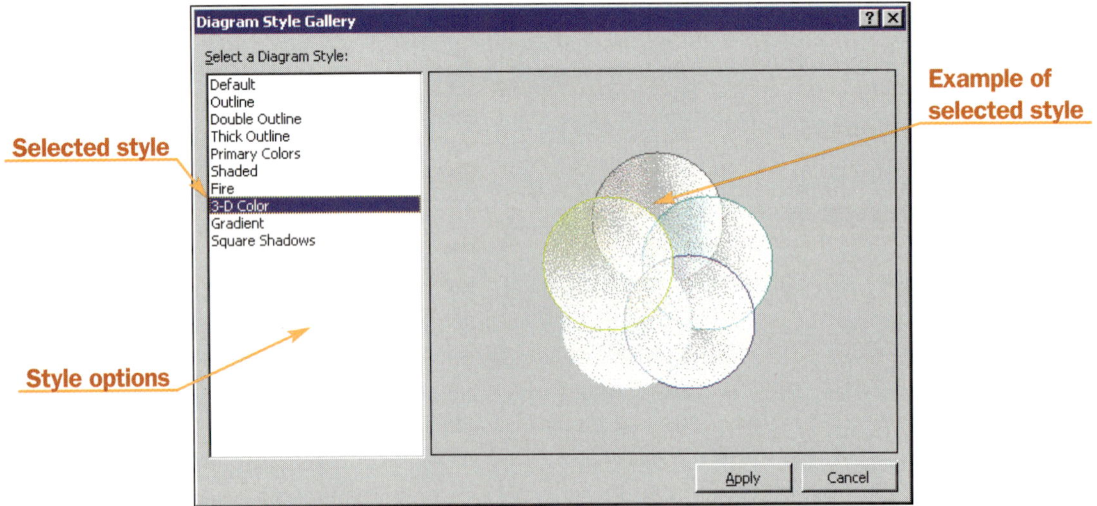

FIGURE 8-8
Diagram Style Gallery dialog box

8. Click **Apply** to change the diagram's format to 3-D Color.

9. Click the **Text Wrapping** button on the Diagram toolbar and click **Behind Text** to position the diagram in a layer behind the text layer. 

10. Drag the diagram to the approximate center of the paragraph and then deselect it. Your screen should look similar to Figure 8-9.

FIGURE 8-9
Completed Venn diagram

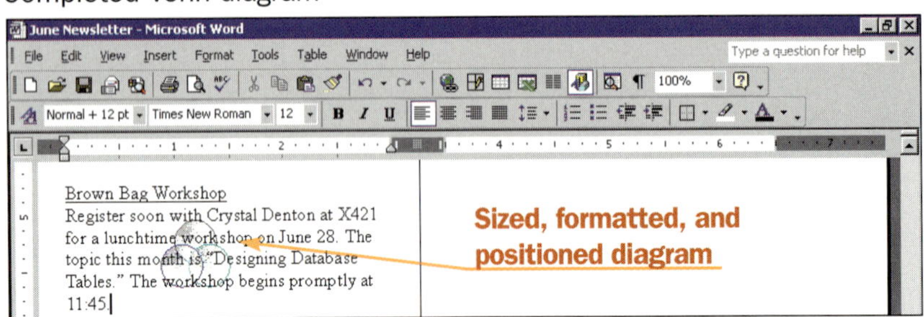

11. Save the document and leave it open for the next Step-by-Step.

Insert and Format a Chart

A *chart* is a picture that represents a set of numerical data or the relationship between multiple sets of numerical data. Inserting a chart such as a bar chart, pie chart, or line chart in a Word document helps readers better understand numerical data. You can embed or link an Excel chart in a Word document, or you can use the Microsoft Graph supplementary application that comes with Office to insert a chart in a Word document from scratch.

A Microsoft Graph datasheet contains many of same features as an Excel worksheet; you enter, select, and edit data in the same way you would if you were working with an Excel worksheet. When you insert a chart using Microsoft Graph, the datasheet contains sample data and a sample chart is created from that data. You must replace the sample data with your actual data. The components of a chart include the plot area, the legend, the Value (Y) axis, the Category (X) axis, and the data points.

To help employees understand the relationship between their contributions and corporate contributions to the United We Care annual charity drive, you want to add a chart to the United We Care Contributions topic in the June newsletter. You call Melody Stackhouse, this year's in-house charity drive director, and ask her for the employee and corporate contributions to date and the total contributions goal. Melody responds with the data shown in Table 8-1. First, you insert a chart and key the data shown in Table 8-1 into the chart's datasheet. Then you format the chart.

TABLE 8-1
Contributions data

	CONTRIBUTIONS
Employee	10,000
Corporate	25,000
Goal	150,000

S TEP-BY-STEP 8.4

1. Verify that the June Newsletter document is open and move the insertion point to the blank line above the Annual Conference paragraph heading.

2. Click **Insert** on the menu bar and click **Object** to open the Object dialog box.

3. Click the **Create New** tab, if necessary, and click **Microsoft Graph Chart** in the Object type list to select it. (*Note:* If you are using Word 2000, click **Microsoft Graph 2000 Chart**.) Your dialog box should look similar to Figure 8-10.

Warning

When you float pictures in a different layer than the text, they may move when you insert additional pictures, charts, or diagrams. If this happens, you need to reposition the picture that has moved. For example, when you insert the chart in Step-by-Step 8.4, the Calgary picture you inserted earlier may move. If this happens, simply drag the picture back to its original position.

STEP-BY-STEP 8.4 Continued

FIGURE 8-10
Object dialog box

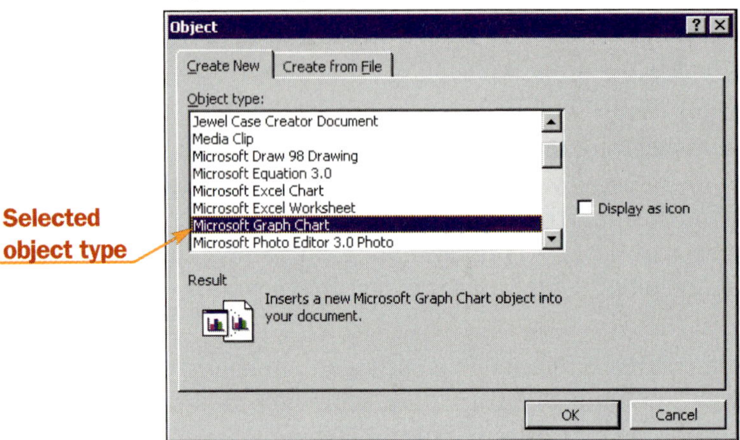

4. Click **OK** to insert a sample chart and view the datasheet containing sample data. Your screen should look similar to Figure 8-11.

FIGURE 8-11
Sample chart and datasheet

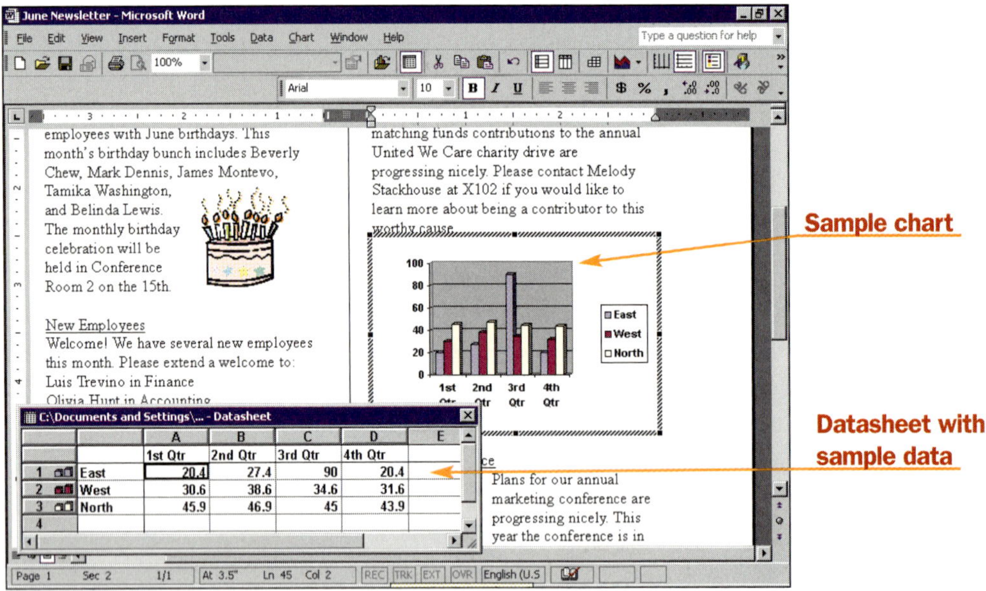

5. Key **Contributions** in the cell immediately below the column A header; key **Employees** in the first cell immediately to the right of the row 1 header; key **10,000** in cell A1; key **Corporate** in the first cell immediately to the right of the row 2 header; key **25,000** in cell A2; key **Goal** in the first cell immediately to the right of the row 3 header; key **150,000** in cell A3. Observe the changes to the sample chart as you make changes to the datasheet.

6. Double-click the **column B**, **column C**, and **column D** header buttons to hide the contents of those columns. Observe the changes to the sample chart as you make changes to the datasheet.

STEP-BY-STEP 8.4 Continued

7. Click the **View Datasheet** button on the Microsoft Graph Standard toolbar to close the Datasheet window. Your screen should look similar to Figure 8-12. 

FIGURE 8-12
Completed chart

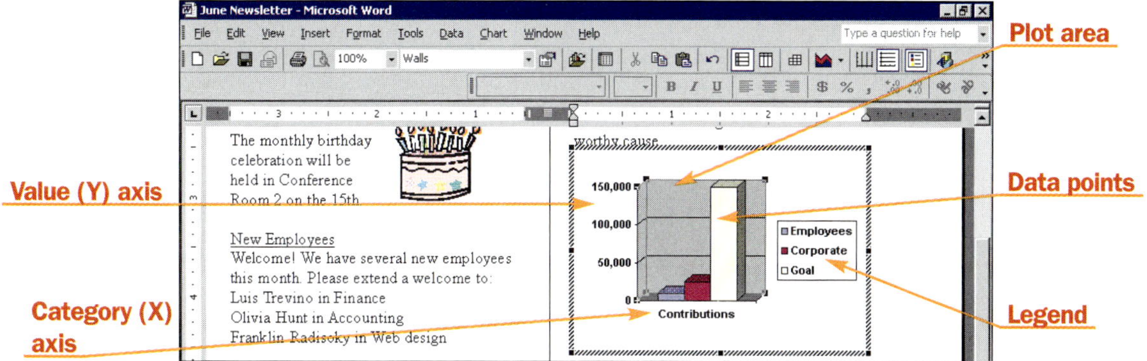

8. Click the **Chart Type** button list arrow on the Microsoft Graph Standard toolbar to view a list of chart types and then click the **Column Chart** icon (first icon in the third row) to change the chart type to a Column chart. 

9. Double-click the gray plot area to open the Format Plot Area dialog box and click the **None** option button for the Area fill color. The dialog box on your screen should look similar to Figure 8-13.

FIGURE 8-13
Format Plot Area dialog box

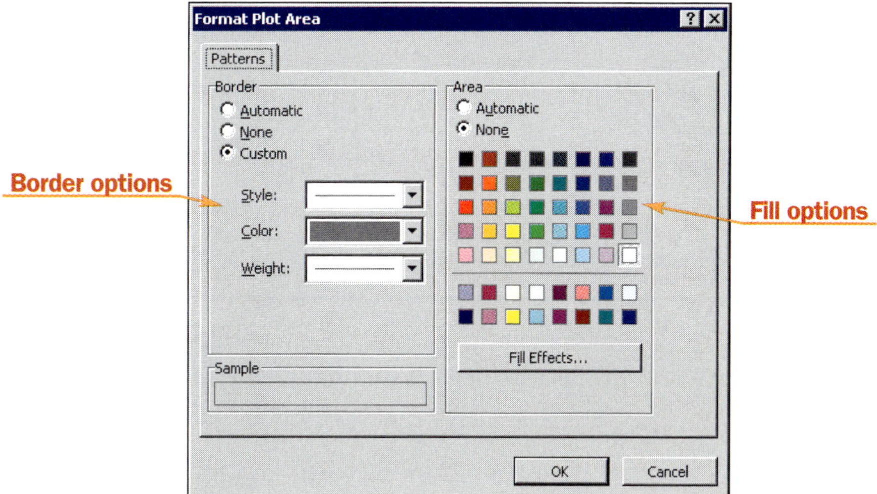

STEP-BY-STEP 8.4 Continued

10. Click **OK**. Your screen should look similar to Figure 8-14.

FIGURE 8-14
Formatted chart

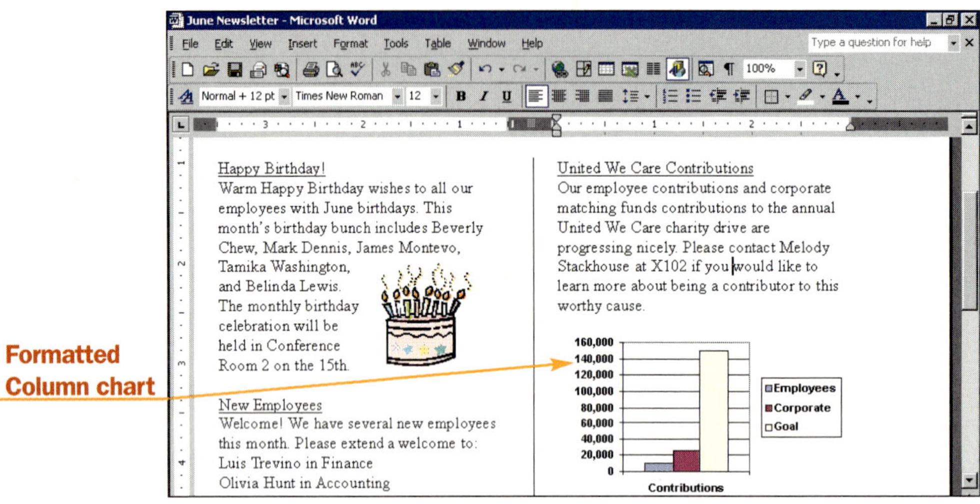

11. Save the document and leave it open for the next Step-by-Step.

Select a Bullet Graphic

To wrap up the June newsletter, you want to emphasize the names of the new employees identified in the New Employees paragraph. One way to do this is to make the list of names a bulleted list. A *bullet* is a graphic object you add to each line of a list of items. You can use the Bullets button on the Formatting toolbar to quickly add bullets to a selected list of items. However, if you want to choose from a variety of available bullet graphics, you use the Bullets and Numbering dialog box to add bullets to a list.

STEP-BY-STEP 8.5

1. Verify that the June Newsletter document is open and then select the list of names in the paragraph below the New Employees heading beginning with the text *Luis Trevino* and ending with the text *Web Design*.

2. Click **Format** on the menu bar, click **Bullets and Numbering**, and then click the **Bulleted** tab, if necessary.

STEP-BY-STEP 8.5 Continued

3. Click a bullet of your choice. Your dialog box should look similar to Figure 8-15.

FIGURE 8-15
Bulleted tab in the Bullets and Numbering dialog box

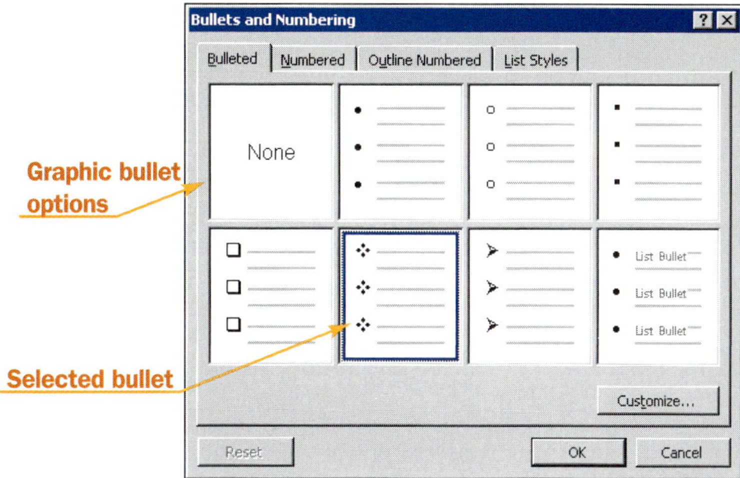

4. Click **OK** to add the bullets to the selected list.

5. Switch to **Print Layout** view, if necessary, and zoom to Whole Page. Your newsletter should look similar to Figure 8-16.

FIGURE 8-16
Completed June newsletter

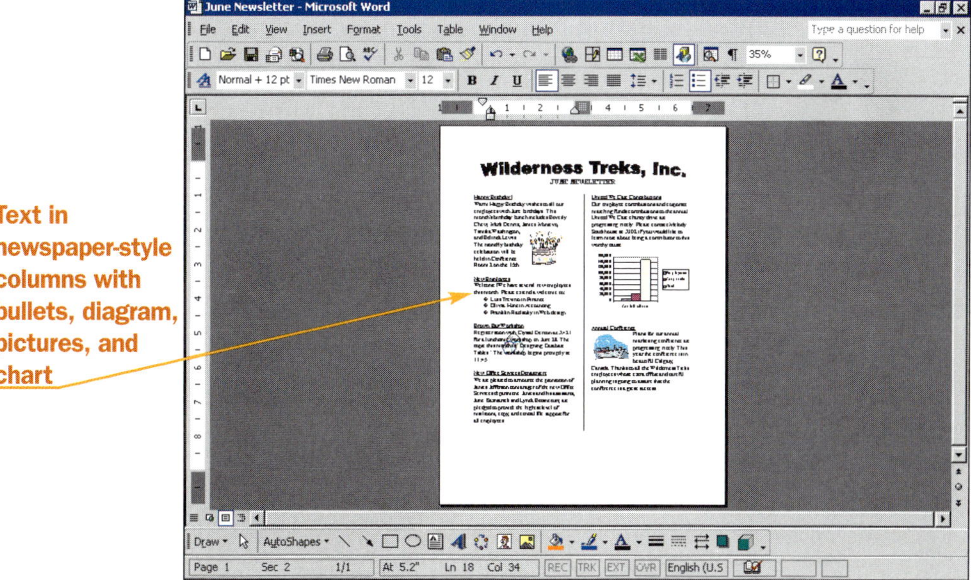

6. Zoom back to **100%** and then save, print preview, and print the document. Finally, close the Drawing toolbar, close the document, and close Word.

SUMMARY

In this lesson, you learned:

- You can format selected text in newspaper-style columns, which allows the text to flow from the leftmost column to the rightmost column.

- To balance the amount of text in each newspaper-style column, you can insert a column break with the Break command on the Insert menu or with the Ctrl + Shift + Enter shortcut key combination.

- Pictures are image files you can insert in an Office document, such as a Word document, Excel worksheet, or PowerPoint slide.

- You can quickly size pictures with the mouse pointer and specify how you want the text above and below the picture to wrap around the picture.

- Diagrams are used to help explain complex relationships and ideas. You can create several different types of diagrams, such as cycle, target, pyramid, radial, and organization chart diagrams.

- You can size and format a diagram and specify how you want the text above and below the diagram to wrap around it.

- A chart is used to represent a set of numerical data or the relationship between multiple sets of numerical data.

- You can use the Microsoft Graph supplemental application that comes with Office to create charts from scratch in a Word document.

- Bullet graphics can be added to selected lists to add emphasis to the lists.

- To choose from a selection of bullet graphics, you can add bullets to a selected list with options in the Bullets and Numbering dialog box.

VOCABULARY *Review*

Define the following terms:

Bullet	Diagram	Newspaper-style columns
Chart	Drawing canvas	Picture
Clip Organizer		

REVIEW *Questions*

TRUE / FALSE

Circle T if the statement is true or F if the statement is false.

T   F   **1.** Most documents, such as letters or reports, are multicolumn documents.

T   F   **2.** You can use the Ctrl + Shift + End shortcut key combination to insert a column break.

T   F   **3.** You position a picture in a different layer than the text when you specify that the text above and below the picture wrap around it.

T   F   **4.** A picture is a figure used with or without text to help explain complex relationships or ideas.

T   F   **5.** The Media Gallery is an area that surrounds a drawing object and helps keep all the parts of the drawing together.

FILL IN THE BLANK

Complete the following sentences by writing the correct word or words in the blanks provided.

1. You can quickly create a chart from scratch in Word by opening the __________ supplementary application.

2. When you create a chart from scratch in Word, you must enter the chart data in the __________.

3. To have text flow from left to right in multiple columns, you must format the text as __________ columns.

4. The default position for inserted pictures is in the same __________ with the text.

5. The diagram you would use to illustrate foundation-based relationships is a(n) __________ diagram.

PROJECTS

 ## PROJECT 8-1

1. Open Word and open Project 8-1 from the data files.

2. Save the document as **Scuba Diving Adventure**.

3. Create newspaper-style columns for the body text beginning with the Pink Beach paragraph heading to the end of the document. Balance the columns by inserting a column break at the Kralendijk paragraph heading.

4. Insert the **Beach** picture located in the data files in the paragraph below the Pink Beach heading paragraph. Size and position the picture attractively.

5. Insert the **Boca Cai** picture located in the data files in the paragraph below the Boca Cai heading paragraph. Size and position the picture attractively.

6. Save the document and then print preview, print, and close it.

PROJECT 8-2

Crystal Denton, the training manager, sends you a draft of a Word document that contains a brief summary of the new Excel training program results. She asks you to review the draft and make any revisions you think are appropriate before she submits the final document to Sloane. Open the **Project 8-2** document and save it as **Training Summary**. Add bullets of your choice to the list of departments whose employees have completed the new Excel training program. Then, using Microsoft Graph, insert a Bar chart (chart with horizontal bars instead of vertical columns) in the document that illustrates the number of trained employees by department. Explore ways to format the chart and then format it as desired. Print preview, print, and close the document.

WEB PROJECT

Melody Stackhouse calls to ask for your help. She is creating a new bulletin board announcement for the United We Care charity drive and would like to add some interesting pictures (clip art) to the announcement. She asks you to find some Web sites she can use to download free pictures. Use the search feature in your Web browser or a search tool such as Google (*www.google.com*) to locate Web sites that offer free clip art that might be appropriate for the announcement document. Print at least three Web pages.

TEAMWORK PROJECT

As an administrative assistant, you are often called upon to create documents containing a variety of diagrams. You want to review how to draw and format the various diagrams available in the Diagram Gallery. Select a classmate to work with you on this project. Then explore creating and formatting at least three different types of diagrams. Create a document containing an example of each type. Using the document, demonstrate to another group of classmates how to create and format the diagrams.

CRITICAL*Thinking*

ACTIVITY 8-1

Beverly Norris, an administrative assistant in the accounting department, meets you for lunch and tells you she is having trouble removing multiple columns from a document. You agree to try to solve Beverly's problem. Using Word online Help, research how to troubleshoot newspaper-style columns and to find a possible solution for Beverly.

Creating a Confirmation Memo and Employee Phone List with Tabs

Use Center, Left, Decimal, and Right Tab Stops to Align Text in Columns

A *center tab stop* allows you to center text at the tab stop and have the text flow left and right from the tab stop. Center tab stops are often used for column headings that appear above columns of text. A *decimal tab stop* allows you to align a column of dollar values on the decimal point. A *right tab stop* allows you to align numbers or text from the right.

The accounting department is receiving invoices from various vendors who are supplying products and services for the annual marketing conference. Bob Davenport, the accounting manager, sends you the e-mail shown in Figure 9-1 asking for payment approval and due dates for the invoices received to date. You respond to Bob's e-mail with an interoffice memo using custom center, left, decimal, and right tab stops to itemize the invoices including their amounts and payment dates. In your memo to Bob Davenport, you use center tab stops to position column headings, left tab stops to position the vendor names, decimal tab stops to position the invoice amounts, and right tab stops to position the payment date.

Did You Know?

When working in a document with multiple paragraphs using different types of tab stops, it is often more efficient to first key the text and then select the text paragraphs to set the appropriate tab stops.

Bob Davenport's e-mail message

Message From: Bob Davenport [davenport@wildernesstreks.biz]
Sent: Wednesday, June 7, 2006 8:30 AM
To: adminasst@wildernesstreks.biz
Subject: Conference vendor invoices

We have received the following invoices and need your approval to pay each invoice plus the date on which you want the invoice paid.

May 15-Calgary Catering-$4,500.00 deposit for banquet
May 29-The Gift House-$3,354.80 for 300 attendee gift baskets
June 1-Baker Limousines-$971.34 for executive limo service to and from airport
June 2-Office Supplies, Inc.-$52.75 for registration supplies

Bob

S TEP-BY-STEP 9.1

1. Start the Word application, if necessary, open the **Step9-1** document from the data files, and switch to Print Layout view, if necessary.

2. Save the document as **Davenport Memo** and display the nonprinting characters, if necessary.

3. Key your name as the FROM variable.

4. Move the insertion point to the bottom of the document.

5. Key **Invoice Date** and press **Tab**. Key **Vendor** and press **Tab**. Key **Invoice Amount** and press **Tab**. Key **Payment Date** and press **Enter**.

6. Key **May 15** and press **Tab**. Key **Calgary Catering** and press **Tab**. Key **$4,500.00** and press **Tab**. Key **June 9** and press **Enter**.

7. Using Figure 9-1 and step 6 as your guides, key the information for the remaining three vendor invoices using June 15 as the payment date for each invoice. Your screen should look similar to Figure 9-2.

STEP-BY-STEP 9.1 Continued

FIGURE 9-2
Vendor payment information

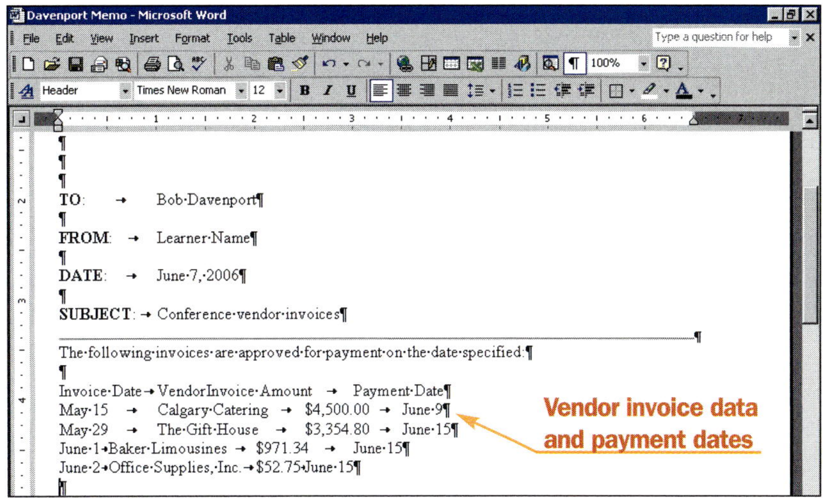

8. Select the column heading paragraph beginning with Invoice Date and ending with Payment Date.

9. Using the Tab Alignment button, the horizontal ruler, and the mouse pointer, set center tab stops at the 1½ inch, 3 inch, and 4½ inch positions.

10. Select the four vendor invoice paragraphs below the column heading paragraph.

11. Using the Tab Alignment button, the horizontal ruler, and the mouse pointer, set a left tab stop at the 1 inch position, a decimal tab stop at the 3 ⅛ inch position, and a right tab stop at the 4 ¾ inch position. Deselect the text but leave the insertion point in the last vendor invoice paragraph. Your screen should look similar to Figure 9-3.

FIGURE 9-3
Vendor payment information with custom tab stops

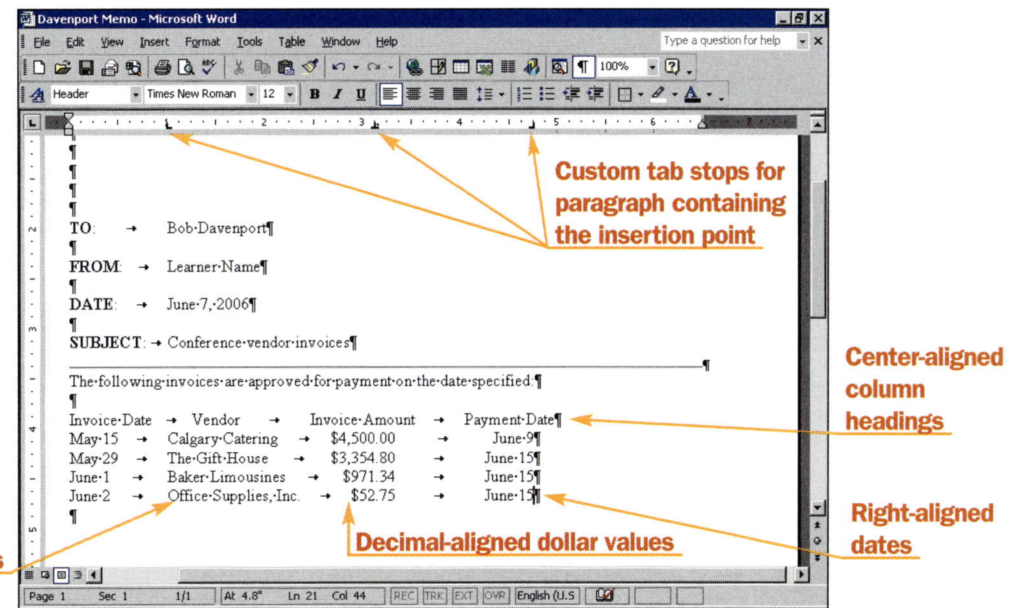

STEP-BY-STEP 9.1 Continued

12. Turn off the nonprinting characters, save the document, and leave it open for the next Step-by-Step.

Apply Special Font Effects and Highlighting

You can add emphasis to text by adding special text effects such as Superscript, Subscript, Strikethrough, and Small caps text effects. The *Superscript* format places text slightly above a line of normal printed text. The *Subscript* format places text slightly below a line of normal printed text. To indicate that text should be deleted, you can format it with the *Strikethrough* text effect, which draws a line through selected text. The *Small caps* effect displays selected text in uppercase characters, and any characters keyed with the Shift key pressed display larger than the remaining characters. The Small caps format is appropriate for headings and titles. You can apply these special text effects to selected text in the Font tab in the Font dialog box. You want to apply the Small caps effect to the column headings.

Another way to add emphasis to text in a document that will be read online is to highlight selected text with color using the Highlight button on the Formatting toolbar. You are going to attach this memo to an e-mail message to Bob Davenport and he will read the memo online; therefore, you want to highlight the Calgary Catering vendor invoice information to draw Bob's attention to it.

Hot Tip

If you frequently use the Superscript or Subscript special text effect in your documents, you can save time by quickly adding Superscript and Subscript buttons to the Formatting toolbar with the Toolbar Options button.

Did You Know?

A very quick way to select a menu command in Word, Excel, or PowerPoint is to use a short-cut menu. For example, a short-cut menu appears whenever you right-click (click with the right mouse button) selected text in a Word document. The menu commands that appear on a short-cut menu depend on the text, cell, or object you right-click. The best way to get familiar with using shortcut menus is to open an Office document, select text, cells, or an object, and then right-click the selection to view the available menu commands.

STEP-BY-STEP 9.2

1. Verify that the **Davenport Memo** document is open and then select the column heading paragraph beginning with Invoice Date and ending with Payment Date.

2. Click the **Format** menu, click **Font** to open the Font dialog box, and click the **Font** tab, if necessary.

3. Click the **Small caps** check box under Effects to insert a check mark and click **Bold** in the Font style list box. Your dialog box should look similar to Figure 9-4.

STEP-BY-STEP 9.2 Continued

FIGURE 9-4
Font dialog box

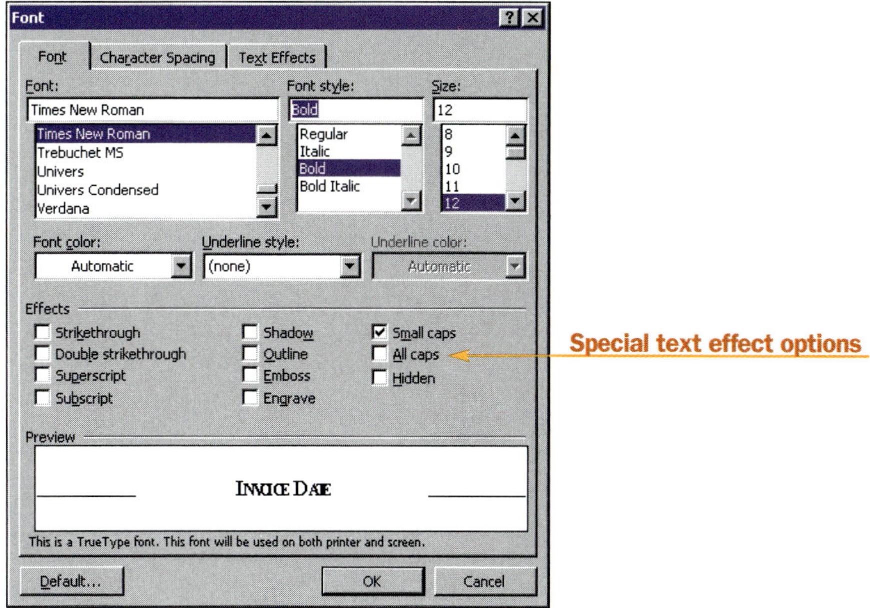

4. Click **OK** and then deselect the column heading paragraph. Your screen should look similar to Figure 9-5.

FIGURE 9-5
Formatted column heading text

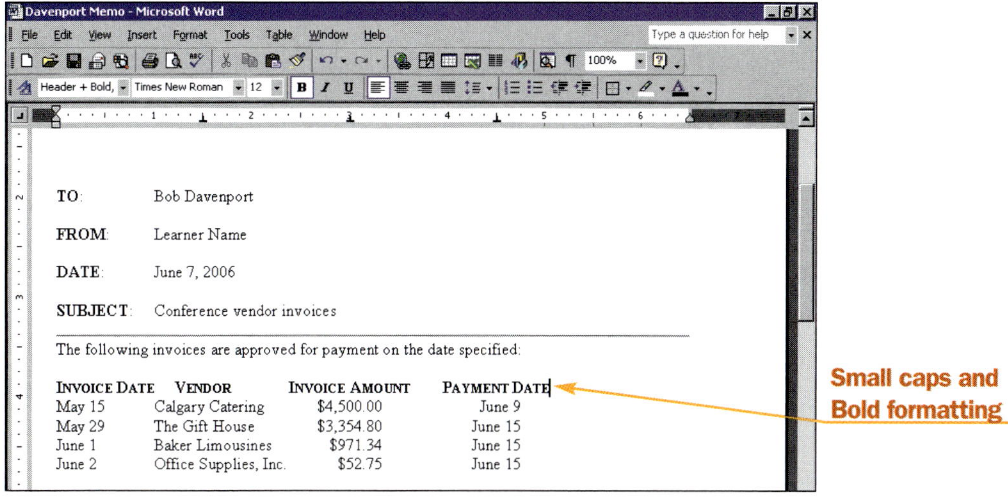

5. Select the **Calgary Catering** vendor invoice paragraph.

6. Click the **Highlight** button list arrow on the Formatting toolbar and click **Yellow** in the color grid. Your screen should look similar to Figure 9-6. 

STEP-BY-STEP 9.2 Continued

FIGURE 9-6
Highlighted paragraph

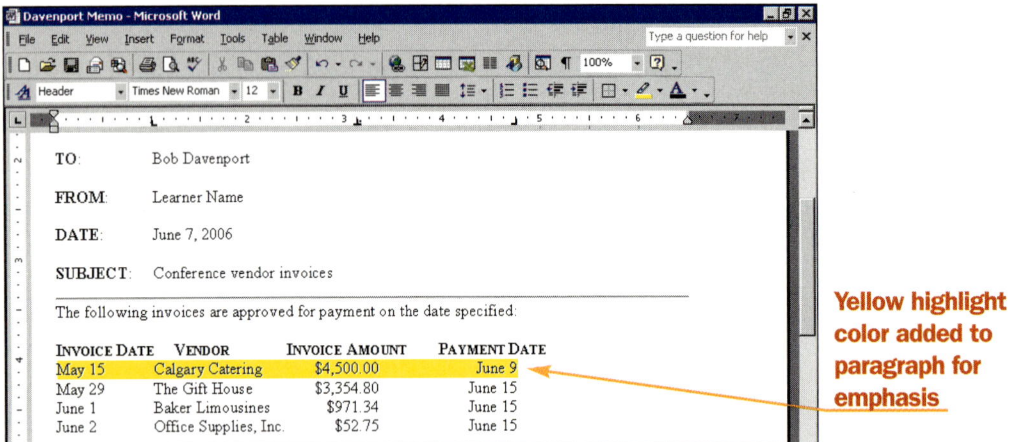

Yellow highlight color added to paragraph for emphasis

7. Save the document and leave it open for the next Step-by-Step.

Insert a Comment

A *comment* is a note you can add to a Word document that is not part of the document text. You use comments to ask questions or add additional information that might be useful to the reader for a document that is being read online. You want to remind Bob that the check for the Calgary Catering vendor invoice should be sent via Federal Express or UPS to assure its quick delivery. You add a comment to the Calgary Catering paragraph to do this.

> **Note** 
>
> If you are using Word 2002, you have the option of keying comment text in a margin balloon in Print Layout view or in the Reviewing Pane in Normal view; however, if you are using Word 2000 you must key comment text in the Reviewing Pane that opens in either Normal view or Print Layout view.

STEP-BY-STEP 9.3

1. Verify that the **Davenport Memo** document is open and then move the insertion point to the end of the highlighted Calgary Catering vendor invoice paragraph.

2. Click the **Insert** menu and click **Comment** to display a Comment balloon containing the insertion point in the right margin of the document. (If you are using Word 2000, the Reviewing Pane opens at the bottom of the Word window.)

3. Key **Please send this check via Federal Express or UPS to assure prompt delivery.** in the Comment balloon. Your screen should look similar to Figure 9-7. (If you are using Word 2000 you must move the mouse pointer over the comment indicator to view the comment text.)

> **Did You Know?** 
>
> The Reviewing toolbar contains buttons you can use to add, edit, and delete comments in a Word document. You can display the Reviewing toolbar with the **Toolbars** command on the **View** menu or by right-clicking any toolbar and clicking **Reviewing** on the shortcut menu.

STEP-BY-STEP 9.3 Continued

FIGURE 9-7
Comment balloon

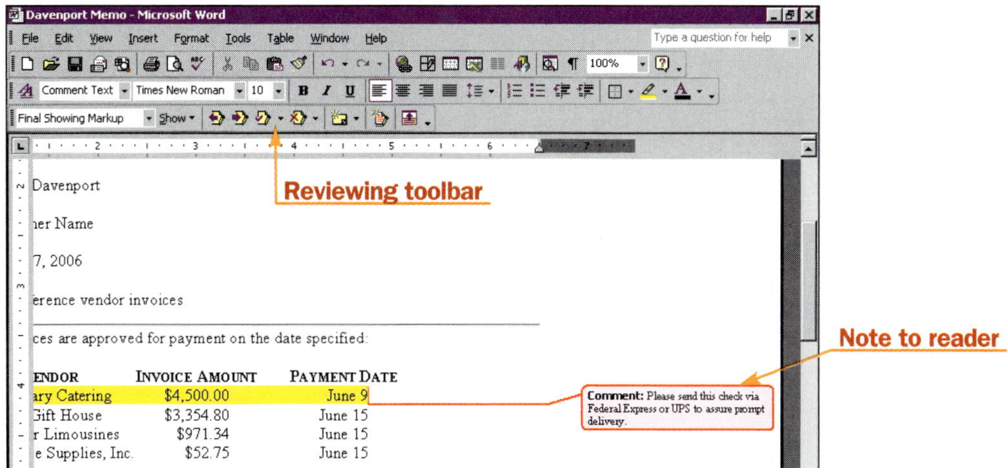

4. Move the insertion point to the end of the document and then save, print preview, and print it, leaving it open for the next Step-by-Step. (If you are using Word 2000, close the Reviewing pane.)

Add an Attachment to an Outgoing E-mail Message

An e-mail *attachment* is a file you include with an outgoing e-mail message. You can quickly add the current Word document to an outgoing e-mail message using the Send To command on the File menu. You are now ready to send the Davenport Memo document as an e-mail attachment to Bob Davenport.

> **Note**
>
> The e-mail address used in the following Step-by-Step is fictitious. Your instructor will provide a valid e-mail address if you are to actually send the e-mail message and attachment.

STEP-BY-STEP 9.4

1. Verify that the **Davenport Memo** document is open and then click **File** on the menu bar, point to **Send To**, and click **Mail Recipient (as Attachment)** to open the e-mail message window.

2. Key **davenport@wildernesstreks.biz** in the To text box.

3. Key **Conference vendor invoices** in the Subject text box.

4. Key **Attached is a memo containing approval, payment dates, and a note about the Calgary Catering invoice.**, press **Enter**, and key your name. Your e-mail message window should look similar to Figure 9-8.

STEP-BY-STEP 9.4 Continued

FIGURE 9-8
E-mail message with attachment

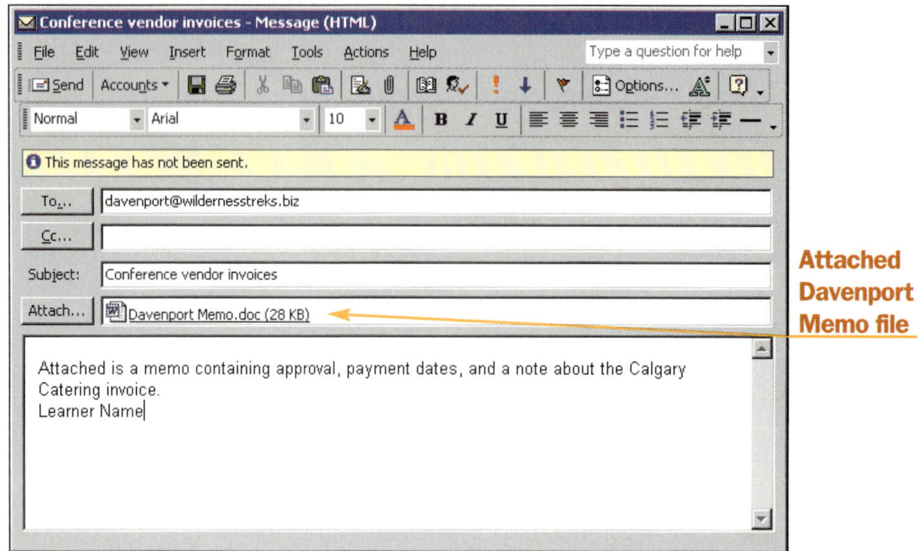

Attached Davenport Memo file

5. If your instructor gives you a valid e-mail address, send the message. Otherwise, go to step 6.

6. Save the e-mail message as **Davenport E-mail** and then print and close it. Close the Word document.

Use Right Tab Stops with Tab Leaders

When you want to help the reader's eye follow across tabbed columns in a document, you can use a tab leader line. A *tab leader line* is a dashed, dotted, or solid line that fills the space to the left of a tab stop. Sloane asks you to create a list of the Austin office employee phone extensions. You create an easy-to-read list of phone extensions by using a right tab and a dotted tab leader line to separate each employee's name and phone extension. Note that you must set the right tab stop and make the leader line selection in the Tabs dialog box.

STEP-BY-STEP 9.5

1. Open the **Step9-5** document from the data files.

2. Save the document as **Employee Phone List**.

3. Select the list of names and phone extensions beginning with Betancourt, Lynda and ending with Yong, J. Q.

4. Click the **Format** menu and click **Tabs** to open the Tabs dialog box.

5. Key **5.5** in the Tab stop position text box, click the **Right** option button, and click the **2 (dotted line)** option button. Your dialog box should look similar to Figure 9-9.

STEP-BY-STEP 9.5 Continued

FIGURE 9-9
Tabs dialog box

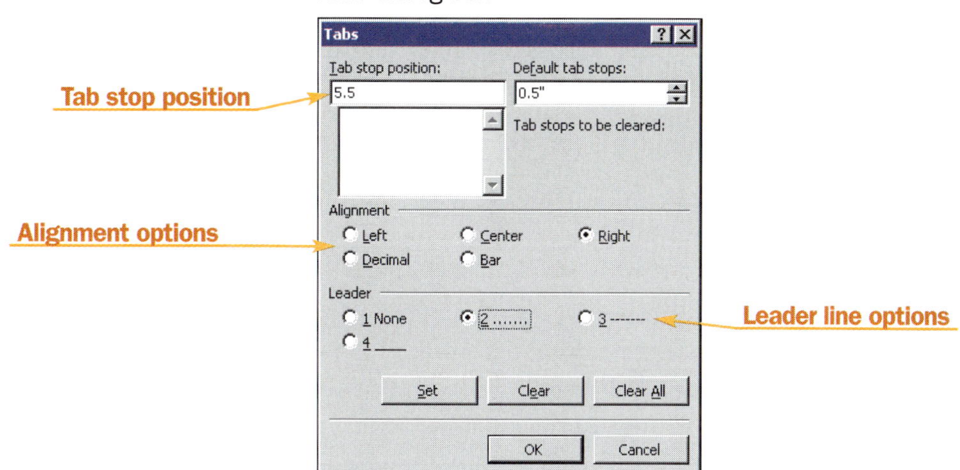

6. Click **OK** to set the right tab stops with dotted leader lines and then deselect the text. Your screen should look similar to Figure 9-10.

FIGURE 9-10
Completed phone list

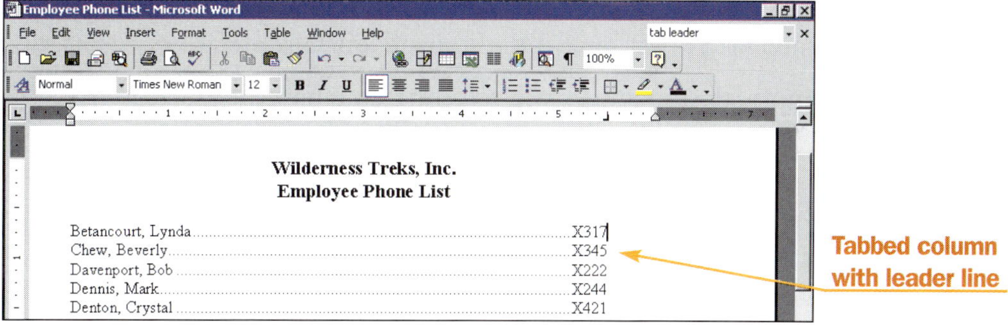

7. Save the document and then print preview, print, and close it.

8. Close the Word application.

SUMMARY

In this job, you learned:

- You can use center tab stops to align column heading text.

- A decimal tab stop is used to align dollar values in a column.

- You can use right tab stops to align numbers or text from the right rather than from the left.

- Superscript, Subscript, Strikethrough, and Small caps are examples of special text effects you can apply to selected text with options in the Font dialog box.

- You can add emphasis to text read online by adding color to the text using the Highlight button on the Formatting toolbar.

- A comment is a note you can add to a Word document that is not part of the document text.

- An attachment is a file you send with an e-mail message.

- When you want to help a reader see across a page of text in columns separated by tabs, you can use tab leader lines, which fill the space to the left of the tab stop.

VOCABULARY *Review*

Define the following terms:

Attachment	Right tab stop	Superscript
Center tab stop	Small caps	Tab leader line
Comment	Strikethrough	
Decimal tab stop	Subscript	

REVIEW *Questions*

TRUE / FALSE

Circle T if the statement is true or F if the statement is false.

T   F   **1.** A right tab stop allows you to center column heading text.

T   F   **2.** The Strikethrough special text effect draws a line through selected text.

T   F   **3.** An e-mail attachment is a file you send along with an e-mail message.

T   F   **4.** A tab leader line can be created using the Tab Alignment button, the mouse pointer, and the horizontal ruler.

T   F   **5.** When working in a document with multiple paragraphs using different types of tab stops, it is a good idea to first key the text, then select the appropriate text and set the tab stops.

FILL IN THE BLANK

Complete the following sentences by writing the correct word or words in the blanks provided.

1. When you need to add additional information or ask the reader a question but do not want to alter the document text, you can insert a(n) __________.

2. The __________ format places text slightly above a line of normal printed text.

3. To add emphasis to text that is being read online, you can add __________ with the Highlight button on the Formatting toolbar.

4. A tab leader line is a(n) __________, __________, or __________ line that fills the space to the left of a tab stop.

5. You can use a(n) __________ tab stop to align dollar values in a column.

PROJECTS

PROJECT 9-1

1. Open Word and open **Project 9-1** from the data files.

2. Save the document as **Expense Analysis Memo**.

3. Set appropriate decimal tab stops to align the dollar values in the Computer Equipment, Office Supplies, and Brochures paragraphs. Space the dollar value columns attractively in the memo.

4. Set appropriate center tab stops to align the column heading text beginning with January and ending with April over each of the dollar value columns.

5. Format the column heading text with the Small caps text effect and Bold style.

6. Save the document and then print preview, print, and close it.

 PROJECT 9-2

You need to complete a budget variance report for Sloane to take to the next staff meeting. Open the **Project 9-2** document and save it as **Budget Variance Report**. Set appropriate tab stops for the column heading text and the dollar value columns. Format the column heading text with the special text effect of your choice. Highlight the Miscellaneous paragraph in yellow and add a comment that says additional details will be provided by Bob Davenport. Save the document and then print preview, print, and close it.

 WEB PROJECT

Crystal Denton calls you to find out more information about the Microsoft Office Specialist (MOS) certification program. Use the search feature in your Web browser or a search tool such as Google (*www.google.com*) to locate Web pages that discuss MOS certification. Print at least two Web pages.

  TEAMWORK PROJECT

As an administrative assistant, you are often called upon to create documents containing text formatted with a variety of special text effects. You want to review the various special text effects available in the Font dialog box. Select a classmate to work with you on this project. Then explore formatting text with the various special text effects. Create a document containing an example of each type of special text effect. Using the document, demonstrate to another group of classmates how to format text with special text effects.

CRITICAL*Thinking*

 ACTIVITY 9-1

Melody Stackhouse drops by your desk and asks you how she can change the default tab stops from .5 inch to .25 inch. Using Word online Help, research how to change the amount of space between the default tab stops and then demonstrate to a classmate how to change the default tab stops from .5 inch to .25 inch. Change the default tab stops back to .5 inch after your demonstration.

Formalizing Meeting Notes Using Styles and Tables

<table>
<tr><td>

OBJECTIVES

Upon completion of this job, you should be able to:

- Find and replace text.
- Apply paragraph and character styles.
- Create and modify tables.
- Insert a page break.
- Create headers and footers.
- Convert a Word document to a Web page.

Estimated Time: 1 hour

</td><td>

VOCABULARY

Automatic page break

Character style

Footer

Header

Heading paragraph

Intranet

Manual page break

Page break

Paragraph style

Style

Table

Table AutoFormat

Web page

</td></tr>
</table>

Finding and Replacing Text

One of the frequent Word document editing tasks is to find text, formatting, or special characters in a document and then replace the text, formatting, or special characters with something else. You can quickly find and replace items in a Word document by using commands on the Edit menu.

When using the Find or Replace features, it is important that you select the most efficient Find criteria in order to narrow the scope of the document search. For example, if you are searching for the whole word *our* you must turn on the Find whole words only option in the Find and Replace dialog box to avoid selecting the three characters *our* contained inside another word such as *hour*. Another important Find criteria to consider is Match case, which allows you to ignore the word *Our* with initial capitalization when you are searching for the word *our* in all lowercase characters. For more information on other Find criteria, see Word online Help.

This morning you attended a meeting of the Conference Planning Committee during which you drafted the meeting notes on your laptop. Now you want to formalize the meeting notes before you distribute them to Sloane and other committee members. To expedite drafting the notes, you keyed WTI as an abbreviation for the company name each time it appeared in the meeting notes. You begin by opening the draft document, finding all instances of the characters WTI, and replacing them with the complete company name Wilderness Treks, Inc.

STEP-BY-STEP 10.1

1. Start the Word application, open the **Step10-1** document from the data files, and switch to Print Layout view, if necessary.

2. Save the document as **Planning Meeting Notes**.

3. Click **Edit** on the menu bar and then click **Replace** to open the Replace tab in the Find and Replace dialog box.

4. Key **WTI** in the Find what text box and press **Tab** to move the insertion point to the next text box.

5. Key **Wilderness Treks, Inc.** in the Replace with text box.

6. Click **More**, if necessary, to expand the dialog box and view the search criteria options.

7. Click the **Match case** and **Find whole words only** check boxes to insert a check mark. Your dialog box should look similar to Figure 10-1.

> **Did You Know?** 
>
> The Select Browse Object button and the Previous and Next Page buttons below the vertical scroll bar are used to quickly find certain document elements such as a comment, table, or picture. You can also use the Select Browse Object button to open the Go To tab or the Find tab in the Find and Replace dialog box. For more information on using the Select Browse Object button, see Word online Help.

FIGURE 10-1
Replace tab in the Find and Replace dialog box

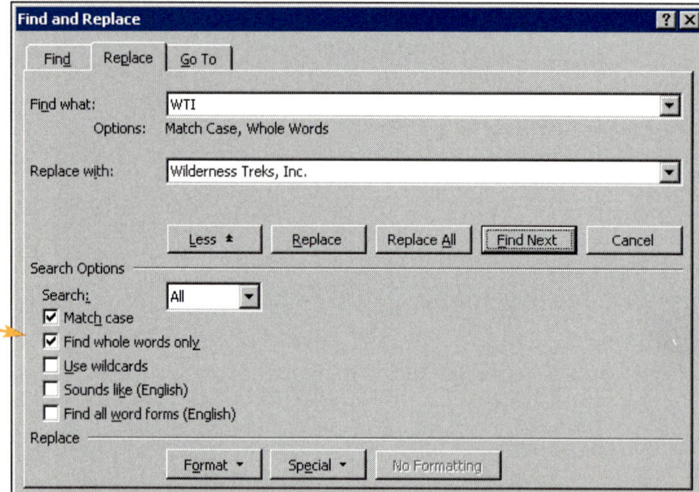

8. Click **Find Next** to find the first instance of WTI and then click **Replace** to replace WTI with Wilderness Treks, Inc.

9. Observe that the next instance of WTI is selected and then click **Replace** and click **OK**. The Replace tab in the Find and Replace dialog box remains open.

10. Key **Sloane's administrative assistant** in the Find what text box.

> **Warning** 
>
> When editing a document with which you are not very familiar, it is a good idea to use the Replace option to carefully replace each instance instead of using the Replace All option. Using Replace All may produce unexpected results and create errors in the document, especially if the Find criteria are not carefully set.

STEP-BY-STEP 10.1 Continued

11. Key your name in the Replace with text box.

12. Replace all three instances of Sloane's administrative assistant with your name.

13. Click **Less** to collapse the Find and Replace dialog box and then close the dialog box.

14. Save the document and leave it open for the next Step-by-Step.

Apply Paragraph and Character Styles

A *style* is a collection of formatting components saved with a document or a document template (such as the Normal template) using a unique name. All the formatting components contained in a style can be quickly applied to selected text all at once. Word contains a number of built-in styles you can apply to selected text by clicking a style name in the Style button list on the Formatting toolbar or the Styles and Formatting task pane. There are two types of styles: paragraph styles and character styles.

Paragraph Styles

A *paragraph style* contains multiple paragraph formatting components such as the line spacing, indenting, and alignment formatting that affects the way a paragraph looks on a page. Paragraph styles are indicated by a paragraph mark (¶) in the styles lists. A *heading paragraph* is a short paragraph that introduces subsequent paragraphs covering the same topic. To give the Planning Meeting Notes document a more professional appearance, you want to apply a paragraph style to each heading paragraph. You use one of the built-in heading styles to do this.

Note

If you are using Word 2000, you can click a style in the Style button list on the Formatting toolbar or use the Style command on the Format menu to open the Style dialog box to view a list of styles. The Styles and Formatting button on the Formatting toolbar and the Styles and Formatting task pane are not available in Word 2000.

Did You Know?

You can create your own custom styles from scratch by selecting all the style components using the New Style button in the Styles and Formatting task pane in Word 2002 or the Style dialog box. You can also select formatted text and create a custom style based on the formats. These custom styles can be saved with the document in which they are applied or saved with the Normal template, which makes the custom styles available for all documents. For more information on creating custom styles, see Word online Help.

S TEP-BY-STEP 10.2

1. Verify that the Planning Meeting Notes document is open. Select the Meeting Objectives heading paragraph and then press and hold the **Ctrl** key and select the remaining heading paragraphs: Budgeting and Reporting, Coordinating Meeting Materials, Speaker Travel Arrangements, Coordinating Attendee Accommodations, Coordinating Travel Arrangements, Supervising Food Service, Managing Registration and Meeting Rooms, and Next Meeting. (*Note:* If you are using Word 2000, combine steps 2, 3, and 4 to select and format each heading paragraph one at a time.)

Warning

Don't forget that a paragraph is any amount of text from a few words to several lines of text followed by a nonprinting paragraph mark. For example, a heading paragraph may consist of just a few words used to introduce a topic, but it is still a complete paragraph because the text is followed by a paragraph mark.

2. Click the **Style** button list arrow on the Formatting toolbar to view a short list of built-in styles.

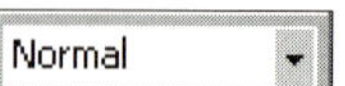

3. Click **Heading 3** to apply the paragraph style to the selected heading paragraphs and then deselect the text. After scrolling to view the top of the document, your screen should look similar to Figure 10-2.

FIGURE 10-2
Formatted heading paragraphs

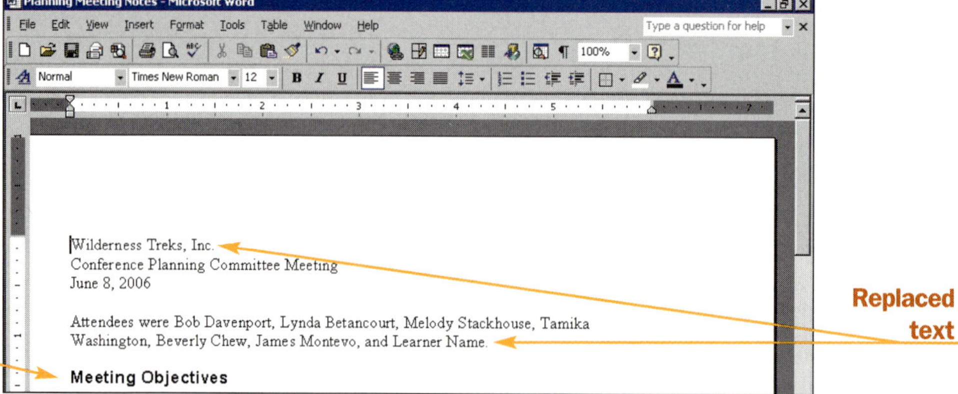

Paragraph formatted with Heading 3 style

Replaced text

4. Select the Wilderness Treks, Inc. title paragraph at the top of the document and apply the **Heading 2** style to the selected paragraph.

5. Select the Wilderness Treks, Inc., Conference Planning Committee Meeting and current date title paragraphs at the top of the document and click the **Center** button on the Formatting toolbar.

6. Deselect the text and then save the document, leaving it open for the next Step-by-Step.

Character Styles

A *character style* contains multiple character formatting components such as Bold, Italic, Underline, or other text effects. Character styles are indicated by an underscored and bolded *a* (**a**) in the styles lists. You want to add emphasis to each of the committee member names by applying a character style to them.

STEP-BY-STEP 10.3

1. Verify that the Planning Meeting Notes document is open. Select **Bob Davenport** in the topic paragraph below the Budgeting and Reporting heading paragraph and then press and hold the **Ctrl** key and select the following names: **Lynda Betancourt**, **Melody Stackhouse**, **Tamika Washington**, **Beverly Chew**, **James Montevo**, and **your name**, which appear in each of the remaining individual topic paragraphs. *Do not select the names in the Attendees paragraph.* (*Note:* If you are using Word 2000, open the Styles dialog box and combine steps 2 through 5 to select and format each name with the Emphasis character style one at a time.)

2. Click the **Styles and Formatting** button on the Formatting toolbar to open the Styles and Formatting task pane. 

3. Click the **Show** list arrow in the Styles and Formatting task pane and click **All styles** to view a list of all styles.

4. Click the **Emphasis** character style in the Styles and Formatting task pane to apply the character style to the selected text and then close the task pane and deselect the text. After scrolling, if necessary, your screen should look similar to Figure 10-3.

FIGURE 10-3
Formatted names

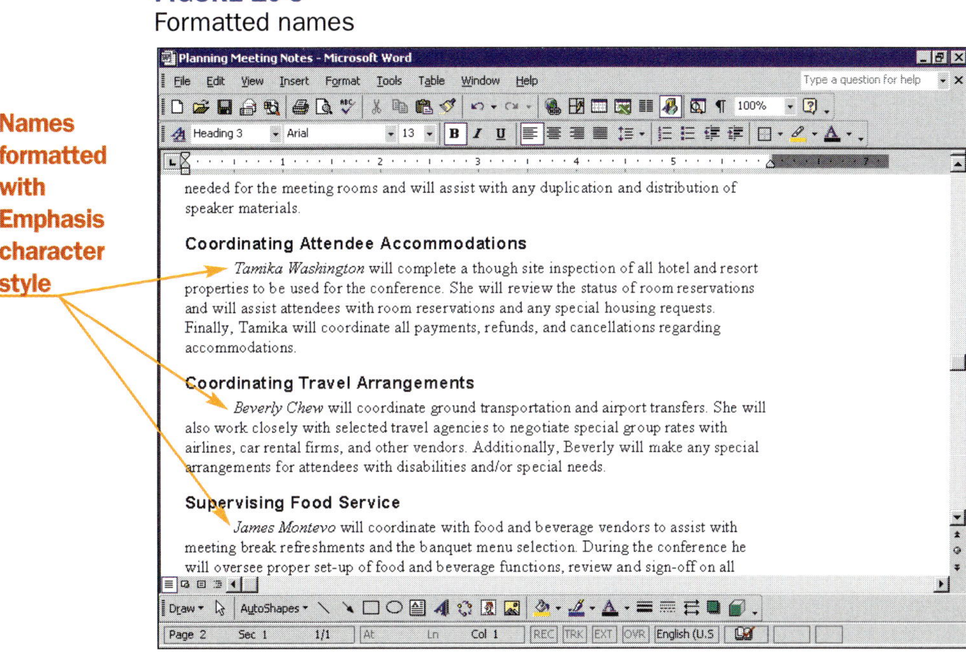

5. Save the document and leave it open for the next Step-by-Step.

Create and Modify Tables

A *table* is a grid organized into columns and rows. A column is a set of information that runs down the page. A row runs across the page. A cell occurs at the intersection of a column and row. You key text and numbers in table cells much in the same way you key text and numbers in Excel worksheet cells. To enhance the readability of the **Planning Meeting Notes** document, you want to place the vendor invoice information in a table.

Convert Text to a Table

You can create a table from scratch using commands on the Table menu, or with the Insert Table button on the Standard toolbar. You then move the insertion point from cell to cell in the table using the Tab key or the directional arrows and key text or numbers in the cells.

Another way to create a table is to convert existing text to a table. When you convert existing text to a table, you specify the number of columns in the table and then select an indicator such as a tab character or paragraph mark to identify which text is placed in which column. You begin by selecting the vendor invoice text and then converting the text to a table.

Did You Know?

A cell in a Word table can be referenced by column and row, for example, A1 for the first column and first row, in the same way a cell in an Excel worksheet is referenced. Because of this, you can perform calculations in a Word table by entering formulas to add, subtract, multiply, or divide the contents of cells using cell references and mathematical operators such as +, −, *, and /. For more information on using formulas in a Word table, see Word online Help.

STEP-BY-STEP 10.4

1. Verify that the Planning Meeting Notes document is open. Select the five paragraphs containing the vendor invoice information beginning with Invoice Date and ending with the last instance of June 15.

2. Click the **Table** menu, point to **Convert**, and click **Text to Table** to open the Convert Text to Table dialog box. Verify that the Number of columns option is 4 and the Tabs option button is selected. Your dialog box should look similar to Figure 10-4.

FIGURE 10-4
Convert Text to Table dialog box

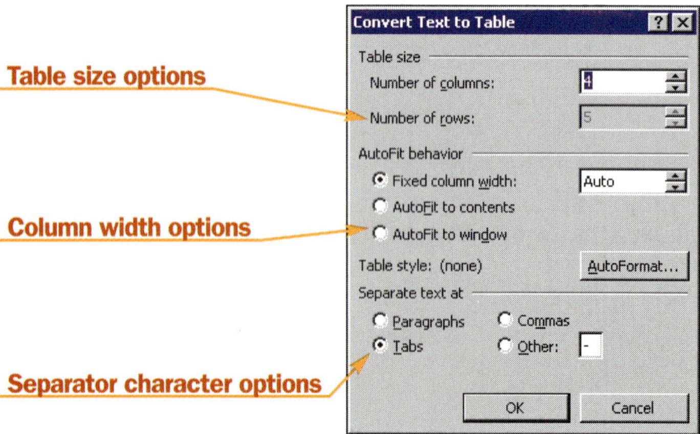

STEP-BY-STEP 10.4 Continued

3. Click **OK** and deselect the table. Your screen should look similar to Figure 10-5.

FIGURE 10-5
Vendor payment table

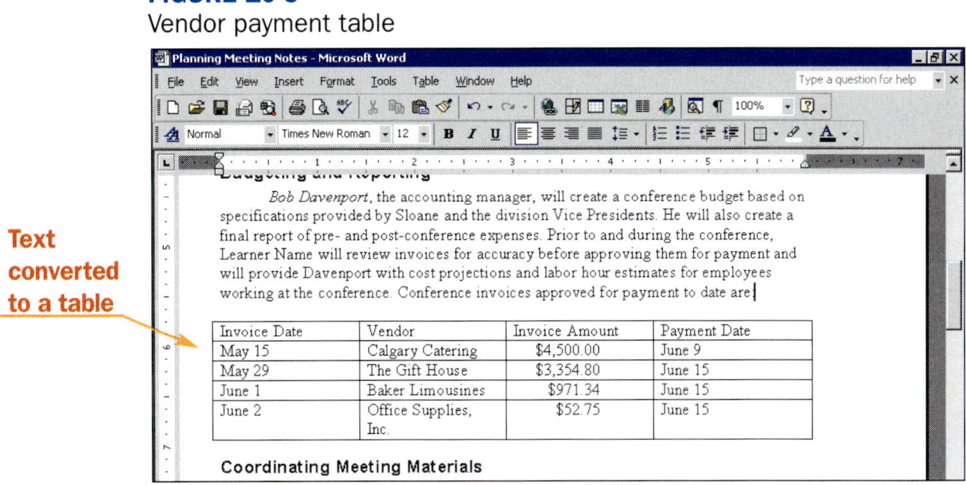

4. Save the document and leave it open for the next Step-by-Step.

Modify a Table

You can quickly insert a cell, a row, or a column in a table with commands on the Table menu. To insert cells, rows, or columns, you first move the insertion point to a row or column to select it, or select multiple rows and columns. Then you click the appropriate commands to insert a cell(s), a row(s) above or below, or a column to the left or right of the selected row or column. You can delete an entire table or selected cells, rows, or columns with the Delete command on the Table menu. You can size columns or rows in the Table Properties dialog box or you can drag a column or row boundary with the mouse pointer to size the row or column. Finally, you can double-click a right column boundary to automatically fit the column size to the column contents.

> **Warning**
>
> You cannot delete selected cells, rows, or columns by pressing Delete. Pressing Delete only deletes the contents of the selected cells. You can delete an entire table by pressing Delete only if you select text above or below the table to be deleted.

You can select an individual cell, row, or column by positioning the mouse pointer inside the left boundary of the cell, outside the left boundary of a row, or immediately above a column. When the mouse pointer is in one of these positions, it becomes a selection pointer. You then simply click the mouse button to make the selection. To select multiple cells, rows, or columns, first position the mouse pointer until it becomes a selection pointer and then drag across the cells, rows, or columns. You can select an entire table or a cell, a row, or a column with the Select command on the Table menu.

STEP-BY-STEP 10.5

1. Verify that the Planning Meeting Notes document is open. Move the insertion point to the last cell in the table (bottom row, right-most column).

2. Click **Table** on the menu bar, point to **Insert**, and click **Rows Below** to insert a row at the bottom of the table.

3. Click in the first cell in the last column (first row, rightmost column) to position the insertion point and then click **Table** on the menu bar, point to **Insert**, and click **Columns to the Right** to insert a column to the right of the selected column. Deselect the new column. Your screen should look similar to Figure 10-6.

FIGURE 10-6
Inserted row and column

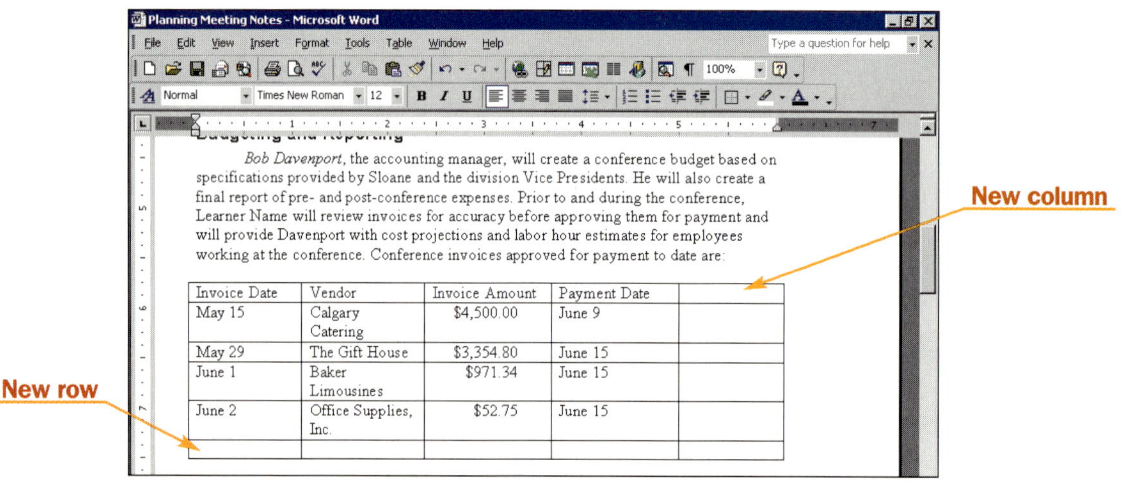

4. Select the new column and click **Table** on the menu bar, point to Delete, and click **Columns**.

5. Select the new row and delete it.

6. Double-click the right boundary of each column to automatically size the column to fit its contents.

7. Save the document and leave it open for the next Step-by-Step.

Apply Table AutoFormats

Table AutoFormat is a table style that contains column width, borders, shading, font and font size formatting, and other formatting components that you might individually apply to a table and its contents. You can quickly give a table a polished and professional look by applying Table AutoFormat. You can also modify the formatting components of a Table AutoFormat style, such as turning borders or shading on or off. You want to preview several Table AutoFormats and then apply one to the vendor invoice table.

Note

If you are using Word 2002, Table AutoFormats are also called table styles. You can create your own custom table styles with the New Style button in the Styles and Formatting task pane. Also, the built-in Table AutoFormats (styles) are available in the Styles and Formatting task pane when you view all the styles. If you are using Word 2000, you can only select from the available built-in Table AutoFormats in the Table AutoFormat dialog box.

S TEP-BY-STEP 10.6

1. Verify that the Planning Meeting Notes document is open and move the insertion point somewhere inside the table, if necessary.

2. Click the **Table** menu and click **Table AutoFormat** to open the Table AutoFormat dialog box.

3. Click the Table AutoFormat of your choice in the Table styles list and preview it. Continue to preview various Table AutoFormat styles.

4. Click the **Table Web 3** Table AutoFormat in the Table styles list and then click **Modify** to open the Modify Style dialog box. (*Note:* If you are using Word 2000, you cannot modify the AutoFormat. Skip steps 5 through 7 and simply apply the Table Web 3 AutoFormat to the table.)

5. Click the **Apply formatting to** list box and click **Header Row**.

6. Click the **Shading Color** button list arrow and click the **Gray 10%** color square (first row, third square). Your dialog box should look similar to Figure 10-7.

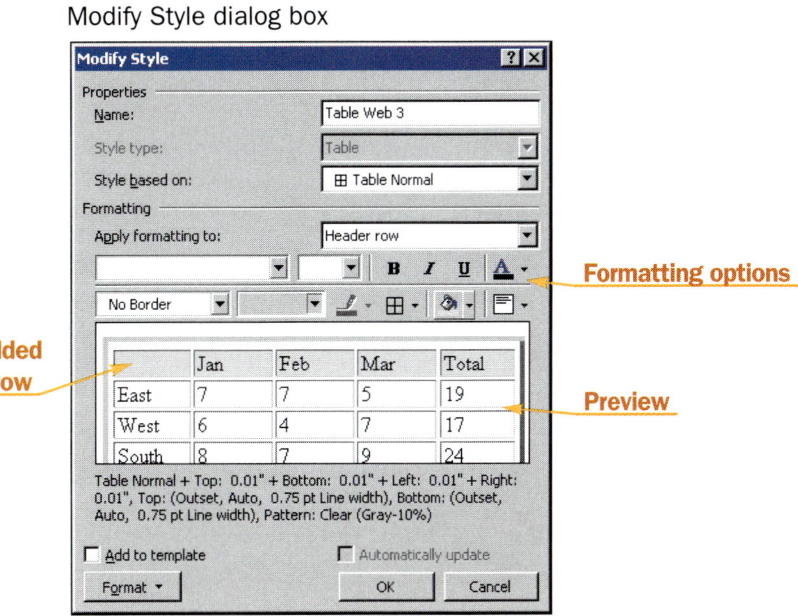

FIGURE 10-7
Modify Style dialog box

7. Click **OK** and then click **Apply** to apply the modified Table AutoFormat style to the vendor payment table.

8. Select the entire table and click the **Center** button on the Formatting toolbar to center the table. 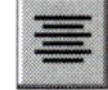

9. Select the cells containing the invoice amounts and the payment dates and click the **Align Right** button on the Formatting toolbar to align the cell contents. Deselect the cells. Your table should look similar to Figure 10-8. 

STEP-BY-STEP 10.6 Continued

FIGURE 10-8
Modified table

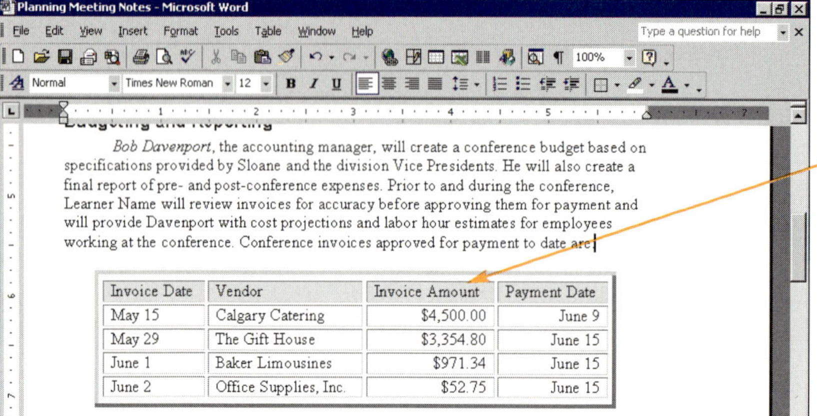

10. Save the document and leave it open for the next Step-by-Step.

Insert a Page Break

A *page break* occurs when one page of a multi-page document ends and another begins. There are two kinds of page breaks: an *automatic page break* created by Word when a page defined by its margins fills with text, and a *manual page break* that you can insert to force text to the next page. Because the Planning Meeting Notes document is a two-page document, you want to insert a manual page break at an attractive location. First, you set the appropriate margins for a report-style document, which are a two-inch top and a one-inch left, right, and bottom margin. Then you insert the page break.

Warning 

Although it is a good idea to print preview all documents, it is especially important to do so for documents that contain both manual and automatic page breaks. When you add, delete, or move text in a document, Word repaginates and adds or deletes automatic page breaks as necessary. However, Word cannot automatically delete or move manual page breaks and just ignores them as it repaginates the document. This can result in inappropriate page breaks throughout the document.

STEP-BY-STEP 10.7

1. Verify that the Planning Meeting Notes document is open, and then set a two-inch top margin and one-inch left, right, and bottom margins.

2. Move the insertion point to the left margin at the Coordinating Meeting Materials heading paragraph.

3. Press **Ctrl + Enter** to insert a manual page break at the position of the insertion point.

STEP-BY-STEP 10.7 Continued

4. Zoom the document to two pages, review it, and then zoom back to 100%.

5. Save the document, leaving it open for the next Step-by-Step.

Create Headers and Footers

A *header* is text that appears at the top of a page and a *footer* is text that appears at the bottom of a page. Headers and footers are used to add additional identifying information to a document, such as page numbers or preparation dates. You want to add the text *Conference Planning Committee*, the page number, and the current date to each page of the Planning Meeting Notes document.

> **Warning** 
>
> Word automatically includes a three-inch Center tab stop and a six-inch Right tab stop for the Header and Footer panes based on the default 1¼-inch left and right margins. If you change your left and right margin settings, you will also have to change the position of the Center and Right tab stops.

STEP-BY-STEP 10.8

1. Verify that the Planning Meeting Notes document is open and move the insertion point to the top of the document, if necessary.

2. Click the **View** menu and click **Header and Footer**.

3. Click the **Switch Between Header and Footer** button on the Header and Footer toolbar to view the Footer pane. 

4. Drag the Center tab stop to the 3¼-inch position and the Right tab stop to the 6½-inch position on the horizontal ruler.

5. Key **Conference Planning Committee** at the left margin of the Footer pane and press **Tab**.

6. Click the **Insert Page Number** button on the Header and Footer toolbar to insert the page number field at the center position and press **Tab**. 

7. Click the **Insert Date** button on the Header and Footer toolbar to insert the current date at the right margin. Your screen should look similar to Figure 10-9. 

FIGURE 10-9
Footer

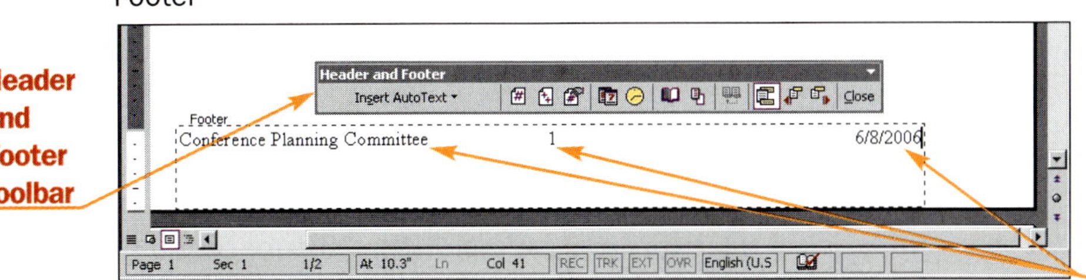

STEP-BY-STEP 10.8 Continued

8. Close the Header and Footer toolbar and then save, print preview, and print the document, leaving it open for the next Step-by-Step.

Convert a Word Document to a Web Page

Sloane calls and suggests you save the Planning Meeting Notes document as a Web page for posting to the company intranet. A *Web page* is a document that contains text and pictures and is linked to other documents. The company *intranet* is a group of internal Web pages used by the Wilderness Treks employees to keep up with information they need to do their various jobs. First, you preview the document to see what it would look like as a Web page, and then you save it as a Web page.

Hot Tip

When you save a Word document as a Web page, it is saved as an HTML document. HTML is the acronym for Hypertext Markup Language. The markup language is used to structure Web pages so that they can be interpreted and presented for viewing by a Web browser.

STEP-BY-STEP 10.9

1. Verify that the Planning Meeting Notes document is still open. Click the **File** menu and click **Web Page Preview** to view the Planning Meeting Notes document in your Web browser.

2. Print the page from your Web browser and then close your Web browser.

3. Click the **File** menu and click **Save as Web Page**.

4. Save the document as a Web page with the name **Planning Meeting Notes**.

5. Close the document and close the Word application.

Did You Know?

When you save a Word document as a Web page, Word may automatically create and save a special folder containing any special HTML instructions and graphic images that must accompany the page. If you move or delete the Web page file, remember to also move or delete its accompanying special folder if one has been created.

SUMMARY

In this job, you learned:

■ You can find text, formatting, or special characters and then replace them with other text, formatting, or special characters using the Find and Replace dialog box.

■ It is important to carefully select the appropriate Find criteria before beginning a find and replace action.

- A style is a group of formatting components, such as line spacing or bold, that you can save with a unique name and then apply all at once to selected text.

- A paragraph style contains paragraph formatting components, such as line spacing, alignment, and indenting, that affect the way a paragraph looks on a page. A character style contains character formatting components, such as font, font size, or italic, that affect the way individual characters look on the page.

- A Word table is a grid organized into columns and rows similar to an Excel worksheet.

- You can create a table from scratch using commands on the Table menu or the Insert Table button on the Standard toolbar. You can also convert existing text separated by tabs or paragraph marks into a table.

- You can add cells, rows, and columns to a table with commands on the Table menu or with the Insert (Cells, Rows, or Columns) button on the Standard toolbar.

- Instead of formatting individual table cells, you can format the entire table at once by applying a Table AutoFormat (also called a table style). You can modify the formatting components contained in a Table AutoFormat or table style.

- A page break occurs when Word fills a page defined by its margins with text. There are two kinds of page breaks: an automatic page break inserted by Word as it paginates a document, and a manual page break you insert to force text to the next page.

- A header is text that appears at the top of a page and a footer is text that appears at the bottom of a page.

- You can preview a Word document as a Web page in your Web browser and then you can save the Word document as a Web page (with an HTML file extension).

VOCABULARY *Review*

Define the following terms:		
Automatic page break	Intranet	Style
Character style	Manual page break	Table
Footer	Page break	Table AutoFormat
Header	Paragraph style	Web page
Heading paragraph		

REVIEW *Questions*

TRUE / FALSE

Circle T if the statement is true or F if the statement is false.

T   F   **1.** It is not important to carefully consider and set Find criteria when using the Find and Replace feature.

T   F   **2.** A style is a group of formatting elements saved with a unique name and applied all at once to selected text.

T   F   **3.** A paragraph style is used to format individual text characters with formatting, such as bold, italic, or font size.

T   F   **4.** You can select and convert text paragraphs to a table by identifying the number of columns and the column separator character such as a tab or paragraph mark.

T   F   **5.** Once you create a table, you cannot add rows and columns to it.

FILL IN THE BLANK

Complete the following sentences by writing the correct word or words in the blanks provided.

1. You can automatically size a table column to fit its contents by ___________ a column's right boundary.

2. A table style is also called a Table ___________.

3. You can insert a(n) ___________ page break to force text to the next page.

4. Text that appears at the bottom of pages in a multipage document is called a(n) ___________.

5. An HTML document that contains text, pictures, and links to other documents is called a(n) ___________ page.

PROJECTS

 **PROJECT 10-1**

1. Open Word and open **Project 10-1** from the data files.

2. Save the document as **Conference Workshop A**.

3. Set a two-inch top margin and one-inch left, bottom, and right margins.

4. Replace all instances of **equipment** with **gear**.

5. Apply the Heading 1 paragraph style to the Wilderness Treks, Inc. title paragraph at the top of the page. Bold the Conference Workshop A and Selecting Backcountry Gear title paragraphs. Then center all three title paragraphs.

6. Apply the Heading 2 paragraph style to the Backcountry Essentials, Backcountry Day Trip Gear, and Backcountry Overnight Trip Gear heading paragraphs.

7. Apply the Strong character style to the words Ms. Elaine Dingle.

8. Create a footer with the text **Conference Workshop A Draft** at the left margin, the page number in the center, and the current date at the right margin. (*Note:* Don't forget to reset the Center and Right tab stops.)

9. Save the document and then print preview, print, and close it.

PROJECT 10-2

You need to save the draft document containing the Conference Workshop B information as a Web page that can be posted to the company intranet so that other employees can review it. Open the **Project 10-2** document, preview it as a Web page, print it from your Web browser, and close your Web browser. Then save the document as a Web page named **Conference Workshop B** and close it.

WEB PROJECT

Sloane sends you an e-mail asking you to find different Web sites where travelers can purchase backcountry equipment. Use the search feature in your Web browser or a search tool such as HotBot (*www.hotbot.com*) to locate Web pages for companies selling backcountry equipment. Print at least five Web pages.

TEAMWORK PROJECT

As an administrative assistant, you are always looking for Office shortcuts to help you get your tasks completed more efficiently. You run into Melody Stackhouse at the coffee bar and she tells you she has started using the Word AutoCorrect feature to quickly insert the company name and other text into her documents. You decide to check out the AutoCorrect feature to see how it can save you time when creating Word documents. Select a classmate to work with you on this project. Then, using online Help and the AutoCorrect command on the Tools menu, explore how to use the AutoCorrect feature to insert pre-keyed and pre-formatted text into a document. Create a document containing several examples and, using the document as your guide, demonstrate to another group of classmates how best to use the AutoCorrect feature.

CRITICAL *Thinking*

ACTIVITY 10-1

An important aspect of your job as an administrative assistant is creating attractively formatted and easy-to-read documents. One way to accomplish this is to use paragraph, character, and table styles. Using the Word 2002 Table Styles dialog box, explore how to create a custom table style (AutoFormat). Then demonstrate to a group of students how to create and apply a custom table style. (*Note:* If you are using Word 2000, use Word online Help to research how to create a custom paragraph style and demonstrate the process to a group of classmates.)

COMPARING AND MERGING DOCUMENTS

<table>
<tr><td>

OBJECTIVES

Upon completion of this job, you should be able to:

- Track changes to a document.
- Compare and merge two documents.
- Use the Thesaurus.
- Indent paragraphs.
- Apply borders and shading to paragraphs.

Estimated Time: 0.5 hour

</td><td>

VOCABULARY

Current document

Indent

Synonym

Target document

Thesaurus

</td></tr>
</table>

Track Changes to a Document

As Sloane's administrative assistant, you are often required to work with other employees to prepare company documents. Sometimes you draft the documents for other employees to review, and sometimes you review documents created by other employees. This review process can be more efficient when you and your coworkers key suggested changes directly in the document being reviewed. Then the document's author can quickly decide to accept or reject the suggested changes.

Setting Track Changes Options

The Track Changes feature allows a reviewer to key suggested changes directly in a document and an author to accept or reject those suggested changes—all while viewing the document on the screen. You begin by setting options for inserted text and formatting changes in the Track Changes dialog box. Then you open and revise a document using the Track Changes feature.

If you are using Word 2000, your Track Changes dialog box options and the way tracked changes are presented in a document are different. Your instructor will provide alternate instructions for Step-by-Step 11.1.

STEP-BY-STEP 11.1

1. Start the Word application, open the **Step11-1** document from the data files, and switch to Print Layout view, if necessary.

2. Save the document as **Conference Workshop C**.

3. Right-click the **TRK** mode indicator on the status bar and click **Options** to open the Track Changes dialog box.

4. Click the **Insertions** list arrow and click **Color only** to have any inserted text appear in a specified color.

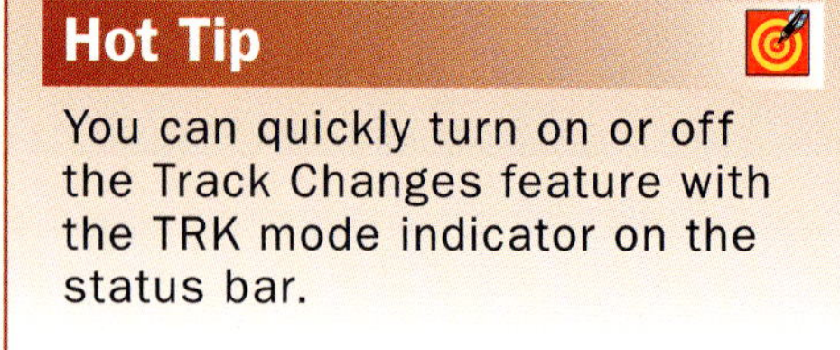

5. Click the **Color** list arrow and click **Red** to have inserted text and other change notations appear in the red color.

6. Click the **Formatting** list arrow and click **Double underline** to have reformatted text appear with a double underline. All other options should remain at their defaults. Your dialog box should look similar to Figure 11-1.

FIGURE 11-1
Track Changes dialog box

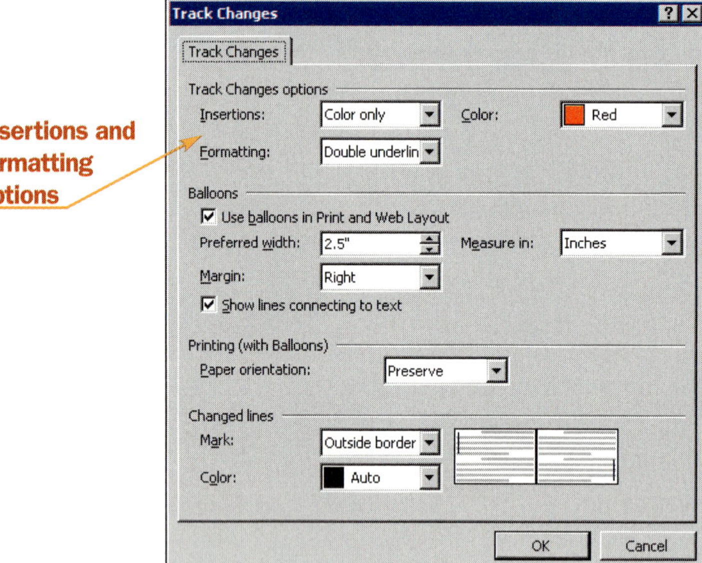

7. Click **OK** to close the Track Changes dialog box.

8. Double-click the **TRK** mode indicator on the status bar to turn on the Track Changes feature.

9. Format the Wilderness Treks, Inc. title paragraph with the Heading 1 style and center it.

10. Bold and center the Conference Workshop C and Clothing for a Backcountry Adventure title paragraphs.

11. Select the Melanie Watson text and key **Margaret Smith** to replace the selected text.

STEP-BY-STEP 11.1 Continued

12. Format the Selecting the Right Boots, Selecting the Right Clothing, and What to Pack for a Two-Day Trip heading paragraphs with the Heading 3 style.

13. Zoom the document to 75%. Your screen should look similar to Figure 11-2.

FIGURE 11-2
Document with tracked changes

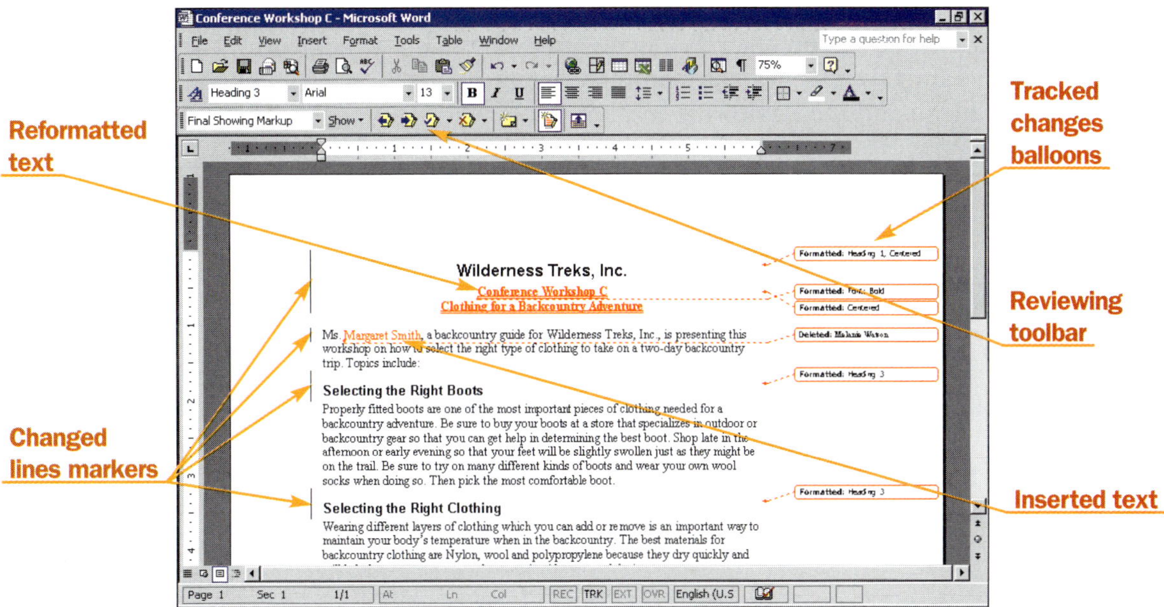

14. Zoom the document to 100% and then save, print preview, print, and close it.

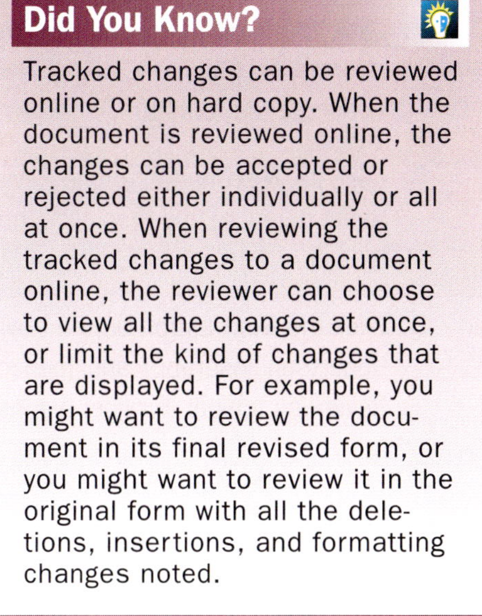

Did You Know?

Tracked changes can be reviewed online or on hard copy. When the document is reviewed online, the changes can be accepted or rejected either individually or all at once. When reviewing the tracked changes to a document online, the reviewer can choose to view all the changes at once, or limit the kind of changes that are displayed. For example, you might want to review the document in its final revised form, or you might want to review it in the original form with all the deletions, insertions, and formatting changes noted.

Accepting or Rejecting Changes

When the Track Changes feature is turned on, the Reviewing toolbar, which you use to accept or reject changes, may automatically appear. If it does not appear, you can display it with the Toolbars command on the View menu or with the toolbars shortcut menu. You can also use a shortcut menu to accept or reject changes. Tamika Washington reviewed your Conference Workshop C document and keyed some suggested changes into the document. You open the document and accept or reject Tamika's changes and comment using both a shortcut menu and the Reviewing toolbar.

Note

If you are using Word 2000, your Reviewing toolbar buttons, your shortcut menu, and the way comments and tracked changes are presented in a document are different. Your instructor will provide alternate instructions for Step-by-Step 11.2.

S TEP-BY-STEP 11.2

1. Open the **Step11-2** document from the data files.

2. Save the document as **Conference Workshop C Revised**.

3. Display the Reviewing toolbar, if necessary.

4. Click the **Display for Review** button list arrow on the Reviewing toolbar and click **Original Showing Markup** to view the original document with all deletions and insertions.

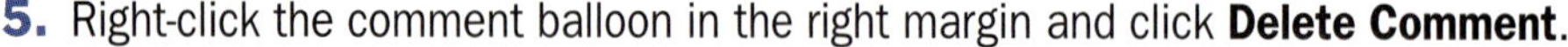

5. Right-click the comment balloon in the right margin and click **Delete Comment**.

6. Right-click the Wilderness Treks, Inc. title paragraph and click **Accept Format Change** to accept the heading style and margin changes.

7. Click the **Next** button on the Reviewing toolbar to select the next changed item (the two reformatted title paragraphs). Then click the **Accept Change** button on the Reviewing toolbar to accept the formatting change.  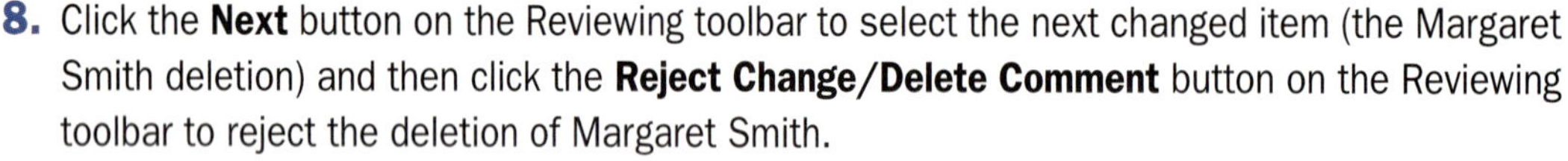

8. Click the **Next** button on the Reviewing toolbar to select the next changed item (the Margaret Smith deletion) and then click the **Reject Change/Delete Comment** button on the Reviewing toolbar to reject the deletion of Margaret Smith. 

9. Click the **Next** button on the Reviewing toolbar to select the next changed item (the Delanie Robertson insertion) and then click the **Reject Change/Delete Comment** button on the Reviewing toolbar to reject the insertion. 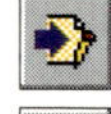

10. Click the **Accept Change** button list arrow on the Reviewing toolbar to view the Accept Change menu and then click **Accept All Changes in Document** to accept all the remaining changes. 

11. Double-click the **TRK** mode indicator on the status bar to turn off the Track Changes feature.

12. Save the document and then print preview, print, and close it.

Compare and Merge Two Documents

When working with others on documents, it is sometimes necessary to combine documents from two authors to get one final document. You can do this with the Compare and Merge feature. When you combine two documents, Word compares the documents and then uses the Track Changes feature to illustrate the changes. Word identifies the documents to be compared and merged as the ***current document*** (the document that is open) and the ***target document*** (the document you choose for comparison). During the compare and merge process, you can choose one of three locations in which to merge the documents and display the document differences: into the current document; into the target document; or into a new third document. You make the choice when you open the Compare and Merge Documents dialog box using the Compare and Merge Documents command on the Tools menu.

You and Belinda Lewis have both drafted information on a conference workshop that Sloane is presenting. You use the Compare and Merge feature to merge Belinda's document and your document into a third document. Then you accept or reject the differences between your document and Belinda's document to create a final document.

> **Note** 
>
> If you are using Word 2000, the document compare and merge process is different. Your instructor will provide alternate instructions for Step-by-Step 11.3.

STEP-BY-STEP 11.3

1. Open the **Step11-3** document from the data files. This is the current document for the compare and merge process.

2. Click the **Tools** menu and click **Compare and Merge Documents** to open the Compare and Merge Documents dialog box.

3. Switch to the data files folder and click the **Step11-3A** filename to select it. (This is the target document for the compare and merge process.) *Warning! Do not double-click the filename!*

STEP-BY-STEP 11.3 Continued

4. Click the **Merge** list arrow in the dialog box to view the Merge menu. The dialog box on your screen should look similar to Figure 11-3.

FIGURE 11-3
Compare and Merge Documents dialog box

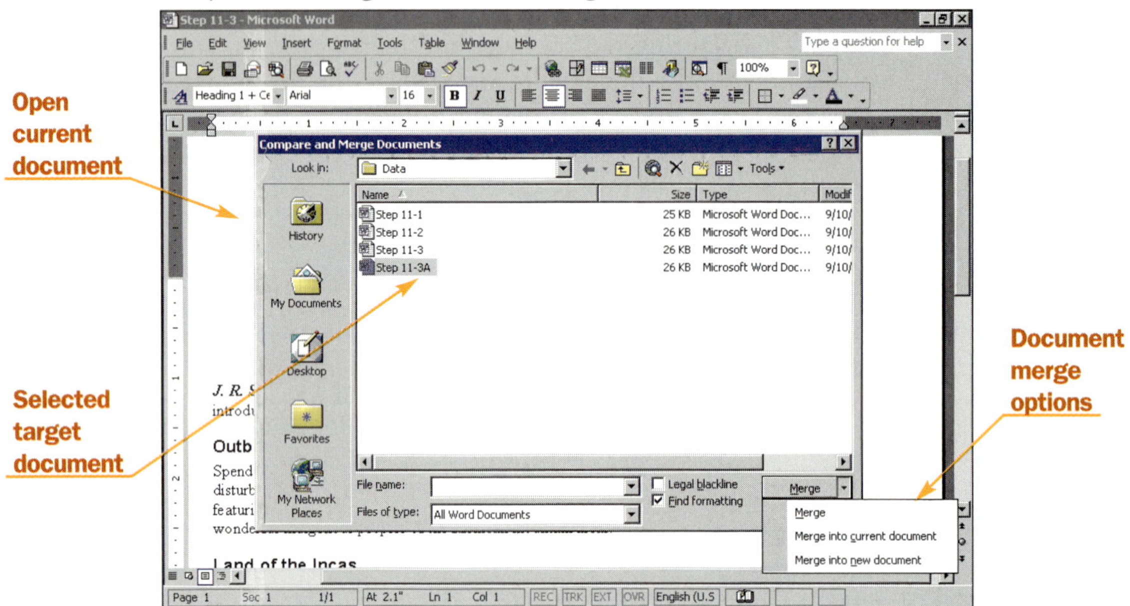

5. Click **Merge into new document** to merge the Step11-3 and Step11-3A documents into a new document.

6. Close the **Step11-3** document. (The Step 11-3A target document never opens.)

7. Save the new merged document as **Conference Workshop D**.

8. Display the Reviewing toolbar, if necessary.

9. Click the **Display for Review** button list arrow, click **Original Showing Markup**, and scroll the document to review the marked changes. 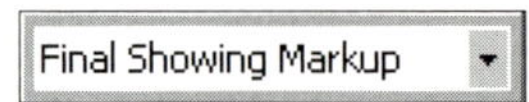

10. Use the shortcut menu method to reject the formatting change to J. R. Sloane.

11. Accept all the remaining changes to the document using the Reviewing toolbar.

12. Save, print preview, and print the document and leave it open for the next Step-by-Step.

Use the Thesaurus

The **Thesaurus** feature enables you to replace a selected word with another word that has the same or a very similar meaning, which is called a **synonym**. You can open the Thesaurus dialog box with the Thesaurus subcommand under the Language command on the Tools menu. You also can open the Thesaurus dialog box with a shortcut menu. You can quickly replace a common word with a synonym without opening the Thesaurus dialog box by using a shortcut menu.

You want to fine-tune the Conference Workshop D document by choosing some different words to describe the Mexico Backpacking Adventure. First, you replace the word *relaxing,* and then you replace the word *natural.*

S TEP-BY-STEP 11.4

1. Verify that the Conference Workshop D document is open. Right-click the word **relaxing** in the first sentence in the topic paragraph below the Mexico Backpacking Adventure heading paragraph, point to **Synonyms**, and click the word **calming** to replace *relaxing* with *calming.*

2. Right-click the word **natural** in the second sentence in the topic paragraph below the Mexico Backpacking Adventure heading paragraph, point to **Synonyms**, and click **Thesaurus** to open the Thesaurus dialog box.

3. Click the word **untreated** (adj.) in the Meanings list and then click the word **organic** in the Replace with Synonym list. Your dialog box should look similar to Figure 11-4.

FIGURE 11-4
Thesaurus dialog box

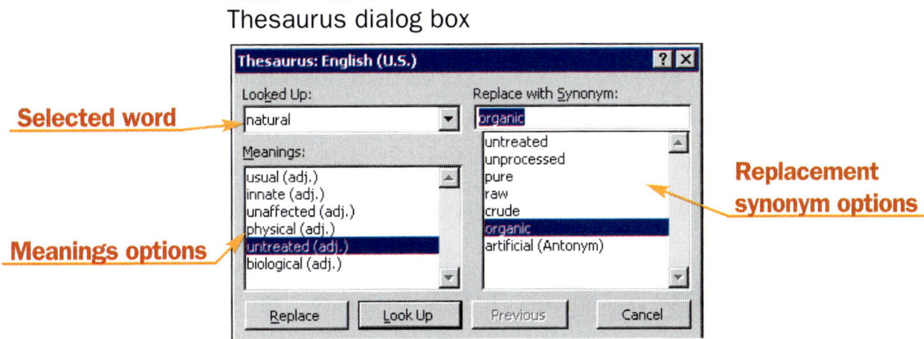

4. Click **Replace** and observe that the word *natural* is replaced with the word *organic.*

5. Save the document and leave it open for the next Step-by-Step.

Indent Paragraphs

You can *indent* a paragraph by moving it away from the left or right margins to help draw attention to the paragraph. Word indentation options allow you to position some, or all, lines of a paragraph to the right of the left margin (or to the left of the right margin). You can indent selected paragraphs with options in the Paragraph dialog box, which you open with the Paragraph command on the Format menu. You also can indent paragraphs with the Increase Indent and Decrease Indent buttons on the Formatting toolbar. Finally, the fastest way to indent selected paragraphs is by dragging the First Line Indent, Hanging Indent, or Left Indent markers to the desired position on the horizontal ruler.

After reviewing the Conference Workshop D document, you decide it would be easier to read if the first line of all the topic paragraphs were indented .25 inch from the left margin. You quickly indent the paragraphs using the First Line Indent marker, the mouse pointer, and the horizontal ruler.

STEP-BY-STEP 11.5

1. Verify that the Conference Workshop D document is open. Using the Ctrl key and the mouse pointer, select all the topic paragraphs. (If you are using Word 2000, combine steps 2 and 3 to select and indent each topic paragraph individually.) Your screen should look similar to Figure 11-5.

Did You Know?

Although it is possible to move the first line of the paragraph to the right of the left margin using a tab formatting mark and a tab stop, a tab formatting mark and an indent are very different formatting features. When you press the Tab key, Word inserts a nonprinting tab formatting mark and moves only that line of a paragraph to the next tab stop on the horizontal ruler. When you indent a paragraph, you can specify which paragraph lines to move and how many spaces to move them.

FIGURE 11-5
Selected topic paragraphs

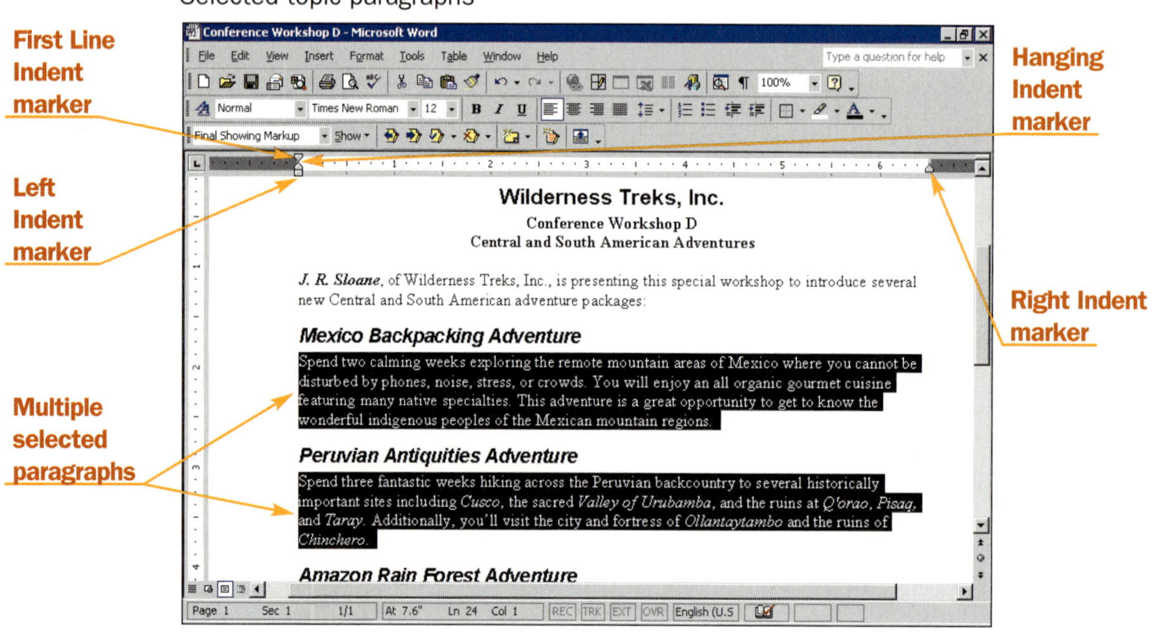

STEP-BY-STEP 11.5 Continued

2. Move the mouse pointer to the First Line Indent marker to the left of the horizontal ruler and then drag the First Line Indent marker to the .25-inch position on the horizontal ruler. Your screen should look similar to Figure 11-6.

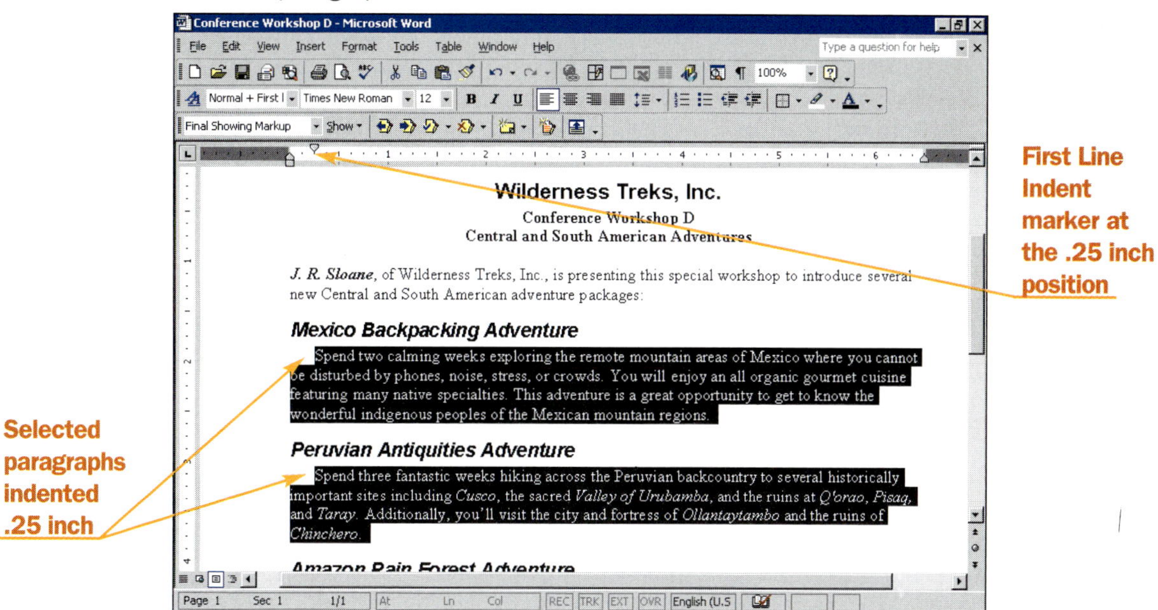

3. Save the document and leave it open for the next Step-by-Step.

Apply Borders and Shading

You can use paragraph borders and shading to add emphasis to an entire paragraph. You can apply borders and shading formatting to a selected paragraph with options in the Borders and Shading dialog box. You open this dialog box with the Borders and Shading command on the Format menu. You also can apply a border to a selected paragraph with the Border button on the Formatting toolbar. You want to add emphasis to the three title paragraphs by adding a 3-point border and 10% Gray shading.

Hot Tip 

When you apply a border to selected paragraphs, the border reaches from margin to margin. To have the border fit more tightly with short title and heading paragraphs, you can indent the paragraphs from the left and right margins after you add the border.

S TEP-BY-STEP 11.6

1. Verify that the Conference Workshop D document is open. Select the three title paragraphs.

2. Click **Format** on the menu bar, click **Borders and Shading** to open the Borders and Shading dialog box, and then click the **Borders** tab, if necessary.

3. Click the **Box** border option in the Setting list, click the Width list arrow and click 3 pt, and then click **Paragraph** in the Apply to list box, if necessary. Your dialog box should look similar to Figure 11-7.

FIGURE 11-7
Borders tab in the Borders and Shading dialog box

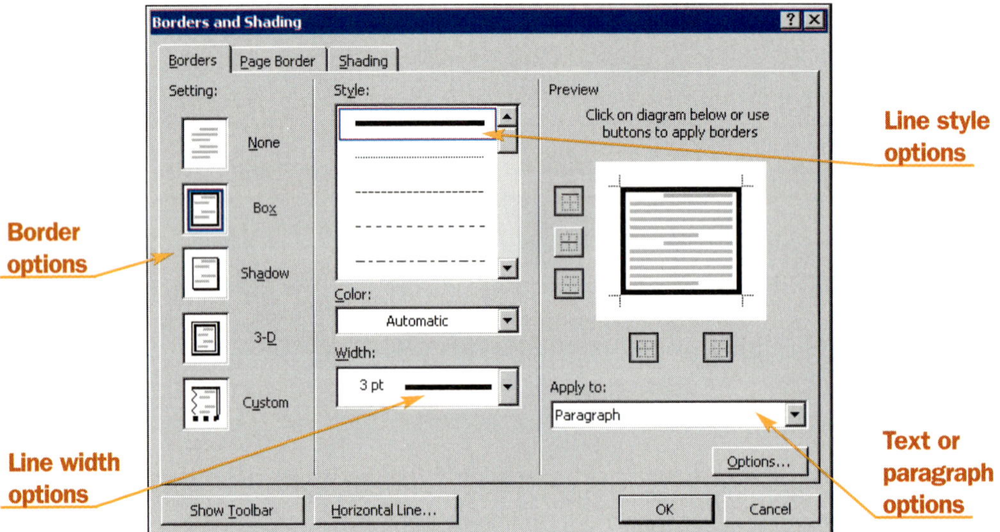

4. Click the **Shading tab** and click Gray-10% option in the Fill color grid. Your dialog box should look similar to Figure 11-8.

FIGURE 11-8
Shading tab in the Borders and Shading dialog box

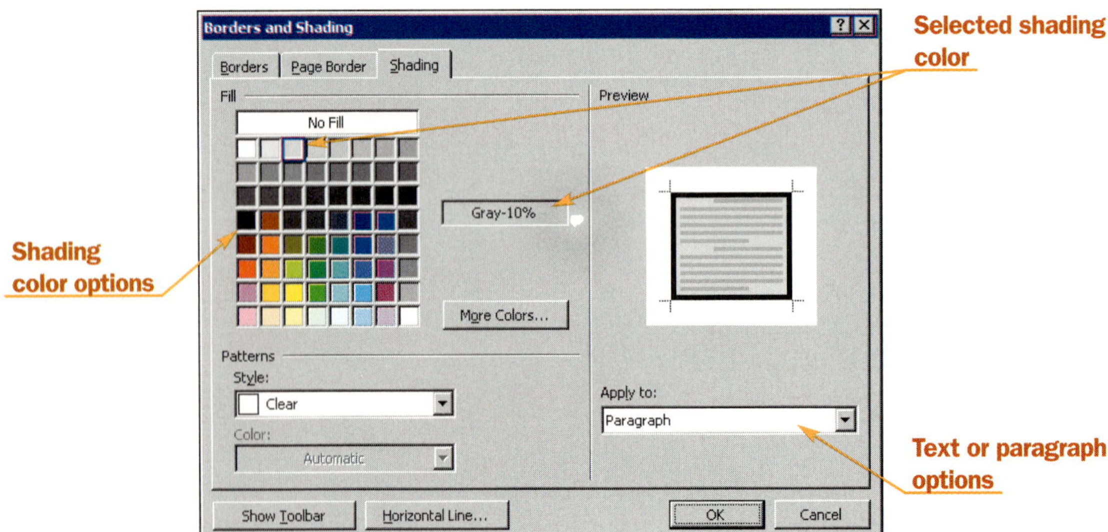

STEP-BY-STEP 11.6 Continued

5. Click **OK** to apply the 3-pt box border and 10% Gray shading.

6. Verify that the three title paragraphs are still selected, and then drag the Left Indent marker to the 1.5-inch position and the Right Indent marker to the 5-inch position on the horizontal ruler. Deselect the title paragraphs. Your screen should look similar to Figure 11-9.

FIGURE 11-9
Formatted title paragraphs

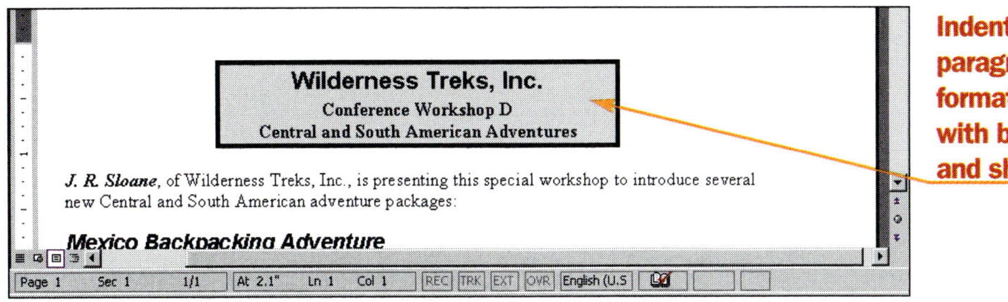

7. Close the Reviewing toolbar and then save, print preview, print, and close the document.

8. Close Word.

SUMMARY

In this job, you learned:

- You can work efficiently on documents with others by keying suggested changes directly into the documents and using the Track Changes feature to review and then accept or reject those changes.

- You can specify how you want tracked changes such as insertions, deletions, and formatting to appear in a document by setting options in the Track Changes dialog box.

- When viewing a document with Tracked Changes turned on, you can accept or reject keyed changes with buttons on the Reviewing toolbar or with a shortcut menu.

- Another way to work with others on documents is to compare two documents and then merge them together using the Track Changes feature to indicate the changes between the current document (the open document) and the target document (the document being compared to).

- The Thesaurus feature allows you to substitute a word for another word. You can open the Thesaurus with a command on the Language submenu that appears on the Tools menu or with the shortcut Synonym menu.

- Indenting paragraphs from the left or right margins adds emphasis to the paragraphs. You can indent the first line of a paragraph from the left margin (First Line Indent), indent all the lines of a paragraph from the left margin (Left Indent), or indent all the lines of a paragraph except the first line (Hanging Indent).

■ Borders and shading are also used to emphasize selected paragraphs. You can apply a border or shading to selected paragraphs with options in the Borders and Shading dialog box. You also can apply a border to selected paragraphs with the Borders button on the Formatting toolbar.

VOCABULARY *Review*

> **Define the following terms:**
>
> Current document   Synonym   Thesaurus
> Indent   Target document

REVIEW *Questions*

TRUE / FALSE

Circle T if the statement is true or F if the statement is false.

T   F   **1.** You can turn on or off the Track Changes feature with the EXT mode indicator.

T   F   **2.** You cannot print a document containing tracked changes.

T   F   **3.** The target document is the open document in a compare and merge process.

T   F   **4.** A synonym is a word that has the same or a very similar meaning as another word.

T   F   **5.** To indent only the first line of a paragraph using the mouse pointer, you drag the Left Indent marker to a position on the horizontal ruler.

FILL IN THE BLANK

Complete the following sentences by writing the correct word or words in the blanks provided.

1.   There are four types of paragraph indents: Left Indent, First Line Indent, Hanging Indent, and __________.

2.   You can apply a border to a selected paragraph with the __________ button on the Formatting toolbar.

3.   You can compare and merge two documents into a separate __________ document.

4.   The __________ enables you to replace a selected word with another word that has the same or similar meaning.

5.   A(n) __________ Indent moves all the lines of a paragraph a specified amount from the left margin.

PROJECTS

PROJECT 11-1

1. Open Word and open **Project 11-1** from the data files.

2. Save the document as **Conference Workshop E**.

3. Set a 2-inch top margin and 1-inch left, bottom, and right margins.

4. Format the Skiing and Camping Equipment, Clothing, and Other Items heading paragraphs with the Heading 3 style.

5. Indent all the topic paragraphs .25 inch from the left margin using the mouse pointer.

6. Create a bulleted list using the bullet graphic of your choice for the list of items following each topic paragraph.

7. Insert a page break to force the Clothing heading paragraph and subsequent paragraphs to a second page.

8. Apply a 2¼-point box border and 10% Gray shading to the introductory paragraph beginning *Mr. Mike Turner*.

9. Use the Thesaurus to change the word *expert* in the first sentence of the introductory paragraph to the word *authority*.

10. Apply the Emphasis character style to the words Mr. Mike Turner. (Word 2002 users: remember to view all styles in the Styles and Formatting task pane.)

11. Create a footer with the text **Conference Workshop E Draft** at the left margin, the page number in the center, and the current date at the right margin. (*Note*: Don't forget to reset the Center and Right tab stops.)

12. Save the document then print preview, print, and close it.

PROJECT 11-2

Melody Stackhouse has drafted the information for the conference workshop describing how to plan for a skiing safari. You need to compare her document draft with your document draft and create a final document. Open the Conference Workshop E document you created in Project 11-1. If you have not completed Project 11-1, do so now. Compare the Conference Workshop E document (the current document) to the Project 11-2 document (the target document) in the data files and merge the two into a third document. If you are asked to resolve a formatting conflict between the documents, select the current document formatting to override. Save the merged document as **Conference Workshop E Revised**. Use the Reviewing toolbar and the shortcut menu to accept or reject the changes as you desire. Then save, print preview, print, and close the document. (If you are using Word 2000, your instruction will provide additional information needed to complete this project.)

WEB PROJECT

James Montevo calls to tell you he just discovered the Web toolbar. He suggests you review the toolbar buttons to see how you could use it to complete some of your tasks more effectively. Create a new blank document and using the toolbar shortcut menu, display the Web toolbar. Explore how to use each of the toolbar buttons. Then demonstrate how to use the Web toolbar to several of your classmates.

TEAMWORK PROJECT

Because much of your time as an administrative assistant is spent creating and editing documents in Word, it is important that you understand how to use the various options in the Formatting dialog boxes. Select a classmate to work with you on this project. Then, using online Help and the Paragraph dialog box, explore how to use the Paragraph dialog box options to set paragraph indents, alignment, line spacing, and other paragraph formatting. Demonstrate how to use these options to another group of classmates.

CRITICAL*Thinking*

ACTIVITY 11-1

An important aspect of your job as an administrative assistant is to assist other employees who might be having a problem using Word features. Several of your coworkers have expressed concerns about indenting paragraphs. You decide to create a list of tips that might help them troubleshoot paragraph indenting problems. Using Word online Help, research indenting troubleshooting tips. Then create a list of tips you can share with others.

Using a Word Document to Create a PowerPoint Presentation

<table>
<tr><td>

OBJECTIVES

Upon completion of this job, you should be able to:

- Create an outline in Outline view.
- Send a Word outline to PowerPoint.
- Change the slide layout and add text to a slide.
- Apply a design template and run a slide show.

Estimated Time: 0.5 hour

</td><td>

VOCABULARY

Design template
Outline view
Placeholder
Slide layout

</td></tr>
</table>

Create an Outline in Outline View

When you are working with a Word document and want to concentrate on the document's structure, you can work with the document in Outline view. In *Outline view*, you can rearrange heading paragraphs and topic paragraphs (also called body text) by moving the paragraphs up or down, or promoting and demoting paragraphs to different outline levels using the mouse pointer or the buttons on the Outlining toolbar. You must format heading paragraphs with one of the built-in heading styles or with an Outline Level format in order to use Outline view features.

> **Did You Know?**
>
> You can create a formal outline using features in the Outline Numbered tab of the Bullets and Numbering dialog box. In this tab you can specify the outline format (I, II, III; A, B, C; and so forth) and you can also customize the numbering format and spacing for each level of the outline.

Sloane is going to open the conference with a short welcoming presentation to be given during the breakfast meeting on the first day of the conference. Sloane drafted a list of topics to be covered in the presentation and asks you to prepare an outline of the topics. First, you open the draft document, switch to Outline view, and format the paragraphs with Outline level formats. Then you rearrange some of the outline paragraphs using the Outlining toolbar.

STEP-BY-STEP 12.1

1. Start the Word application and open the **Step12-1** document from the data files.

2. Save the document as **Conference Outline**.

3. Click the **Outline View** button to the left of the horizontal scroll bar to switch to Outline view.

4. Observe that the Outlining toolbar automatically appears. Your toolbar may be docked below the Standard toolbar or in some other position on your screen. Your screen should look similar to Figure 12-1.

Hot Tip

When you want to use heading paragraphs and body text in an outline, but you do not want to change their formatting by applying heading styles, you can apply an Outline level format to the paragraphs. You first select a paragraph, then open the Paragraph dialog box with the **Paragraph** command on the **Format** menu, and select the appropriate Outline level format from the Outline level list box. You can also apply Outline level formatting to selected paragraphs in Outline view with the **Outline Level** button on the Outlining toolbar.

FIGURE 12-1
Document in Outline view

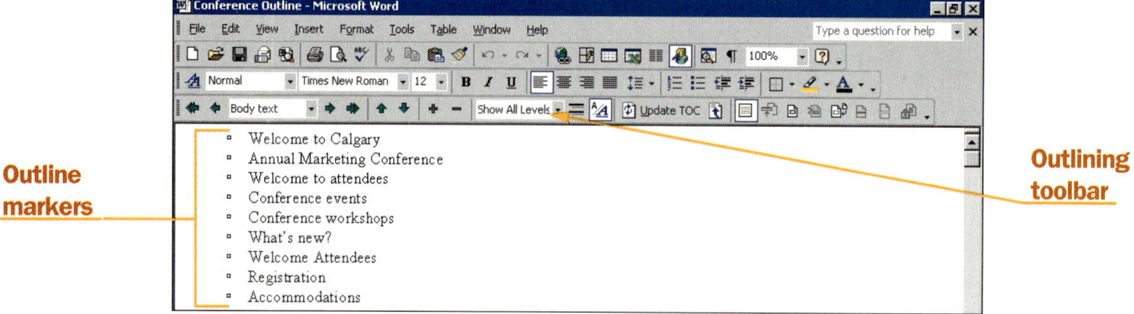

5. Move the insertion point to the Welcome to Calgary paragraph, if necessary, click the **Outline Level** button list arrow on the Outlining toolbar, and click **Level 1** to apply the Level 1 format to the paragraph. Observe the Level 1 outline marker to the left of the paragraph. (If you are using Word 2000, click the Promote button on the Outlining toolbar to promote the paragraph to Level 1.)

6. Move the insertion point to the Annual Marketing Conference paragraph, click the **Outline Level** button list arrow on the Outlining toolbar, and click **Level 1**. Observe the Level 1 outline marker to the left of the paragraph. (If you are using Word 2000, click the Promote button on the Outlining toolbar to promote the paragraph to Level 1. Word 2000 automatically formats the text with heading styles.)

7. Select the **Welcome to attendees**, **Conference events**, **Conference workshops**, and **What's new?** paragraphs, click the **Outline Level** button list arrow on the Outlining toolbar, and click **Level 2**. Observe the Level 2 outline marker to the left of the each paragraph. (If you are using Word 2000, click the Demote button on the Outlining toolbar to demote the selected paragraphs to Level 2.)

STEP-BY-STEP 12.1 Continued

8. Apply the Level 1 format to the following paragraphs: Welcome Attendees, Events, Workshops, and What's New at Wilderness Treks, Inc.? (If you are using Word 2000, combine steps 8 and 9 and, using the Promote and Demote buttons, promote or demote the paragraphs to Level 1 or Level 2 as noted.)

9. Apply the Level 2 format to the remaining paragraphs. Your screen should look similar to Figure 12-2.

FIGURE 12-2
Welcome to Calgary outline

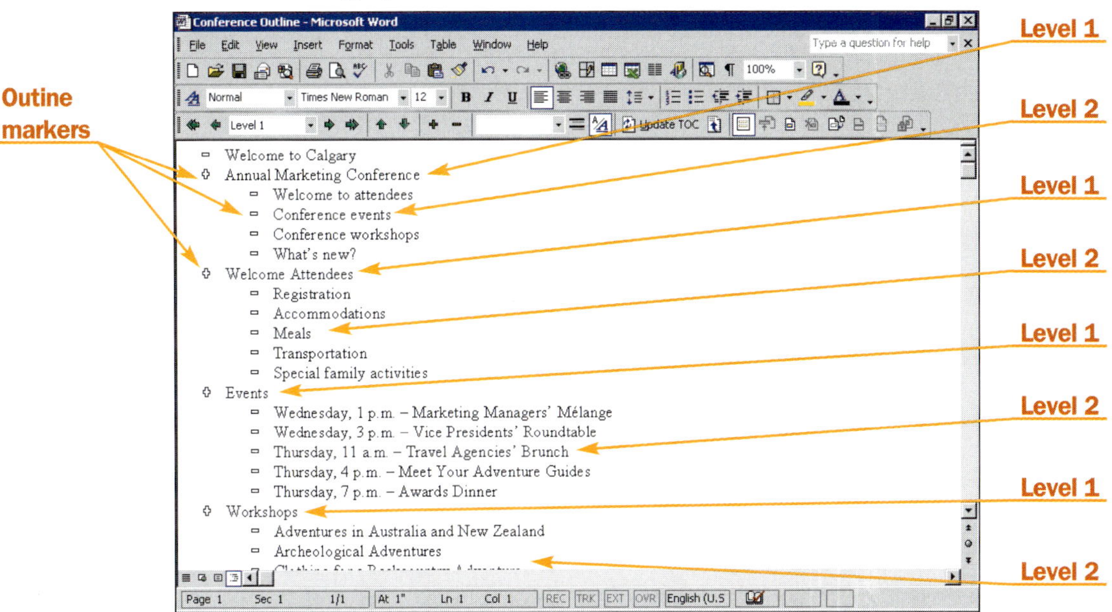

10. Click the Level 2 outline marker for the What's new? paragraph to select the paragraph.

11. Click the **Move Up** button on the Outlining toolbar twice to move the What's new? paragraph up two places to reposition the paragraph below the Welcome to attendees Level 2 paragraph. Your screen should look similar to Figure 12-3.

FIGURE 12-3
Repositioned What's new? paragraph

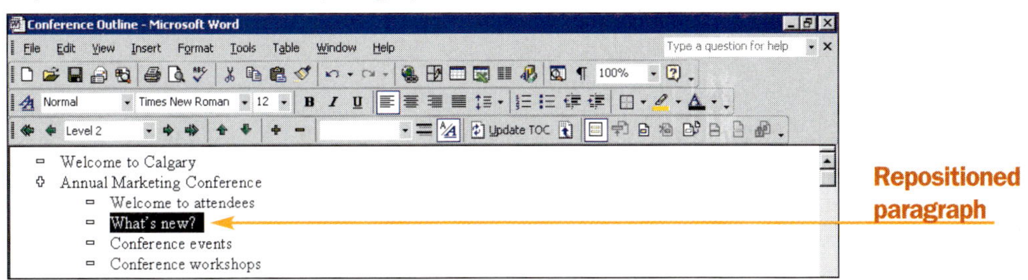

12. Click the **Show Level** button list arrow on the Outlining toolbar and click **Show Level 1** to show the Level 1 paragraphs and hide the Level 2 paragraphs. (If you are using Word 2000, click the Show Heading 1 button on the Outlining toolbar.)

STEP-BY-STEP 12.1 Continued

13. Click the Level 1 outline marker for the What's New at Wilderness Treks, Inc.? paragraph to select the paragraph and the two hidden Level 2 paragraphs below it.

14. Click the **Move Up** button on the Outlining toolbar twice to reposition the selected paragraphs below the Welcome Attendees Level 1 paragraph. 

15. Click the **Show Level** button list arrow on the Outlining toolbar and click **Show All Levels** to view both the Level 1 and Level 2 paragraphs. Deselect the paragraphs. Your screen should look similar to Figure 12-4. (If you are using Word 2000, click the Show All Headings button on the Outlining toolbar.)

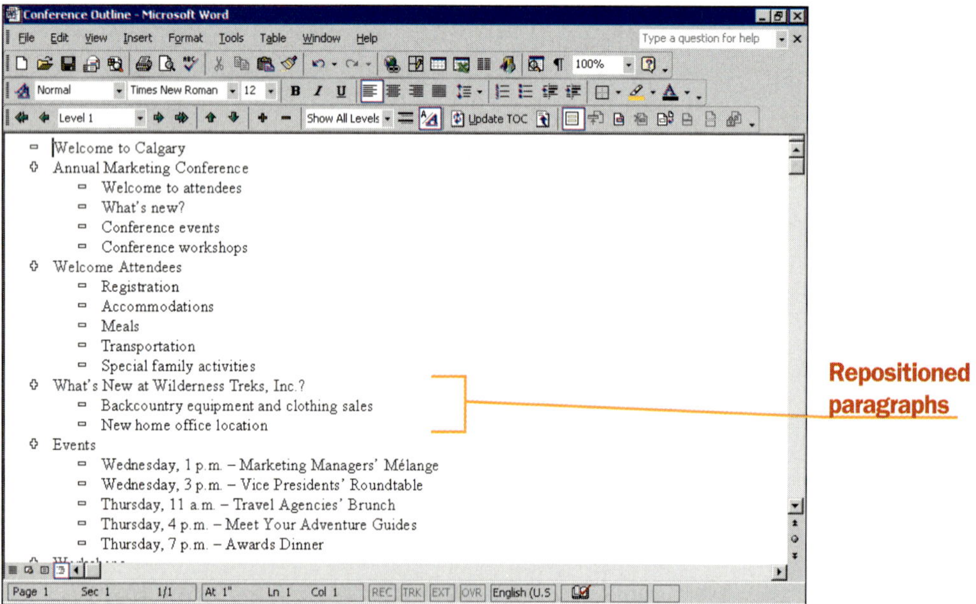

FIGURE 12-4
Repositioned What's New at Wilderness Treks, Inc.? paragraphs

16. Save the document and leave it open for the next Step-by-Step.

Send a Word Outline to PowerPoint

Y ou can quickly create a PowerPoint presentation by sending a Word outline to PowerPoint. It is not necessary to first open PowerPoint before you send a Word outline to PowerPoint to create a new presentation. PowerPoint automatically opens and creates a new presentation containing Title and Text slides based on the outline. All Level 1 (or Heading 1) formatted paragraphs create a new slide with the Level 1 (or Heading 1) formatted text as the slide's title. All following Level 2 (or Heading 2) formatted paragraphs become bulleted list text on the slide. You can also use a Word outline to create a PowerPoint presentation by first opening the PowerPoint application and then clicking the **Open** button on the Standard toolbar, switching to the folder where the outline document is stored, changing the Files of type to **All Outlines** to view all the outline documents, and then opening the desired outline to create a new presentation. You can also open the PowerPoint application, click **Insert** on the menu bar, and click **Slides from Outline** to locate and insert new slides based on a Word outline document.

Now that you have an outline of the topics Sloane is going to discuss at the conference's opening breakfast, you send it to PowerPoint to create the presentation Sloane will use while discussing the topics.

S TEP-BY-STEP 12.2

1. Verify the Conference Outline document is still open. Click **File** on the menu bar, point to **Send To**, and click **Microsoft PowerPoint** to send the Word document to the PowerPoint application.

2. Save the new PowerPoint presentation as **Sloane Comments**. Your screen should look similar to Figure 12-5.

Sloane Comments presentation

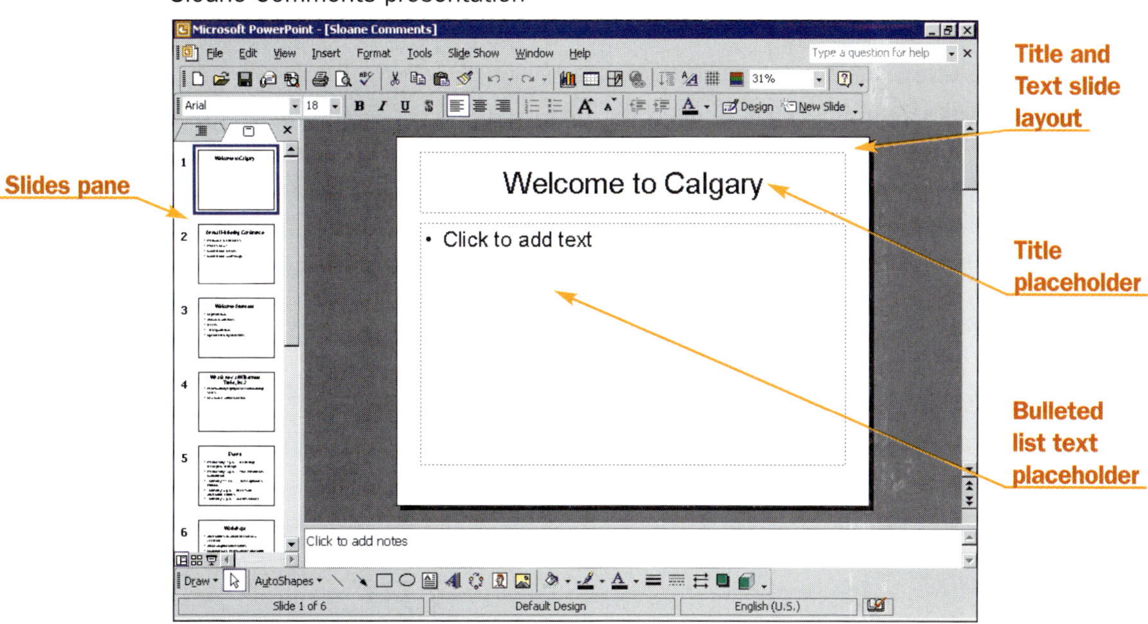

3. Close the **Conference Outline** document and close Word.

4. Leave the Sloane Comments presentation and PowerPoint open for the next Step-by-Step.

Change a Slide Layout and Add Text to a Slide

A *slide layout* controls the way items, such as text, pictures, charts, and so forth, are positioned on a slide. Text and other objects are positioned on slides in a boxed area called a *placeholder*. The basic slide layout is called the Title and Text layout, which contains placeholders for title text and for bulleted list text. Other slide layouts include Blank, Title Slide, Title Only, and various Content layouts containing some combination of title, text, picture, chart, diagram, and table placeholders.

The first slide contains the title of the entire presentation. Because only Title and Text slides are created from a Word outline document, you need to change the slide layout for the first slide to Title Slide. Then you need to add Sloane's name, title, and the company name to the title slide.

STEP-BY-STEP 12.3

1. Verify that the Sloane Comments presentation is open. Click **Format** on the menu bar and click **Slide Layout** to open the Slide Layout task pane. (If you are using PowerPoint 2000, the Slide Layout dialog box opens.)

2. Click the **Title Slide** layout in the Text Layouts section of the Slide Layout task pane to apply the Title Slide layout to the first slide. Your screen should look similar to Figure 12-6. (If you are using PowerPoint 2000, double-click the **Title Slide** layout in the Slide Layout dialog box.)

> ### Note
>
> There are a number of differences between PowerPoint 2000 and PowerPoint 2002. For example, in PowerPoint 2000, the Title and Text slide layout is called the Bulleted List slide, and slide layouts are selected from the New Slide or Slide Layout dialog box rather than from the Slide Layout task pane. Additionally, the slide layout selections available in PowerPoint 2000 are not as extensive as those in PowerPoint 2002. Also, the Normal view Slides pane is not available in PowerPoint 2000. As you work through the next two Step-by-Step activities, alternate instructions are presented for PowerPoint 2000 users. Additionally, PowerPoint 2000 users' screens will look similar to, but not exactly like, the illustrations.

FIGURE 12-6
Title slide

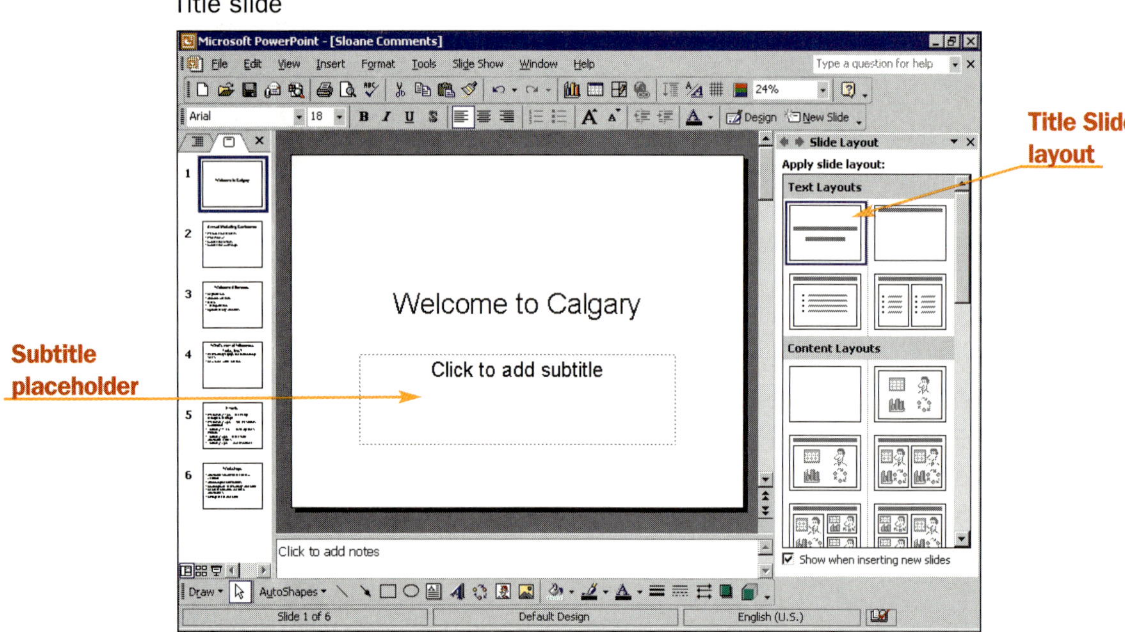

3. Scroll to view the remaining slides and then return to the title slide.

STEP-BY-STEP 12.3 Continued

4. Click inside the **Click to add subtitle** placeholder to position the insertion point and key **J. R. Sloane**. Press **Enter**. Key **President** and press **Enter**. Key **Wilderness Treks, Inc.** (If you are using PowerPoint 2000 click the **Click to add text** placeholder.) Your screen should look similar to Figure 12-7.

FIGURE 12-7
Added subtitle text

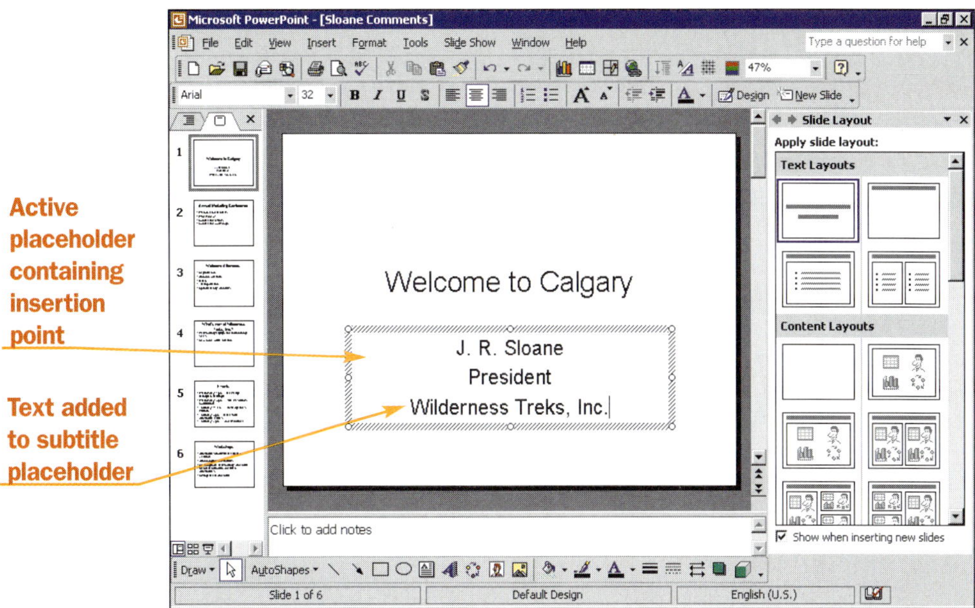

Active placeholder containing insertion point

Text added to subtitle placeholder

5. Click in the gray area outside the slide to deselect the subtitle placeholder.

6. Close the Slide Layout task pane, if necessary, and save the presentation, leaving it open for the next Step-by-Step.

Apply a Design Template and Run a Slide Show

A *design template* is a template that controls the overall look of a presentation: the color scheme; the font, font styles, and font sizes for titles and bulleted list text; background graphics; placeholder arrangement; and text alignment. You can create a new presentation based on a design template, or you can apply a design template to an existing presentation. Design templates give a presentation a very polished and professional appearance.

The Sloane Comments presentation must have a very professional look, so you apply a design template to it. Then you view the entire presentation as a slide show to review how the slides will look when they are presented by Sloane during the breakfast meeting.

Did You Know? 

If you create a new presentation in PowerPoint 2002 with the New command on the File menu, the New Presentation task pane opens, displaying options for creating a blank presentation and creating a presentation from a design template. If you create a presentation by sending a Word outline to PowerPoint, the Blank design template (blank presentation) is applied.

STEP-BY-STEP 12.4

1. Verify that the Sloane Comments presentation is open. Click the **Slide Design** button on the Formatting toolbar to open the Slide Design task pane. (If you are using PowerPoint 2000, click the **Apply Design Template** command on the Format menu to open the Apply Design Template dialog box.) 

2. Click the **Edge** design template in the Slide Design task pane to apply it to all slides in the presentation. Your screen should look similar to Figure 12-8. (If you are using PowerPoint 2000, double-click the **Straight Edge** design template in the Apply Design Template dialog box.)

FIGURE 12-8
Sloane Comments with applied design template

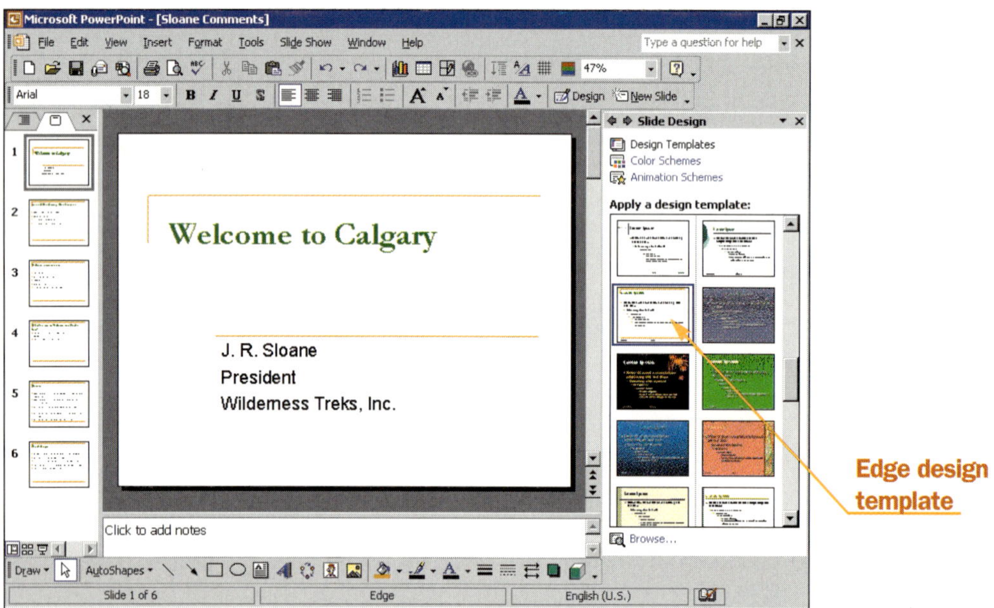

3. Click the **Slide Show** button in the lower-left area of the PowerPoint window to view the presentation as a slide show. 

4. Click the left mouse button or press the right arrow key to move from slide to slide until you have reviewed all the slides.

5. Click the **Print** button on the Standard toolbar to print all the slides.

6. Save the presentation and close it.

SUMMARY

In this job, you learned:

■ You can use Outline view to modify a document's structure by moving paragraphs up and down in the document.

- You can create an outline in Outline view by formatting paragraphs with built-in heading styles or Outline Level formats; then you can view different outline levels and move, promote, and demote outline paragraphs with buttons on the Outlining toolbar.

- A quick way to create a PowerPoint presentation is to send a Word outline document to PowerPoint.

- When you send a Word outline document to PowerPoint, Level 1 (or Heading 1) text becomes the title of a Title and Text slide. The following Level 2 (or Heading 2) text becomes bulleted list text in the Title and Text slide.

- A slide layout controls the positioning of text placeholders, pictures, charts, tables, and so forth on a slide.

- A design template controls the overall appearance of a presentation including the color scheme, fonts, placeholder arrangement, text alignment, and background graphics.

VOCABULARY *Review*

Define the following terms:

Design template	Placeholder	Slide layout
Outline view		

REVIEW *Questions*

TRUE / FALSE

Circle T if the statement is true or F if the statement is false.

T   F   **1.** You can rearrange heading and topic paragraphs with toolbar buttons in Outline view.

T   F   **2.** Outline level paragraph formatting allows you to format paragraphs that can be promoted or demoted to different outline levels without changing the text's font, font size, or other formatting attributes.

T   F   **3.** You cannot open a Word outline document in PowerPoint to create a presentation.

T   F   **4.** When you send a Word outline document to PowerPoint, the resulting presentation is automatically formatted with the Edge design template.

T   F   **5.** You must first open the PowerPoint application before you can send a Word outline to it to create a new presentation.

FILL IN THE BLANK

Complete the following sentences by writing the correct word or words in the blanks provided.

1. You must format paragraphs with the built-in __________ or __________ in order to use the Outline view features.

2. A(n) __________ is used to position objects such as text, pictures, and charts on a slide.

3. The __________ controls the way text, pictures, charts, and tables appear on a slide.

4. To control the overall look of a presentation, you can apply a(n) __________.

5. When you send a Word outline to PowerPoint, all the slides are created with the __________ layout.

PROJECTS

PROJECT 12-1

1. Open Word and open **Project 12-1** from the data files.

2. Save the document as **Workshop D Outline** and view it in Outline view.

3. Promote all the Heading 3 formatted heading paragraphs to Level 1 using the Outlining toolbar.

4. Demote all the Body Text formatted paragraphs (topic paragraphs) to Level 2 using the Outlining toolbar. (If you are using Word 2000, demote all the Normal formatted paragraphs to Level 2.)

5. Send the Workshop D Outline document to PowerPoint and then save and close the document.

6. Save the PowerPoint presentation as **Workshop D,** print the slides, and close the presentation.

PROJECT 12-2

You need to edit the Workshop D presentation you created in Project 12-1 to apply the Title Slide layout to the first slide and apply an attractive design template. Open the **Workshop D** presentation you created in Project 12-1. If you have not yet completed Project 12-1, do so now. Apply the Title Slide layout to the first slide and the design template of your choice to all the slides. Print the slides and save and close the presentation.

WEB PROJECT

You have lunch with June Kazmarick who tells you she is working on several presentations for the conference; however, her supervisor is not pleased with the design templates she is using. She asks if you know where she can download free PowerPoint design templates for her supervisor's review. Using your Web browser's search tool or a search engine such as Google (*www.google.com*), search for Web sites offering free PowerPoint design templates. Print at least three Web pages.

 **TEAMWORK PROJECT**

Sloane just received a copy of a presentation based on a unique design template from one of the Wilderness Treks, Inc. clients and would like you to create a custom design template based on this presentation. Select a classmate to work with you on this project. Then, using PowerPoint online Help, research how to create a design template from an existing presentation. Finally, demonstrate how to do this to another group of classmates using an existing presentation of your choice.

CRITICAL *Thinking*

ACTIVITY 12-1

Because most businesses are increasingly relying on their employees to create attractive presentations to support internal and external company communications, it is important for an administrative assistant to have strong PowerPoint skills, such as being able to effectively use a variety of slide layouts. Open the PowerPoint application and apply at least three different slide layouts to the title slide. Then demonstrate how to use the layouts to a group of classmates. (If you are using PowerPoint 2000, open PowerPoint and create a new presentation based on the Blank Presentation design template.)

BUSINESS WEEK TWO

COMMAND SUMMARY

WORD FEATURE	MENU COMMAND	KEYSTROKE	TOOLBAR BUTTON	JOB
Accept Change	Accept (Insertion, Deletion, Formatting)			11
Attachment	File, Send To, Mail Recipient (as Attachment)			9
Borders and Shading	Format, Borders and Shading			11
Bullet graphic	Format, Bullets and Numbering			8
Character styles	Format, Styles and Formatting	Ctrl + Shift + S	Normal	10
Chart object	Insert, Object, Microsoft Graph Chart			8
Chart type	Chart, Chart Type			8
Column break	Insert, Break	Ctrl + Shift + Enter		8
Columns	Format, Columns			8
Comment	Insert, Comment	Alt + Ctrl + M		9
Compare and Merge	Tools, Compare and Merge Documents			11
Convert text to table	Table, Convert, Text to Table			10
Delete Comment	Delete Comment			11
Diagram layout			Layout	8
Drawing toolbar	View, Toolbars, Drawing			8
Find and Replace	Edit, Find; Edit, Replace	Ctrl + F; Ctrl + H		10
Header and Footer	View, Header and Footer			10
Highlights				9
Insert a diagram	Insert, Diagram			8
Insert a picture	Insert, Picture, From File			8
Insert columns	Table, Insert, Columns to the Left or Columns to the Right			10
Insert rows	Table, Insert, Rows Above or Rows Below			10

WORD FEATURE	MENU COMMAND	KEYSTROKE	TOOLBAR BUTTON	JOB
Move Paragraphs Up				12
Next (Change)				11
Outline Level Formatting	Format, Paragraph (Normal and Print Layout views)		Level 1	12
Outline view	View, Outline	Alt + Ctrl + O		12
Paragraph styles	Format, Styles and Formatting	Ctrl + Shift + S Alt + Ctrl + 1 (Heading 1) Alt + Ctrl + 2 (Heading 2) Alt + Ctrl + 3 (Heading 3)	Normal	10
Preview document as a Web page	File, Web Page Preview			10
Reject Change	Reject (Insertion, Deletion, Formatting)			11
Review tracked changes			Final Showing Markup	11
Save document as a Web page	File, Save as Web Page			10
Send a Word document to PowerPoint	File, Send To, Microsoft PowerPoint			12
Show Outline Levels			Show Level 9	12
Switch Between Header and Footer				10
Tab leaders	Format, Tabs			9
Table AutoFormat	Format, Styles and Formatting; Table, Table AutoFormat			10
Text effects	Format, Font			9
Thesaurus	Tools, Language, Thesaurus	Shift + F7		11
Track Changes	Tools, Track Changes	Ctrl + Shift + E	TRK	11
Track Changes options			TRK ; Show	11
Wrap text				8

COMMAND SUMMARY

OUTLOOK FEATURE	MENU COMMAND	KEYSTROKE	TOOLBAR BUTTON	JOB
Calendar Day view	View, Day		Day	7
Calendar Month view	View, Month	Alt + Equal sign	Month	7
Calendar Week view	View, Week	Alt + Hyphen	Week	7
Calendar Work Week view	View, Work Week		Work Week	7

OUTLOOK FEATURE	MENU COMMAND	KEYSTROKE	TOOLBAR BUTTON	JOB
Calendar	View, Go To, Calendar	Ctrl + Y		7
Contacts	View, Go To, Contacts	Ctrl + Y		7
Go to Today	View, Go To, Today		Today	7
New Appointment	File, New, Appointment Actions, New Appointment	Ctrl + Shift + A	New	7
New Contact	File, New, Contact Actions, New Contact	Ctrl + Shift + C	New	7
New Message to Contact	Actions, New Message to Contact			7
Print	File, Print	Ctrl + P		7
Save and Close		Alt + S	Save and Close	7
Save and New				7

COMMAND SUMMARY

POWERPOINT FEATURE	MENU COMMAND	KEYSTROKE	TOOLBAR BUTTON	JOB
Print a presentation	File, Print	Ctrl + P		12
Run a Slide Show	Slide Show, View Show	F5		12
Save a presentation	File, Save; Save As	Ctrl + S		12
Slide Design task pane	Format, Slide Design		Design	12
Slide Layout task pane	Format, Slide Layout			12

REVIEW *Questions*

TRUE/FALSE

Circle T if the statement is true or F if the statement is false.

T F **1.** You must format paragraphs with the built-in heading styles or Outline Level formatting to use the Outline view features to create an outline.

T F **2.** You open the Track Changes dialog box with the TRK mode indicator on the status bar.

T F **3.** Each Outlook folder has several different views, or ways, to look at the items in the folder.

T F **4.** A diagram is used to represent a set of numerical data, or the relationship between multiple sets of numerical data.

T F **5.** Special text effects that can add emphasis to text are available in the Paragraph dialog box.

T F **6.** A paragraph style contains multiple paragraph formatting elements, such as line spacing, indenting, and alignment.

T F **7.** When you compare and merge documents, all changes must be merged into the target document.

T F **8.** A slide design controls the way text, pictures, charts, and other objects are positioned on slides in placeholders.

T F **9.** A Table AutoFormat is a type of style that contains column width, borders, shading, font, font size, and other formatting necessary to create attractive and easy-to-read tables.

T F **10.** The Clip Organizer contains picture, sound, video, and other media files or clips you can insert in Office XP documents.

MATCHING

Match the correct term in Column 1 to its description in Column 2.

Column 1

____ 1. Synonym

____ 2. Event

____ 3. Style

____ 4. Drawing canvas

____ 5. Outline view

____ 6. Item

____ 7. Manual page break

____ 8. Newspaper-style columns

____ 9. Tab leader line

____ 10. Placeholder

Column 2

A. A page break inserted by the user to force text to another page

B. Multicolumn text in which the text fills a column and then flows to the right to fill the next column

C. An e-mail message, appointment, or contact entered in an Outlook Inbox, Calendar, or Contacts folder

D. A word that has the same or similar meaning to another word

E. A dashed, dotted, or solid line that fills the space to the left of a custom tab stop

F. Boxed area on a slide that is used to position text, pictures, and other objects

G. An activity entered in an Outlook Calendar that lasts 24 hours or longer

H. An area that surrounds drawing objects and helps to position them in a document

I. A collection of formatting components saved with a unique name

J. A Word document view that allows you to structure a document by moving, promoting, or demoting paragraphs

CRITICAL *Thinking*

PROJECT 1

Sloane asks you to draft a newsletter-style document highlighting the new Central and South American travel adventure packages that are being promoted during the annual marketing conference. The document is to be e-mailed to various clients in advance of the conference. Open the **Unit 2 Review Project 1** document from the data files. Use margin settings, newspaper columns, pictures (from the Clip gallery or other sources), text wrapping, diagrams, character styles, paragraph styles, fonts, font size, borders, shading, headers, and footers as you desire to create an informative, interesting, and appealing promotional document. Save the document as **New Adventures Promotion** and then print preview, print, and close it.

PROJECT 2

You now need to distribute the New Adventures Promotion document to a list of clients via an e-mail attachment. Open the **Unit 2 Review Project 2** document from the data files and print it. Using the information in the document, create four new Outlook Contact items. Then, create an e-mail message from Sloane to each contact announcing the new travel adventures and attach the **New Adventures Promotion** document you created in Project 1 to each message. (If you have not yet completed Project 1, do so now.) Save the e-mail messages. If your instructor provides valid e-mail addresses, send the e-mail messages.

ADVANCED *Challenge*

An important way to save time when creating mailing labels, form letters, and envelopes for clients whose name and address information is already in your Outlook Contacts folder is to begin the merge process directly from Outlook. To do this, you must first open your Outlook Contacts folder and select the contact items to be included in the merge process. Then, you use the Mail Merge command on the Tools menu to specify the contact fields to include, the document to merge to, and the type of merge (mailing labels, envelopes, form letters, or catalog). After you set these parameters, Word opens with the specified new or existing main document. You then use the Insert Merge Fields button on the Mail Merge toolbar (*Note:* Do not use the Address Block button) to insert the appropriate fields (usually name and address fields) in the main document. Finally, you proceed with the mail merge process to create the merged documents.

Sloane wants you to create 5260 Address mailing labels for the Washington, Gartner, Gonzales, and Yang contacts you added to your Contacts folder in Project 2. (If you have not added the contacts to your Contacts folder, do so now.) First, open your Contacts folder, then select the four contacts and proceed with the merge process following the instructions in various dialog boxes that appear including the Mail Merge Helper in Word. (Leave the Only selected records and All contact fields options turned on in the Outlook Mail Merge Contacts dialog box.) Use a new blank main document and insert only the Full_Name, Job_Title, and Business_Address fields. If you are using Word 2002, don't forget to propagate the labels with the Propagate Labels button on the Mail Merge toolbar. Preview the merge before merging to a new document. Save the main document as **Contact Main Document** and save the finished label document as **Contact Labels**. Remember to delete the four contact records.

BUSINESS WEEK THREE: WORKSHEETS AND PRESENTATIONS

Unit 3

Estimated Time for Unit 3: 4 hours

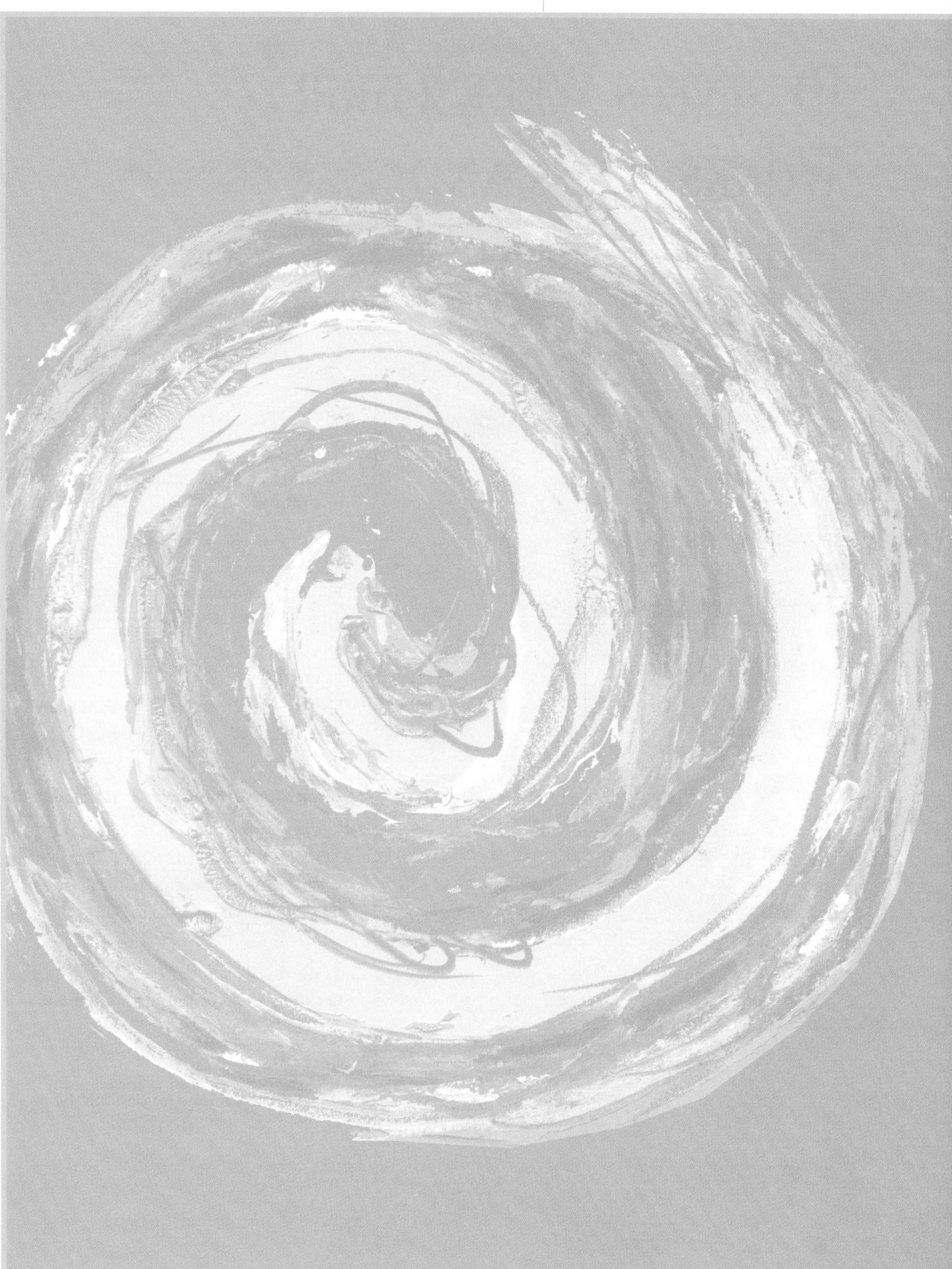

CREATING AND FORMATTING BUDGET DATA AND CHARTS

OBJECTIVES

Upon completion of this job, you should be able to:

- Insert rows and cells.
- Create linking formulas containing 3-D references.
- Copy formulas with relative and absolute cell references.
- Insert comments.
- Check spelling.
- Create and format charts.
- Set page setup options and a print area.
- Save a workbook as a Web page.

Estimated Time: 1.5 hours

VOCABULARY

3-D references

Absolute cell reference

Comment

Fill handle

Grouping

Linking formulas

Mixed cell reference

Print area

Relative cell reference

Insert Rows and Cells

During this Monday morning's meeting with Sloane, you learn that at the close of the annual marketing conference, Sloane and the vice presidents are staying in Calgary for an additional two days to begin working on the budget for the coming year. Sloane asks you to prepare a preliminary annual budget based on data provided by Bob Davenport, the accounting manager. Davenport sent you an Excel workbook with three worksheets: Budget, Revenues, and Expenses, and included the projected revenue and expense data in the worksheets.

You begin by opening Davenport's workbook and, because you expect to make a number of revisions, you insert the current date and time on all three worksheets. Then, based on a phone call you just received from Davenport, you insert new cells on one of the worksheets in the workbook and add additional expense data to the cells. Finally, you insert a new row on two of the worksheets.

As you work with Davenport's workbook, you may notice some spelling errors. For now, just ignore them. You correct any spelling errors later in this job.

Did You Know?

You can select multiple worksheets and then perform the same action (inserting, editing, and formatting) on all the selected worksheets. This action is called **grouping**. To group adjacent worksheets, you click the first sheet tab and then press and hold the **Shift** key while clicking the last sheet tab in the group. To group nonadjacent sheet tabs, use the **Ctrl** key. When finished inserting, editing, or formatting the grouped worksheets, you must remember to ungroup them by clicking an individual sheet tab that is not part of the group to select only that worksheet. You can also ungroup worksheets by right-clicking any sheet tab in the group and clicking the Ungroup Sheets command on the shortcut menu.

S TEP-BY-STEP 13.1

1. Start the Excel application, open the **Step13-1** workbook from the data files, and click the **Budget** sheet tab, if necessary.

2. Save the workbook as **Annual Budget**.

3. Press and hold the **Shift** key and click the **Expenses** sheet tab to group all three worksheets. Observe that all three sheet tabs are white, indicating that they are selected or grouped. The sheet tabs on your screen should look similar to Figure 13-1.

FIGURE 13-1
Grouped worksheets

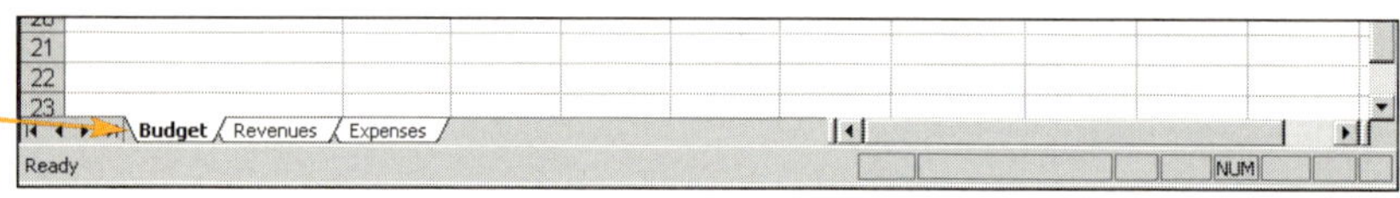

4. Click cell **A3** to activate it, key **=NOW()**, and press **Enter** to insert the current date and time.

5. Select the range **A3:G3** and click the **Merge and Center** button on the Formatting toolbar to merge all the cells in the range and center the date and time in the merged cells. 

6. Click the **Revenues** sheet tab and observe the inserted and formatted date and time; click the **Expenses** sheet tab and observe the inserted and formatted date and time; click the **Budget** sheet tab.

7. Group the Revenues and Expenses worksheets using the **Ctrl** key.

STEP-BY-STEP 13.1 Continued

8. Click the row 4 heading to select the entire row, click **Insert** on the menu bar, and click **Rows** to insert a blank row between the date and time row and the column header row. Your screen should look similar to Figure 13-2.

FIGURE 13-2
Inserted row on two grouped worksheets

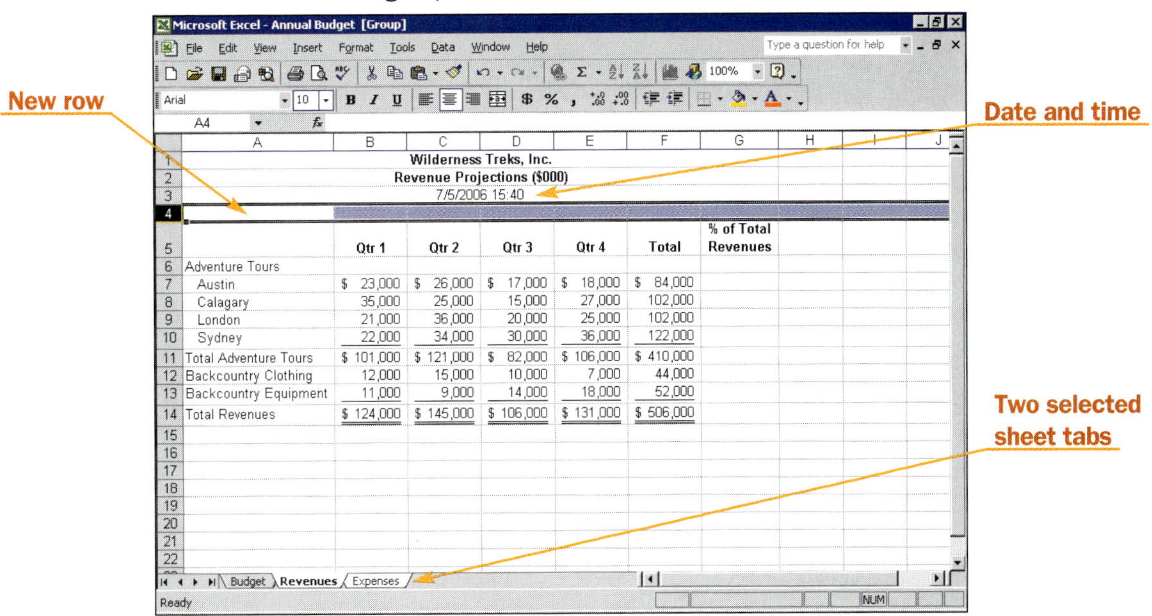

9. Activate cell **A1**, click the **Expenses** sheet tab to verify the new row is inserted on the Expenses worksheet, and click the **Budget** sheet tab.

10. Click the **Expenses** sheet tab and select the range **A12:G12**.

11. Click the **Insert** menu, click **Cells**, verify the **Shift cells down** option button is selected, and click **OK** to insert new cells in the selected range, moving the remaining cells down one row. Your screen should look similar to Figure 13-3.

FIGURE 13-3
Inserted cells

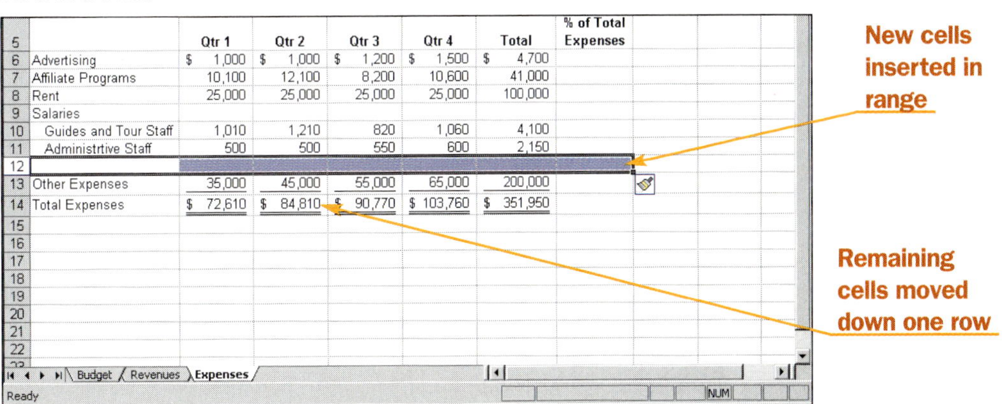

STEP-BY-STEP 13.1 Continued

12. Key **Web Site and Other IT Expenses** in cell A12; key **1200** in cells B12, C12, D12, and E12. 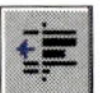 (*Note*: If the Extend list formats and formulas check box in the Edit tab of the Options dialog box is turned on, Excel assumes the new cells in the range A12:G12 are part of a list and automatically adds a formula to cell F12 to sum the range based on the similar formulas in cells F11 and F13.) Use the **AutoSum** button to calculate the total expenses for the new data in cell F12, if necessary.

13. Activate cell **A12** and click the **Decrease Indent** button to remove the indentation.

14. Double-click the column A right boundary to size the column to fit its contents. Your screen should look similar to Figure 13-4.

FIGURE 13-4
New expense data

	A	Qtr 1	Qtr 2	Qtr 3	Qtr 4	Total	% of Total Expenses		
1		Wilderness Treks, Inc.							
2		Expense Projections ($000)							
3		7/5/2006 15:49							
4									
5		Qtr 1	Qtr 2	Qtr 3	Qtr 4	Total	% of Total Expenses		
6	Advertising	$ 1,000	$ 1,000	$ 1,200	$ 1,500	$ 4,700			
7	Affiliate Programs	10,100	12,100	8,200	10,600	41,000			
8	Rent	25,000	25,000	25,000	25,000	100,000			
9	Salaries								
10	Guides and Tour Staff	1,010	1,210	820	1,060	4,100			
11	Administrtive Staff	500	500	550	600	2,150			
12	Web Site and Other IT Expenses	1,200	1,200	1,200	1,200	4,800			
13	Other Expenses	35,000	45,000	55,000	65,000	200,000			
14	Total Expenses	$ 73,810	$ 86,010	$ 91,970	$ 104,960	$ 356,750			

15. Click the **Budget** sheet tab and save the workbook, leaving it and the Budget worksheet open for the next Step-by-Step.

Create Linking Formulas Containing 3-D References

You can create formulas that span multiple worksheets in the same workbook. Cell references from one worksheet included in a formula on another worksheet are called *3-D references*, and such formulas are called *linking formulas*. You now need to summarize revenue and expense data on the Budget worksheet by creating linking formulas with 3-D references to the data on the Revenues and Expenses worksheets. You begin by activating a cell in the Budget worksheet that will contain the linking formula. Then you key the equal sign to indicate you are creating a formula and use the mouse pointer to build the formula by selecting the appropriate worksheet and cells.

Did You Know?

When executing formulas that multiply or divide cell values, Excel calculates the results up to 15 decimal places. If you then choose to display the results with fewer decimal places (for example, no decimal places, which is appropriate for financial data), your worksheet totals may reflect rounding errors. To solve this problem, you can use the ROUND function with your multiplication or division formulas, which allows you to have Excel round its calculations to the same number of decimal places you display in the worksheet. To learn more about using the ROUND function, see Excel online Help.

S TEP-BY-STEP 13.2

1. Verify the Annual Budget workbook is still open and you are viewing the Budget worksheet. Click cell **B6** to activate it.

2. Key **=** to begin the formula, click the **Revenues** sheet tab to view the Revenues worksheet, and click cell **B11** to select the cell's contents. Observe the formula bar and note that the formula you are building now includes the Revenues worksheet and cell B11 3-D references.

3. Press **Enter** to finalize the formula and return to the Budget worksheet. Activate cell **B6** on the Budget worksheet, if necessary, and observe that the linking formula calculates the adventure tours revenues for the first quarter. Your screen should look similar to Figure 13-5.

Linking formula with 3-D references

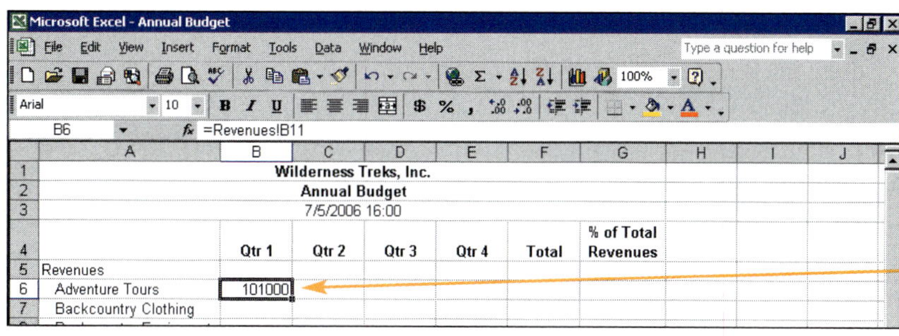

4. Activate cell **B7** on the Budget worksheet, key **=**, click the **Revenues** sheet tab, click cell **B12**, and press **Enter** to create a linking formula that calculates the first quarter revenues for the Backcountry Clothing line.

5. Activate cell **B8** on the Budget worksheet, if necessary, and create a linking formula that calculates the first quarter revenues for the Backcountry Equipment line.

6. Activate cell **B9** on the Budget worksheet, if necessary, and key **=Sum(**.

7. Drag to select the range **B6:B8**. Your formula should look like Figure 13-6.

Formula with Sum function

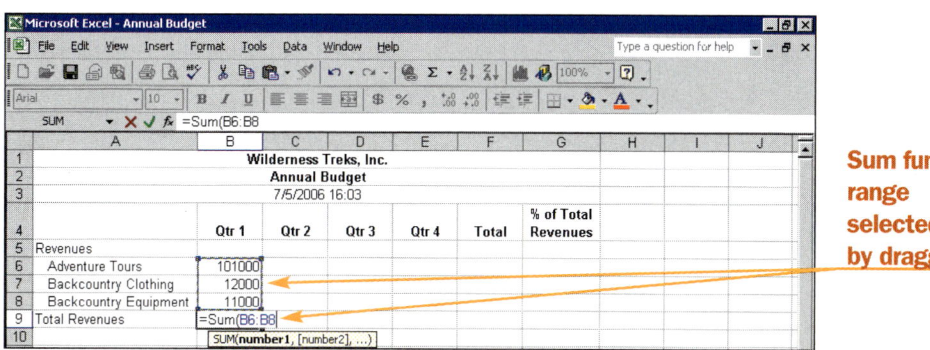

STEP-BY-STEP 13.2 Continued

8. Press **Enter** to finalize the formula that calculates the total first quarter revenues. (Note that Excel automatically adds the closing parenthesis for you.)

9. Activate cell **B12** on the Budget worksheet, key **=**, click the **Expenses** sheet tab, click cell **B6**, and press **Enter** to create a linking formula with 3-D references that calculates the advertising expenses for the first quarter.

10. In cells B13 and B14, create linking formulas with 3-D references that calculate the first quarter Affiliate Programs and Rent expenses, respectively.

11. Activate cell **B15**, key **=**, click the **Expenses** sheet tab, click cell **B10**, press the **Plus (+)** key, and click cell **B11** to build a linking formula that calculates the total salaries for the first quarter. The formula bar on your screen should look similar to Figure 13-7.

FIGURE 13-7
Linking formula with multiple cell references

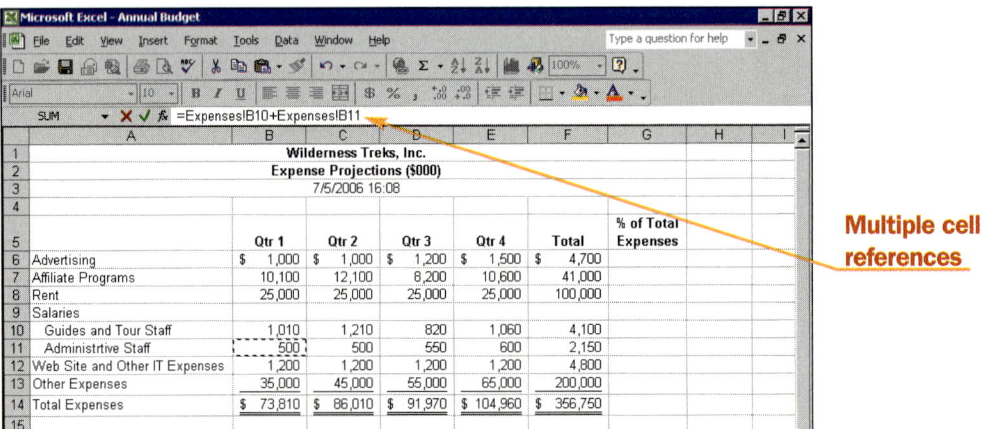

12. Press **Enter** to finalize the formula and return to the Budget worksheet.

13. Activate cell **B16** on the Budget worksheet, if necessary, and create a linking formula with 3-D references that calculates the total Other Expenses for the first quarter by adding the values in cell B12 and cell B13 (Web Site and Other IT Expenses and Other Expenses) on the Expenses worksheet.

14. Activate cell **B17** on the Budget worksheet, if necessary, and create a formula using the Sum function to calculate total expenses.

STEP-BY-STEP 13.2 Continued

15. Activate cell **B19** on the Budget worksheet, if necessary, key **=**, click cell **B9**, press the **Minus (-)** key, and click cell **B17** to create a formula that calculates gross profit (revenues minus expenses) for the first quarter. Your screen should look similar to Figure 13-8.

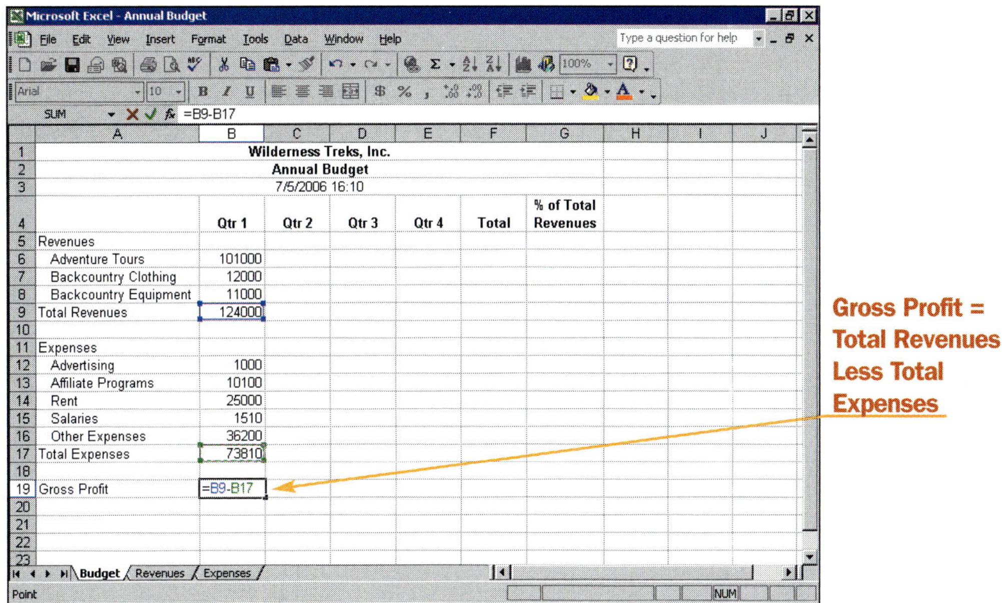

16. Press **Enter** to finalize the formula.

STEP-BY-STEP 13.2 Continued

17. Select the nonadjacent cells **B6**, **B9**, **B12**, **B17**, and **B19** using the **Ctrl** key and format the cell contents with the Currency Style and no decimal places using the Formatting toolbar. Select the ranges **B7:B8** and **B13:B16** using the **Ctrl** key and format the cell contents with the Comma Style and no decimal places using the Formatting toolbar. Select the nonadjacent cells **B8** and **B16** using the **Ctrl** key and apply the Underline format using the Formatting toolbar. Activate cell **B19** and apply the **Double Accounting** underline format using the Font tab in the Format Cells dialog box. After activating cell A1, your screen should look similar to Figure 13-9.

FIGURE 13-9
Formatted first quarter values

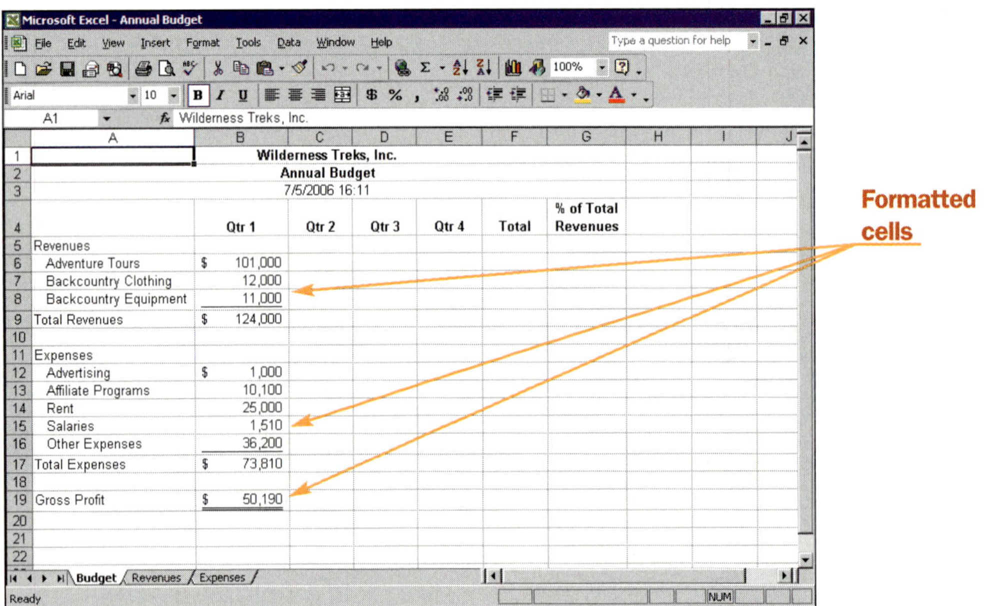

18. Save the workbook and leave it and the Budget worksheet open for the next Step-by-Step.

Copy Formulas with Relative and Absolute Cell References

In order to save time when building a worksheet and creating formulas, you can copy formulas to other cells rather than recreating the formulas from scratch. There are three ways to copy formulas: with relative cell references, absolute cell references, and mixed cell references. You want to copy the formulas you created to calculate the first quarter budget values to the second, third, and fourth quarters. You do this by copying the formulas with relative cell references.

Hot Tip 

The *fill handle* is the small square at the lower-right corner of a selected cell or range of cells. When you place the mouse pointer on the fill handle, the pointer becomes a small black cross-hair pointer. When you drag the fill handle down or to the right to adjacent cells, you copy the cells' contents, including formulas. There are many special ways to use the fill handle. For more information on different ways use the fill handle, see Excel online Help.

Relative Cell References

When you copy a formula containing a *relative cell reference*, the cell reference changes, relative to the cell from which the formula was copied. For example, if cell E1 contains the formula =C1+D1 and you copy the formula down to cell E2, Excel recognizes that cell E2 is one row down from cell E1 and changes the copied formula to =C2+D2 to reflect this. By default, Excel copies all references as relative cell references.

You can use the Copy and Paste commands on the Edit menu, or the Copy and Paste buttons on the Standard toolbar to copy formulas. However, if you are copying formulas to adjacent cells, the fastest way to copy them is with the fill handle. You begin by copying the formula that calculates the first quarter adventure tour revenues to the second, third, and fourth quarters using the fill handle.

$TEP-BY-STEP 13.3

1. Verify that the Annual Budget workbook is open and you are viewing the Budget worksheet. Click cell **B6** to activate it and move the mouse pointer to the cell's fill handle. Your screen should look similar to Figure 13-10.

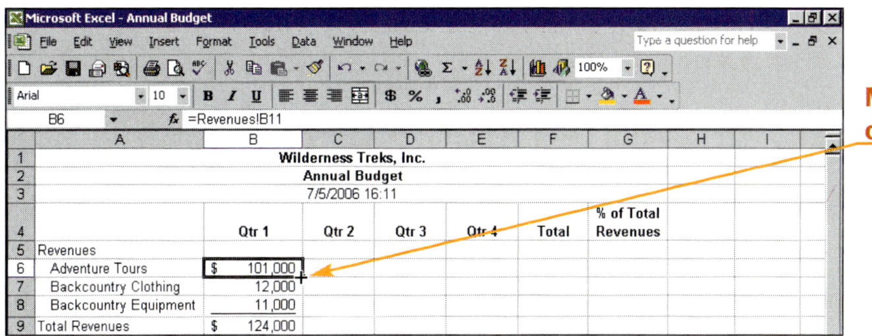

2. Press and hold the left mouse button and drag the fill handle to the right to cell **E6**, then release the mouse button to copy the formula in cell B6 to cells C6, D6, and E6. AutoFit the columns to their contents, if necessary, then activate cell **C6**. Observe the formula bar and note that the original formula in cell B6 (=Revenues!B11) was copied to cell C6 with a relative cell reference (=Revenues!C11). Observe the value in cell C6 and note that the Currency Style with zero decimal places formatting also was copied. Activate cells **D6** and **E6** and review the copied formula in the formula bar and the copied formatting in the cells.

3. Select the range **B7:B19** and drag the fill handle to the range **E7:E19** to copy the remaining formulas and formatting from the first quarter to the second, third, and fourth quarters.

STEP-BY-STEP 13.3 Continued

4. Select the range **B6:F19** and use the AutoSum button on the Standard toolbar to calculate the totals and then deselect the range. AutoFit the columns to their contents, if necessary. Add the appropriate underline formatting to cells **F8**, **F16**, and **F19**. Activate cell **A1**. Your screen should look similar to Figure 13-11.

FIGURE 13-11
Budget totals

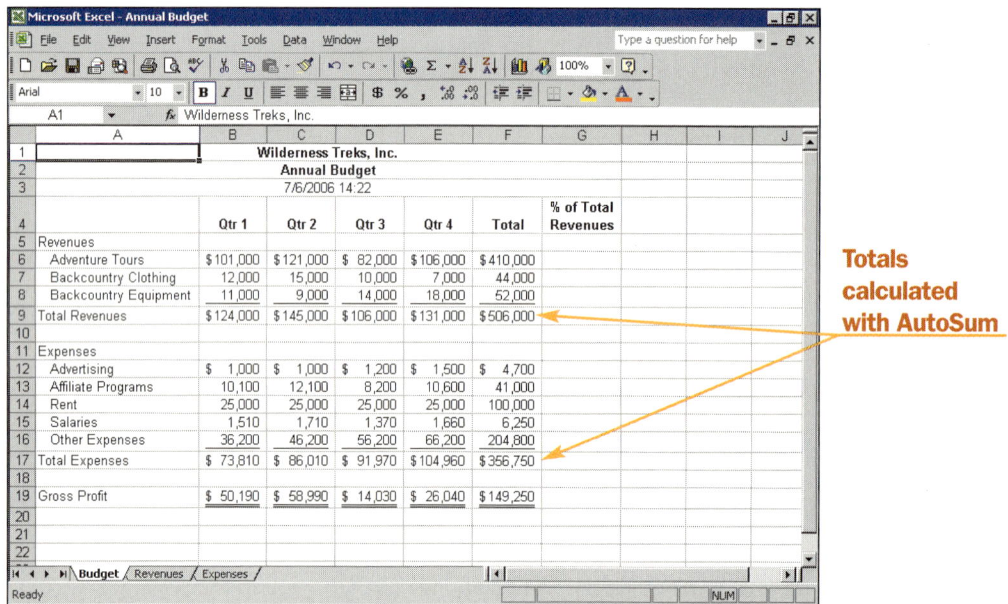

Totals calculated with AutoSum

5. Save the workbook and leave it and the Budget worksheet open for the next Step-by-Step.

Absolute and Mixed Cell References

When you copy a formula containing an *absolute cell reference*, the cell reference does not change, relative to the cell from which the formula was copied. You create a formula with an absolute cell reference when you know you are going to copy the formula and you do not want the cell reference to change; for example, when you want to divide a number of different values by a single value. You indicate an absolute cell reference by adding the dollar sign ($) to the column and row indicators in the cell reference. For example, if you want a formula to contain an absolute cell reference to cell C1, you indicate that absolute cell reference as C1. A *mixed cell reference* is one in which only one component of the reference (either the column indicator or the row indicator) cannot be changed when the formula is copied. Examples of mixed cell references include $C1 (the column reference is held absolute when the formula is copied to the right) or C$1 (the row reference is held absolute when the formula is copied down).

Hot Tip

When creating an absolute or mixed cell reference you can either key the appropriate dollar sign ($) or you can use the F4 key to insert the dollar sign(s) as you create the formula. The F4 key has four options you can cycle through by pressing it multiple times: absolute cell reference (C1), mixed cell reference (C$1), mixed cell reference ($C1), and relative cell reference (no dollar signs).

When analyzing financial data, it is important to know the percentage of individual revenue and expense amounts to their totals and the percentage of gross profit to total revenues. To help Sloan and the vice presidents evaluate the annual budget data, you add formulas to the Budget, Revenues, and Expenses worksheets that calculate several percentages. You begin by calculating the percentage of adventure tours revenues to total revenues. You do this by dividing the adventure tours revenues by the total revenues and then formatting the result as a percentage with one decimal place. Then you copy the formula to calculate the percentage of backcountry clothing and equipment revenues to total revenues.

STEP-BY-STEP 13.4

1. Verify that the Annual Budget workbook is open and you are viewing the Budget worksheet. Click cell **G6** to activate it, key **=**, click cell **F6**, press the **Forward Slash** (/) key, click cell **F9**, and press the **F4** key to build a formula containing an absolute cell reference. The formula on your screen should look similar to Figure 13-12.

FIGURE 13-12
Formula with absolute cell reference

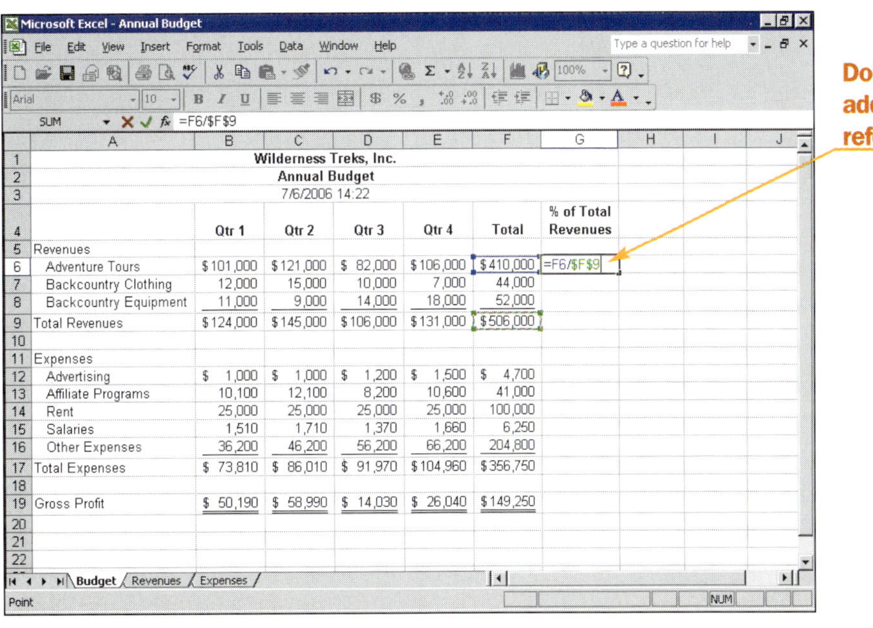

2. Press **Enter** to finalize the formula.

3. Activate cell **G6**, if necessary, click the **Percent Style** button on the Formatting toolbar, and click the **Increase Decimal** button on the formatting toolbar to format the cell contents as a percentage with one decimal point. 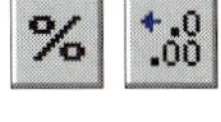

4. Use the fill handle to copy the formula and formatting in cell G6 to adjacent cells G7 and G8.

5. Activate cell **G17** and create a formula containing an absolute reference that calculates total expenses as a percentage of total revenues. Format the cell with the Percent Style and one decimal place.

6. Copy the formula in cell G17 and paste it into nonadjacent cell G19 using the **Copy** and **Paste** buttons on the Formatting toolbar.  

STEP-BY-STEP 13.4 Continued

7. Click the **Revenues** sheet tab and insert formulas in the appropriate cells to calculate the percentage of total revenues applicable to each branch, to Backcountry Clothing, and to Backcountry Equipment. Format the cells containing the formulas with the Percent Style and one decimal place. Your screen should look similar to Figure 13-13.

FIGURE 13-13
Percentage of total revenues

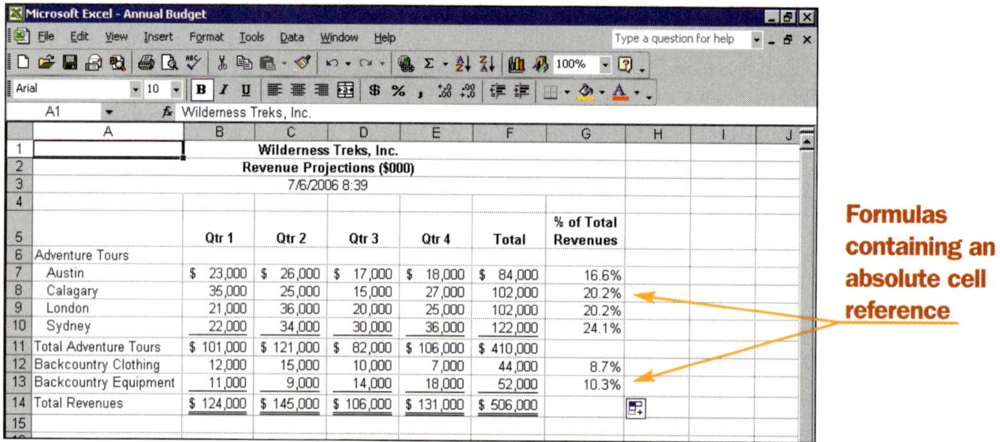

8. Click the **Expenses** sheet tab and insert formulas in the appropriate cells to calculate the percentage of total expenses applicable to each expense category. Format the cells containing the formulas with the Percent Style and one decimal place. Your screen should look similar to Figure 13-14.

FIGURE 13-14
Percentage of total expenses

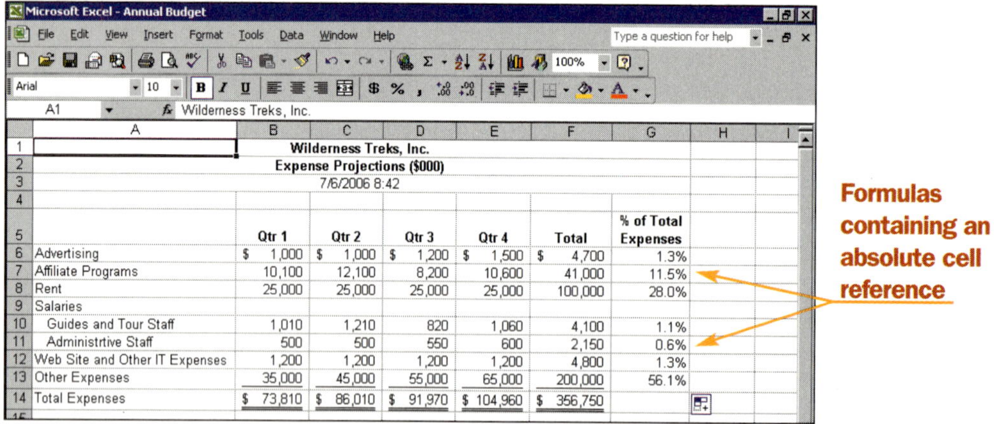

9. Click the **Budget** sheet tab, click cell **A1**, and save the workbook leaving it and the Budget worksheet open for the next Step-by-Step.

Insert Comments

A *comment* is a note you can insert in a cell to add an additional explanation about the cell's contents. When you insert a comment in a cell, a small red comment indicator appears in the upper-left corner of the cell. To read a comment, simply move the mouse pointer to the cell containing the comment indicator. You want to remind Sloane and the Vice Presidents that the preliminary revenue and expense estimates were provided by Bob Davenport. You can easily do this by inserting comments in the Budget worksheet.

STEP-BY-STEP 13.5

1. Verify that the Annual Budget workbook is open and you are viewing the Budget worksheet. Click cell **F9** on the Budget worksheet to activate it, click the **Insert** menu, and click **Comment** to add a comment to cell F9.

2. Key **Preliminary revenue data provided by Bob Davenport.** in the Comment box.

3. Click cell **A1** to activate it and observe the small, red comment indicator in cell F9. Move the mouse pointer to cell F9 (*do not click the cell*) to read the comment text. Your screen should look similar to Figure 13-15.

FIGURE 13-15
Comment

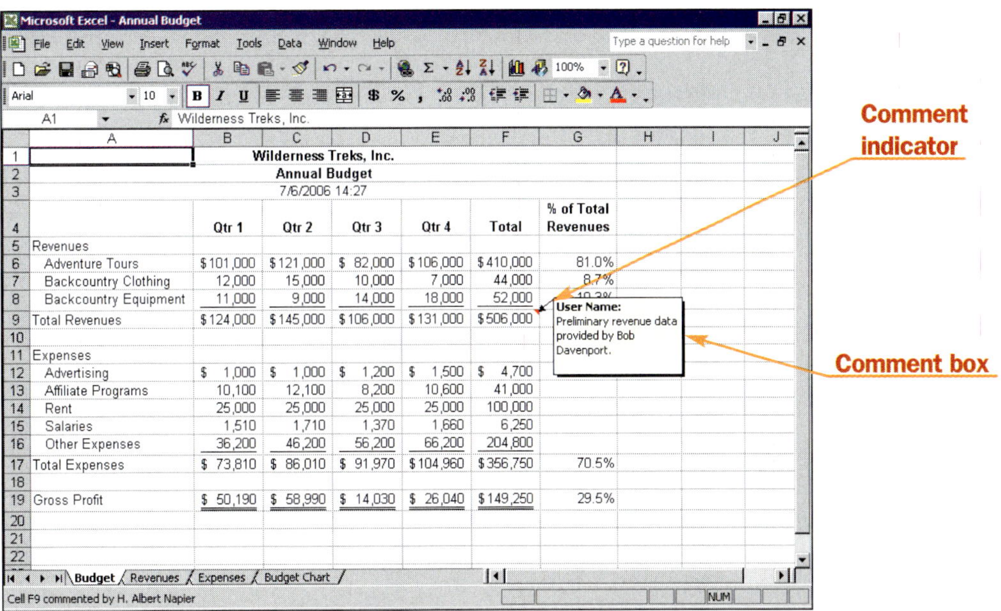

4. Insert a comment in cell **F17** that states the preliminary expense data was provided by Bob Davenport.

5. Save the workbook and leave it and the Budget worksheet open for the next Step-by-Step.

Check Spelling

An important part of preparing a worksheet is to be certain that there are no spelling errors. Before you print any of the Annual Budget worksheets, you need to check the spelling on the worksheets. Spell checking a worksheet is similar to spell checking a Word document. You can use the Spelling command on the Tools menu or the Spelling button on the Standard toolbar to begin the spell checking process. You can also spell check an individual worksheet, or you can check the spelling on multiple worksheets at one time by grouping them.

Note

The Annual Budget workbook contains two deliberately misspelled words; however, you may have inadvertently introduced other misspellings as you worked in the workbook. As you complete Step-by-Step 13.6, remember to correct any additional misspelled words that may appear.

STEP-BY-STEP 13.6

1. Verify that the Annual Budget workbook is open and you are viewing the Budget worksheet. Use the **Shift** key to group the Budget, Revenues, and Expenses worksheets, then click cell **A1** to activate it.

2. Click the **Spelling** button on the Standard toolbar to begin the process and open the Spelling  dialog box. Excel finds a misspelled word on the Expenses worksheet. Your dialog box should look similar to Figure 13-16. Note that your name may appear as a misspelling prior to Adminstrtive.

Did You Know?

When you spell check a worksheet, the spelling in any comments you inserted is also checked.

FIGURE 13-16
Spelling dialog box

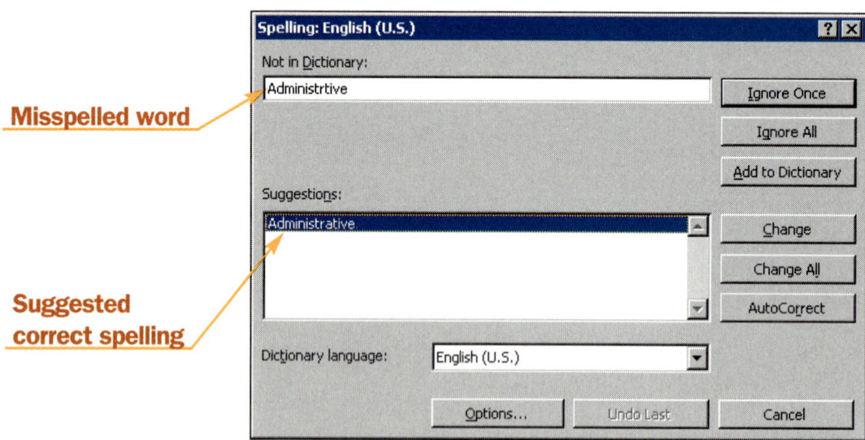

3. Click **Change** to correct the misspelled word *Administrtive* to *Administrative*. Excel then finds a misspelled word on the Revenues worksheet.

4. Click **Change** to correct the misspelled word *Calagary* to *Calgary*. Excel finds no misspelled words on the Budget worksheet.

STEP-BY-STEP 13.6 Continued

5. Click **OK** to complete the spell checking process.

6. Ungroup the worksheets, click the **Budget** sheet tab, click cell **A1**, and save the workbook, leaving it and the Budget worksheet open for the next Step-by-Step.

Create and Format Charts

You can help worksheet readers better understand complex values, such as budget data, by using charts to illustrate that data. To create a chart, you must first select the cells that contain the headings and data to be charted and then you create the chart with the Chart Wizard. A chart can be placed on its own chart sheet in the workbook, or it can be embedded as an object on the worksheet that contains the data. After you create a chart, you can use the Chart menu or Chart toolbar to edit the chart.

When you create a new chart, the Chart toolbar should automatically appear either docked with the Standard and Formatting toolbars or floating in its own window, depending on where it was last displayed. If it does not automatically appear, you can show it with the Toolbars command on the View menu or with the toolbar shortcut menu.

Create a Chart on Its Own Chart Sheet

You want to add a column chart to the Annual Budget workbook that shows the relationship between total revenues, total expenses, and gross profit. You begin by selecting the column headings and data and then using a shortcut key to create a default column chart on its own sheet.

STEP-BY-STEP 13.7

1. Verify that the Annual Budget workbook is open and you are viewing the Budget worksheet. Select the nonadjacent ranges **A4:E4**, **A9:E9**, **A17:E17**, and **A19:E19** using the **Ctrl** key.

2. Press the **F11** key to create a default column chart on the Chart1 sheet. Observe that the X axis was determined by the longer side of the selected data—the column headings; and the Y axis was determined by the shorter side of the selected data—the row headings.

Did You Know?

You can quickly create a default column chart on its own chart sheet by selecting the headings and data to be charted and then pressing the F11 key. When Excel reads your selected cells, it *guesses* the Category (X) axis and Value (Y) axis of the chart based on the way the cells are selected. The longer side of the selection becomes the X axis and the shorter side of the selection becomes the Y axis. If Excel makes an incorrect guess about which values to place on the X or Y axis and the resulting chart does not explain the data appropriately, you can switch the data orientation with a button on the Chart toolbar.

STEP-BY-STEP 13.7 Continued

3. Rename the Chart1 sheet tab as **Budget Chart** and then drag the Budget Chart sheet tab to the right and drop it after the Expenses worksheet tab. Your screen should look similar to Figure 13-17.

FIGURE 13-17
Budget Chart

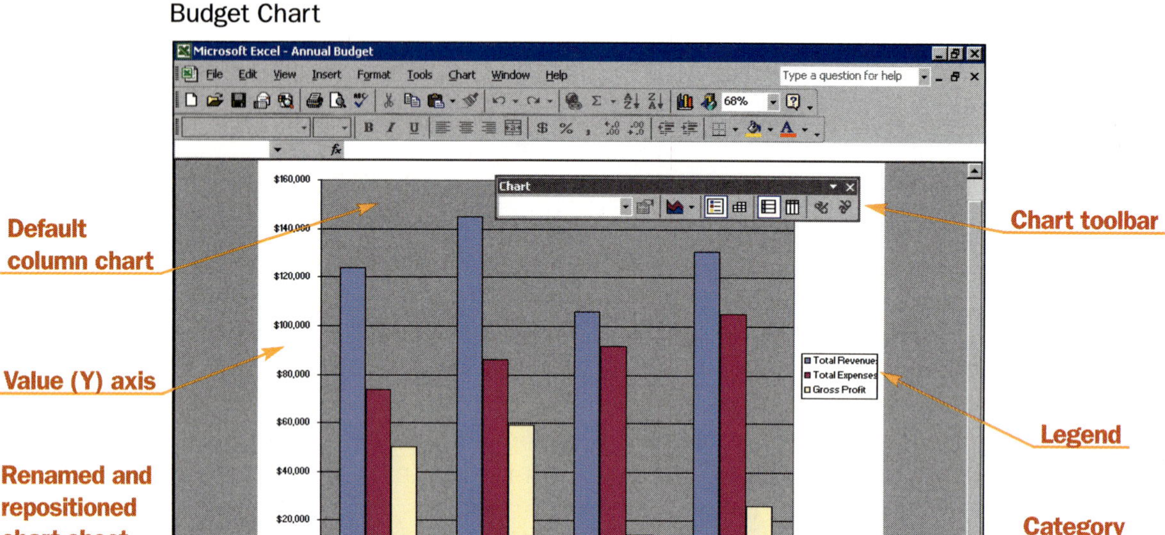

4. Double-click a Total Revenues data point and change the fill color to red in the Format Data Series dialog box. Then change the Total Expenses data series fill color to blue and the Gross Profit data series fill color to green. Remember to press **Esc** to deselect any selected chart object such as a selected data series before going to the next step.

5. Double-click the **Legend**, click the **Placement** tab in the Format Legend dialog box, click the **Bottom** option button, and click **OK** to reposition the legend at the bottom of the chart.

6. Save the workbook and leave it open for the next Step-by-Step.

Create a Chart as an Embedded Object on a Worksheet

Pie charts are used to illustrate the relationship of individual data points to the total of all the data points and by definition have only one data series.

You want to add a pie chart to the Revenues worksheet to illustrate the relationship of each branch office's adventure tours revenues to total adventure tours revenue. First, you select the headings and data to be charted and then you use the Chart Wizard to create the embedded chart.

STEP-BY-STEP 13.8

1. Verify that the Annual Budget workbook is open. Click the **Revenues** sheet tab and select the nonadjacent ranges **A7:A10** and **F7:F10** using the **Ctrl** key.

2. Click the **Chart Wizard** button on the Standard toolbar to open the Chart Wizard Step 1 of 4 dialog box, click **Pie** in the Chart type list, and click the **3-D chart type** (second option in first row). Your dialog box should look similar to Figure 13-18. 

FIGURE 13-18
Chart Wizard Step 1 of 4 dialog box

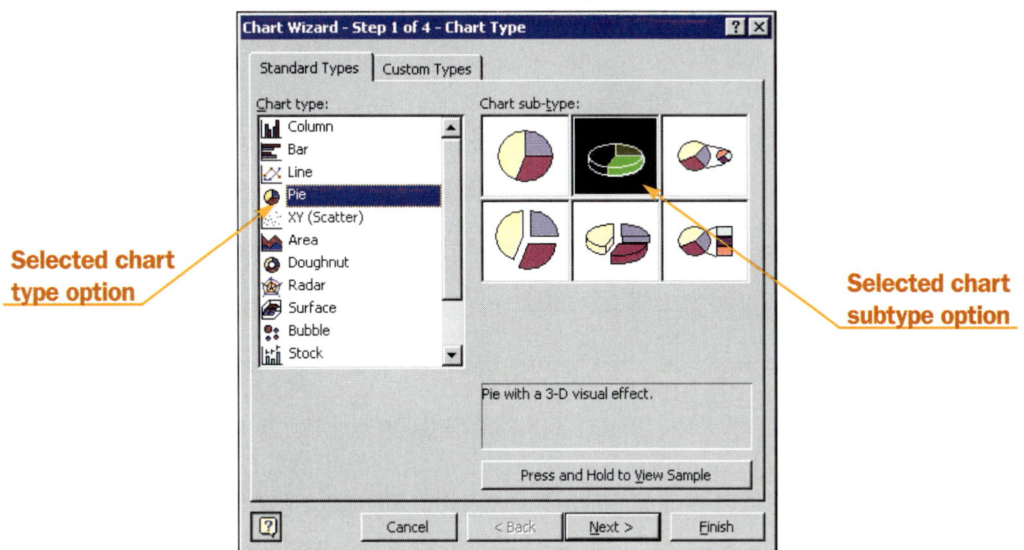

3. Click **Next** to go to the Chart Wizard Step 2 of 4 dialog box. The Series in columns option button is automatically selected, which appropriately displays the data in a pie chart with a legend. Click **Next** to go to the Chart Wizard Step 3 of 4 dialog box.

STEP-BY-STEP 13.8 Continued

4. Key **Adventure Tours Revenues** in the Chart title text box. Click the **Legend** tab and click the **Show legend** check box to remove the check mark. Click the **Data Labels** tab and click the **Category name** and **Percentage** check boxes to insert a check mark. (If you are using Excel 2000, click the **Show label and percent** option button.) Your dialog box should look similar to Figure 13-19.

FIGURE 13-19
Chart Wizard Step 3 of 4 dialog box

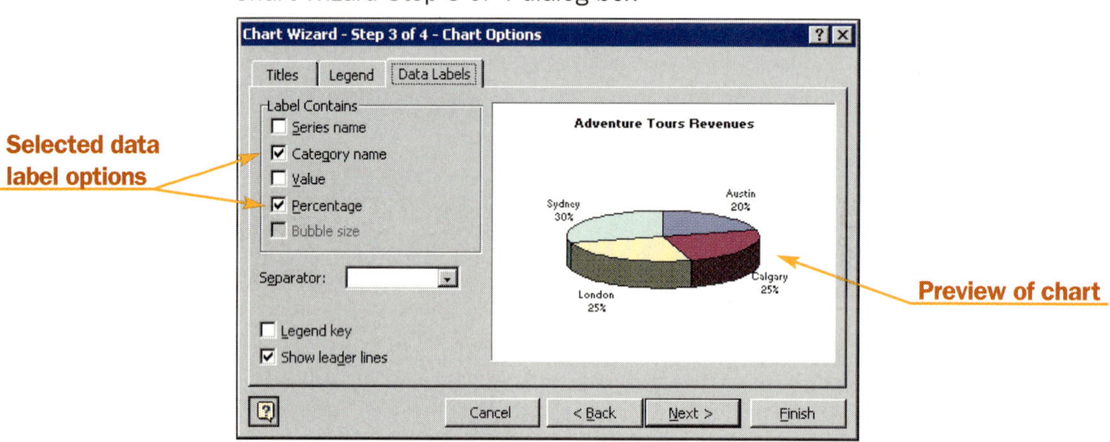

5. Click **Next** to go to the Chart Wizard Step 4 of 4 dialog box. Verify that the option As object in is selected and click the Revenues worksheet from the drop-down list, if necessary. Then click **Finish** to insert the 3-D pie chart as an embedded object in the Revenues worksheet.

6. Drag the selected chart object downward until its upper-left corner is at cell B17. Your screen should look similar to Figure 13-20. Resize the chart, if necessary.

FIGURE 13-20
Embedded chart object

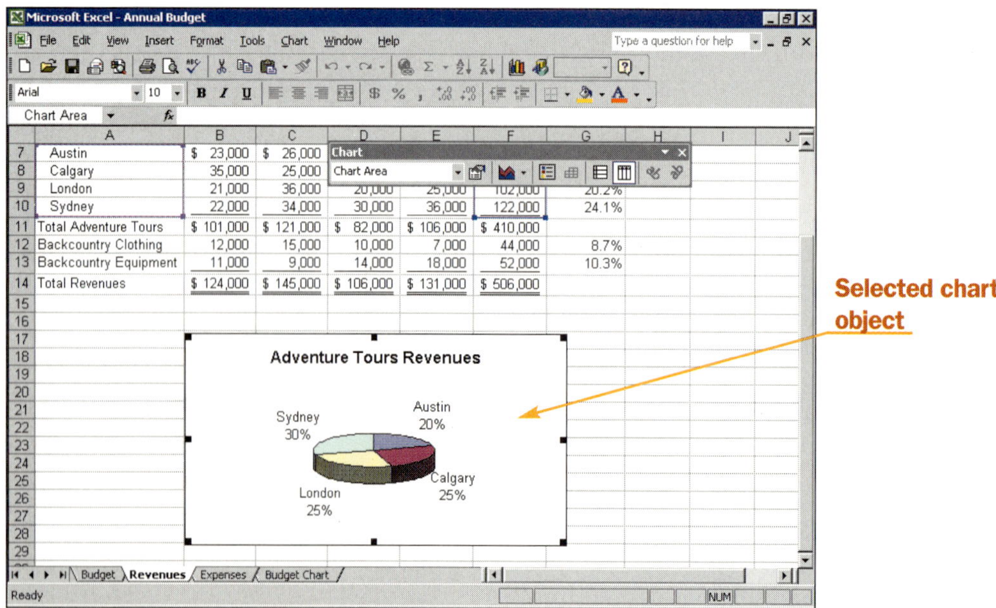

STEP-BY-STEP 13.8 Continued

7. Click the London data point to select the entire data series and then click the London data point a second time (*do not double-click*) to select only the London data point in the series. Right-click the selected data point and click Format Data Point to open the Format Data Point dialog box and change the data point fill color to red. Change the Sydney data point fill color to blue, the Austin data point fill color to green, and the Calgary data point fill color to yellow. Click in the worksheet outside the chart object to deselect it.

8. Click the **Budget** sheet tab, click cell **A1** to activate it, and then save the workbook, leaving it and the Budget worksheet open for the next Step-by-Step.

Set Page Setup Options and a Print Area

You can change worksheet orientation from Portrait to Landscape and vice versa, set margins, specify rows and columns to print, and set other print options in the Page Setup dialog box. When you work with a large worksheet, you may frequently print only a small range of cells instead of the entire active area of the worksheet. You can specify a range of cells to print, called a **print area**, by keying the print area range in the Sheet tab of the Page Setup dialog box. You also can specify a print area by first selecting a range of cells and then clicking the Set Print Area subcommand under the Print Area command on the File menu.

To review the Annual Budget worksheets, you want to print the Budget, Revenues, Expenses, and Budget Chart sheets in Landscape orientation. To take advantage of the increased width of the paper, you also want to widen the left and right margins. Finally, Bob Davenport calls and asks you to print him the data portion of the Revenues worksheet only. As you review the printed worksheets, you notice that the second title line in cell A2 on the Budget worksheet is missing the ($000) reference that indicates all the values are in thousands. You complete the annual budget by editing the contents of cell A2 to add the ($000) reference using the formula bar.

> **Did You Know?** 
>
> When you have an embedded chart on a worksheet and want to print only the chart and not the data, first click the chart to select it. Then when you preview and print the worksheet, only the chart is previewed and printed. If you do not select the embedded chart, both the data and the chart are previewed and printed.

STEP-BY-STEP 13.9

1. Verify that the Annual Budget workbook is open and you are viewing the Budget worksheet. Group the Budget, Revenues, Expenses, and Budget Chart sheets using the **Shift** key.

2. Click **File** on the menu bar, click **Page Setup** to open the Page Setup dialog box, click the **Page** tab, if necessary, and click the **Landscape** option button.

3. Click the **Margins** tab, key **1.5** in the Left and Right margin text boxes, and click **Print Preview** to preview the new page setup. Scroll to view each of the pages and then return to the Budget worksheet page. Print the worksheets and chart sheet and then ungroup the sheets.

STEP-BY-STEP 13.9 Continued

4. Click the **Revenues** sheet tab, if necessary, and select the range **A1:G14**. Click the **File** menu, point to **Print Area**, and click **Set Print Area**. Then print preview and print the revenues data.

5. Click the **Revenues** sheet tab, if necessary, click the **File** menu, point to **Print Area**, and click **Clear Print Area** to remove the print area setting from the worksheet. Deselect the range.

6. Click the **Budget** sheet tab, if necessary, and click cell **A2** to activate it. Click in the **formula bar** at the end of the Annual Budget text, press the **Spacebar**, key **($000)**, and press **Enter**.

7. Save the workbook, leaving it and the Budget worksheet open for the next Step-by-Step.

Save a Workbook as a Web Page

Sloane stops by your desk to discuss the annual budget worksheets. Some of the vice presidents have asked for a copy of the worksheets prior to the end-of-conference meeting. Sloane suggests you save the entire workbook as a Web page so that it can be posted to the company intranet. Then each of the vice presidents can view the worksheets as time permits. You begin by previewing the workbook as a Web page and then you save it as a Web page.

Did You Know?

If you save an entire workbook or an individual worksheet as a Web page with the Interactivity option turned on, viewers can actually manipulate the data, create formulas, format cells, and perform other actions while viewing the Web page in their Web browser. Any changes made by the viewer are only made to the open Web page (not to the original saved Web page) and are lost when the viewer closes his or her Web browser. If the viewer wants to save the changes, he or she must export the Web page back to Excel, creating a new workbook. For more information on saving a workbook or worksheet as a Web page with interactivity, see Excel online Help.

STEP-BY-STEP 13.10

1. Verify that the Annual Budget workbook is open and you are viewing the Budget worksheet. Click the **File** menu, and click **Web Page Preview** to launch your Web browser and view the workbook as a Web page. Maximize your Web browser, if necessary. Your screen should look similar to Figure 13-21.

FIGURE 13-21
Web Page Preview

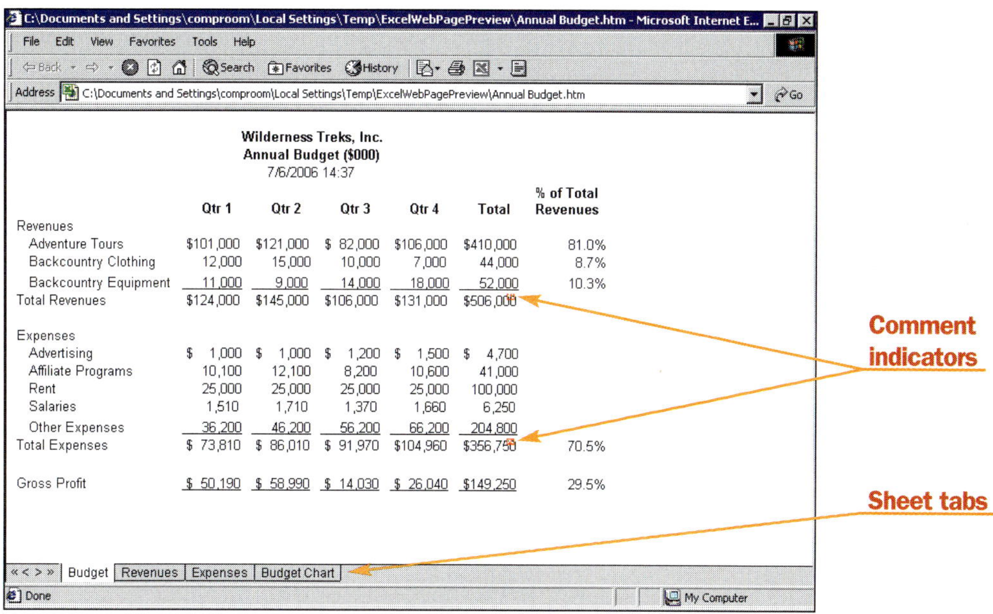

2. Click each sheet tab to view the worksheet or chart as a Web page and then close your Web browser.

3. Click the **File** menu, and click **Save as Web Page** to open the Save As dialog box.

4. Verify that the Entire Workbook option button is selected and click **Save**.

5. Close the workbook and close Excel.

SUMMARY

In this job, you learned:

- You can insert rows, columns, and a range of cells in a worksheet.

- You can group or select multiple adjacent or nonadjacent worksheets in order to perform the same action on the selected worksheets at one time.

- Formulas that span multiple worksheets in the same workbook are called linking formulas with 3-D references.

- By default, Excel copies formulas with relative cell references—cell references that change relative to the cell from which the formula was copied. When you do not want cell references to change in a copied formula, you use dollar signs ($) to create absolute or mixed cell references.

- The fastest way to copy cell contents including formulas to adjacent cells is with the fill handle.

- A comment is a note you can insert in a cell to provide additional explanatory information.

- It is important to remember to check the spelling on your worksheets.

- You can use charts based on Excel worksheet data to help readers better understand that data. Excel charts can be placed on their own chart sheet or can be embedded as an object on a worksheet that contains the charted data.

- You can use the Page Setup dialog box to change the margins, paper orientation, and other print options.

- To print a range of cells instead of the entire active worksheet, you can first select the range and then set that range as the print area.

- You can save an entire workbook or an individual worksheet as a Web page.

VOCABULARY *Review*

Define the following terms:

3-D reference	Fill handle	Mixed cell reference
Absolute cell reference	Grouping	Print area
Comment	Linking formulas	Relative cell reference

REVIEW *Questions*

TRUE / FALSE

Circle T if the statement is true or F if the statement is false.

T   F   **1.** You use the Alt key when grouping nonadjacent worksheets.

T   F   **2.** By default, Excel copies formulas with mixed cell references.

T   F   **3.** The fastest way to copy a formula to adjacent cells is with the Copy and Paste buttons on the Formatting toolbar.

T   F   **4.** You can press the F4 key to create a relative cell reference.

T   F   **5.** You cannot save an entire workbook as a Web page with interactivity.

FILL IN THE BLANK

Complete the following sentences by writing the correct word or words in the blanks provided.

1. To bold the contents of cell C1 on three worksheets at one time, you must first __________ the worksheets.

2. Formulas that span worksheets are called _____________ formulas.

3. The cell reference E5 is a(n) _____________ cell reference.

4. To add additional explanatory information to a worksheet cell, you can insert a(n) _____________.

5. To quickly create a default column chart from selected Excel data, you can press the _____________ key.

PROJECTS

PROJECT 13-1

1. Open Excel and open the **Project 13-1** workbook from the data files.

2. Save the workbook as **Sydney Budget**.

3. Group the Budget and Expenses worksheets and insert a row at row 2. Add the heading text **Sydney Branch** in the new cell A2.

4. Click cell **A3** and, using the formula bar, edit the heading text to add the thousands reference ($000). Then ungroup the worksheets.

5. Create linking formulas with 3-D references from the Budget worksheet to the Expenses worksheet to calculate the first quarter expenses. Then copy the formulas to the second, third, and fourth quarters.

6. Create formulas on the Budget worksheet to calculate the total expenses and gross profit for each quarter and the total revenues and expenses for all four quarters. Format the worksheet appropriately for financial data.

7. Click cell **G14** on the Budget worksheet and create a formula with an absolute reference that calculates the percentage of total expenses to total revenues. Format the result as a percentage with one decimal place. Copy the formula to cell **G16**.

8. Click cell **G6** on the Expenses worksheet and create a formula with an absolute reference that calculates the percentage of advertising expense to total expenses. Format the result as a percentage with one decimal place. Copy the formula to the range **G7:G8** and **G10:G12**.

9. Spell check the worksheets.

10. Set a print area on the Budget worksheet to print only the total expenses and gross profit data. Print the worksheet and then clear the print area.

11. Group the worksheets, change the paper orientation to Landscape and the left and right margins to 1.25, and print the worksheets. Then ungroup the worksheets, save the workbook, and close it.

PROJECT 13-2

Bob Davenport sends you an e-mail asking you to make some changes to the Sydney branch office annual budget workbook. He asks you to add a comment to the total adventure tours revenue value indicating that the data was provided by Liz Bourke in the Sydney office. He also asks you to add two formulas to the Budget worksheet to calculate the quarters with the minimum and maximum adventure tours revenues using the MIN and MAX functions. Finally, he asks you to save the workbook as a Web page to be posted to the company intranet. Open the **Sydney Budget** workbook you completed in Project 13-1. If you haven't completed the project, do so now. Save the workbook as **Sydney Budget with Comment** and insert the requested comment in cell F6. Insert the minimum and maximum quarterly revenue row headings and formulas in the range A18:B19. (Use Excel online Help, if necessary, to review the MIN and MAX functions.) Save the workbook and print the worksheets. Then preview the workbook as a Web page, save it as a Web page, and close it.

WEB PROJECT

Sloane calls to tell you that a very important international client is visiting the Austin headquarters next Tuesday and asks you to arrange for two-day hotel accommodations, limousine service to and from the airport, and dinner reservations for four on Tuesday evening. The dinner reservations should be at a restaurant that offers Texas food specialties. Using your Web browser's search tool or a search engine such as HotBot (*www.hotbot.com*), search for Web sites you can use to make the necessary arrangements. Print at least five Web pages.

TEAMWORK PROJECT

Melody Stackhouse sends you an e-mail message advising that she has several new summer interns on staff and wants you to present a 30-minute brown bag lunch review of several useful Excel features for the interns on next Thursday. She asks you to discuss and demonstrate how to move the contents of selected cells, how to clear cell contents, how to freeze and unfreeze panes, how to modify row height and column width, how to insert and delete worksheets in a workbook, and how to apply an AutoFormat to worksheets. Select two classmates to help you with this project. Then using Excel online Help, if necessary, review Melody's selected Excel topics. Then, using workbooks of your choice, discuss and demonstrate how to use the specified Excel features.

CRITICAL*Thinking*

ACTIVITY 13-1

As Sloane's administrative assistant, you are often called on to assist other employees to complete critical projects. One of the difficult situations you sometimes experience is locating information in a workbook that you did not create and with which you are not familiar. Excel provides three features that can help in this situation: Find and Replace, Go To, and AutoFilter. Using Excel online Help, review how to use options in the Find and Replace dialog box, how to use the Go To dialog box options, and how to turn on and off and use AutoFilter. Using the workbooks of your choice, practice using these features and then demonstrate the features to a classmate.

EDITING PRESENTATION SLIDE AND TITLE SLIDE MASTERS

<table>
<tr><td>

OBJECTIVES

Upon completion of this job, you should be able to:

- Create a presentation using the AutoContent Wizard.

- Modify a presentation using the title slide and slide masters.

- Insert, delete, and move slides and modify slide text.

- Preview and print slides and handouts.

Estimated Time: 0.5 hour

</td><td>

VOCABULARY

AutoContent Wizard

Slide master

Title slide master

</td></tr>
</table>

Create a Presentation Using the AutoContent Wizard

You are asked to chair a meeting of the Conference Planning Committee to be held this afternoon from 2:00 to 2:30 p.m. The purpose of this afternoon's meeting is to have each committee member report on the status of his or her conference responsibilities. Because of time constraints on several committee members' schedules, the meeting must be brief and to the point. To maximize the short time available, you create a PowerPoint presentation you can run from your laptop to help clarify the meeting agenda and direct the meeting's progress. You begin by creating a presentation using the AutoContent Wizard, and then you modify the presentation's design and text.

The *AutoContent Wizard* allows you to save time by quickly creating a presentation for a common business purpose, such as selling a product or service, an employee orientation, or an employee brainstorming session. Presentations created with the AutoContent Wizard have a default design template applied and sample text inserted on a number of slides. You simply modify the design template and sample text to suit your needs.

STEP-BY-STEP 14.1

1. Start the PowerPoint application and click the **From AutoContent Wizard** link in the New Presentation task pane to launch the AutoContent Wizard. (If you are using PowerPoint 2000, click the **AutoContent Wizard** option button in the PowerPoint dialog box and click **OK** to launch the AutoContent Wizard.)

2. Click **Next** to choose the presentation type.

3. Click the **Projects** button and click **Reporting Progress or Status** in the list box. Your AutoContent Wizard dialog box should look similar to Figure 14-1.

Did You Know?

You can use the PowerPoint Meeting Minder feature to key minutes during a meeting and create action items (to do items) for meeting attendees while running a slide show. Simply right-click to view the slide show shortcut menu and then click **Meeting Minder**. Key the minutes in the Meeting Minutes text box or set the action items options in the Action Items tab. For more information on using the Meeting Minder feature, see PowerPoint online Help.

FIGURE 14-1
AutoContent Wizard presentation type

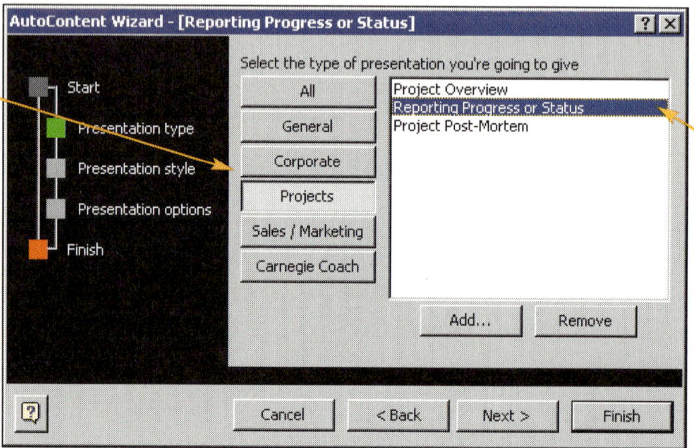

4. Click **Next** to choose the presentation style.

5. Click the **On-screen presentation** option button, if necessary, and click **Next** to choose the presentation options.

6. Key **Conference Planning Committee Meeting** in the Presentation title text box, click the **Date last updated** check box to remove the check mark, and click the **Slide number** check box to insert a check mark, if necessary. Your AutoContent Wizard dialog box should look similar to Figure 14-2.

STEP-BY-STEP 14.1 Continued

FIGURE 14-2
AutoContent Wizard presentation options

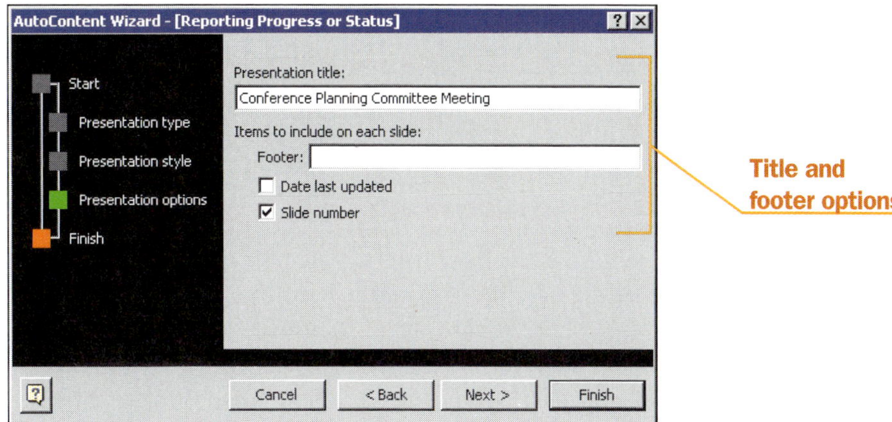

7. Click **Next** and then click **Finish** to complete the AutoContent Wizard process.

8. Select the name that appears in the Subtitle Area placeholder on the title slide and key your name, if necessary. Then click outside the slide to deselect the placeholder contents.

9. Scroll to view all the slides and their sample text and then view Slide 1 (title slide).

10. Save the presentation as **Conference Planning Committee Meeting** and leave it open for the next Step-by-Step.

Modify a Presentation Using the Title Slide and Slide Masters

The *slide master* allows you to control the formatting for all the slides (except the title slide) in a presentation, including font, font size, color schemes, bullet graphics, headers and footers, and other elements. The *title slide master* allows you to control the formatting on any title slides in the presentation. Making changes to the title slide and slide masters enables you to format all the slides automatically, instead of manually formatting each slide. The elements you see on the title and slide masters are based on the design template applied to the slides.

You want to use the slide and title masters to remove the footer from any title slides in the presentation, change the design template's color scheme, change the title text default font, center the title text on all slides, change the first-level bullet graphic on all title and text slides, and insert a picture on all slides except the title slide.

Change the Slide Color Scheme, Font, Font Color and Text Alignment Using the Title Slide Master

You begin by modifying the title slide master. First, you view the title slide master, and then you change the slide color scheme, change the default font from Times New Roman to Arial, delete a graphic object, and delete the Footer Area and Number Area placeholders. Then you center-align the subtitle text and change its font color to white.

You can manually format a slide to override the formatting in the slide or title master; however, if you first manually format slides *and then modify the slide or title slide masters*, your manually formatted slides are not changed based on the changes to the masters. In other words, although you can an override the slide or title slide master formatting, the slide or title master formatting cannot automatically override your manual formatting. For this reason, it is a good idea to make slide or title slide master changes first and then make any individual slide formatting changes you desire.

Hot Tip

If you delete placeholders on a slide or slide title master, you can restore them by clicking the Master Layout button on the Slide Master View toolbar.

S TEP-BY-STEP 14.2

1. Verify the Conference Planning Committee Meeting presentation is still open and you are viewing Slide 1 (title slide). Click the **View** menu, point to **Master**, and click **Slide Master** to view the title slide master. (If you are using PowerPoint 2000, click **View** on the menu bar, point to **Master**, and click **Title Master**.)

2. Click the **Slide Design** button on the Formatting toolbar to view the Slide Design task pane and then click the **Color Schemes** link in the task pane to view the alternate color schemes for the design template. Click the second color scheme in the first row (blue background). (If you are using PowerPoint 2000, click the **Format** menu, and click **Slide Color Scheme**. Then click the second color scheme and click **Apply to All**.) Your screen should look similar to Figure 14-3.

STEP-BY-STEP 14.2 Continued

FIGURE 14-3
Modified color scheme

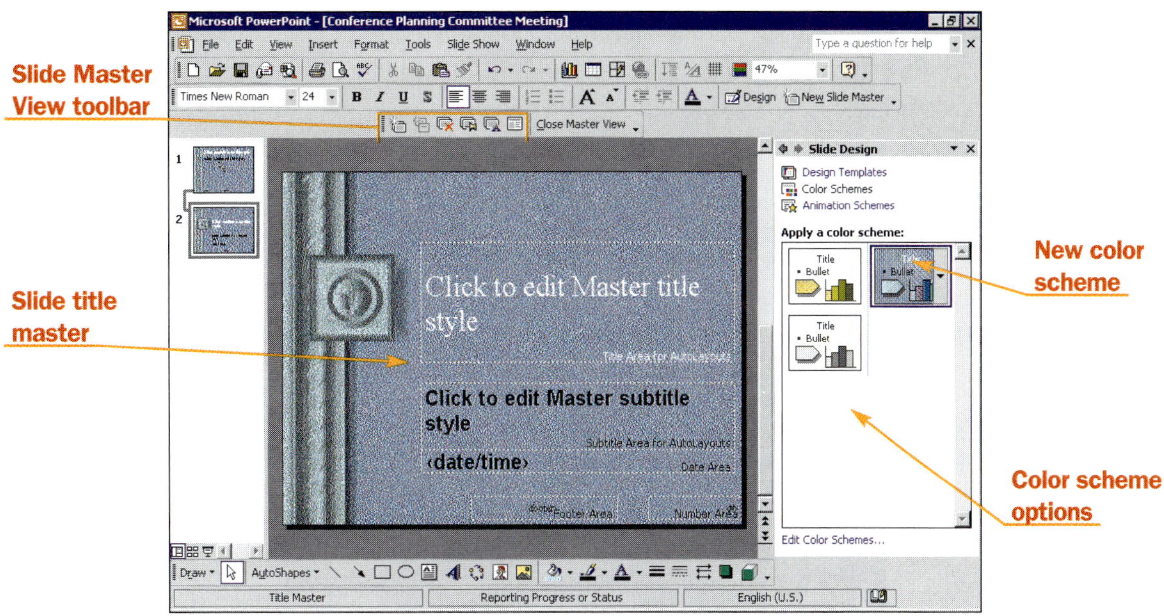

3. Click the **Format** menu, and click **Replace Fonts**. Verify that Times New Roman appears in the Replace text box. Click the **With** text box list arrow and click **Arial**, if necessary. Your Replace Fonts dialog box should look similar to Figure 14-4.

FIGURE 14-4
Replace Font dialog box

4. Click **Replace** and then click **Close**. Observe that the sample text in the Title Area placeholder is now formatted with the Arial font.

5. Click the large square graphic object to the left of the Title Area placeholder to select it and then press **Delete** to delete it.

6. Click the **Footer Area** placeholder, press and hold the **Shift** key, and click the **Number Area** placeholder to select both placeholders. Then press **Delete** to delete them.

STEP-BY-STEP 14.2 Continued

7. Click the **subtitle area** placeholder text to select it and then click the **Center** button on the Formatting toolbar to center-align the text. Click the **Bold** button on the Formatting toolbar to remove the bold formatting, click the **Font Color** button list arrow on the Drawing toolbar, and click **White** in the color grid. Deselect the placeholder contents. Your title slide master should look similar to Figure 14-5.

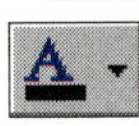

FIGURE 14-5
Modified slide title master

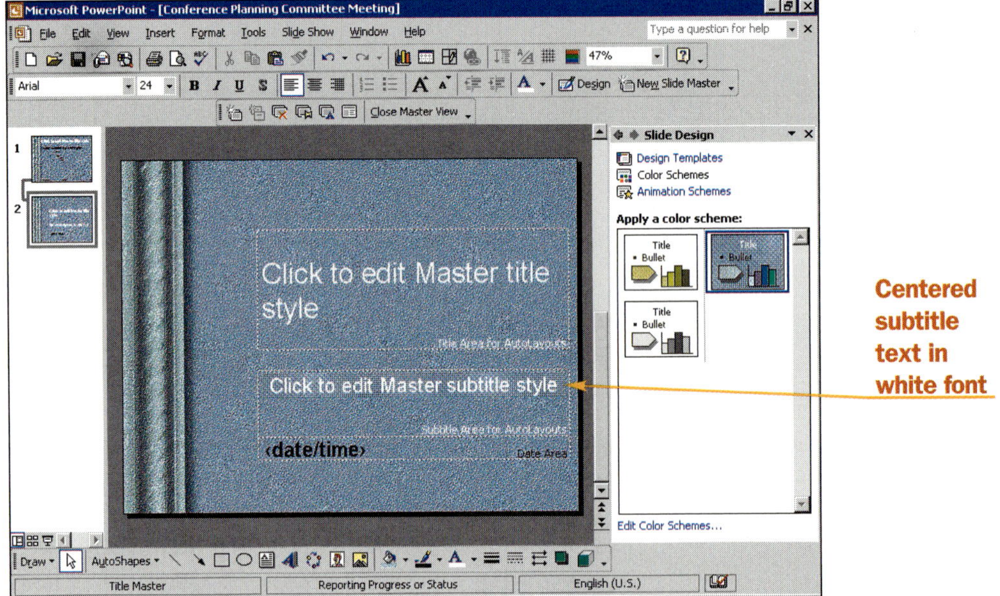

Centered subtitle text in white font

8. Scroll up to view the slide master.

9. Save the presentation and leave it open for the next Step-by-Step.

Modify Text Alignment, Bullet Graphics, and Font Color Using the Slide Master

Next you want to center the title text on all slides (except the title slide), change the first-level bullet graphic shape and color, change the font color for the bulleted text and slide number, and insert a picture that appears on all slides except the title slide.

When you insert a picture on a slide, you can then format that picture using buttons on the Picture toolbar or with options in the Format Picture dialog box. Depending on the type of picture you insert, you may be able to recolor the picture components, change the picture from color to black and white, and make other editing changes. To quickly view the Format Picture dialog box, simply right-click the picture and click **Format Picture** from the shortcut menu.

S TEP-BY-STEP 14.3

1. Verify that the Conference Planning Committee Meeting presentation is open and you are viewing the slide master. Click in the **Title Area** placeholder and click the **Center** button on the Formatting toolbar to center the title text.

2. Click the first-level bullet text in the object area placeholder to select the first-level bullet, click the **Format** menu, and click **Bullets and Numbering** to open the Bullets and Numbering dialog box.

3. Click **Customize**, click the graphic object of your choice from the Wingdings font grid, and click **OK** to select a new graphic object for the first-level bullet. (If you are using PowerPoint 2000, click **Character** to view the Wingdings graphic characters.)

4. Click the **Color** list arrow in the Bullets and Numbering dialog box and click the **White** color on the color grid to change the graphic object's color to white. Click **OK** to close the dialog box and accept all the changes to the first-level graphic bullet. Click outside the slide to deselect the first-level bullet text.

5. Press and hold the **Shift** key and click the object area placeholder boundary and the Number Area placeholder boundary to select the placeholders' contents. Then click the **Font Color** button on the Drawing toolbar to change the text color in the selected placeholders to white. Click the **Bold** button on the Formatting toolbar twice to remove the Bold formatting in the Object Area placeholder. Click outside the slide to deselect the placeholders.

6. Click the **Insert Clip Art** button on the Drawing toolbar to view the Insert Clip Art task pane. Key **Calgary** in the Search text box and click the **Search** button to search for appropriate clips. If the search word Calgary does not produce results, try other search words, such as buildings, cities, or Canada. (If you are using PowerPoint 2000, click the **Insert ClipArt** button to open the Insert Clip Art dialog box. Search for appropriate clips using keywords such as cities or Canada.)

STEP-BY-STEP 14.3 Continued

7. Insert the clip of your choice in the slide master, position it in the lower-right corner of the object area placeholder, and size it with the mouse pointer so that it is no larger than ½-inch wide by ½-inch high. Edit the picture as desired using the Picture toolbar or the Format Picture dialog box. Your slide master should look similar to Figure 14-6.

FIGURE 14-6
Modified slide master

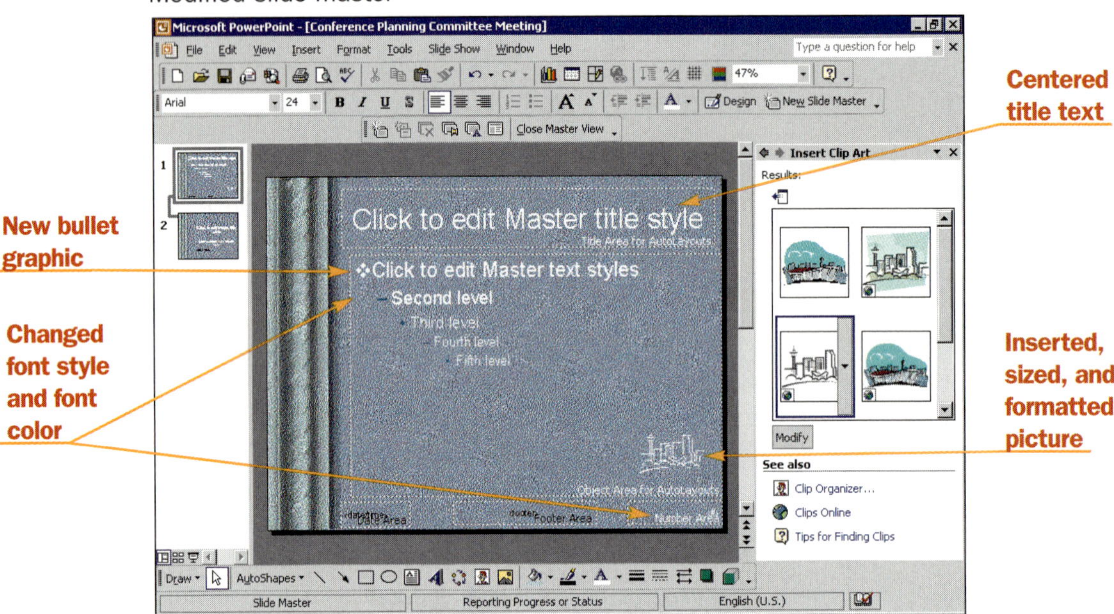

8. Click the **Normal View** button below the Outline pane to close the slide master and switch to Normal view. Close the task pane, if necessary.

9. Scroll the slides to view the changes and then return to Slide 1 (title slide).

10. Save the presentation and leave it open for the next Step-by-Step.

Insert, Delete, and Move Slides and Modify Slide Text

Now that you have made the changes to the title slide and slide masters, you are ready to finalize customizing the presentation by adding and removing slides, repositioning slides, and editing the sample text. You begin by inserting a new text and title (bulleted list) slide following the title slide and adding text to the slide. Then you delete unwanted slides, reposition the summary slide, and modify the text on the remaining slides.

Hot Tip 

If you need to view all the slides in a presentation and then delete or reposition some of the slides, first switch to Slide Sorter view. Using Slide Sorter view, you can quickly select individual slides or multiple adjacent slides using the Shift + click method, and nonadjacent slides using the Ctrl + click method, and then delete the slides or drag them to a new location.

STEP-BY-STEP 14.4

1. Verify that the Conference Planning Committee Meeting presentation is open and you are viewing Slide 1 (title slide). Click the **New Slide** button on the Formatting toolbar to insert a new text and title slide. Click the **Title and 2-Column Text** layout in the task pane. (If you are using PowerPoint 2000, click the **New Slide** button on the Standard toolbar and click **New Slide**. Then double-click the **2 Column Text** slide layout.)

2. Key **Attendees** in the title placeholder. Key the following list of attendee names in the first bulleted list placeholder, pressing **Enter** after each name except the last name: **Bob Davenport**, **Lynda Betancourt**, **Melody Stackhouse**, and **Tamika Washington**. Key the following list of attendee names in the second bulleted list placeholder, pressing **Enter** after each name except the last name: **Beverly Chew**, **James Montevo**, and your name. Drag the middle sizing handle, as necessary, on the first bulleted list placeholder to size it so that no name wraps to a second line. Your slide should look similar to Figure 14-7.

FIGURE 14-7
Attendees slide

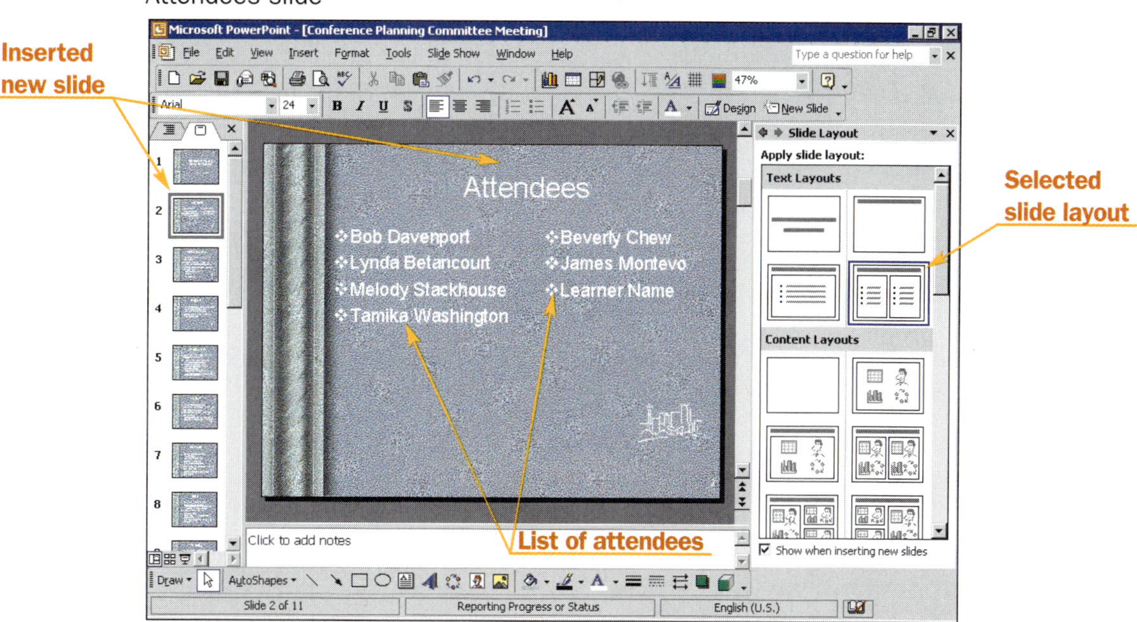

3. Click the **Slide Sorter View** button below the Outline pane to switch to Slide Sorter view.

4. Click **Slide 7** to select it, press and hold the **Shift** key, and click **Slide 10** to select the adjacent Slides 7, 8, 9, and 10. Then press **Delete** to delete the slides.

5. Drag Slide 3 (Status Summary) and drop it in front of Slide 7 (Goals for Next Review).

STEP-BY-STEP 14.4 Continued

6. Double-click **Slide 3** (Progress) to edit it in Normal view. Select all the bulleted list text and key the following list, pressing **Enter** at the end of each item except the last item: **Conference budget**, **Meeting materials**, **Speakers' travel and workshops**, **Hotel accommodations**, **Travel arrangements**, **Food and beverage service**, and **AV equipment**. Your Slide 3 should look similar to Figure 14-8.

FIGURE 14-8
Edited slide text

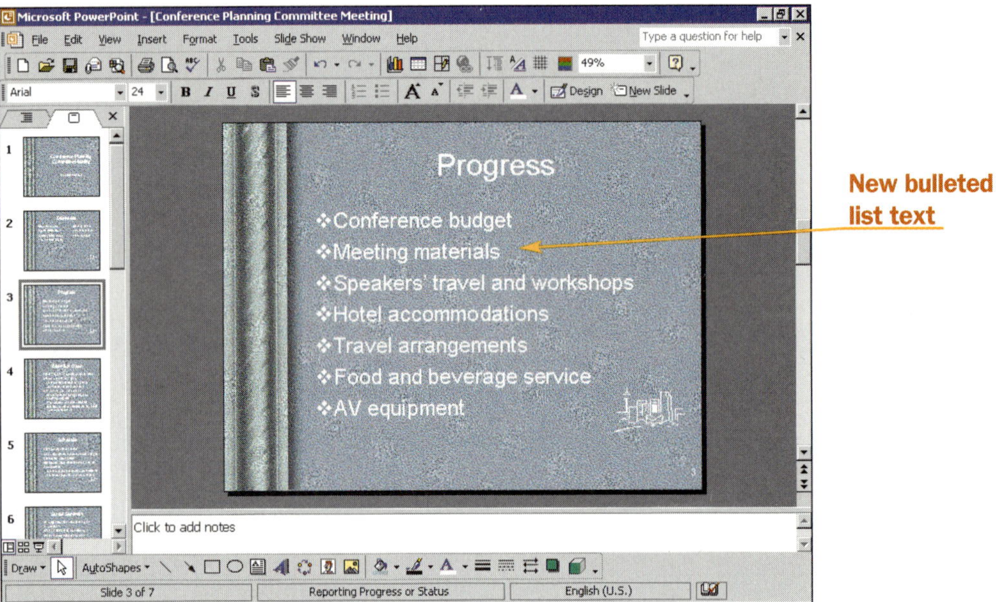

7. Delete the bulleted list text on Slides 4 through 7 and then switch to **Slide Sorter** view. Your Slide Sorter view should look similar to Figure 14-9.

STEP-BY-STEP 14.4 Continued

FIGURE 14-9
Revised slides

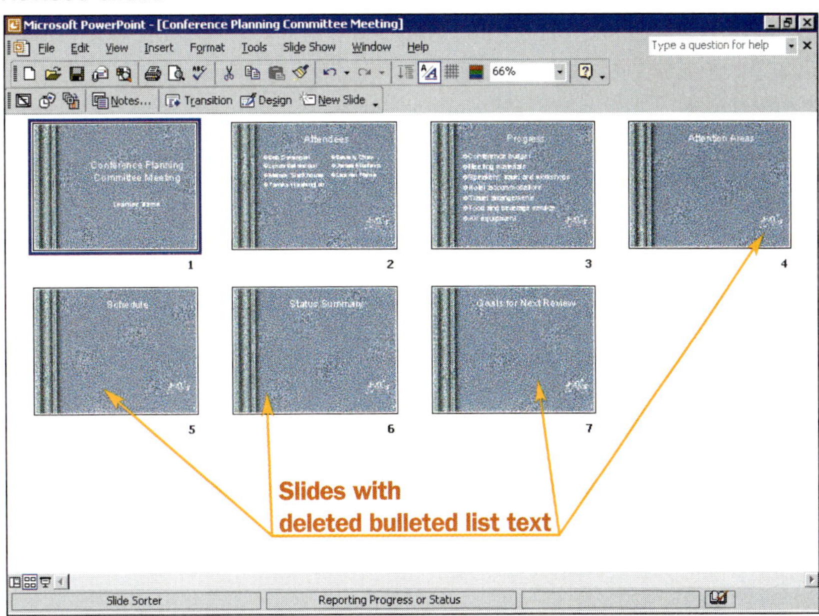

8. Double-click **Slide 1** (title slide) to return to Normal view and run the slide show. Then save the presentation, leaving it open for the next Step-by-Step.

Preview and Print Slides and Handouts

You want to print a copy of each slide for your files and you also want to print a handout containing the slides for the meeting attendees. Just as with any Office document, it is a good idea to print preview your presentation before you actually print the slides or the handouts.

Hot Tip

You can add header, footer, date, and page number information to audience handouts by modifying placeholders in the Handout Master. To view the Handout Master, click **View** on the menu bar, point to **Master**, and click **Handout Master**.

STEP-BY-STEP 14.5

1. Verify that the Conference Planning Committee Meeting presentation is open and you are viewing Slide 1 (title slide). Click the **Print Preview** button on the Standard toolbar. (If you are using PowerPoint 2000, you cannot print preview your slides. Skip steps 2 and 3.)

2. Click the **Next Page** button on the Print Preview toolbar to view the next slide. Continue until all slides are previewed, and then click the **Previous Page** button on the Print Preview toolbar until you are again viewing Slide 1 (title slide).

Warning

The Print dialog box remembers your last option settings during the same PowerPoint session. If you are unable to use the Previous Page or Next Page buttons in Print Preview, open the Print dialog box and verify that the Print Range options are set correctly for what you are trying to preview. For example, if you are trying to preview all the slides, the All option button should be turned on.

3. Click the **Print** button on the Print Preview toolbar to open the Print dialog box, set your print options, and click **OK** to print the slides. (If you are using PowerPoint 2000, click the **Print** command on the **File** menu, set your print options to print the slides, and click **OK**.)

4. Click the **Print What** button list arrow on the Print Preview toolbar and click **Handouts (3 slides per page)** to preview the audience handout layout that includes lines beside each slide that attendees can use to take notes during the meeting. Your Print Preview should look similar to Figure 14-10. (If you are using PowerPoint 2000, click the **Print** command on the **File** menu, click **Handouts** in the Print what list, click **3** in the Slides per page list, and click **OK**.)

FIGURE 14-10
Handout in Print Preview

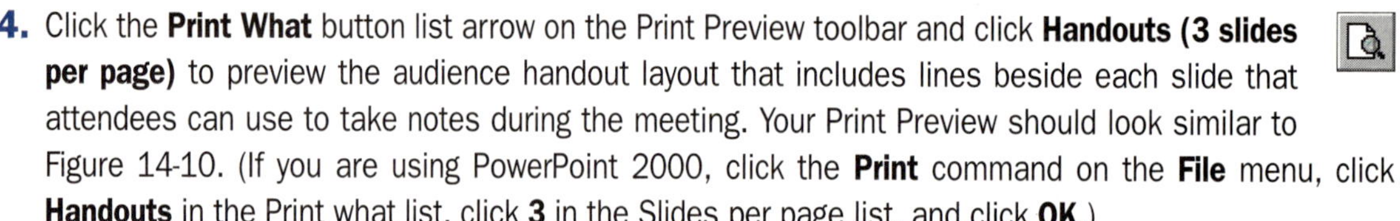

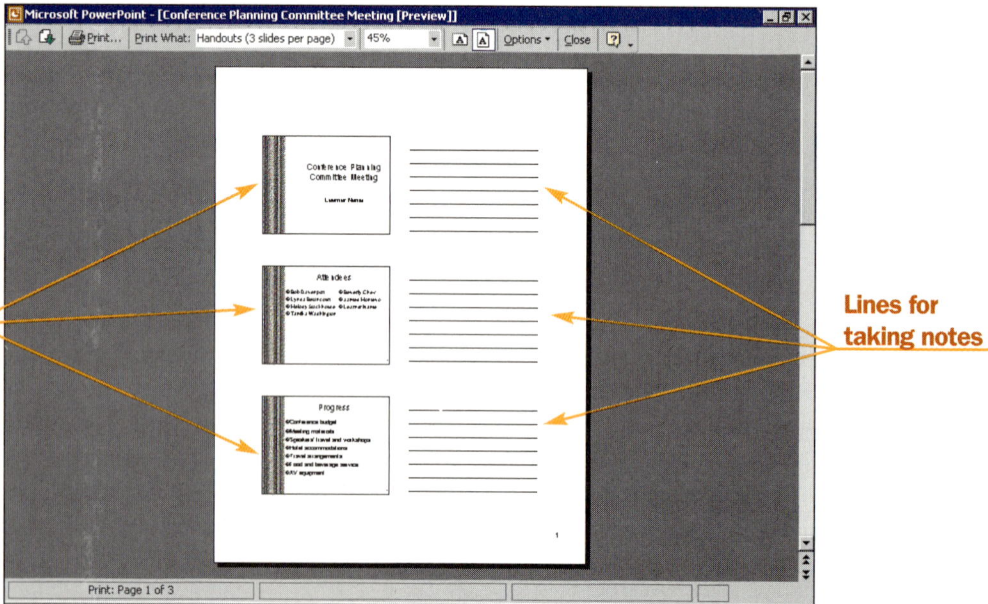

STEP-BY-STEP 14.5 Continued

5. Print the handout and close Print Preview. (If you are using PowerPoint 2000, skip this step.)

6. Save the presentation, close it, and close PowerPoint.

SUMMARY

In this job, you learned:

- You can quickly create a presentation containing sample text and with a design template already applied by using the AutoContent Wizard.

- The title slide master controls the formatting on any title slides in a presentation and the slide master controls the formatting on all other slides in a presentation.

- You can quickly replace one font with another for all the slides in a presentation.

- You can change the type, style, and color of bullet graphics used on all text and title slides in a presentation by modifying the graphic object on the slide master.

- You can change text font, color, and alignment on all slides in a presentation by modifying the slide and slide title masters.

- Slide Sorter view is used to view all the slides in a presentation at one time and to quickly delete or reposition slides.

- You can preview and print presentation slides or handouts.

VOCABULARY *Review*

Define the following terms:

AutoContent Wizard   Slide master   Title slide master

REVIEW *Questions*

TRUE / FALSE

Circle T if the statement is true or F if the statement is false.

T   F   **1.** The AutoContent Wizard is helpful when you want to quickly create a presentation for a common business purpose, such as a sales meeting, or to report financial data.

T   F   **2.** You cannot delete the placeholders on a slide or slide title master.

T   F   **3.** You can select multiple placeholders on a slide or slide title master using the Alt key.

T   F   **4.** To insert a picture on all slides except the title slide, you can position the picture on the title slide master.

T   F   **5.** You can use the Shift + click and Ctrl + click methods to select multiple slides in Slide Sorter view.

FILL IN THE BLANK

Complete the following sentences by writing the correct word or words in the blanks provided.

1. The ___________ allows you to control the formatting on all title slides in a presentation.

2. When you need to reposition slides in a presentation, you can first view the slides in ___________ view.

3. You can key meeting notes and action items directly into a presentation during a slide show by using the ___________ feature.

4. The handout layout that contains lines on which notes can be taken has ___________ slide miniatures per page.

5. To replace one font with another on all slides in a presentation, you use the ___________ command on the ___________ menu.

PROJECTS

 PROJECT 14-1

1. Start PowerPoint and open the **Project 14-1** presentation from the data files.

2. Save the presentation as **Revised Sloane Comments**.

3. Apply the design template of your choice to the presentation.

4. View the slide master and change the design color scheme. Change the title text alignment, change the first-level bullet graphic shape and color, and change the default font. Change the text font size, if necessary, so that all text is attractively positioned within its placeholder.

5. Click **View** on the menu bar, click **Header and Footer**, add the slide number to all the slides in the presentation except the title slide, and add "Go Calgary!" as a footer.

6. View the slide title master and insert the picture of your choice. Then size and position the picture attractively on the master. Change the title and subtitle text font color.

7. Close the slide title master and run the slide show. Make any additional formatting changes you desire to the slide and slide title masters after viewing the slide show.

8. Save the presentation and run the slide show. Then print preview and print the individual slides and a handout with six slide miniatures per page.

9. Close the presentation.

PROJECT 14-2

Sloane calls you from the airport to tell you that Wilderness Treks, Inc. has lost a major client who is unhappy with the company's approach to the client's needs and with the company's methods of solving customer problems. Sloane needs you to create a presentation that can be used to guide a meeting with the marketing and sales staff to discuss the client loss. The meeting will take place just as soon as Sloane reaches the office, in about 45 minutes. Using the AutoContent Wizard, create a presentation containing five slides that Sloane can use with the marketing and sales staff to break the bad news about the client loss. Edit the presentation masters and individual slide text as desired. Save the presentation as **Sales and Marketing Meeting** and run the slide show. Make any additional changes to the slide and title slide master necessary after running the slide show. Print preview and print the slides as a handout for the meeting attendees.

WEB PROJECT

You have lunch with Beverly Harris, who tells you that she is scheduled to make a presentation using PowerPoint at the next meeting of the Administrative Assistants Association. She has no previous experience in giving presentations and asks you where she can find some helpful tips. Using your Web browser's search tool or a search engine such as Google (*www.google.com*), search for Web sites where Beverly can find useful tips on how to prepare for and give presentations. Print at least three Web pages.

TEAMWORK PROJECT

As Sloane's administrative assistant, you are frequently called on to speak to groups of other employees or conduct meetings with other employees. You often use a PowerPoint slide show to help you and the other employees focus on the topics being discussed. The PowerPoint Rehearse Timings feature allows you to practice or rehearse running a slide show and then add timings (run time) to each slide. Then you can set the slide show up to have the slides advance automatically as you are speaking to the group. Select a classmate to help you with this project. Using PowerPoint online Help, research how to use the Rehearse Timings feature and how to set up a slide show to advance the slides automatically based on the rehearsed timings. Finally, using the presentation of your choice, demonstrate to a group of other classmates how to rehearse and set slide timings and how to run a slide show with automatically advancing slides based on those rehearsed timings.

CRITICAL*Thinking*

ACTIVITY 14-1

It is possible to add sound and video to a PowerPoint presentation; however, both sound and video should be used only when they enhance the presentation's message. Using PowerPoint online Help, research how to insert sound and video clips in a presentation, if necessary. Then, using the PowerPoint presentation of your choice, demonstrate to another classmate how to locate an appropriate sound clip or video clip in your Clip Organizer and how to insert it on a slide. Set the appropriate options for the clip to run automatically while the slide is being viewed. Finally, run the slide show to view or hear the clip.

LINKING EXCEL DATA TO A PRESENTATION

Insert Hyperlinks in a Workbook

After Sloane and the vice presidents review the annual budget workbook posted to the company intranet, they ask Davenport to make several changes to the data. Davenport sends you another workbook containing the revised data, and tells you Sloane wants to be able to quickly relate the adventure tours revenue summary data on the Budget worksheet to the individual branch office adventure tours revenue data on the Revenues worksheet. You solve this problem with hyperlinks.

A *hyperlink* is text or an object that is associated with the path to text or an object at another location: somewhere else in the same document or a different document. It is likely you have used hyperlinks on Web pages to load other Web pages in your Web browser. You also can create hyperlinks in Office documents. For example, an Excel worksheet hyperlink can link to a new location in the same worksheet, another worksheet, another workbook, another Office document, or a Web page.

Create a Hyperlink Using Cell Contents

You begin by opening the workbook with the revised budget data and creating a hyperlink from the cell on the Budget worksheet that contains the total adventure tours revenue to the cell on the Revenues worksheet that contains the total adventure tours revenue.

Hot Tip

To follow a hyperlink in a worksheet cell, click the hyperlink. To simply activate a cell that contains a hyperlink *without following the hyperlink*, press and hold the mouse button briefly when pointing to the cell.

Did You Know?

To edit a hyperlink in an Excel workbook, activate the cell that contains the hyperlink and then open the Insert Hyperlink dialog box. You can make any changes necessary to options in the dialog box including removing the hyperlink. If you do not want the hyperlink underlined, simply click the Underline button on the Formatting toolbar to remove the hyperlink's underline formatting.

STEP-BY-STEP 15.1

1. Start the Excel application and open the **Step15-1** workbook from the data files. Click the Budget sheet tab, if necessary.

2. Save the workbook as **Revised Budget Data**.

3. Click cell **F6** to activate it and then click the **Insert Hyperlink** button on the Standard toolbar to open the Insert Hyperlink dialog box.

4. Click **Place in This Document** in the Link to bar, click **Revenues** in the Or select a place in this document list box, and key **F11** in the Type the cell reference text box. Your Insert Hyperlink dialog box should look similar to Figure 15-1.

FIGURE 15-1
Insert Hyperlink dialog box

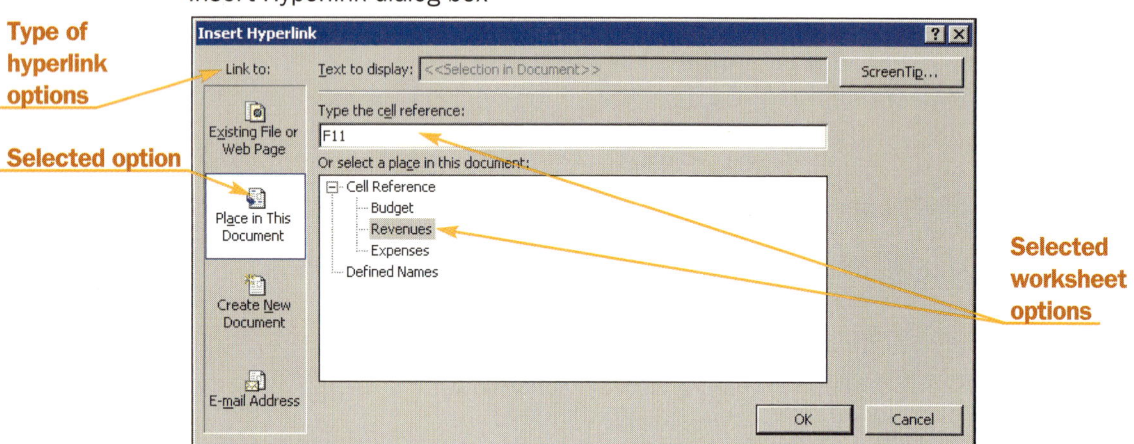

5. Click **OK** and click cell **A1** to activate it. Observe that the value in cell F6 is now blue and underlined, indicating a hyperlink. Your screen should look similar to Figure 15-2.

FIGURE 15-2
Hyperlink in cell

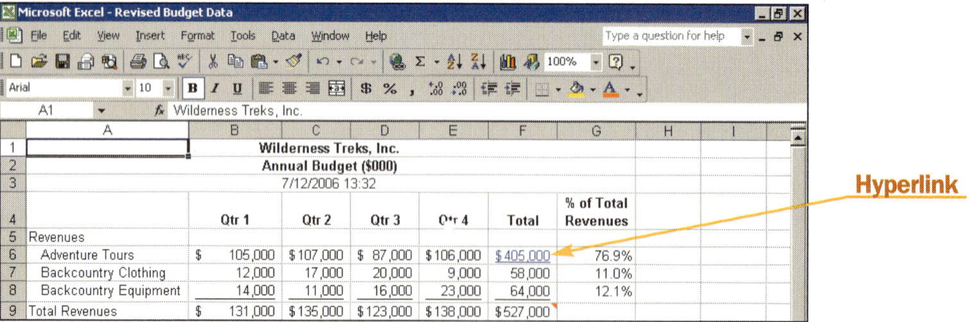

6. Click the hyperlink in cell F6 to view the Revenues worksheet and the active cell F11.

7. Save the workbook and leave it and the Revenues worksheet open for the next Step-by-Step.

Create a Hyperlink Using a Drawing Object

Drawing objects, such as circles, squares, lines, rectangles, arrows, and special shapes called AutoShapes, are often used in Excel to enhance worksheets and charts to make them more attractive to the user. The Drawing toolbar contains features and buttons you can use to create and edit drawing objects. To create a drawing object, you select the object using a Drawing toolbar button and drag the mouse pointer in the document to create the object.

You also can assign a hyperlink to a drawing object. You need to make it easy for Sloane and other workbook users to quickly return to the Budget worksheet after clicking the adventure tours hyperlink to view the adventure tours revenues. You draw a left arrow object on the Revenues worksheet and use it to create a hyperlink back to the Budget worksheet.

Did You Know?

The Drawing toolbar is available in Word, Excel, and PowerPoint and the features and buttons you use to create and edit drawing objects work exactly the same way in all three Office applications.

S TEP-BY-STEP 15.2

1. Verify that the Revised Budget Data workbook is open and you are viewing the Revenues worksheet. Click the **Drawing** button on the Standard toolbar to view the Drawing toolbar, which usually appears anchored at the bottom of the Excel window above the status bar.

2. Click the **AutoShapes** button on the Drawing toolbar, point to Block Arrows, and click the **Left Arrow** shape (second shape in the first row) to turn on the AutoShape feature. Move the mouse pointer to the top-center of cell **H11** and drag down and to the right to the bottom-center of cell **I11**. Release the mouse button when your left arrow drawing object looks similar to the object in Figure 15-3.

FIGURE 15-3
Left arrow drawing object

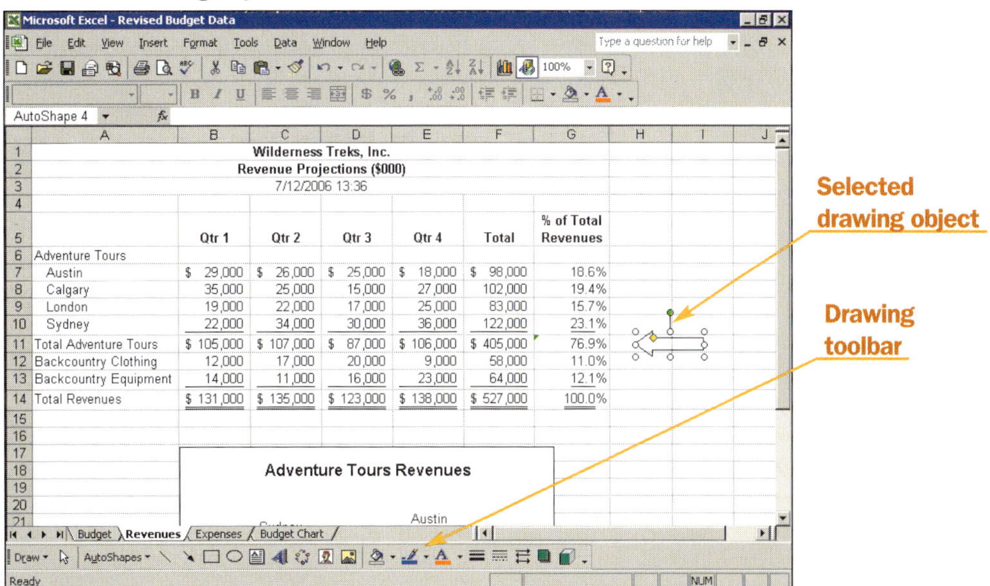

STEP-BY-STEP 15.2 Continued

3. Observe the selection or sizing handles around the object and then click the **Fill Color** button list arrow on the Drawing toolbar and click the Red color on the color grid to fill the object with color. *Do not deselect the object.* 

4. Click the **Insert Hyperlink** button on the Standard toolbar, click **Budget** in the Or select a place in this document list box, key **F6** in the Type the cell reference text box, and click **OK**. Then click cell **A1** to activate it and deselect the left arrow drawing object.

5. Move the mouse pointer to the left arrow drawing object (*do not click*) and observe that the mouse pointer changes to a hand pointer indicating a hyperlink. Click the left arrow drawing object hyperlink to view the Budget worksheet with cell F6 activated.

6. Close the Drawing toolbar, click cell **A1** to activate it, and save the workbook, leaving it and the Budget worksheet open for the next Step-by-Step.

Link Excel Data and Charts to Slides

You can copy a range of Excel data or a chart and paste it into a PowerPoint slide as a *linked object*. When you link an Excel object in a PowerPoint slide, you create a reference (or link) to the original Excel worksheet. In PowerPoint you use the Paste Special command on the Edit menu to paste a linked Excel object.

Link Excel Data to a Slide

Sloane sends you an e-mail asking that you prepare a PowerPoint presentation that can be used to direct the budget review meeting to be held in Calgary immediately after the annual conference. You are to include data from the Revised Budget Data workbook in the presentation. You begin by creating a new presentation based on a design template. Then you add the appropriate slides and insert linked objects containing the data from the Budget, Revenues, and Expenses worksheets.

STEP-BY-STEP 15.3

1. Verify that the Revised Budget Data workbook is open and you are viewing the Budget worksheet. Start PowerPoint and click the **From Design Template** hyperlink in the New Presentation task pane to create a new presentation based on a design template. (If you are using PowerPoint 2000, click the **Design Template** option button in the PowerPoint dialog box and click **OK**.)

2. Click the design template of your choice in the Slide Design task pane. (If you are using PowerPoint 2000, click the design template of your choice in the New Presentation dialog box and click **OK** and then double-click the **Title Slide** layout.)

3. Save the presentation as **Annual Budget Meeting**.

4. Key **Annual Budget Meeting** and **J. R. Sloane** in the title and subtitle areas in Slide 1 (title slide).

STEP-BY-STEP 15.3 Continued

5. Click the **New Slide** button on the Formatting toolbar to insert a new text and title slide following Slide 1 (title slide) then click the **Title Only** layout in the Slide Layout task pane to change the slide's layout. (If you are using PowerPoint 2000, click the **Common Tasks** button on the Formatting toolbar, click **New Slide**, and double-click the **Title Only** slide layout.)

6. Key **Budget Data** in the title placeholder and then deselect the placeholder.

7. Click the **Excel** button on the task bar to view the Budget worksheet in the Revised Budget Data workbook. Select the range **A1:G19** and click the **Copy** button on the Standard toolbar to copy the range to the Office Clipboard.

8. Click the **PowerPoint** button on the task bar, click **Edit** on the menu bar, and click **Paste Special** to open the Paste Special dialog box. Click the **Paste link** option button, verify that Microsoft Excel Worksheet Object is selected in the As list, and click **OK** to insert the linked Excel object. Your slide should look similar to Figure 15-4.

FIGURE 15-4
Linked Excel object

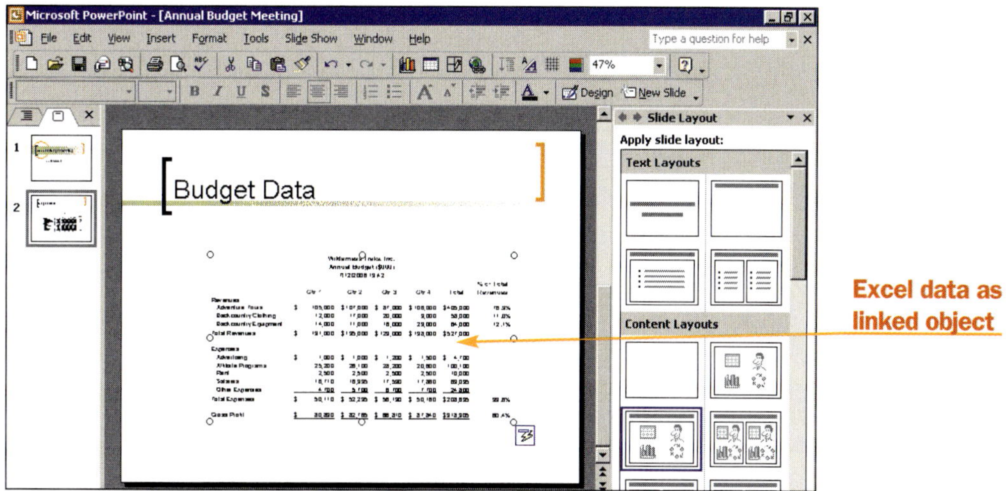

9. Size and position the linked Excel object attractively on the slide using the mouse pointer and then deselect the object. (Remember to use the **Ctrl** key to size the object from the center and to drag a corner sizing handle to size the object proportionally.)

10. Insert a new **Title Only** slide following Slide 2 (Budget Data) and key **Revenue Data** in the title placeholder.

11. Switch to **Excel**, click the **Revenues** sheet tab, and copy the range **A1:G14** to the Office Clipboard.

12. Switch to **PowerPoint**, open the **Paste Special** dialog box, and paste link the range as an Excel worksheet object on the slide. Size and position the linked worksheet object attractively on the slide.

STEP-BY-STEP 15.3 Continued

13. Insert a new **Title Only** slide with the title text **Expense Data** following Slide 3 (Revenue Data). Then paste link the data in the range **A1:G14** on the **Expenses** worksheet in the Revised Budget Data workbook on the slide. Size and position the linked worksheet object attractively on the slide.

14. Switch to **Slide Sorter** view. Your screen should look similar to Figure 15-5.

FIGURE 15-5
Slides with linked Excel data

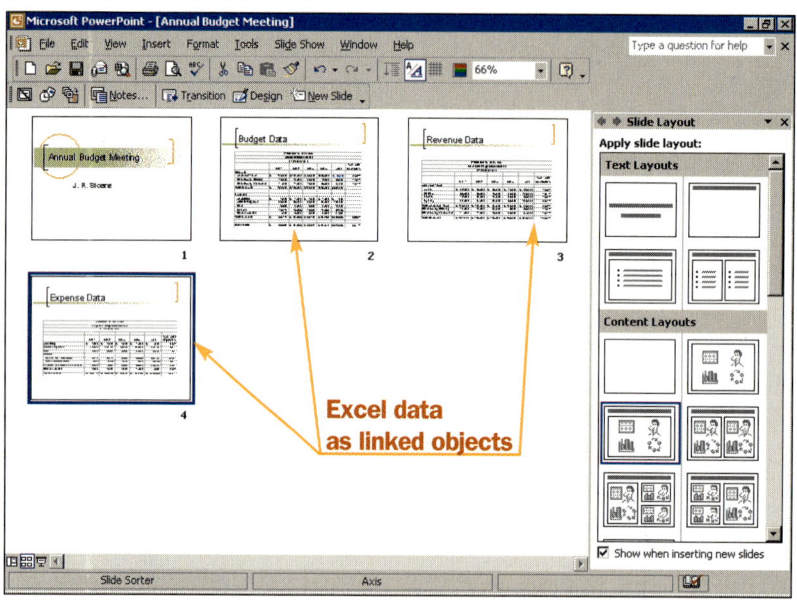

15. Switch back to **Normal** view, save the presentation, and leave it and the Excel workbook open for the next Step-by-Step.

Link an Excel Chart to a Slide

Now you want to link the Budget Chart and the embedded revenues chart on the Revenues worksheet to slides in the presentation. You follow the same process to link Excel chart objects as you do to link Excel data objects.

STEP-BY-STEP 15.4

1. Verify that the Annual Budget Meeting presentation is open and you are viewing Slide 4. Create a new **Title Only** slide with the title text **Budget Chart** following Slide 4 (Expense Data).

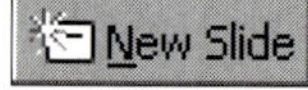

2. Switch to **Excel**, click the **Budget Chart** sheet tab, and click the white chart area to select the entire chart. (Note the selection handles around the chart area indicating that the entire chart is selected.) Copy the chart to the Office Clipboard.

STEP-BY-STEP 15.4 Continued

3. Switch to **PowerPoint** and paste link the chart object on the slide. Size and position the chart object attractively with the mouse pointer.

4. Create a new **Title Only** slide with the title text **Revenue Chart** following Slide 5 (Budget Chart).

5. Switch to **Excel**, click the **Revenues** sheet tab, click the embedded chart to select it, and copy the chart to the Office Clipboard.

6. Switch to **PowerPoint** and paste link the chart object on the slide. Size and position the chart object attractively with the mouse pointer.

7. Switch to **Slide Sorter** view. Your screen should look similar to Figure 15-6.

FIGURE 15-6
Slides with linked Excel charts

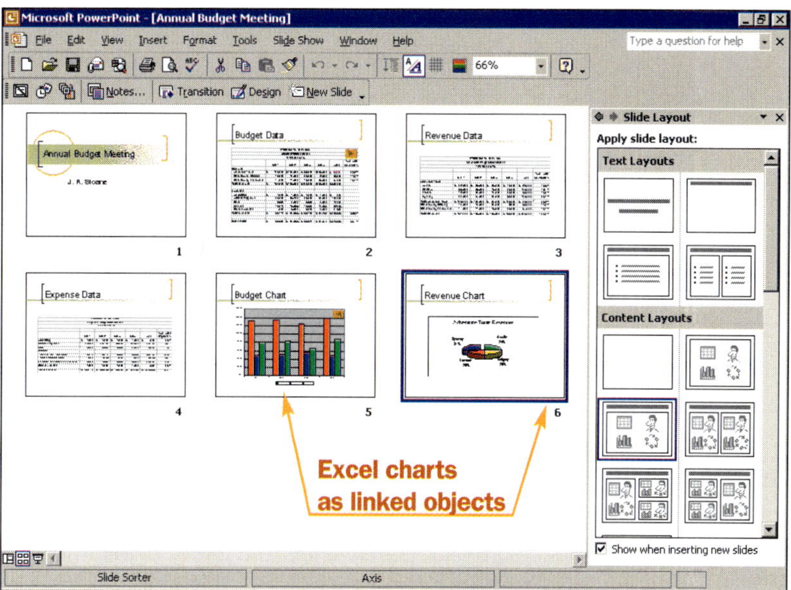

8. Switch to **Excel**, group the Budget, Revenues, and Expenses worksheets and click **A1** to activate it on all three worksheets. Ungroup the worksheets, leaving the Budget worksheet active, and then save and close the workbook. Close Excel.

9. Switch to **PowerPoint**, if necessary, switch to **Slide 1** in **Normal** view, and run the slide show. Then save the presentation leaving it open for the next Step-by-Step.

Edit a Linked Excel Object in a Slide

A linked Excel object must be edited in its original workbook. For example, when you link an Excel object to a PowerPoint slide, you edit the object in PowerPoint by double-clicking it to open the original Excel source workbook in the Excel application. Any changes you make to the original Excel workbook are reflected in the object in the PowerPoint slide.

After reviewing the Annual Budget Meeting slide show you decide that the Sydney slice of the adventure tours revenues pie chart should be emphasized to show that Sydney has the largest projected tour revenues. You can do this by modifying the pie chart to explode by dragging the Sydney slice away from the rest of the pie.

STEP-BY-STEP 15.5

1. Verify that the Annual Budget Meeting presentation is open and you are viewing Slide 1 (title slide). Scroll to view Slide 6 and double-click the linked chart object to open the Excel application and the Revenues worksheet in the Revised Budget Data workbook.

2. Click the embedded chart to select it and click the pie object in the chart to select the entire pie. Then click the **Sydney** slice (blue slice) to select only that slice of the pie. Drag the Sydney slice upward and to the left slightly to move it away from the other pie slices. Press **Esc** twice to deselect the Sydney slice and the embedded chart. Your screen should look similar to Figure 15-7.

FIGURE 15-7
Exploded pie chart

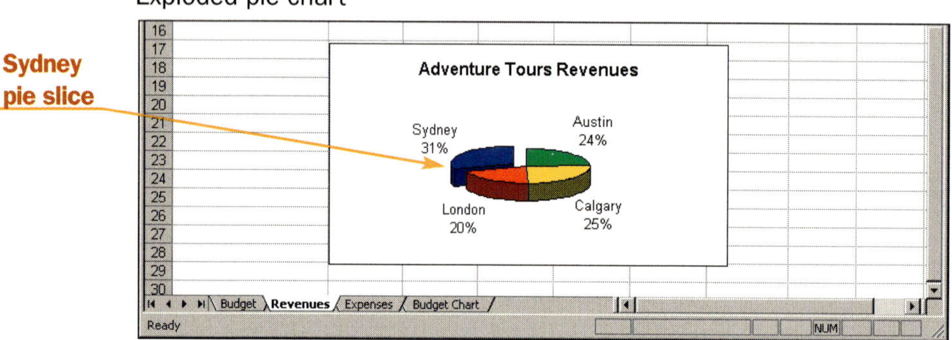

3. Print preview and print the Budget and Revenues worksheets and then save and close the workbook and close Excel. Switch to PowerPoint, if necessary, and observe that the pie chart in the linked Excel chart object on Slide 6 is also exploded. Deselect the linked chart object.

4. Save the presentation and leave it open for the next Step-by-Step.

Insert Hyperlinks in a Presentation

You can use hyperlinks in a PowerPoint presentation to link from one slide to another, to another presentation, to another Office document, or to a Web page. Using hyperlinks to link from one slide to another within the same presentation is an easy way to quickly show related slides during a slide show, rather than simply showing the slides in sequential order. You can use text, drawing objects, or action buttons to create hyperlinks in PowerPoint.

Sloane wants to be able to quickly show the appropriate chart slide following each data slide while running the Annual Budget Meeting slide show. You draw action buttons with the mouse pointer to create hyperlinks to help Sloane navigate from data slide to chart slide and back again.

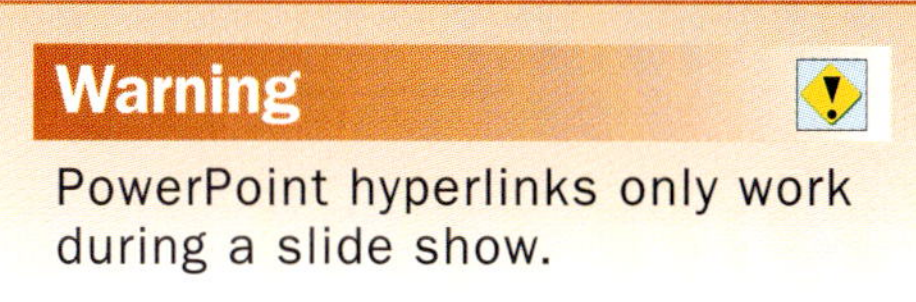

STEP-BY-STEP 15.6

1. Verify that the Annual Budget Meeting presentation is open and then scroll to view Slide 2 (Budget Data). Click **Slide Show** on the menu bar, point to **Action Buttons**, and click the **Forward or Next** action button icon (second icon in the second row).

2. Move the mouse pointer to the upper-right corner of the worksheet object and drag down and to the right to create an action button approximately 1/2 inch wide by 1/2 inch tall. Release the mouse button to open the Action Settings dialog box.

3. Click the **Hyperlink to** list arrow and click **Slide** to open the Hyperlink to Slide dialog box. Click **5. Budget Chart** and click **OK** twice to create the action button with hyperlink and close both dialog boxes. Your screen should look similar to Figure 15-8.

FIGURE 15-8
Action button hyperlink

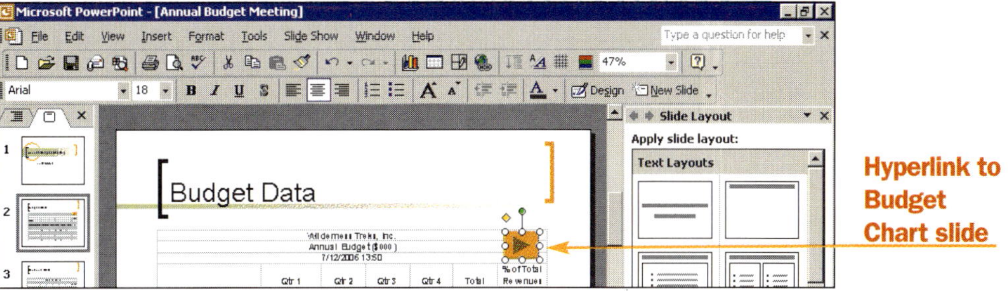

4. Run the slide show and click the action button hyperlink to quickly show Slide 5 (Budget Chart). Then press **Esc** to stop the slide show.

5. Verify you are viewing Slide 5 (Budget Chart) in Normal view and then click **Slide Show**, point to Action Buttons, and click the **Back or Previous** action button icon (first icon in second row). Draw an action button approximately 1/2 inch by 1/2 inch in the upper-right corner of the chart object. Create a hyperlink to the 2. Budget Data slide.

6. Run the slide show and click the action button hyperlink to show Slide 2 (Budget Data) and then stop the slide show.

7. Create actions buttons on Slide 3 (Revenue Data) and Slide 6 (Revenue Chart) that can be used to navigate between the two slides. Run the slide show and test your action button hyperlinks.

8. Scroll to view Slide 1, save the presentation, and then print preview and print the slides and handouts with two slides per page. Close the presentation and close PowerPoint.

SUMMARY

In this job, you learned:

- A hyperlink is text or an object that is associated with the path to text or an object at a different location.

- You can create hyperlinks between worksheets in the same Excel workbook to make navigating between related worksheets easier.

- You can use the Drawing toolbar to create drawing objects such as arrows, circles, rectangles, and AutoShapes and then use the drawing objects as hyperlinks.

- A range of Excel data or an Excel chart can be copied and then pasted as a linked object on a PowerPoint slide.

- When you edit a linked Excel object on a PowerPoint slide, you open the original source workbook and changes in the workbook are then reflected in the linked object.

- You can create hyperlinks between slides in a PowerPoint presentation to help navigate to and from related slides.

VOCABULARY *Review*

Define the following terms:
Hyperlink   Linked object

REVIEW *Questions*

TRUE / FALSE

Circle T if the statement is true or F if the statement is false.

T   F   **1.** Drawing objects can be used in an Excel workbook to enhance the appearance of a worksheet or to create hyperlinks.

T   F   **2.** To create a linked Excel worksheet or chart object, you can click the Paste button on the Standard toolbar.

T   F   **3.** The process for creating a linked Excel chart object is different than the process for creating a linked Excel data object.

T   F   **4.** Creating hyperlinks from slide to slide allows a presenter to quickly show related slides instead of showing slides in sequential order during a slide show.

T   F   **5.** To activate a worksheet cell that contains a hyperlink without following the link, you must press and hold the mouse button for a brief time while pointing to the cell.

FILL IN THE BLANK

Complete the following sentences by writing the correct word or words in the blanks provided.

1. A text __________ generally appears in blue and underlined in an Excel worksheet.

2. __________ are special shapes such as block arrows you can draw with the mouse pointer.

3. A linked Excel object must be edited in the original __________.

4. To create a linked Excel worksheet or chart object, you use the __________ command on the Edit menu.

5. To __________ a pie chart, you drag slices away from each other.

PROJECTS

PROJECT 15-1

1. Start Excel and open the **Project 15-1** workbook from the data files.

2. Save the workbook as **Calgary Budget**.

3. Use the Chart Wizard to embed a 3-D exploded pie chart on the Expenses worksheet that shows each expense category's percentage of total expenses. The chart title is Calgary Expenses. Show the legend at the bottom of the chart and do not add data labels.

4. Activate cell **F14** on the Budget worksheet and create a hyperlink that links to cell **F13** on the Expenses worksheet.

5. Draw an object of your choice on the Expenses worksheet and use it to create a hyperlink to cell **F14** on the Budget worksheet. Format the object as desired.

6. Test the hyperlinks and then print preview, print, and save the workbook. Leave it open for the next project.

PROJECT 15-2

L. D. Meeker, the director of marketing and sales for Canada, asks you to create a PowerPoint presentation containing the Calgary branch office budget data and chart. Create the presentation using a design template and save it as **Calgary Budget**. Key the text **Calgary Budget** and **L. D. Meeker** on the title slide and insert the budget and expense data and chart from the Calgary Budget workbook as linked objects on Title Only slides in the presentation. Size and position the linked objects attractively on the slides. Create action button hyperlinks from and to the Expense Data and Expense Chart slides. Test the hyperlinks. Print preview and print the slides and handouts with four slides per page. Then close the presentation and close PowerPoint.

WEB PROJECT

As an administrative assistant, you are always looking for ways to improve your productivity when working in Excel workbooks. Use your Web browser to locate the Microsoft Excel Tips and Tricks Web page and print the page. Then choose two tips that you find particularly useful and demonstrate the tips to a classmate.

TEAMWORK PROJECT

You want to know more about linking cells on the same worksheet and about linking cells in different workbooks. Select a classmate to help you with this project, and then use Excel online Help to research how to link cells on the same worksheet or between different workbooks. Then, using the workbooks of your choice, demonstrate to a group of classmates how to link cells on the same worksheet using the Paste Options button and how to link cells on different workbooks using a formula. (If you are using Excel 2000, you do not have a Paste Options button, so only complete the linking workbooks portion of this project.)

CRITICAL *Thinking*

ACTIVITY 15-1

It is sometimes necessary to manage the hyperlinks in Office documents by copying, moving, or deleting them. Using Excel or PowerPoint online Help, if necessary, research how to copy, move, and delete hyperlinks. Then, using the workbook or presentation of your choice, demonstrate to another classmate how to manage hyperlinks in a workbook or presentation.

USING CHARTS AND TABLES IN A PRESENTATION

Create and Format a Table on a Slide

A PowerPoint table is a grid of columns and rows used to organize text and data on a slide. You can create and format a table on a PowerPoint slide in much the same way you create and format a table in a Word document. You can use the Insert Table button on the Standard toolbar to select the number of table columns and rows from a grid. In PowerPoint, you also can use the Table command on the Insert menu to insert a table by specifying the number of columns and rows in the Insert Table dialog box. Also, just as it does in Word, the Tables and Borders toolbar contains buttons that allow you to draw and format a table, including its outside boundary, rows and columns.

Sloane reviewed the short presentation you prepared for the workshop on the new Central and South American adventure tours and sends you the e-mail shown in Figure 16-1 requesting some modifications be made to the presentation. You begin by inserting a new Title Only slide at the end of the workshop presentation and then you draw a table on the slide into which you key the departure information. The table needs a column for the tour name, a column for the tour departure dates, and four rows—one for each new tour.

FIGURE 16-1
Sloane e-mail message

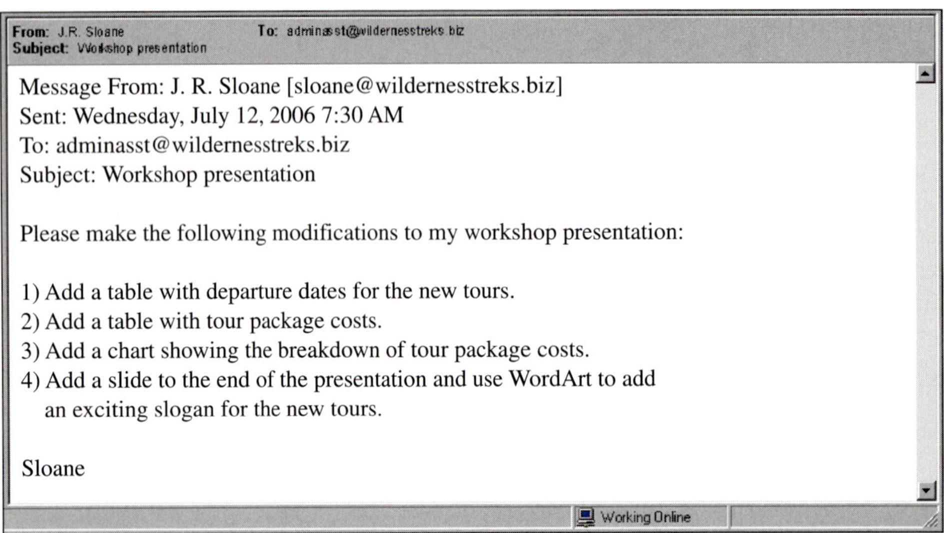

S TEP-BY-STEP 16.1

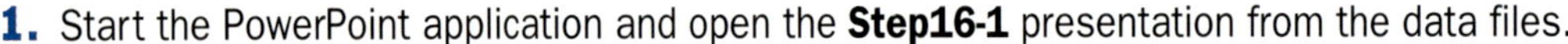

1. Start the PowerPoint application and open the **Step16-1** presentation from the data files.

2. Save the presentation as **Revised Workshop D**.

3. Scroll to view Slide 5 (the Galapagos Adventure slide) and insert a new blank slide. Change the slide layout to Title Only. Key **Departure Dates** as the slide title and then deselect the placeholder. If you are using PowerPoint 2002, close the task pane.

4. Click the **Tables and Borders** button on the Standard toolbar to display the Tables and Borders toolbar. It may appear floating in its own window or docked at the top of the screen above the slide work area. 

STEP-BY-STEP 16.1 Continued

5. Click the **Draw Table** button on the Tables and Borders toolbar, if necessary, to turn the  mouse pointer into a drawing pointer. Then move the drawing pointer to the upper-left side of the slide below the title placeholder. Your screen should look similar to Figure 16-2.

FIGURE 16-2
Drawing pointer

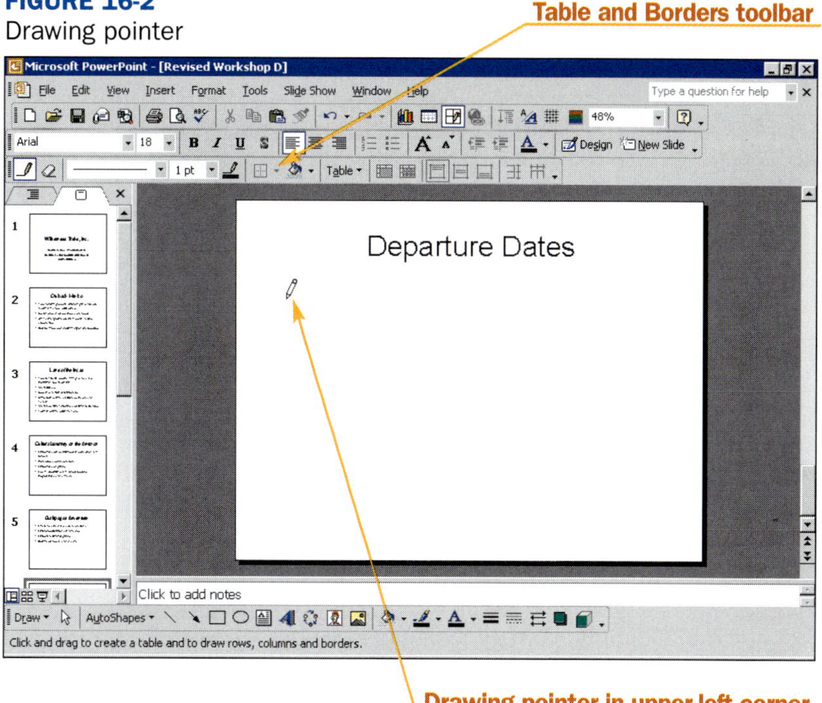

6. Using Figure 16-3 as your guide, drag the drawing pointer downward and to the right to create the outside boundaries of the table. Drag the drawing pointer from the left table boundary to the right table boundary three times to create four rows. Drag the drawing pointer downward from the top table boundary to the bottom table boundary to create two columns. (*Note*: You can use the Eraser button on the Drawing toolbar to change the mouse pointer to an eraser pointer and then drag the eraser pointer over a row or column boundary to remove it.)

STEP-BY-STEP 16.1 Continued

FIGURE 16-3
New table

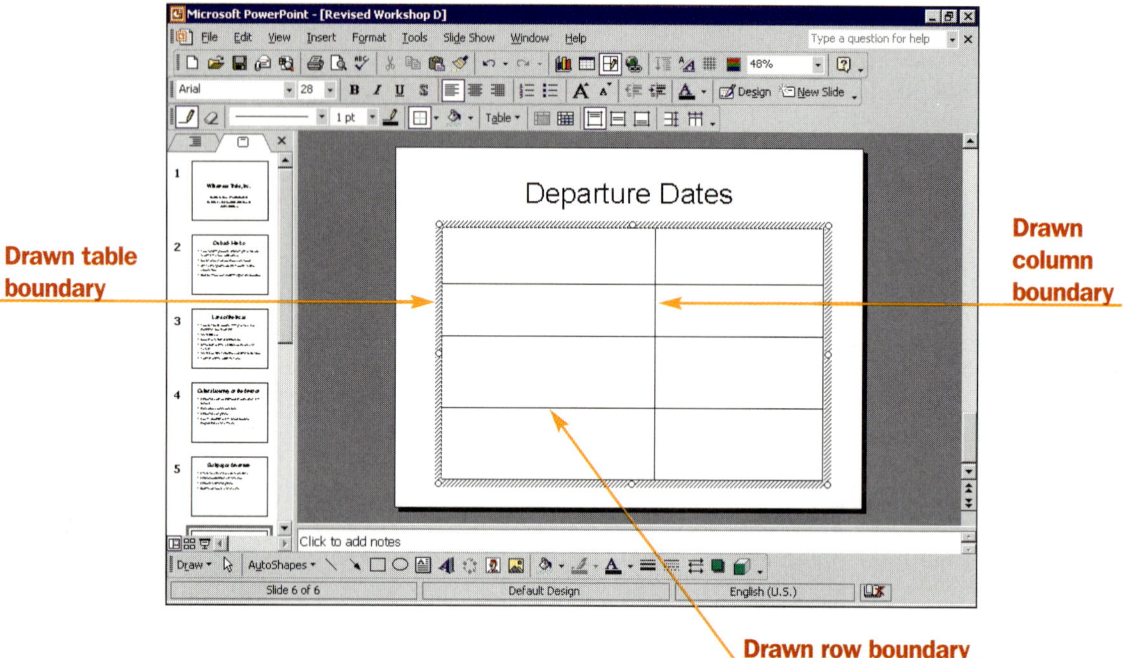

7. Click the **Draw Table** button on the Tables and Borders toolbar to turn off the drawing pointer.

8. Position the mouse pointer over the first column until the mouse pointer becomes a small black selection pointer and then drag the selection pointer to the right to select both columns.

9. Click the **Distribute Rows Evenly** button on the Tables and Borders toolbar to reposition the row boundaries so that there is equal distance between them. Then click the **Center Vertically** button on the Tables and Borders toolbar to center the cell contents vertically in each cell. (If you are using PowerPoint 2000, there is no Distribute Rows Evenly button on the Tables and Borders toolbar. Use the mouse pointer to drag the row boundaries to size all the rows approximately the same size.)

STEP-BY-STEP 16.1 Continued

10. Click in the leftmost cell in the first row to deselect the columns and position the insertion point. Key **Outback Mexico** and press **Tab**; key **8/23 and 12/15** and press **Tab**; key **Land of the Incas** and press **Tab**; key **9/15 and 1/23** and press **Tab**; key **Cultural Journey on the Amazon** and press **Tab**; key **10/17 and 2/13** and press **Tab**; key **Galapagos Adventure** and press **Tab**; and key **11/8 and 3/25** (do not press **Tab**). Select the date column and click the **Center** button on the Formatting toolbar to center the dates in each cell then deselect the column. Your slide should look similar to Figure 16-4.

FIGURE 16-4
Completed departure table

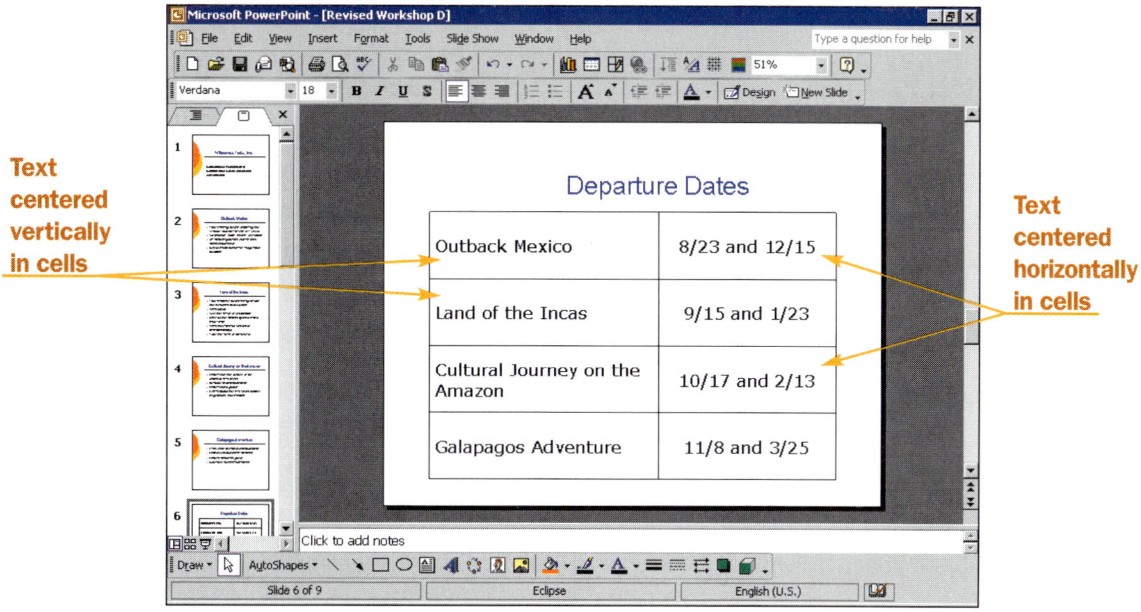

Outback Mexico	8/23 and 12/15
Land of the Incas	9/15 and 1/23
Cultural Journey on the Amazon	10/17 and 2/13
Galapagos Adventure	11/8 and 3/25

11. Save the presentation and leave it open for the next Step-by-Step.

12. Close the Tables and Borders toolbar.

Embed a Word Table Object on a Slide

Another way to create a table on a slide is to embed a Word table. You can embed an existing Word table by copying the Word table to the Office Clipboard and then pasting it on a slide as an *embedded Word table* object. To edit an embedded Word table, you double-click it to access the Word editing features. You want to add a new Title Only slide to the end of the presentation and then embed a Word table containing the new adventure tour costs on the slide.

STEP-BY-STEP 16.2

1. Verify that the Revised Workshop D presentation is open and you are viewing Slide 6 (the Departure Dates slide). Insert a new Title Only slide and then, if you are using PowerPoint 2002, close the task pane. Key **Tour Costs** as the slide title and then deselect the placeholder.

2. Open the **Step16-2** Word document from the data files. Copy the table to the Office Clipboard and then switch to PowerPoint and Slide 7 (the Tour Costs slide) in the Revised Workshop D presentation.

3. Click the **Edit** menu and click **Paste Special** to open the Paste Special dialog box. Click the **Paste** option button, if necessary, and click **Microsoft Word Document Object** in the As list. Your dialog box should look similar to Figure 16-5.

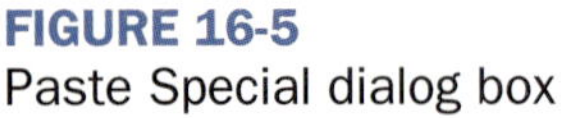
FIGURE 16-5
Paste Special dialog box

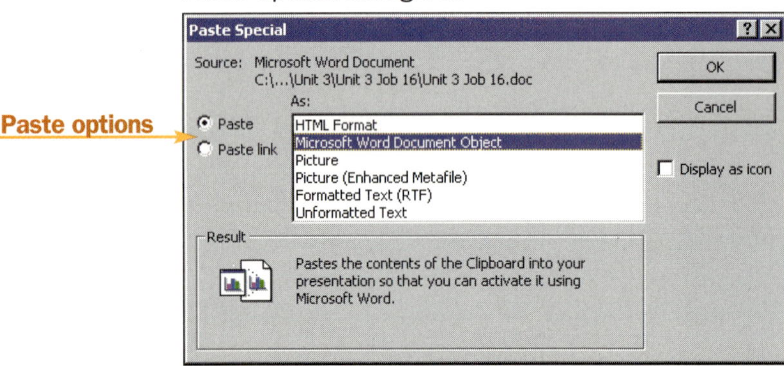

4. Click **OK** to embed the Word table object on the slide.

5. Size the embedded Word object attractively with the mouse pointer and then save the presentation, leaving it open for the next Step-by-Step. Close the Word document.

Create an Embedded Chart Object on a Slide

You can create an embedded chart object on a slide from scratch just as you did in Word by using the Microsoft Graph supplementary application. You can click the Object command on the Insert menu to start Microsoft Graph. PowerPoint offers several slide layouts that include an icon for launching Microsoft Graph as well. You add a new Title and Content slide to the end of the presentation, launch Microsoft Graph, and create a pie chart illustrating the tour cost breakdown.

STEP-BY-STEP 16.3

1. Verify that the Revised Workshop D presentation is open and you are viewing Slide 7 (the Tour Costs slide). Insert a new Title and Content slide and key **Tour Cost Breakdown** as the slide title and then deselect the placeholder. (If you are using PowerPoint 2000, use the Chart slide layout.)

2. Click the **Insert Chart** icon in the content placeholder to open Microsoft Graph and view the datasheet and sample data. (If you are using PowerPoint 2000, double-click the chart placeholder.)

3. Double-click the column B, C, and D column header buttons to hide these columns. Key **Costs** in the cell immediately below the column A header button. Using Figure 16-6 as your guide, key the row 1–4 header text and the corresponding values in column A.

FIGURE 16-6
Completed datasheet

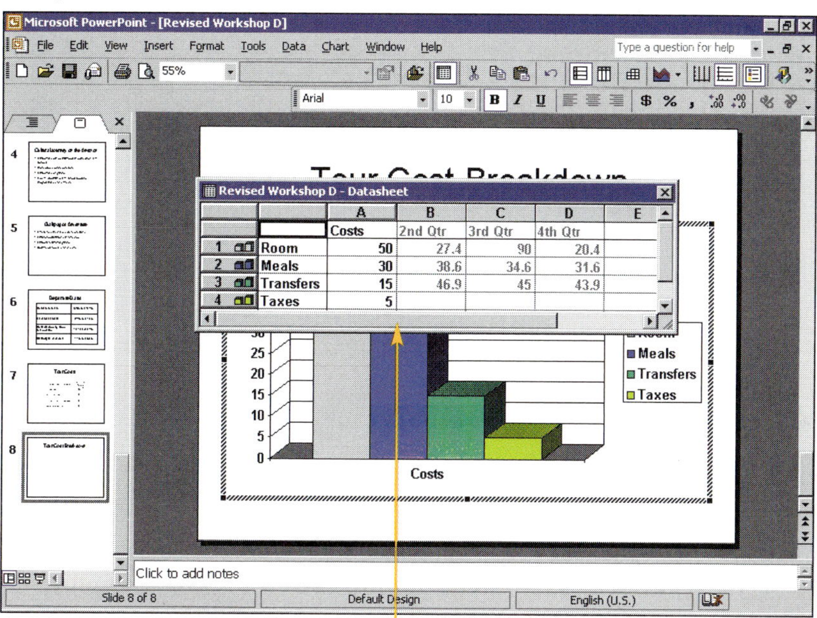

Datasheet with new values and hidden columns

4. Close the datasheet, format the chart as a 3-D Pie Chart, and switch the data to By Column, if necessary, using buttons on the Microsoft Graph Standard toolbar. Delete the legend and show data labels with the category names and percentages. Format the Room data point slice with the red color and the Meals data point slice with the yellow color. Explode the Meals pie slice, resize the plot area to be larger, and remove the plot area border. Then deselect the chart object. Your pie chart should look similar to Figure 16-7.

STEP-BY-STEP 16.3 Continued

FIGURE 16-7
Completed pie chart

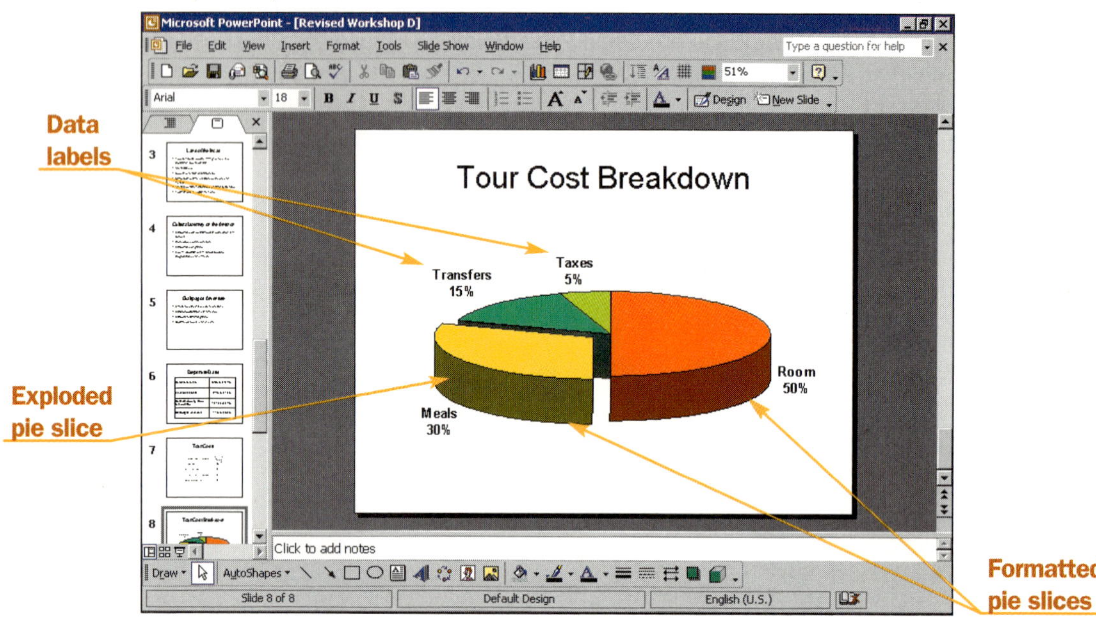

5. Save the presentation and leave it open for the next Step-by-Step.

Customize a Slide Background and Create a WordArt Object

After applying a design template, you can customize individual slides by adding or removing the background color or image and by adding drawing objects such as WordArt. *WordArt* is specially formatted text you can add to a slide and then change its font, color, and shape. You create WordArt with a button on the Drawing toolbar and then format it with buttons on the WordArt toolbar.

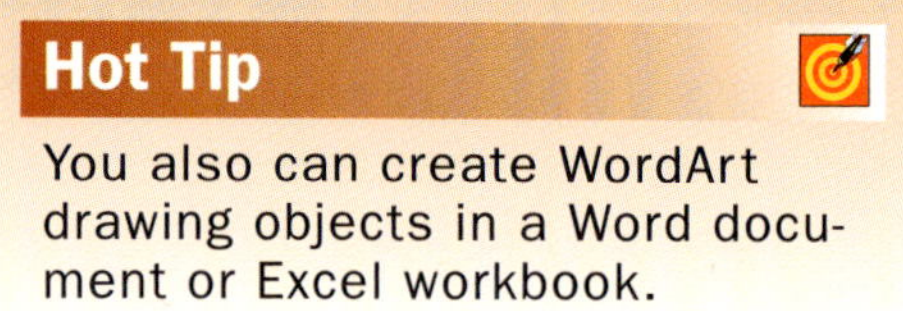

Hot Tip

You also can create WordArt drawing objects in a Word document or Excel workbook.

You now need to apply a design template to the Revised Workshop D presentation and make any necessary adjustments to the slide master. Then you need to add a slide at the end of the presentation, remove its background graphics, and create a WordArt drawing object to indicate the end of the slide show.

Warning

The Office spell checking feature *does not* check the spelling of WordArt text.

S TEP-BY-STEP 16.4

1. Verify that the Revised Workshop D presentation is open and you are viewing Slide 8 (the Tour Cost Breakdown slide). Insert a new blank slide and then apply the Eclipse design template to the presentation. Change the color scheme to the first scheme in the second row (white background with red and gold accent colors). (If you are using PowerPoint 2000, select a design template with a white background and a red and gold color scheme.)

2. View the slide master, center the contents of the title placeholder on all the slides, and then close the slide master and return to Slide 9 in Normal view.

3. Verify you are viewing Slide 9, click the **Format** menu, and click **Background** to open the Background dialog box. Click the **Omit background graphics from master** check box to insert a check mark. Your dialog box should look similar to Figure 16-8.

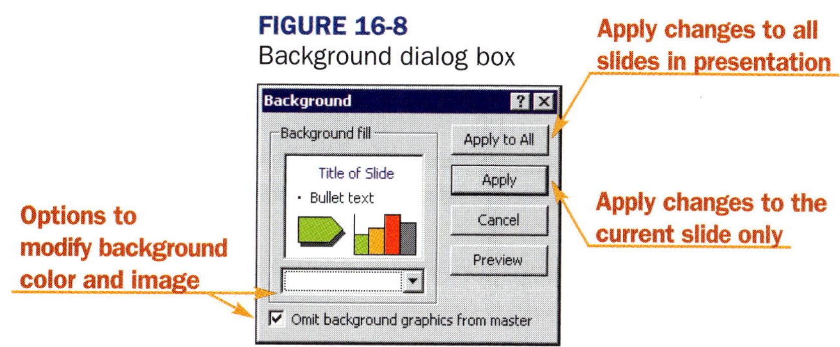

FIGURE 16-8
Background dialog box

4. Click **Apply** to remove the background graphics from Slide 9. (*Note:* Do not click Apply to All.)

5. Click the **Insert WordArt** button on the Drawing toolbar to open the WordArt Gallery dialog box. Click the fourth WordArt style in the first row and click **OK**. Key **Viva Adventure!** in the Edit WordArt Text dialog box and change the font size to 60 and bold the text. Your dialog box should look similar to Figure 16-9. 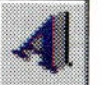

STEP-BY-STEP 16.4 Continued

FIGURE 16-9
Edit WordArt Text dialog box

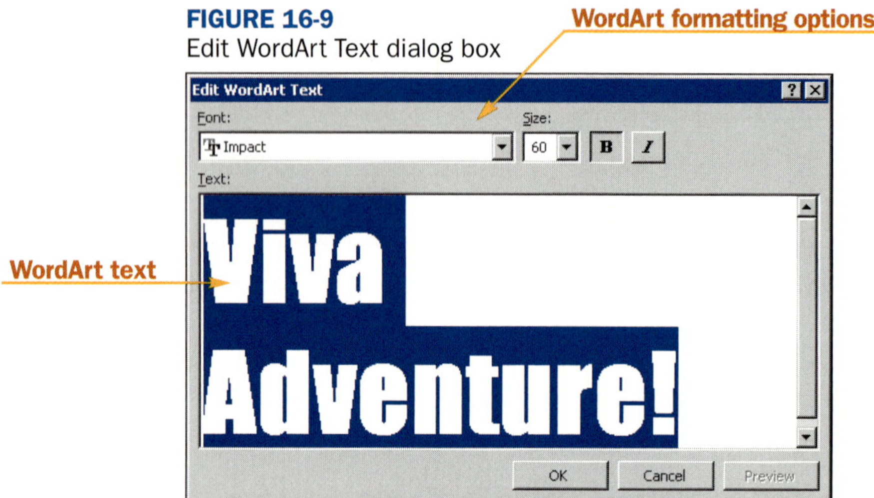

6. Click **OK** to insert the WordArt object on the slide. Observe the round selection/sizing handles around the selected WordArt object. Click the **Fill Color** button list arrow on the Drawing toolbar and click the red color on the grid to fill the WordArt object with the red color. Your slide should look similar to Figure 16-10. 

FIGURE 16-10
Edited WordArt object

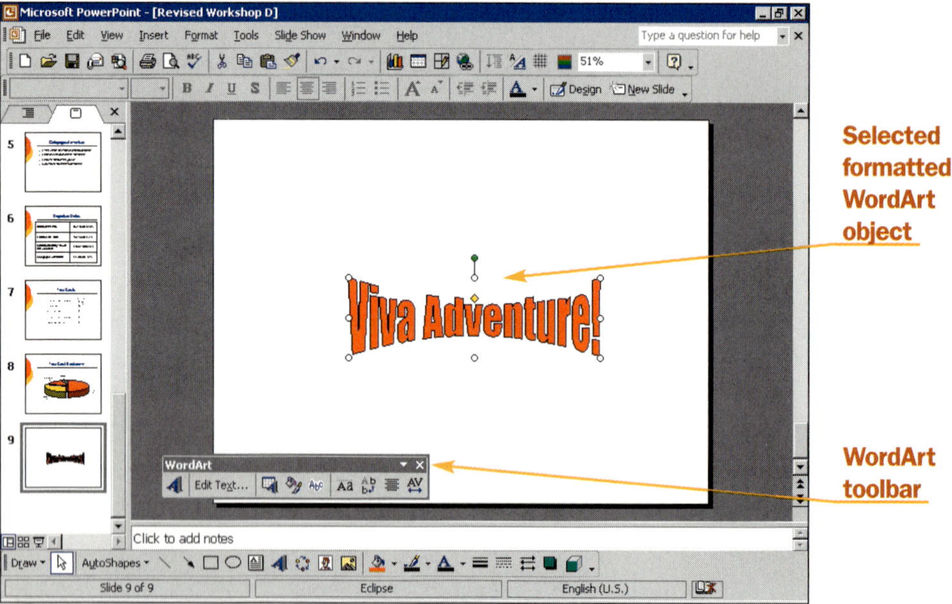

STEP-BY-STEP 16.4 Continued

7. Scroll to view Slide 1 (the title slide) and run the slide show. At the end of the slide show make any adjustments to the individual slides you think necessary (such as repositioning the embedded table or chart objects).

8. Save the presentation, close it, and close PowerPoint.

SUMMARY

In this job, you learned:

- You can create and edit a table on a PowerPoint slide much as you create and edit a table in a Word document.

- You can use a drawing pointer to draw a table on a slide, including its outside boundaries, row boundaries, and column boundaries.

- You can embed a Word table object on a PowerPoint slide using the Copy and Paste Special commands.

- The Microsoft Graph supplementary application can also be used to create an embedded chart from scratch on a slide.

- You can change the background color or remove the background image from the current slide or all slides in a presentation.

- WordArt is a special type of text drawing object you can size, position, and format.

VOCABULARY *Review*

Define the following terms:
Embedded Word table   WordArt

REVIEW *Questions*

TRUE / FALSE

Circle T if the statement is true or F if the statement is false.

T   F   **1.** A table on a PowerPoint slide is created and formatted very differently than a table in a Word document.

T   F   **2.** You can use the mouse pointer to draw a table on a PowerPoint slide.

T   F   **3.** The Draw Table button is found on the Drawing toolbar.

T   F   **4.** A copied Word table can be embedded on a PowerPoint slide using the Paste Special command.

T   F   **5.** If you draw a table with uneven rows and columns you can then distribute those rows or columns evenly with a button on the Tables and Borders toolbar.

FILL IN THE BLANK

Complete the following sentences by writing the correct word or words in the blanks provided.

1. The ___________ button on the PowerPoint Standard toolbar is used to create a table by selecting the number of columns and rows from a grid.

2. ___________ is a text drawing object that can be sized, repositioned, and formatted.

3. An existing Word table can be ___________ on a PowerPoint slide and then edited with Word formatting features.

4. To center text vertically in a table cell, you can use the Center Vertically button on the ___________ toolbar.

5. To create a chart from scratch on a PowerPoint slide, you can use the ___________ supplementary application.

PROJECTS

PROJECT 16-1

1. Start PowerPoint and create a new blank presentation and save it as **Conference Planning Meeting**.

2. Key **Conference Planning Committee Meeting** and today's date as title and subtitle on the title slide.

3. Insert a new Title Only slide and key **Attendees** as the slide title.

4. Draw a seven row by two column table on Slide 2 (the Attendees slide) and distribute the rows evenly. The first column should be approximately one-third the table width. Center the text vertically in the cells. Then position the insertion point in the leftmost cell in the first row.

5. Key **Davenport** and press **Tab**; key **Conference budget** and press **Tab**; key **Betancourt** and press **Tab**; key **Meeting materials** and press **Tab**; key **Stackhouse** and press **Tab**; key **Speakers' workshops** and press **Tab**; key **Washington** and press **Tab**; key **Hotel accommodations** and press **Tab**; key **Chew** and press **Tab**; key **Travel arrangements** and press **Tab**; key **Montevo** and press **Tab**; key **Food and beverage** and press **Tab**; key **your name** and press **Tab**; key **Audio-visual equipment**. (*Note:* Do not press **Tab**.)

6. Insert a new Title Only slide and key **Vendor Payments** as the slide title. Then open the **Project 16-1** Word document from the data files, copy the table to the Office Clipboard, and paste the table as an embedded Microsoft Word Document Object on the new Slide 3 (the Vendor Payments slide). Size and position the embedded Word table object attractively on the slide.

7. Apply the design template of your choice to the presentation and change the color scheme, if desired.

8. Insert a blank slide at the end of the presentation and remove any background images and color (if the background is not white). Add **Committee Meeting** as a WordArt text object in 66-point font using any style you desire from the WordArt Gallery. Fill the WordArt object with a color that compliments the design template color scheme.

9. Save the presentation and leave it open for the next project.

10. Close the Word document and application.

PROJECT 16-2

After reviewing the Conference Planning Meeting presentation, you decide to make a few changes to make the presentation more attractive. Verify that the Conference Planning Meeting presentation you created in Project 16-1 is open. If you have not completed Project 16-1, do so now. Save the presentation as **Revised Meeting** and then double-click the embedded Word table object on Slide 3 (the Vendor Payments slide) to edit the object. Change the table text font to Arial and the font color to a color that compliments the design template color scheme. Bold the table column heading text. Resize any columns with the mouse pointer, if necessary. Then deselect the table object. Select the WordArt object on Slide 4 and resize and reposition it. Use the WordArt Shape button on the WordArt toolbar to change the object's shape. Use the Format WordArt button on the WordArt toolbar to change the object's fill color and border color. Run the slide show and then preview and print the slides. Print audience handouts with three slides per page. Save and close the presentation and close PowerPoint.

WEB PROJECT

Your co-workers frequently ask you which search engine or directory to use when they are looking for information on the World Wide Web. Use your Web browser and search for Web sites that provide information on how search engines such as AltaVista and directories such as Yahoo! work. Print at least three Web pages.

TEAMWORK PROJECT

Sloane suggests you should consider publishing the conference presentations as Web pages on the company intranet. Select a classmate to work with you on this project. Then, using PowerPoint online Help, research how to preview and publish a presentation as a Web page. Finally, using the presentation of your choice, demonstrate this process to several of your classmates.

CRITICAL *Thinking*

ACTIVITY 16-1

Sloane wants to take home a copy of the Revised Workshop D presentation in order to review it later in the evening but doesn't have PowerPoint loaded on the home computer. Using PowerPoint online Help, research how you can prepare the presentation so that it can be viewed on a computer that does not have PowerPoint installed. Then create a Word document containing a brief description of how to do this.

ADDING TRANSITIONS AND ANIMATIONS TO A PRESENTATION

OBJECTIVES

Upon completion of this job, you should be able to:

- Add transition effects to slides.
- Add an animation scheme to a presentation.
- Add custom animations to slide objects.
- Set up a slide show to run automatically.

Estimated Time: 0.5 hour

VOCABULARY

Animation

Animation scheme

Custom animation

Transition effects

Unattended mode

Add Transition Effects to Slides

Slide *transition effects* are special motion effects used to introduce a slide during a slide show. Transition effects create the motion viewers see as a presenter progresses through a slide show from one slide to another. Examples of transition effects include a wiping down across the screen motion, or a motion similar to window blinds closing. You can add transition effects to slides by clicking the Slide Transition command on the Slide Show menu. You can also add transition effects in Slide Sorter view with the Slide Transition button on the Slide Sorter toolbar.

After reviewing the conference presentation containing the welcome to attendees information, Sloane suggests that the presentation can be made more exciting and interesting if a different design template is applied and if slide transition effects are added. You begin by opening the reviewed presentation, changing the design template and color scheme, and then previewing transition effects with and without sound. Finally, you apply a transition effect to all the slides.

Note 

If you are using PowerPoint 2000, you do not have a Slide Transition task pane. You apply slide transition effects and set automatic timings in the Slide Transition dialog box. You then can run the slide show to test the transitions and timings.

Hot Tip 

You can change the speed of transition effects and add sound effects. If you are using PowerPoint 2002, you can apply sound effects along with the transition effects in the Slide Transition task pane.

STEP-BY-STEP 17.1

1. Start the PowerPoint application, open the **Step17-1** presentation from the data files, and save it as **Final Sloane Comments**.

2. Apply the Network design template with a white background and the red and gold color scheme. (If you are using PowerPoint 2000, apply a design template and color scheme of your choice.)

3. Switch to Slide Sorter view, verify that Slide 1 is selected, and click the **Slide Transition** button on the Slide Sorter toolbar to open the Slide Transition task pane. (If you are using PowerPoint 2000, the Slide Transition dialog box opens.)

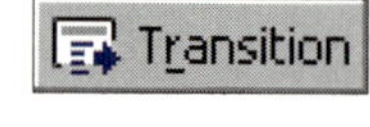

> **Warning**
>
> Whether or not you use transition effects with or without sound depends on a presentation's purpose, content, and audience. Remember that excessive movement and sound can annoy some audience members, so consider using these effects only when they enhance the presentation's message.

4. Click **Blinds Horizontal** in the Apply to selected slides list in the Slide Transition task pane. Observe the transition effect for Slide 1 (the title slide) shown in Figure 17-1 and on your screen. Note the star-shaped Transition Effect icon below Slide 1. (If you are using PowerPoint 2000, click the **Blinds Horizontal** effect in the Effect list and click **Apply**. The Transition Effect icon is a small slide icon.)

FIGURE 17-1
Blinds Horizontal slide transition effect

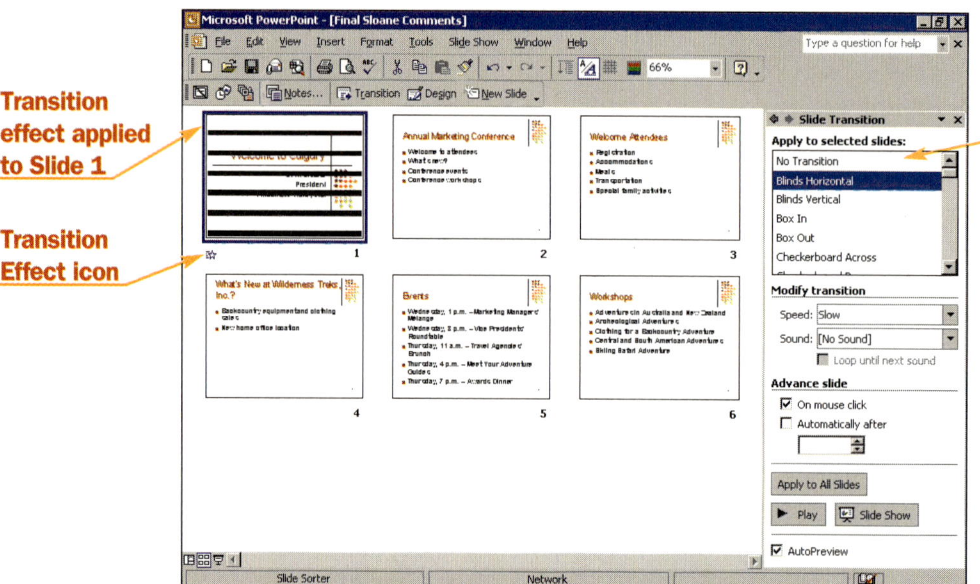

5. Click the **Transition Effect** icon below Slide 1 to repeat the transition effect preview. Then continue to preview several different slide transition effects for Slide 1.

STEP-BY-STEP 17.1 Continued

6. Click **Newsflash** in the Apply to selected slides list in the Slide Transition task pane. Click the **Speed** list arrow in the Slide Transition task pane and click **Medium** to change the transition effect speed. Click the **Sound** list arrow and click **Camera** to add sound as part of the transition effects. (*Note:* If your computer does not have a sound card and speakers, you won't be able to hear the sound effect.) Click the **Apply to All Slides** button in the Slide Transition task pane to apply the Newsflash transition effect, transition speed, and sound effect to all slides. Your screen should look similar to Figure 17-2. (If you are using PowerPoint 2000, open the Slide Transition dialog box and apply the transition effect of your choice at Medium speed to all slides.)

FIGURE 17-2
Transition and sound effect options

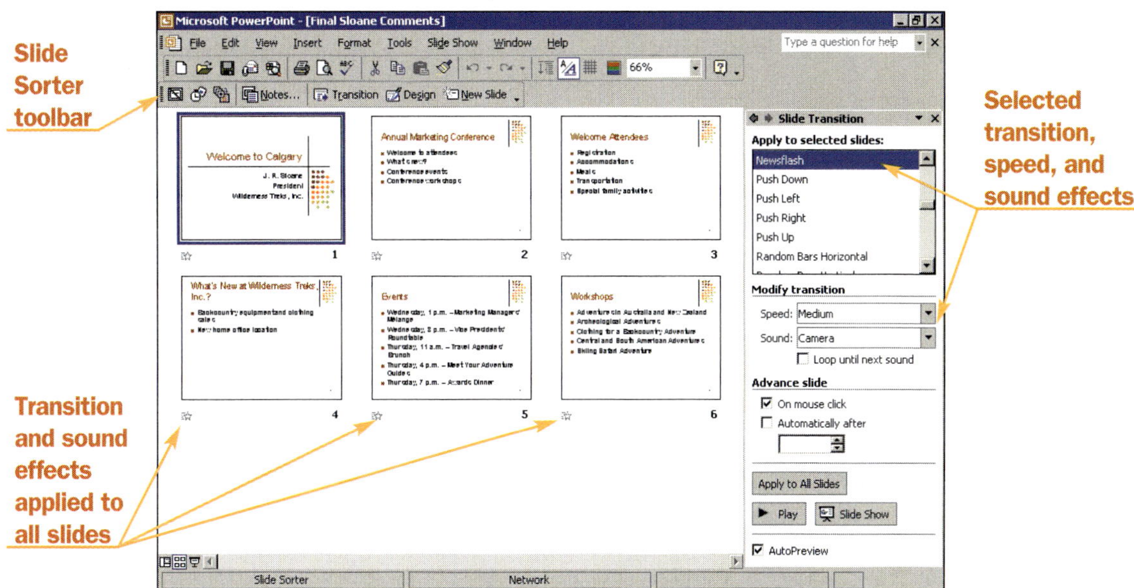

7. Click the **Slide Show** button in the Slide Transition task pane to run the slide show from the selected Slide 1. Advance the slides to view the transition effects. Then return to Normal view. (If you are using PowerPoint 2000, click the **Slide Show View** button to run the slide show and then return to Normal view.)

8. Save the presentation and close it. If you are using PowerPoint 2002, close the task pane.

Add an Animation Scheme to a Presentation

Another way to add interest and excitement to a slide show is to add animation. *Animation* includes special visual and sound effects added to text and other slide objects. When you want to add visual effects to slide title text, bullet text, and text paragraphs, you can quickly do so by applying several preset visual effects together in a set called an *animation*

Note

PowerPoint 2000 does not have animation schemes. If you are using PowerPoint 2000, you may read but not do the following Step-by-Step 17.2. Your instructor may provide alternate instructions for this Step-by-Step.

scheme. PowerPoint 2002 provides a number of animation schemes, ranging from subtle animation to more dramatic animation. You can apply an animation scheme to one or more slides in a presentation using options in the Slide Design task pane. Sloane also asks you to apply an animation scheme to the Final Workshop D presentation.

Hot Tip

When you run a slide show for slides with an applied animation scheme, you may be required to manually advance bulleted items in a list.

S TEP-BY-STEP 17.2

1. Open the **Step17-2** presentation from the data files and save it as **Final Workshop D.** Switch to Slide Sorter view and click **Slide 2** (the Outback Mexico slide) to make it the active slide.

2. Click the **Slide Design** button on the Slide Sorter toolbar to open the Slide Design task pane and then click the **Animation Schemes** hyperlink to view the various animation schemes.

Warning

Some animation schemes also include a transition effect. If you apply an animation scheme to a presentation that already has transition effects applied, the original transition effects are turned off and the animation scheme controls the transition and animation effects for the presentation.

3. Click the **Fade in one by one** animation scheme in the Subtle group in the Slide Design task pane. Observe the animation on your screen and in Figure 17-3. Note the star-shaped Animation icon below Slide 2.

FIGURE 17-3
Fade in one by one animation scheme

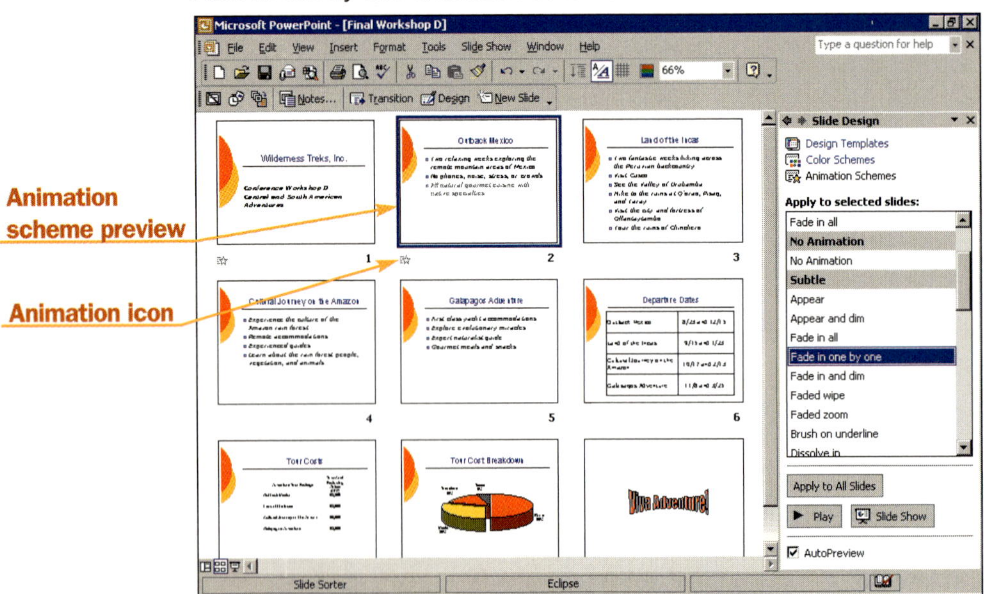

4. Click the star-shaped **Animation** icon below Slide 2 to repeat the animation scheme preview. Then continue to preview several different animation schemes for Slide 2.

STEP-BY-STEP 17.2 Continued

5. Select Slides 1 through 8 using the Shift + click method and apply the Ellipse motion animation scheme in the Exciting group to the selected slides.

6. Observe the animation scheme preview. Your screen should look similar to Figure 17-4.

FIGURE 17-4
Ellipse motion animation scheme

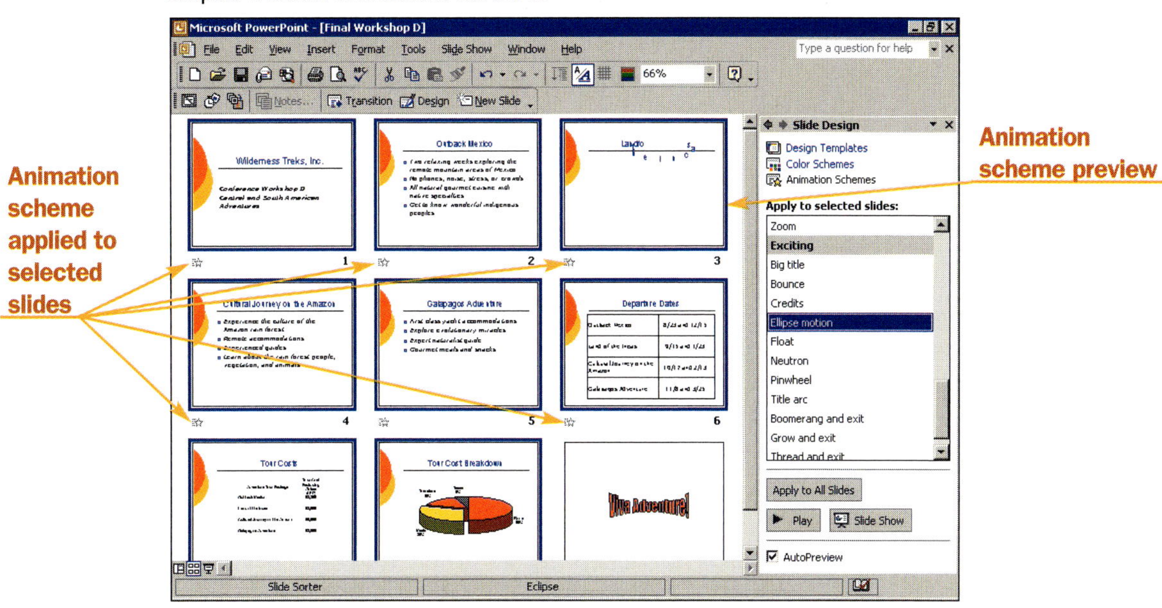

7. Click the **Slide Show** button in the Slide Design task pane to run the slide show. Click as necessary to advance the animation on each slide and to advance to the next slide.

8. Switch to Slide 1 in Normal view, save the presentation, and leave it open for the next Step-by-Step. Close the task pane.

Add Custom Animation to Slide Objects

In addition to applying an animation scheme that contains preset animation and transition effects, you can also apply *custom animation* effects to individual components on each slide. For example, you can apply one animation effect to title text and a different effect to bullet text on the same slide. You also can apply custom animation effects to images, charts, and other objects. If you are using PowerPoint 2002, you can apply custom animation effects with options in the Custom Animation task pane and then set the speed, timing, and presentation method in the Effects Options dialog box.

> **Note** 
>
> PowerPoint 2000 does not have an Animation Effects task pane. If you are using PowerPoint 2000, you can apply custom animation effects using options in the Custom Animation dialog box. You open the dialog box with the Custom Animation command on the Slide Show menu, or with a shortcut menu.

Sloane is pleased with the transitions and animations you added to the two conference presentations, but suggests you add some additional custom animation effects to the chart and marketing slogan in the Final Workshop D presentation. You apply custom animation effects to the chart on Slide 8 (the Total Cost Breakdown slide) so that the pie chart appears—slice by slice—after the slide title appears. You then add custom animation effects to the marketing slogan on Slide 9 so that it first spins and then grows larger. You modify these custom animations to run automatically when each slide is presented.

Hot Tip

When you have multiple custom animations on a slide, each animation effect has an order number and plays in sequence based on that number. You can control the order in which the animation effects are presented by reordering the animation effects.

S TEP-BY-STEP 17.3

1. Verify that the Final Workshop D presentation is open and then save it as **Final Workshop D With Custom Animation**. (If you are using PowerPoint 2000, open the **Step17-2** presentation from the data files and save it as **Final Workshop D With Custom Animation**.)

2. Scroll to view Slide 8 (the Total Cost Breakdown slide) and then click the **Slide Show** menu and click **Custom Animation** to view the Custom Animation task pane. (If you are using PowerPoint 2000, first select the embedded object and then click the same menu commands. The Custom Animation dialog box opens. Skip steps 3 through 8 and instead click the **Entry** animation and sound list arrow and click **Appear**. Click the **Introduce chart elements** list arrow and click **by Category**. Then click **OK**. Then go to step 9.)

3. Observe the Ellipse motion animation icon added to the title text in the previous Step-by-Step. Your Slide 8 should look similar to Figure 17-5.

FIGURE 17-5
Slide 8 with animation notations

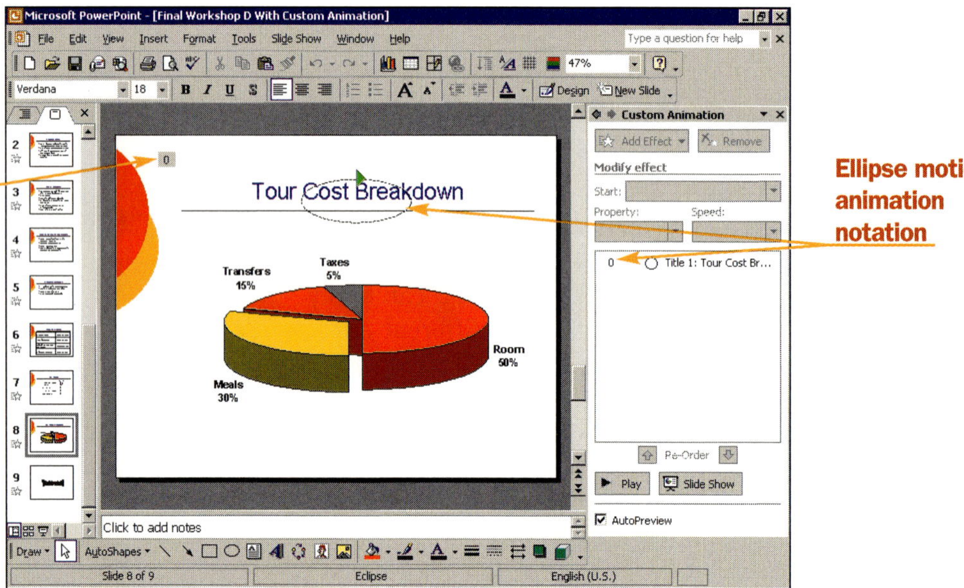

STEP-BY-STEP 17.3 Continued

4. Click the embedded pie chart object to select it. Then click the **Add Effect** button in the Custom Animation task pane to view a menu of animation types. Point to **Entrance** and click **Appear**. (If necessary, click **More Effects** to open the Add Transition Effects dialog box and click **Appear**.) Observe the new animation effect added to the animation effects list in the Custom Animation task pane and the animation number tag to the left of the chart object. Your screen should look similar to Figure 17-6.

Appear custom animation added to chart object

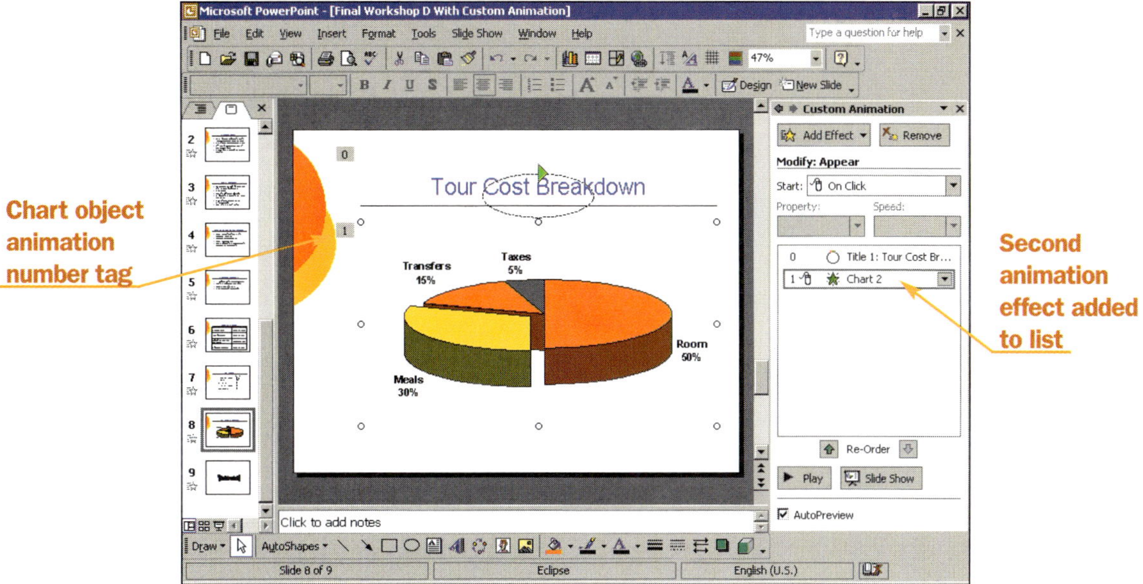

5. Click the **Chart 2 animation item** list arrow in the Custom Animation task pane to view the options menu for the Chart 2 animation item. Then click **Effect Options** to open the Appear effect options dialog box. Click the **Timing** tab.

6. Click the **Start** list arrow and click **After Previous** to have the chart appear after the title text animation. Key **1** in the Delay text box to have the chart objects begin appearing one second after the previous animation. Your dialog box should look similar to Figure 17-7.

Timing tab

STEP-BY-STEP 17.3 Continued

7. Click the **Chart Animation** tab. Then click the **Group chart** list arrow and click **By category** to have the pie slices appear one at a time. Your dialog box should look similar to Figure 17-8.

FIGURE 17-8
Chart Animation tab

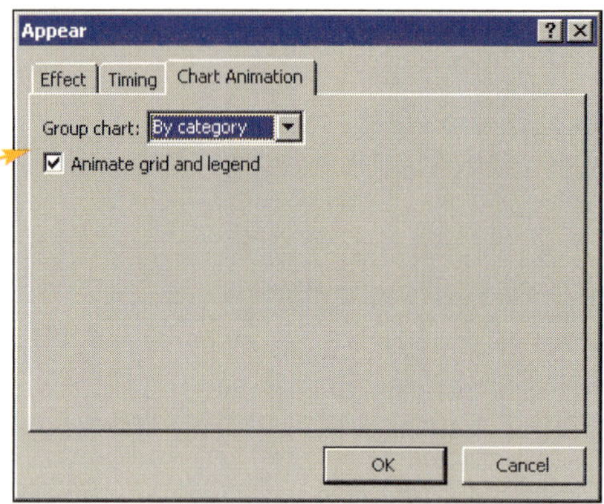

8. Click **OK** to apply the start, timing, and chart group animations. Observe the chart object animations and then click the **Play** button in the Custom Animation task pane to preview all the slide animations in sequence.

9. View Slide 9 and select the WordArt object, click the **Add Effect** button in the Custom Animation task pane, point to **Emphasis**, and click **Spin**. Observe the new animation effect added to the animation effects list in the Custom Animation task pane and the animation number tag to the left of the object. Click the **Viva Adventure! animation item** list arrow in the Custom Animation task pane and click **Start With Previous** to start the animation automatically when the slide appears. (If you are using PowerPoint 2000, select the WordArt object and open the Custom Animation dialog box. Apply the entry animation effect of your choice and click **OK**. Skip steps 10 and 11.)

10. Click the **Add Effect** button, point to **Emphasis**, and click **Grow/Shrink**. Observe the second animation effect added to the animation effects list in the Custom Animation task pane. Click the second **Viva Adventure! animation item** list arrow in the Custom Animation task pane and click **Start After Previous** to start the animation automatically after the previous animation.

11. Click the **Play** button in the Custom Animation task pane to preview all the animations on the slide.

12. Close the Custom Animation task pane, view Slide 1, and run the slide show to view all the animations. (If you are using PowerPoint 2002, the animations on Slides 8 and 9 run automatically—no need to click. If you are using PowerPoint 2000, click to advance the custom animations on Slides 8 and 9.)

13. Save the presentation and leave it open for the next Step-by-Step.

Set Up a Slide Show to Run Automatically

A slide show presentation can be set up to run in an ***unattended mode***. This is useful when a presenter needs to move around the room and can't physically advance the slides. Unattended slide shows are also frequently used at trade shows and conferences where they run from beginning to end in a continuous loop from an unattended computer (sometimes called a kiosk). A kiosk-style presentation is often used to introduce new products or provide general information to those passing by the unattended computer.

Sloane calls to tell you that Slides 1 through 6 and Slide 9 from the Final Workshop D With Custom Animation presentation must also to be set up to run in a kiosk-style unattended presentation on a computer placed near the conference workshop registration desk. Sloane expects this type of unattended presentation will interest conference participants and convince them to register for the workshop. You begin by saving a copy of the presentation. Then you hide Slides 7 and 8, set automatic timings for the remaining slides, and then modifying the slide show setup options for the presentation.

S TEP-BY-STEP 17.4

1. Verify that the Final Workshop D With Custom Animation presentation is open and then save it as **Final Workshop D for Kiosk**.

2. Switch to Slide Sorter view and select Slides 7 and 8 using the Shift + click method. Click the **Hide Slide** button on the Slide Sorter toolbar to hide both slides.

3. Select Slides 1 through 6 and Slide 9 using the Ctrl + click method. Click the **Slide Transition** button on the Slide Sorter toolbar to view the Slide Transition task pane.  Click the **Automatically after** check box in the Slide Transition task pane to turn on the automatic slide and animation advance feature. Key **2** in the Automatically after text box to set the automatic timing to two seconds. Click the **On mouse click** check box in the Slide Transition task pane to turn off the option to advance slides with the mouse. Your screen should look similar to Figure 17-9. (If you are using PowerPoint 2000, click **Apply to All** in the Slide Transition dialog box and then select Slide 1 before going to Step 4.)

STEP-BY-STEP 17.4 Continued

FIGURE 17-9
Slides with automatic timing

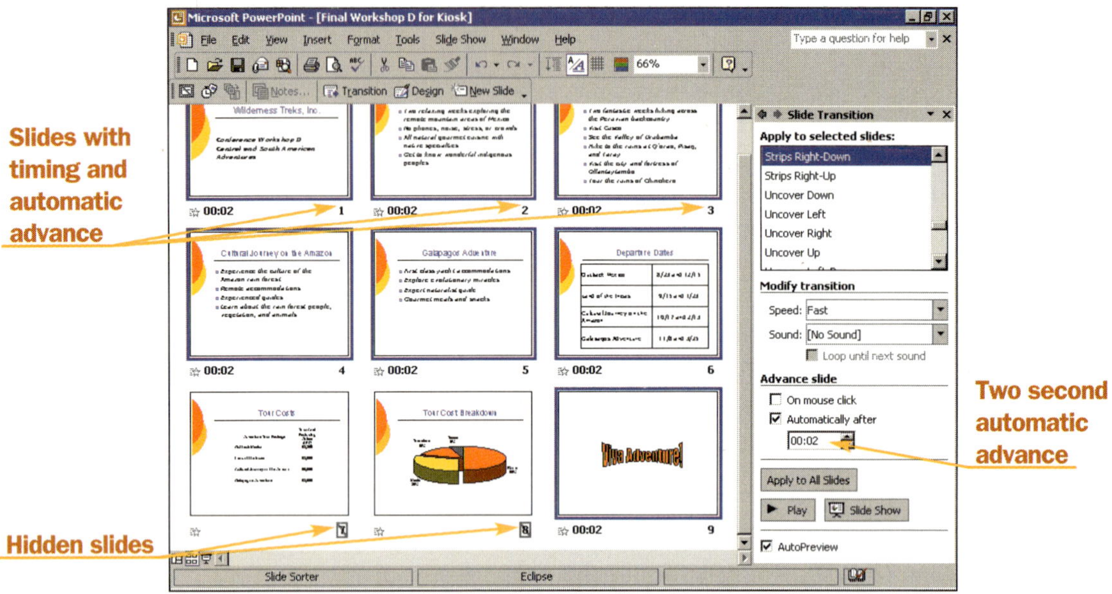

4. Run the Slide Show to preview the automated slide advance and animations and then save the presentation.

5. Click the **Slide Show** menu and click **Set Up Show** to open the Set Up Show dialog box. Then click the **Browsed at a kiosk (full screen)** option button. Observe that the Loop continuously until 'Esc' and Using timings, if present options are automatically selected. Your dialog box should look similar to Figure 17-10.

FIGURE 17-10
Set Up Show dialog box

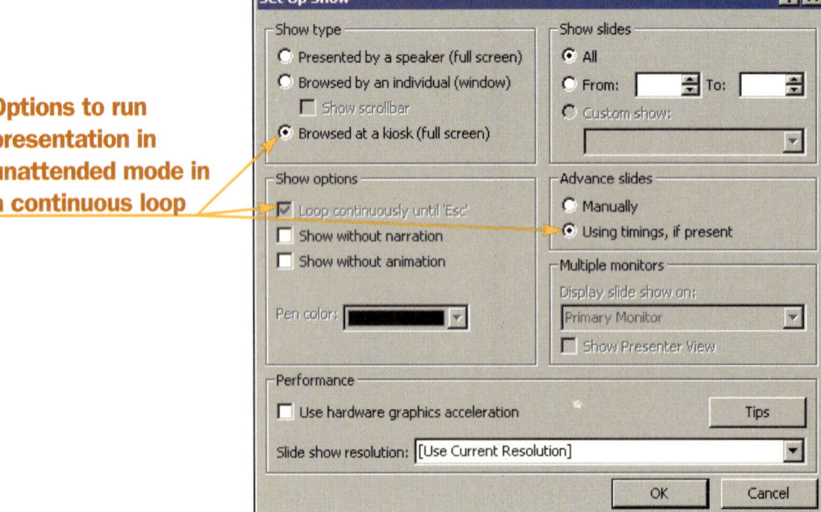

STEP-BY-STEP 17.4 Continued

6. Click **OK** and then run the slide show to view it in a continuous loop.

7. Save the presentation and close it and close PowerPoint.

SUMMARY

In this job, you learned:

- Transition effects are special motion effects used to introduce a slide during a slide show.

- Animation includes special visual and sound effects added to text and other slide objects.

- To quickly add a transition effect and animation to title, bulleted list, and paragraph text to one or several slides, you can apply an animation scheme.

- Custom animation effects are applied to individual slide objects and then modified to set the presentation method, timing, speed, and other options.

- You can set up a slide show to run in unattended mode in the Set Up Show dialog box.

VOCABULARY *Review*

Define the following terms:		
Animation	Custom animation	Unattended mode
Animation scheme	Transition effects	

REVIEW *Questions*

TRUE / FALSE

Circle T if the statement is true or F if the statement is false.

T   F   **1.** A set of preset text animation effects with or without transition effects that can be applied all at once is called an animation scheme.

T   F   **2.** Special motion effects viewers see as a slide show progresses from one slide to another are called animation effects.

T   F   **3.** You can alter the speed at which transition effects take place.

T   F   **4.** You cannot hide slides in a slide show.

T   F   **5.** It is a good idea to add as many transition and animation effects as you possibly can to every PowerPoint presentation you create.

FILL IN THE BLANK

Complete the following sentences by writing the correct word or words in the blanks provided.

1. The __________ button on the Slide Sorter toolbar is used to add transition effects to one or more slides.

2. __________ includes special visual and sound effects added to text and other slide objects.

3. You can click the __________ below a slide in Slide Sorter view to preview the slide's animation.

4. An unattended computer on which slide show presentations are run automatically in a continuous loop is sometimes called a(n) __________.

5. A motion effect that you can apply to one or more slides that is similar to opening and closing window blinds is called a(n) __________ effect.

PROJECTS

PROJECT 17-1

1. Start PowerPoint, open the **Project 17-1** presentation from the data files, and save it as **Confidential Meeting With Animation**.

2. Apply the design template and color scheme of your choice. Make any modifications to font alignment, font style, and font size that you desire.

3. Apply the transition effect of your choice to all the slides and then run the slide show to view the transitions.

4. Apply the animation scheme of your choice to all the slides and then run the slide show to view the animations.

5. Set two-second automatic timings for all the slides and then run the slide show to view the automatic timings.

6. Save the presentation and close it.

PROJECT 17-2

After Sloane shows L. D. Meeker the difference transition and animation effects can make to a presentation, Meeker calls you and asks that you revise the presentation containing the Calgary budget data to include some of these special effects. Meeker leaves it up to you to select the appropriate combination of transition and animation effects. Open the **Project 17-2** presentation from the data files and save it as **Revised Calgary Budget**. (*Note:* Click **No** or **Cancel** if asked to update the links.) Apply the design template and color scheme of your choice. Make any additional changes you think necessary to assure the presentation is professional looking and attractive. Then apply appropriate transition and/or animation effects to the presentation.

  ## WEB PROJECT

Because of all your hard work on the conference, Sloane suggests you spend an additional four days in the Calgary area after the conference at the company's expense. You decide you want to visit the town of Banff and Lake Louise, which has a glacier coming right down to the lake. Using your Web browser, locate at least five Web pages you can use to plan your four-day stay at Lake Louise, including transportation to Lake Louise and back to the Calgary airport; hotel or lodge accommodations; and activities during your stay. Print the Web pages.

  ## TEAMWORK PROJECT

 Melody Stackhouse calls and asks for your help. She has a very large slide show presentation that her supervisor uses for employee orientation. However, each employee orientation group may need to view different slides from the presentation and rarely does any group view all the slides. She is tired of having to hide and unhide slides each time the presentation is used and asks if you can think of a better way to handle the problem. You think creating custom shows stored within the large presentation may be the answer. Select a classmate to help you with this project. Then, using PowerPoint online Help, research how to set up and run a custom show. Using the presentation of your choice, demonstrate to a group of classmates how to set up and run a custom show.

CRITICAL*Thinking*

 ## ACTIVITY 17-1

 Melody calls back with another question. She needs to know if there is a way to show a hidden slide during a slide show. You tell her that you will research the problem and get back to her shortly. Using PowerPoint online Help, research how to view a hidden slide during a slide show. Then, using the presentation of your choice, demonstrate to a classmate how to hide a slide and then view the hidden slide during a slide show.

CREATING SPEAKER NOTES AND AUDIENCE HANDOUTS

<table>
<tr><td>

OBJECTIVES

Upon completion of this job, you should be able to:

- Modify the notes master.
- Create speaker notes.
- Modify the handout master.
- Send a presentation to Word to create audience handouts.

Estimated Time: 0.5 hour

</td><td>

VOCABULARY

Handout master

Notes master

Speaker notes pages

</td></tr>
</table>

Modify the Notes Master

Sloane is pleased with the Final Sloane Comments conference presentation you prepared and asks you to create a set of speaker notes pages for it. *Speaker notes pages* are printed pages that contain a picture of a slide, header and footer placeholders, and a text box in which you key text related to the slide. Sloane plans to use the speaker notes pages to list key topics to be mentioned during the slide show.

The *notes master* is used to control the layout of speaker notes pages in the same way that the slide master is used to control the layout of individual slides. Before you create the speaker notes pages, you first modify the presentation's notes master to add Sloane's name in a header, today's date, and Calgary Conference in a footer.

$\mathcal{S}$TEP-BY-STEP 18.1

1. Start the PowerPoint application, open the **Step18-1** presentation from the data files, and save it as **Final Sloane Comments With Notes**.

2. Click the **View** menu, point to **Master**, and click **Notes Master** to view the notes master. Observe the Header, Date, Footer, Number, and Notes Body Area placeholders.

3. Zoom the view to 75% and click the <**header**> text placeholder in the Header Area placeholder to select it. Then key **J. R. Sloane**.

4. Click the <**date/time**> text placeholder in the Date Area placeholder. Then click the **Insert** menu and click **Date and Time** to open the Data and Time dialog box. Click the fourth date option to select it and click the **Update automatically** check box to insert a check mark. Click **OK** to insert the current date and time as an automatically updated field.

5. Scroll to view the Footer Area placeholder and click the <**footer**> text placeholder to select it. Key **Calgary Conference** and deselect the text box. Zoom the view to Fit. Your screen should look similar to Figure 18-1.

FIGURE 18-1
Modified notes master

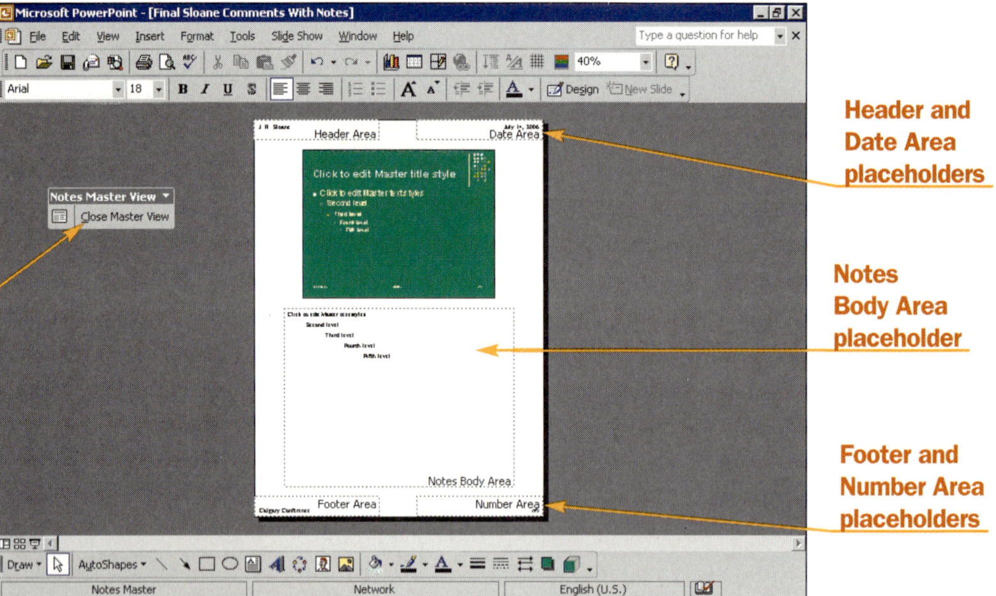

6. Return to **Normal** view.

7. Save the presentation and leave it open for the next Step-by-Step.

Create Speaker Notes

You create speaker notes pages in Notes Page view and then preview and print the pages using options in Print Preview view and the Print dialog box. You add the following text to speaker notes pages in the Final Sloane Comments With Notes presentation:

Slide 2—Remember to introduce the Wilderness Treks employees on hand.

Slide 4—Remember to mention the new Web site URL and our new address.

Slide 6—Remind attendees to sign up for the Central and South American adventures workshop.

STEP-BY-STEP 18.2

1. Verify that the Final Sloane Comments With Notes presentation is open and you are viewing Slide 1 (the title slide). Click the **View** menu and click **Notes Page** to view Slide 1 in Notes Page view and then scroll to view Slide 2 (the Annual Marketing Conference slide). Zoom the view to 75%, if necessary.

2. Click in the Notes Body Area placeholder to position the insertion point and key **Remember to introduce the Wilderness Treks employees on hand.** Deselect the placeholder. Your screen should look similar to Figure 18-2.

FIGURE 18-2
Slide 2 notes page

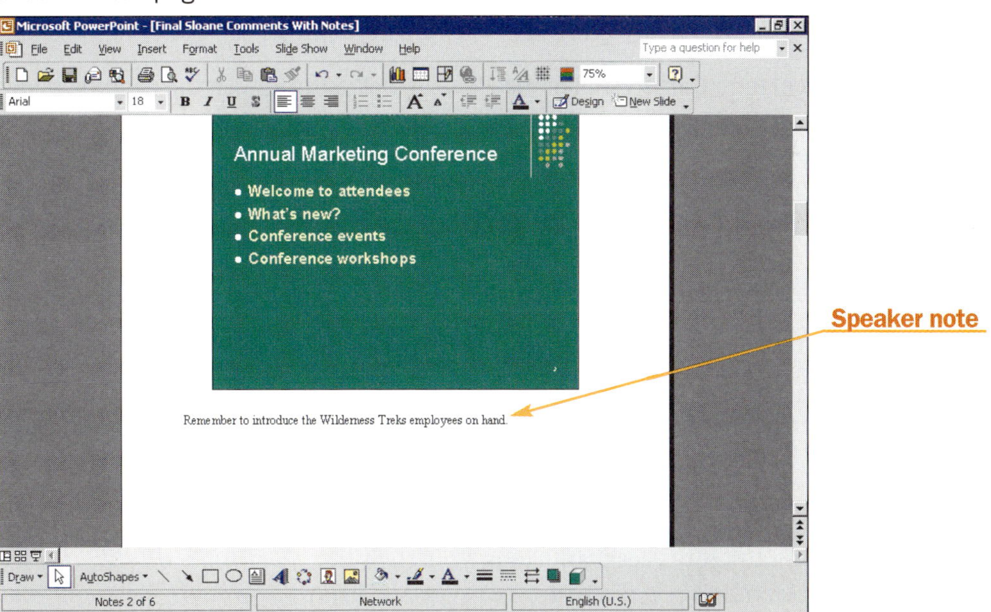

3. Scroll to view Slide 4 and key **Remember to mention the new Web site URL and our new address.** in the Notes Body Area placeholder.

4. Scroll to view Slide 6 and key **Remind attendees to sign up for the Central and South American adventures workshop.** in the Notes Body Area placeholder. Then zoom the view to Fit.

STEP-BY-STEP 18.2 Continued

5. Switch to **Normal** view, scroll to view Slide 1, and save the presentation.

6. Print preview using the Notes Pages option and then print the pages. Switch to **Normal** view and leave the presentation open for the next Step-by-Step. (If you are using PowerPoint 2000, you will not be able to print preview the notes pages.)

Modify the Handout Master

The *handout master* controls the layout of audience handout pages you create in PowerPoint. Sloane calls to remind you to create a set of audience handout pages with two slides per page and with appropriate headers and footers for the Final Sloane Comments With Notes presentation. You begin by modifying the handout master to add the header and footer text and then you preview and print the audience handout pages.

STEP-BY-STEP 18.3

1. Verify that the Final Sloane Comments With Notes presentation is open and you are viewing Slide 1 (the title slide). Click the **View** menu, point to **Master**, and click **Handout Master** to view the handout master. Zoom the view to 75%.

2. Key **Welcome to Calgary** in the <header> text placeholder; key **July** and the current year (**200X**) in the <date/time> text placeholder; and key **Wilderness Treks, Inc.** in the <footer> text placeholder.

3. Switch to **Normal** view, print preview the slides using the Handouts (2 slides per page) option, and print the handout pages. Then switch to **Normal** view.

4. Save the presentation and close it.

Send a Presentation to Word to Create Audience Handouts

Sloane drops by your desk and tells you that the Workshop D presentation is going to be reviewed in a marketing directors' meeting this afternoon and you need to create handout material for the meeting. Another way to create audience handouts is by sending a PowerPoint slide show to Word. You can create PowerPoint slide show handouts in Word in a variety of layouts. You open the presentation in PowerPoint and send it to Word using a layout that provides blank lines below each embedded slide.

> **Hot Tip** 
>
> When you send a PowerPoint presentation to Word, you have the option of embedding or linking the slides in the resulting Word document. If you embed the slides, you can then modify them in the Word document without changing the slides in the original presentation. If you link the slides to the Word document, all changes are made in the original presentation.

STEP-BY-STEP 18.4

1. Open the **Step18-4** presentation from the data files.

2. Click **File**, point to **Send To**, and click **Microsoft Word** to open the Send To Microsoft Word dialog box. (If you are using PowerPoint 2000, the Write Up dialog box opens.)

3. Click the **Blank lines below slides** option button and then click the **Paste** option button, if necessary. Your dialog box should look similar to Figure 18-3.

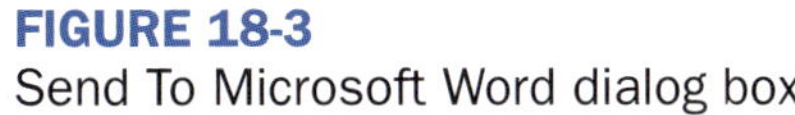

FIGURE 18-3
Send To Microsoft Word dialog box

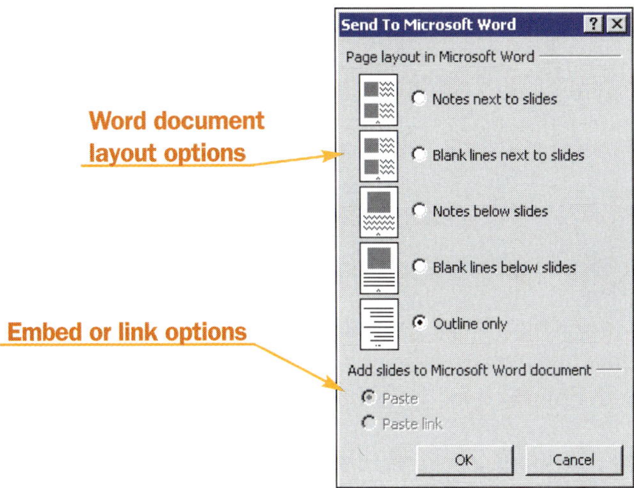

4. Click **OK** to send the presentation to Word. (It may take a few seconds for the Word document to be created.)

5. Save the Word document as **Workshop D Handouts** and then scroll to view all the pages.

6. Print preview, print, and close the Word document and close Word.

7. Close the presentation and close PowerPoint.

SUMMARY

In this job, you learned:

- Speaker notes pages are printed pages that contain the picture of a slide, header and footer text, and notes or comments related to the slide pictured.

- The notes master controls the layout of speaker notes pages.

- The handout master controls the layout of the audience handout pages you create in PowerPoint.

- You can send a PowerPoint presentation to Word to create a Word document containing embedded or linked slides. You can choose from several different layouts for the Word document.

VOCABULARY *Review*

Define the following terms:

Handout master   Notes master   Speaker notes pages

REVIEW *Questions*

TRUE/FALSE

Circle T if the statement is true or F if the statement is false.

T   F   **1.** The slide master is used to control the layout of audience handout pages.

T   F   **2.** The notes master is used to control the layout of notes pages.

T   F   **3.** When you send a PowerPoint presentation to Word, you can either embed or link the slides in the resulting Word document.

T   F   **4.** You can control the layout of PowerPoint audience handouts with the layout master.

T   F   **5.** When you send a PowerPoint presentation to Word to create handout material, the document always has one slide per page with lines below the slide.

FILL IN THE BLANK

Complete the following sentences by writing the correct word or words in the blanks provided.

1. The <header> text placeholder in the notes master is used to key __________ text.

2. In the handout or notes master you can use the __________ command on the Insert menu to insert a date field that automatically updates.

3. Speaker __________ pages are often used to help a speaker keep track of the important topics he or she must discuss during a slide show.

4. When you send a PowerPoint presentation to Word with __________ slides, any modifications you make to the slides in the resulting Word document are not made in the original presentation.

5. The __________ master is used to control the layout of audience handouts you create in PowerPoint.

PROJECTS

PROJECT 18-1

1. Start PowerPoint, open the **Project 18-1** presentation from the data files, and save it as **Meeting Notes and Handouts**.

2. Modify the notes master to add Sloane's name as a header and today's date in the footer.

3. Add the following text as notes in Notes Page view: Slide 2—**Ask each attendee his/her view of our situation.**; Slide 3—**Poll the attendees for their understanding of what went wrong.**; Slide 4—**Remind attendees to submit a list of goals and expectations and time frame in which to accomplish them.**

4. Print preview the notes pages, print them, and then return to **Normal** view.

5. Save the presentation and close it.

PROJECT 18-2

Meeker calls and asks you to create a Word document that can be used as a handout at the Calgary office's budget meeting. Open the **Project 18-2** presentation from the data files and click **Cancel** to not update the link. Then send the presentation to Word to create a Word document with linked slides and blank lines beside the slides. Save the document as **Calgary Budget Meeting** and then print preview and print the document. Then close the Word document, close Word, close the PowerPoint presentation, and close PowerPoint.

WEB PROJECT

As an administrative assistant, it is important that you continue your ongoing professional development. You think the Web might be a good place to look for information of interest to an administrative assistant. Using your Web browser and a search tool such as Google (*www.google.com*), locate at least three Web sites containing information useful to the professional development of an administrative assistant. Print the Web pages.

TEAMWORK PROJECT

Sloane asks you for information about broadcasting the conference presentations over the company intranet to interested employees who can then critique the presentations. Select a classmate to help you with this project. Then, using PowerPoint online Help, review the basics of broadcasting an online presentation. Finally, describe the process to a group of classmates.

CRITICAL*Thinking*

ACTIVITY 18-1

Melody Stackhouse calls and asks for your help. She needs to be able to open a specific Excel workbook during a slide show, but she isn't sure how to do it. Using PowerPoint online Help, research how to set up another application or program to run from a PowerPoint presentation. Then using the Excel workbook and PowerPoint presentation of your choice, demonstrate to a classmate how to set up the application or program to run from PowerPoint.

BUSINESS WEEK THREE

COMMAND SUMMARY

EXCEL FEATURE	MENU COMMAND	KEYSTROKE	TOOLBAR BUTTON	JOB
AutoShapes	Drawing toolbar, AutoShapes			15
AutoSum			Σ	13
Chart	Insert, Chart	F11		13
Clear print area	File, Print Area, Clear Print Area			13
Comment	Insert, Comment			13
Copy	Edit, Copy	Ctrl + C		13
Decrease indent	Format, Cells	Ctrl + 1		13
Drawing toolbar	View, Toolbars, Drawing			15
Fill color	Format, Cells	Ctrl + 1		15
Increase decimal	Format, Cells	Ctrl + 1		13
Insert cells	Insert, Cells			13
Insert hyperlink	Insert, Hyperlink	Ctrl + K		15
Insert rows	Insert, Rows			13
Merge and center	Format, Cells	Ctrl + 1		13
Page setup	File, Page Setup			13
Paste	Edit, Paste	Ctrl + V		13
Paste link	Edit, Paste Special			15
Percent Style	Format, Style Format, Cells	Ctrl + 1	%	13
Save a Web page	File, Save As Web Page			13
Set print area	File, Print Area, Set Print Area			13
Spelling	Tools, Spelling	F7		13
Underline	Format, Cells	Ctrl + 1		13
Web page preview	File, Web Page Preview			13

COMMAND SUMMARY

POWERPOINT FEATURE	MENU COMMAND	KEYSTROKE	TOOLBAR BUTTON	JOB
Action buttons	Slide Show, Action Buttons			15
Animation schemes	Format, Slide Design		Design	17
Bold	Format, Font	Ctrl + B	B	14
Bulleted list	Format, Bullets and Numbering			14
Center vertically				16
Color schemes	Format, Slide Design		Design	16
Custom animation	Slide Show, Custom Animation			17
Distribute rows evenly				16
Draw table				16
Fill color				16
Font color	Format, Font		A	14
Handout master	View, Master, Handout Master			18
Hide slides				17
Insert clip art	Insert, Picture, Clip Art			14
Insert WordArt	Insert, Picture, WordArt			16
New slide	Insert, New Slide	Ctrl + M	New Slide	14
Normal view	View, Normal			15
Notes master	View, Master, Notes Master			18
Notes Page view	View, Notes Page			18
Numbered list	Format, Bullets and Numbering			14
Paste link	Edit, Paste Special			15
Print	File, Print	Ctrl + P	Print...	14
Print preview	File, Print Preview			14
Print What?			Slides	14
Replace fonts	Format, Replace Fonts			14
Send to Word	File, Send To, Microsoft Word			18
Set up a slide show	Slide Show, Set Up Show			17
Slide Design task pane	Format, Slide Design		Design	14
Slide master	View, Master, Slide Master			14
Slide show	Slide Show, View Show	F5		15
Slide Sorter view	View, Slide Sorter			15
Slide transition effects	Slide Show, Slide Transition		Transition	17

REVIEW *Questions*

TRUE/FALSE

Circle T if the statement is true or F if the statement is false.

T F   1.   A mixed cell reference is one in which only one component of the reference cannot be changed when a formula is copied to another location.

T F   2.   To create an absolute cell reference you insert an asterisk (*) before both the column and row indicators.

T F   3.   You can view multiple slides and then move or delete them in Slide Transition view.

T F   4.   Drawing objects, such as AutoShapes, cannot be used as hyperlinks.

T F   5.   You can use hyperlinks to navigate between worksheets in an Excel workbook or between slides in a PowerPoint presentation.

T F   6.   You can create a table on a PowerPoint slide by drawing the table's outside boundary and its row and column boundaries.

T F   7.   You can use the Microsoft Graph supplementary application to create an embedded chart from scratch on a PowerPoint slide.

T F   8.   PowerPoint slide shows that run in a continuous loop on unattended computers are often used at trade shows and conferences.

T F   9.   The notes master is used to control the layout of individual slides.

T F   10.   The cell reference D26 is a mixed cell reference.

MATCHING

Match the correct term in Column 1 to its description in Column 2.

<table>
<tr><td>Column 1</td><td colspan="2">Column 2</td></tr>
<tr><td>____ 1. Absolute</td><td>A.</td><td>Selecting multiple worksheets in order to perform the same action on all the worksheets at one time</td></tr>
<tr><td>____ 2. AutoContent Wizard</td><td>B.</td><td>Specially formatted text drawing objects</td></tr>
<tr><td>____ 3. Hyperlink</td><td>C.</td><td>A table copied from a Word document and pasted into a PowerPoint slide that must be edited with Word features</td></tr>
<tr><td>____ 4. Linked object</td><td></td><td></td></tr>
<tr><td>____ 5. Grouping</td><td>D.</td><td>Special motion effects used to introduce a slide during a slide show</td></tr>
<tr><td>____ 6. Embedded Word table</td><td></td><td></td></tr>
<tr><td>____ 7. WordArt</td><td>E.</td><td>An object or text associated with the path to text or an object at another location</td></tr>
<tr><td>____ 8. Slide transition effects</td><td>F.</td><td>A pre-designed set of visual effects applied to one or more slides</td></tr>
<tr><td>____ 9. Animation scheme</td><td></td><td></td></tr>
<tr><td>____ 10. Animation</td><td>G.</td><td>A step-by-step process for quickly creating a slide show that has already had a design template applied and slides containing sample text</td></tr>
<tr><td></td><td>H.</td><td>Special visual and sound effects added to text and other slide objects</td></tr>
<tr><td></td><td>I.</td><td>A cell reference (both column and row) that does not change when a formula is copied down or to the right</td></tr>
<tr><td></td><td>J.</td><td>An object copied from a source application document and pasted into a destination application document in such a way that it must be edited with the tools of the source application</td></tr>
</table>

CRITICAL*Thinking*

 **PROJECT 1**

J. L. Stackhouse sends you a workbook containing the data for the London budget and asks that you finalize the worksheets by creating the appropriate formulas. Open the **Unit 3 Review Project 1** workbook from the data files and save it as **London Budget**. On the Expenses worksheet, create a formula to calculate the percentage of total expenses for the Advertising expense category. Then copy the formula with appropriate absolute references for the remaining expense categories using the fill handle. On the Budget worksheet, create linking formulas to the Expenses worksheet as needed to calculate the expenses for each quarter. Create formulas to calculate the total expenses and gross profit for each quarter and the annual totals. Create a formula to calculate the percentage of total revenues for total expenses and gross profit. Create an embedded chart on the Budget worksheet (using the chart type and subtype of your choice) that shows the relationship between adventure tours revenues, total expenses, and gross profit for each of the four quarters. Format the chart objects as desired. Print the worksheets and save and close the workbook.

PROJECT 2

You want to create a PowerPoint presentation that can be used to direct Stackhouse's London budget discussion at the budget meeting following the Calgary conference. Create a new blank presentation, apply the design template of your choice, and save it as **Stackhouse Budget Presentation**. Use the slide and slide title masters to make changes to the title and other slide layouts. Add Stackhouse's name and the text **London Budget** to the title slide.

Insert three Title only slides following the title slide. On the first new slide (Slide 2), embed the Budget data from the London Budget workbook; on the second new slide (Slide 3), embed the Expenses data; and on the third new slide (Slide 4), embed the Budget chart. Add appropriate titles to the three slides. Size and position the embedded objects attractively.

Insert a new Title and Content slide at the end of the presentation and create a pie chart from scratch showing the percentage of total expenses for each London branch expense category. (If you are using PowerPoint 2000, insert a new Chart slide and then create the pie chart.) Get your data from the Expense worksheet in the London Budget workbook. Format the chart objects as desired. Add an appropriate title to the slide.

Use action buttons to create hyperlinks to and from the slides containing data and the slides containing charts illustrating that data. Apply slide transition effects, an animation scheme, or custom animation to the presentation as desired. Run the slide show to test the hyperlinks and the animations.

Modify the handout master to include Stackhouse's name and today's date. Then print preview the slides and print the slides and audience handouts using the handout layout of your choice. Save the presentation and then close it.

ADVANCED *Challenge*

Because so many of your coworkers have asked you about creating slide shows in PowerPoint, you have been holding a series of "brown bag" luncheon seminars on creating presentations. Next Wednesday's topics are "The Importance of Selecting the Right Font" and "Embedding Fonts in a PowerPoint Presentation." Using PowerPoint online Help, research these two topics. Then create a PowerPoint presentation containing useful information on these two topics. Format the slides attractively.

BUSINESS WEEK FOUR: DATABASES

Unit 4

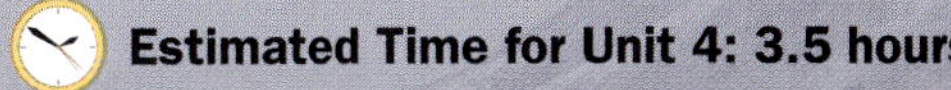 **Estimated Time for Unit 4: 3.5 hours**

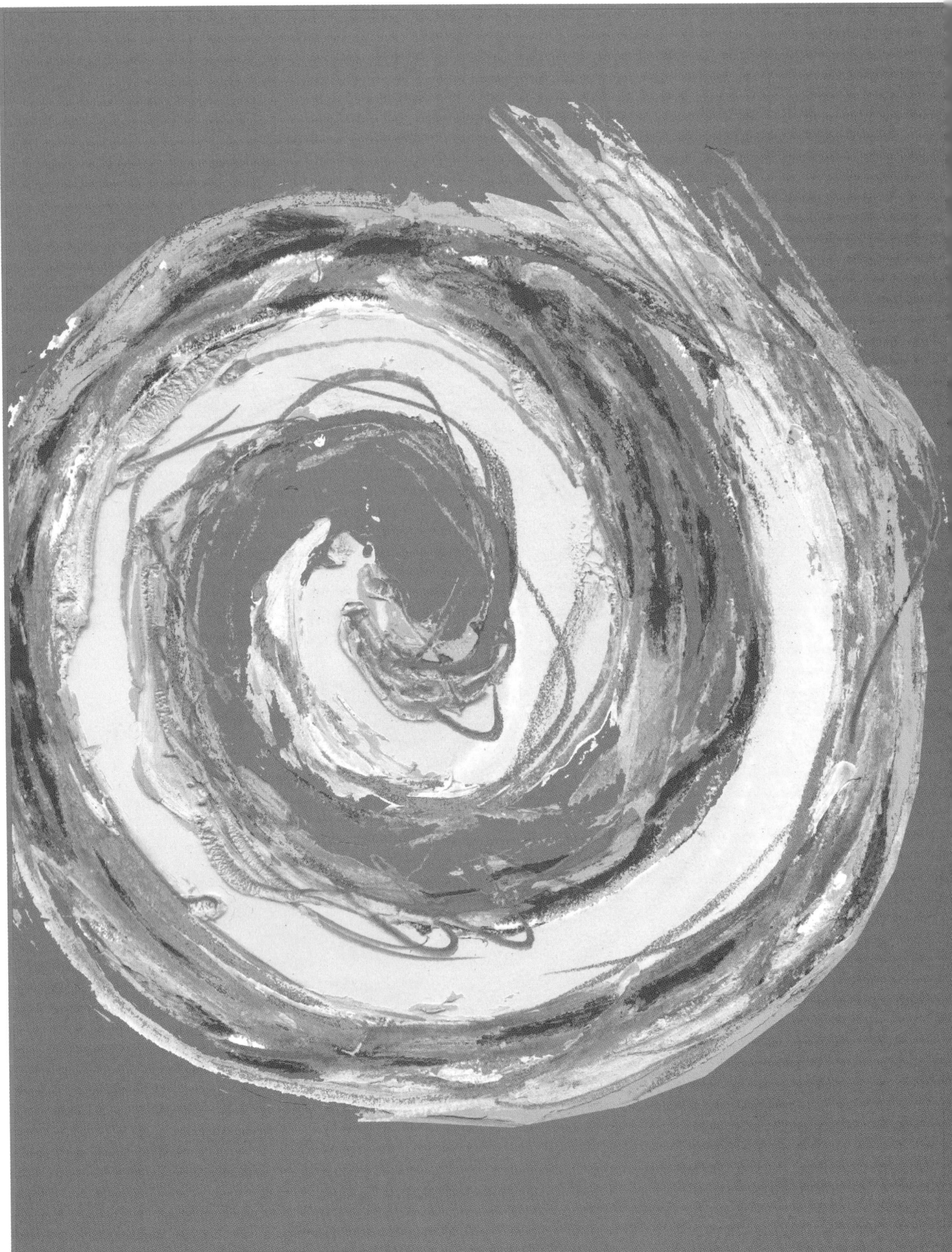

CREATING A DATABASE

Create a New Database

A *database* is a collection of related information. The most common example of a manual database is a hardcopy phone book that contains name, address, and telephone number data for individuals or businesses. Today, most businesses use electronic databases to store and access related information. Wilderness Treks, Inc. uses Microsoft Access databases to store and manage much of its business information. An Access database can contain multiple objects, such as tables, queries, forms, and reports. (You work with queries, forms, and reports in later jobs.) Each object type identifies how the data is stored in the database and how it is viewed. You can view different types of objects by clicking buttons on the Objects bar in the Database window.

At this Monday morning's meeting with Sloane, you are given several new assignments for the week, including creating a new database that contains vendor and attendee information for the annual marketing conference. You begin by creating a blank database.

Hot Tip 

Microsoft Access uses a relational database management model, which means you can relate each piece of information to other pieces of information by joining them. For example, a database may contain a table with vendor information. Another table may contain the orders placed with these vendors. Vendor and order information from these two tables can be joined or combined to create purchasing reports.

STEP-BY-STEP 19.1

1. Start the Access application and verify that the New File task pane is open. Click the **Blank Database** hyperlink in the New File task pane to open the File New Database dialog box. (If you are using Access 2000, click the **Blank Access database** option button in the Microsoft Access dialog box and click **OK**.)

2. Switch to the folder that contains your solution files, key **mdbConference** in the File name text box, and click **Create** to create the blank database. Your screen should look similar to Figure 19-1.

> **Did You Know?** 
>
> The Leszynski naming convention (LNC) is a frequently used naming method for databases and database objects that uses one of the following naming prefixes: *tbl* for table; *qry* for query; *frm* for form; *rpt* for report; *mcr* for macro; *dap* for data access page; and *mdb* for database. The LNC naming convention is followed in this text.

FIGURE 19-1
Blank mdbConference database

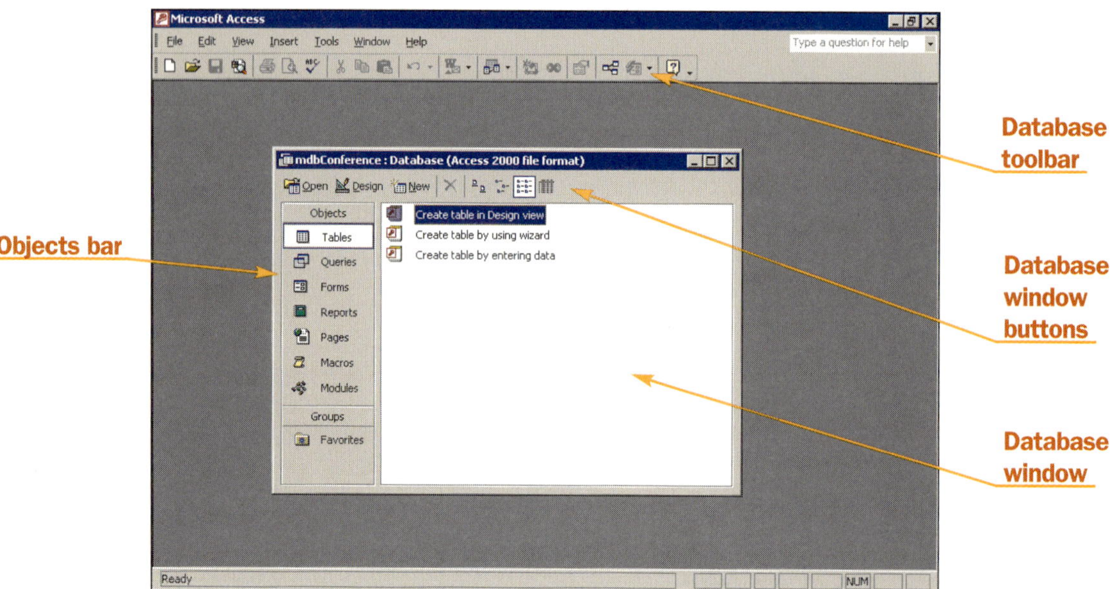

3. Leave the database open for the next Step-by-Step.

Create a Table Using the Table Wizard

Tables are the center point of every Access database because tables are the objects that contain stored data. A database usually contains multiple tables, with each table containing information about a specific topic, such as vendors or customers. An Access *table* is similar to an Excel worksheet; however, rows are called records and columns are called fields. A *record* is an entry that spans a

> **Did You Know?** 
>
> When you use the Table Wizard, you can select individual sample fields to be included in your new table by clicking the button with the single right-pointing arrow. You can include all the sample fields by clicking the button with the double right-pointing arrow. You can remove individual sample fields from your new table by selecting a field and clicking the button with the single left-pointing arrow, or remove all the fields by clicking the button with the double left-pointing arrow.

row in a table and a *field* is a category of specific information entered in a column for each record. For example, in a table containing vendor information, each row is a separate vendor record. The names, addresses, contact numbers, and so forth for each vendor are entered in separate fields (or columns) in that vendor's record.

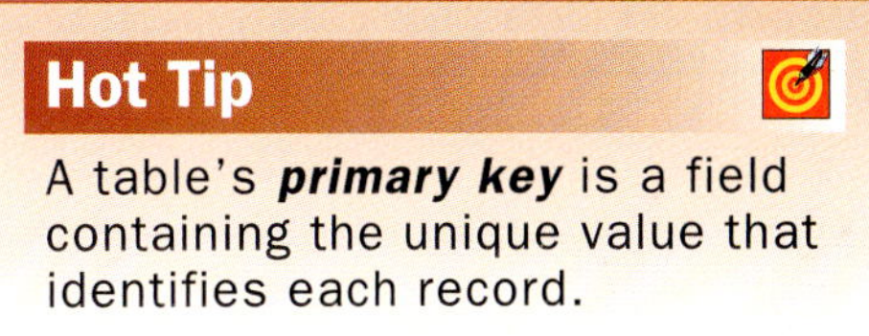

A quick way to create a table is to use the Table Wizard. The *Table Wizard* allows you to create a table based on one of many commonly used table templates containing predefined fields. You create a new table with conference vendor information based on the Suppliers table template.

STEP-BY-STEP 19.2

1. Verify that the mdbConference database is open. Click the **Tables** button in the Objects bar, if necessary, to view the table objects.

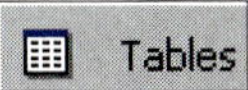

2. Double-click **Create table by using wizard** in the Database window to start the Table Wizard. Verify that the Business option button is selected. Then scroll the Sample Tables list and click **Suppliers**.

3. Click the button with the double right-pointing arrows to select all the sample fields for your new table. Then scroll the Fields in my new table list, click **Notes**, and click the button with the single left-pointing arrow to remove the Notes field. Your Table Wizard should look similar to Figure 19-2.

FIGURE 19-2
Sample fields in Table Wizard

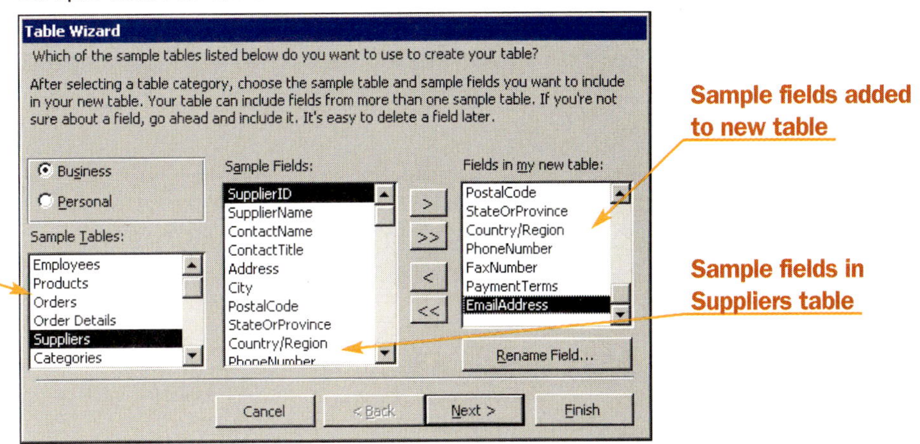

Sample business tables

Sample fields added to new table

Sample fields in Suppliers table

STEP-BY-STEP 19.2 Continued

4. Click **Next** and key **tblVendors** in the What do you want to name your table? text box. Click the **Yes, set a primary key for me.** option button to select it, if necessary. Your dialog box should look similar to Figure 19-3.

FIGURE 19-3
Table name and primary key options

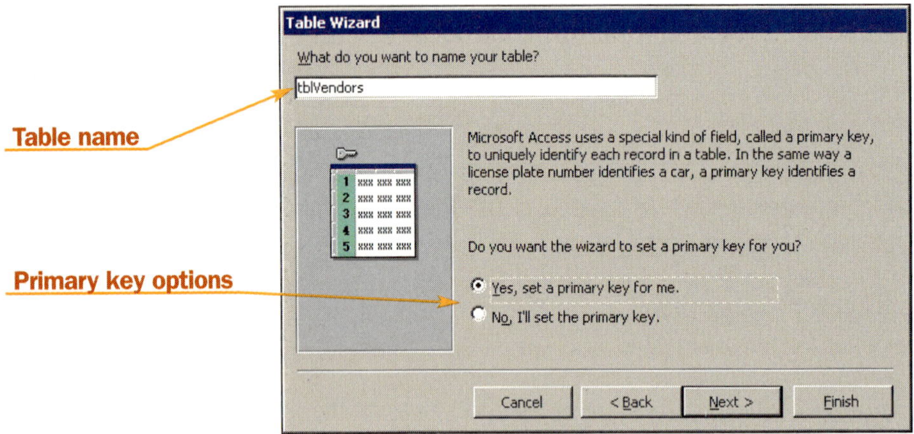

5. Click **Next**, and click the **Enter data directly into the table.** option button to select it, if necessary. Then click **Finish** to create the Vendor table. Your screen should look similar to Figure 19-4.

FIGURE 19-4
Empty tblVendors table

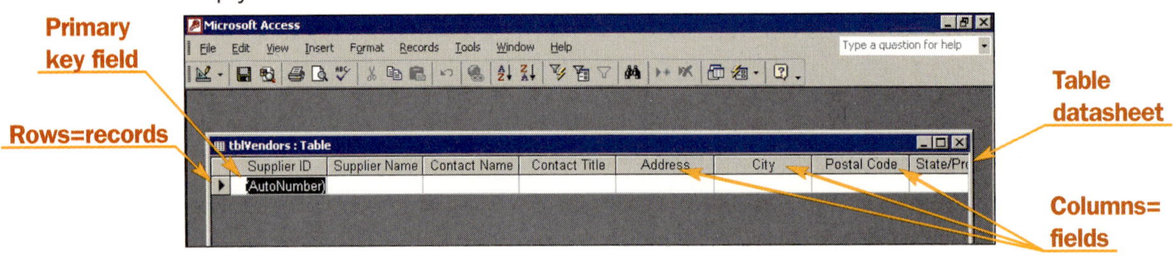

6. Click the **Close** button on the table title bar to close the table and observe the new tblVendors table object. Your screen should look similar to Figure 19-5.

FIGURE 19-5
tblVendors table in the Database window

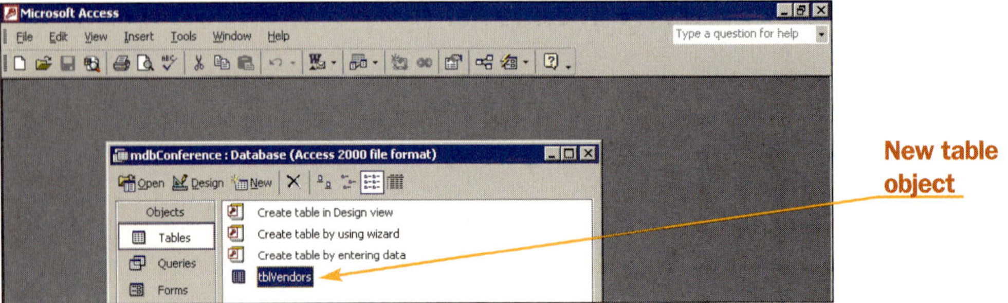

7. Leave the database open for the next Step-by-Step.

Enter Records in a Table

You enter data in a table by opening the table in *Datasheet view* and keying the data for each record directly into the table *datasheet*, a grid of columns and rows, in much the same way you enter data into an Excel worksheet. You can click any field in the table datasheet to position the insertion point or you can use the Enter key or the Tab and Shift + Tab keys to move the insertion point from field to field. The values you key are entered and stored in the table when you press Enter after the last field entry or press the down arrow to move the insertion point to a new record (row).

The current list of conference vendor information in Figure 19-6 was compiled by Beverly Harris, who is also working on the conference. You use this list to enter the vendor data in the new table.

Warning

If you are using Access 2000, the PostalCode field in the tblVendors table is formatted to show a U.S. numeric Zip+4 postal code. This is an inappropriate data type and formatting property for international postal codes that use a combination of numbers and letters. In step 1 of Step-by-Step 19.3, you are given additional instructions to remove this formatting. Field data types and properties are reviewed in more detail in Job 20.

FIGURE 19-6
Vendor list

	Vendor #1	Vendor #2	Vendor #3	Vendor #4	Vendor #5
Supplier Name	Calgary Catering	The Gift House	Baker Limousines	Office Supplies, Inc.	Malloy Temps
Contact Name	Joan Wilson	Lois Childress	Dave Baker	Mark Nguyen	Lillian Jones
Contact Title	Manager	Manager	Owner	Manager	Director
Address	1102 Meridian St.	7803 Cannon Dr.	9382 W 19th Ave.	3201 Denton Dr.	1103 Highfield Ave.
City	Calgary	Austin	Calgary	Austin	Calgary
Postal Code	T2A1X2	78746-7803	T2E7A2	78735-3201	T2P0T9
State or Province	AB	TX	AB	TX	AB
Country/Region	Canada		Canada		Canada
Phone Number	(403) 555-9210	(512) 555-8967	(403) 555-1782	(512) 555-5678	(403) 555-2234
Fax Number	(403) 555-9211	(512) 555-8968	(403) 555-1783	(512) 555-5679	(403) 555-2235
Payment Terms	2/10, net 30	net 30	net 30	2/10, net 30	net 30
E-mail Address	jw@cc.biz	childress@gifthouse.biz	limo@xeon.net	orders@offsup.biz	ljones@malloytemps.biz

STEP-BY-STEP 19.3

1. Verify that the mdbConference database is open and click the **Tables** button in the Objects bar, if necessary, to view table objects. Then double-click **tblVendors** to open the table in Datasheet view. (If you are using Access 2000, you must remove the formatting from the PostalCode field before continuing to step 2. Click the **Design View** button on the Table Datasheet toolbar, click the PostalCode field to select it, drag to select the contents of the Input Mask properties in the Field Properties pane, and press **Delete**. Click the **Save** button on the Table Datasheet toolbar and then click the **Datasheet View** button on the Table Datasheet toolbar to return to Datasheet view. Continue to step 2.)

2. Press **Tab** to move the insertion point to the Supplier Name field in the first record. Key **Calgary Catering** and press **Tab** to move the insertion point to the Contact Name field. Key **Joan Wilson** and press **Tab**. Key **Manager** and press **Tab**. Continue to key the remaining data for the current record in the appropriate fields using Figure 19-6 as your guide.

STEP-BY-STEP 19.3 Continued

3. Press **Enter** to save the data for the first record and move the insertion point to the second record. Observe that the Supplier ID number is automatically added for the first record (Calgary Catering). Then press **Tab** to move the insertion point to the Supplier Name field for the second record. Key **The Gift House** and press **Tab**. Continue to add the remaining data for The Gift House using Figure 19-6 as your guide. Then press **Enter** to store the data and move the insertion point to record number 3.

4. Using Figure 19-6 as your guide, enter the data for the remaining three vendors. When you have entered all the vendor data, your screen should look similar to Figure 19-7.

FIGURE 19-7
Data in the tblVendors table

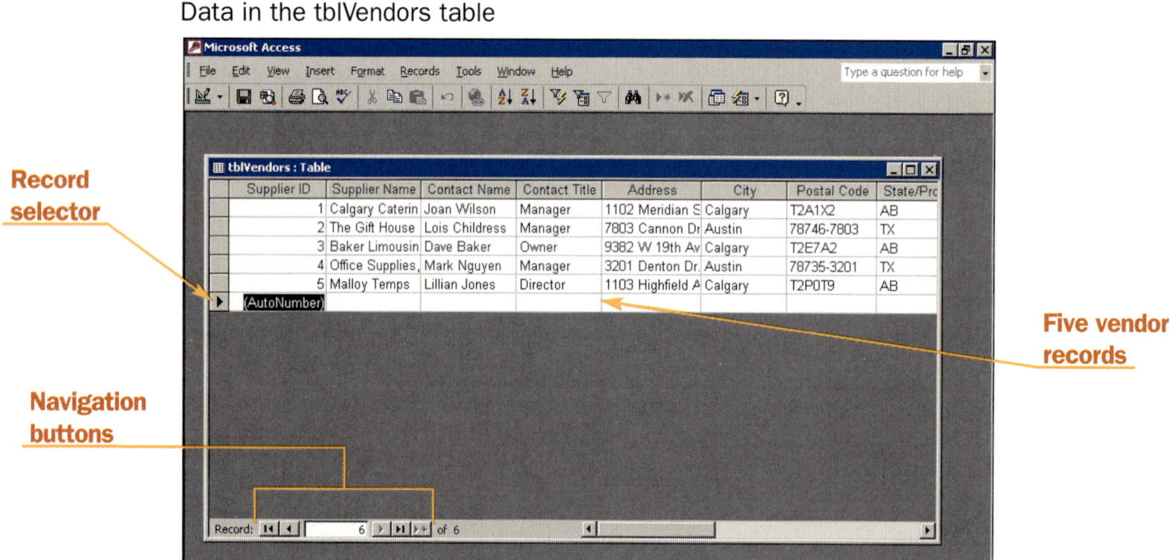

5. Leave the tblVendors table open in Datasheet view for the next Step-by-Step.

Navigate Among Records

Often it is necessary to select a specific record to delete it, or to select a specific field in a record to edit the field's contents. You can click the *record selector* located to the left of the Supplier ID field to select an entire record. You can use the *navigation buttons* at the bottom of the datasheet to move the insertion point to the first record, the next record, the previous record, or the last record. You can click any field in a record to position the insertion point in the field. You can select the entire field by moving the mouse pointer to the field's left boundary until the mouse pointer becomes a large white plus pointer and then clicking the field. You can also use the Tab and Shift + Tab keys to select a field's entire contents.

Hot Tip

To delete a selected record you can press **Delete**, click the **Delete Record** command on the **Edit** menu, or click the **Delete Record** button on the Table Datasheet toolbar.

Did You Know?

The right-pointing arrow on the record selector indicates the record is activated for editing. The pencil icon on the record selector indicates that changes to the record are not yet saved.

Beverly Harris calls to give you updated information on the Baker Limousines vendor. The phone number should be (403)555-1772 and the fax number should be (403)555-1773. You navigate to the Baker Limousines record and correct the data.

STEP-BY-STEP 19.4

1. Verify that the tblVendors table is open in Datasheet view. Then click the previous record navigation button (button with the left pointing arrow) until the record selector indicates record number 3, Baker Limousines, is active for editing.

2. Press **Tab** until the Phone Number field for the Baker Limousines record is selected. Key **(403) 555-1772**. Drag to select the number 8 in the Fax Number field for the Baker Limousines record and key **7**. Your screen should look similar to Figure 19-8.

FIGURE 19-8
Edited Baker Limousines record

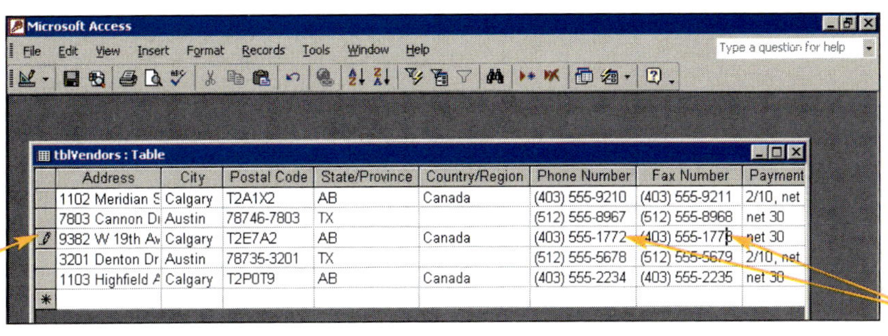

3. Press the down arrow to move the insertion point to the next record, saving the changes to the Baker Limousines record.

4. Leave the tblVendors open in Datasheet view for the next Step-by-Step.

Format and Print a Datasheet

All of the data in each field in the tblVendors table is not currently visible in Datasheet view because the table was created with a default column width that is not wide enough to view all of the data in each field. You can change the column width for a column by clicking the column heading to select the entire column and then clicking the Column Width command on the Format menu. You also can fit the column width automatically to the appropriate size with the mouse pointer by double-clicking the right boundary of a column heading. If you drag across all the

column headings to select all the columns and then double-click the right boundary of the last column, you automatically fit all the columns to their appropriate size at one time. You select and size all the columns to their best fit and then print the datasheet.

STEP-BY-STEP 19.5

1. Verify that the tblVendors table is open in Datasheet view. Then drag across the column headings to select all the columns. (The mouse pointer will be a black selection pointer.)

2. Double-click the right boundary of the last column (the Email Address field) to size all the columns to their best fit. Then click in the Supplier Name field for record number 1 to deselect the columns and view the formatted datasheet. Your screen should look similar to Figure 19-9.

FIGURE 19-9
Formatted tblVendors datasheet

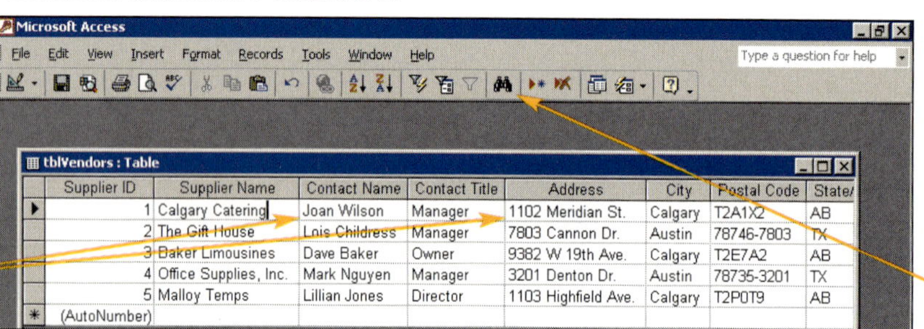

3. Click the **Print** button on the Table Datasheet toolbar to print the datasheet.

4. Close the table and click **Yes** to save the changes to the table layout.

5. Close the database and close Access.

SUMMARY

In this job, you learned:

- A database is a collection of related information. Modern electronic databases contain multiple objects, such as tables, queries, forms, and reports.

- At the heart of an Access database is its tables where the data is stored.

- A database table consists of rows called records and columns called fields.

- You can use the Table Wizard to quickly create a table using table templates that contain sample fields.

- A primary key is the unique identifier for each record.

- To enter data in a table, you first open the table in Datasheet view and then key the data in fields in the table datasheet, which is similar to an Excel worksheet.

- When entering data in a table datasheet, you can move the insertion point from field to field by pressing the Tab and Shift + Tab keys.

- You can use the navigation buttons at the bottom of the table datasheet to activate the first record, the previous record, the next record, or the last record for editing.

- You can click the record selector to select an entire record and then delete it with the keyboard, a toolbar button, or a menu command.

- You can select the entire contents of a field by moving the mouse pointer to the field's left boundary and clicking or by pressing the Tab or Shift + Tab keys.

- Datasheet column boundaries can be sized with a menu command or the mouse pointer as necessary to view the entire contents of fields.

- You can print the table datasheet with a menu command or the Print button on the Table Datasheet toolbar.

VOCABULARY *Review*

Define the following terms:

Database	Navigation buttons	Record selector
Datasheet	Primary key	Table
Datasheet view	Record	Table Wizard
Field		

REVIEW *Questions*

TRUE/FALSE

Circle T if the statement is true or F if the statement is false.

T   F   1. The business yellow pages phone book is an example of a manual database.

T   F   2. Table objects are the center point of an Access database.

T   F   3. A primary key is the unique field that identifies each record in a table.

T   F   4. You can select an entire record by clicking its record selector.

T   F   5. The pencil icon on the record selector indicates changes to a record have been saved.

FILL IN THE BLANK

Complete the following sentences by writing the correct word or words in the blanks provided.

1. A(n) _________ is a collection of related information.

2. You enter data in a table in _________ view.

3. You can quickly create a new table with the _________.

4. A table _________ is a grid of columns and rows similar to an Excel worksheet.

5. You can use the _________ buttons located at the bottom of the table datasheet to activate a specific record for editing.

PROJECTS

PROJECT 19-1

1. Start Access and create a new blank database named **mdbAdventures**.

2. Create a new table named **tblTours** using the Table Wizard and the Events table template. Add all the sample fields to the new table except the Notes field. Let Access set the primary key.

3. Enter the data shown in Figure 19-10 in the table datasheet in Datasheet view. (*Note*: The date, time, and amount fields in the Events template are preformatted. Simply enter the values as shown without the slashes, colons, and other formatting. Also carefully observe the column headings to enter the data in the appropriate fields. You will not be entering data in all the fields at this time.)

FIGURE 19-10
Tours data

	Tour #1	Tour #2	Tour #3	Tour #4
Event Name	Outback Mexico - 1	Outback Mexico - 2	Land of the Incas - 1	Land of the Incas - 2
Location	Mexico	Mexico	Peru	Peru
Start Date	08/23/06	12/15/06	09/15/06	01/23/07
End Date	09/06/06	12/29/06	09/29/06	02/05/07
Start Time	08:00 AM	08:00 AM	08:00 AM	08:00 AM
End Time	08:00 PM	08:00 PM	08:00 PM	08:00 PM
Required Staffing	5	5	7	7
Confirmed	No	No	No	No
Available Space	15	15	20	20
Cost per Person	2300	2300	3500	3500
Event Description	Two weeks exploring the remote mountain areas of Mexico.	Two weeks exploring the remote mountain areas of Mexico.	Two weeks hiking across the Peruvian backcountry viewing important Inca sites.	Two weeks hiking across the Peruvian backcountry viewing important Inca sites.

	Tour #5	Tour #6	Tour #7	Tour #8
Event Name	Cultural Journey on the Amazon - 1	Cultural Journey on the Amazon - 2	Galapagos Adventure - 1	Galapagos Adventure - 2
Location	Brazil	Brazil	Ecuador	Ecuador
Start Date	10/17/06	02/13/07	11/08/06	03/25/07
End Date	10/31/06	02/26/06	11/17/06	04/04/06
Start Time	08:00 AM	08:00 AM	08:00 AM	08:00 AM
End Time	08:00 PM	08:00 PM	08:00 PM	08:00 PM
Required Staffing	12	12	10	10
Confirmed	No	No	No	No
Available Space	30	30	25	25
Cost per Person	6500	6500	8000	8000
Event Description	Two weeks at a remote hideaway on the Amazon river.	Two weeks at a remote hideaway on the Amazon river.	Ten-day yachting tour of the Galapagos Islands off the coast of Ecuador.	Ten-day yachting tour of the Galapagos Islands off the coast of Ecuador.

4. Close the table and close the database.

PROJECT 19-2

After double-checking your new tours data, you find you have to make a few changes before you print a list of the tour records. Open the **mdbAdventures** database you created in Project 19-1 and open the **tblTours** table in Datasheet view. Change the Outback Mexico tours' available space to 20. Change the Land of the Incas tours' start time to 7:00 AM. Change the Cultural Journey on the Amazon – 1 tour available space to 20. Change the Galapagos Adventure tours' end time to 5:00 PM. Size all the columns to fit and print the datasheet. Then close the table and save the new layout. Close the database.

WEB PROJECT

Now that you are responsible for creating and working with some of the Wilderness Treks databases, you would like to become more familiar with tips and tricks for working with the Access application. Using your Web browser and a search tool, such as AltaVista (*www.altavista.com*), locate Web sites offering Access tips and tricks. Print at least four Web pages.

TEAMWORK PROJECT

It is frequently necessary for you to view a group of specific records in a database table; for example, all of the tours in Mexico or all of the vendors in Calgary, by filtering a table. It is also sometimes necessary to rearrange records in a database table in a specific order, such as alphabetically by location by sorting a table. Select a classmate to assist you with this project and then research how to perform a simple sort on a table in Datasheet view. Then research how to filter a table by form and by selection. Using the database table of your choice, demonstrate simple sorting and filtering in Datasheet view. Remove all filters and sorts before closing the database and do not save the changes to the table.

CRITICAL*Thinking*

ACTIVITY 19-1

Melody Stackhouse wants to quickly create a database for her training information. You suggest that she use the Database Wizard. Using Access online Help, review working with the Database Wizard. Then demonstrate to another classmate how to create a new database named **mdbTraining** using the Contact Management Database Wizard. Review all the objects automatically created in the database.

Creating Tables in Design View

Create a Table in Design View

Design view allows you to view, add, modify, or delete fields in an existing table. You also can create a new table in Design view and then manually add the appropriate fields to the table. Sloane asks you to add a table to the mdbConference database that can be updated with attendee information at the conference registration desk. You create the new table from scratch in Design view.

As you work in an Access database, your changes are saved in the open database. In order to protect the database data files for Jobs 20 through 24, you are instructed to create a copy of each database data file in Windows Explorer and rename it before beginning each job. This enables you to make your changes to the copied database.

Hot Tip

The Design view window consists of two panes: the Fields pane at the top of the window and the Field Properties pane at the bottom of the window. You add and delete fields and define their data type in the Fields pane and set the properties for a selected field in the Field Properties pane.

STEP-BY-STEP 20.1

1. Open Windows Explorer, switch to the data files, copy the **mdbStep20-1** database and paste it in the folder that contains your solution files. Rename the pasted database **mdbConferenceJob20**. Close Windows Explorer, open Access, and open the **mdbConferenceJob20** database. Click the **Tables** button on the Objects bar, if necessary, to view the table objects.

2. Double-click **Create table in Design view**. Your screen should look similar to Figure 20-1.

FIGURE 20-1
New table in Design view

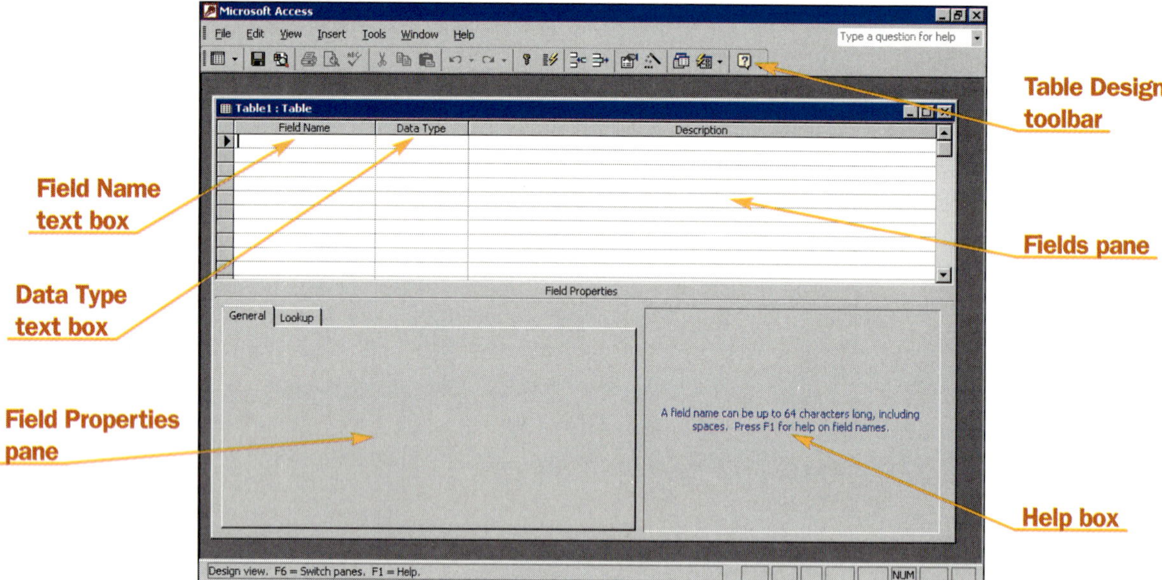

3. Leave the new table open in Design view for the next Step-by-Step.

Add Fields to a Table

When you add a field to a table you must assign a data type to the field. The *data type* identifies the type of data a field can contain: text, numbers, date and time, currency, hyperlinks, or other data types. It is important to select the correct data type for each field to insure that the appropriate kind of data is entered in each field. After considering the kinds of data you need to record for each attendee, you draft the list of table fields shown in Figure 20-2.

FIGURE 20-2
Field names and data types

Field Name	DataType	Description
AttendeeID	AutoNumber	Unique identifying number
Title	Text	Mr., Ms., or Miss
FirstName	Text	
LastName	Text	
Company	Text	
Address	Text	
City	Text	
StateOrProvince	Text	
PostalCode	Text	
Country	Text	
HomePhone	Text	
WorkPhone	Text	
CellPhone	Text	
FaxNumber	Text	
EmailAddress	Text	
RegistrationDate	Date/Time	
WorkshopA	Yes/No	Adventures in Australia and New Zealand
WorkshopB	Yes/No	Archeological Adventures
WorkshopC	Yes/No	Clothing for a Backcountry Adventure
WorkshopD	Yes/No	Central and South American Adventures
WorkshopE	Yes/No	Skiing Safari Adventure
SpouseName	Text	
ChildrenNames	Text	

You use the AutoNumber data type to allow Access to automatically insert a unique identifying number for each attendee record. The Text data type allows you to enter alphabetic characters, numbers not used in a calculation, and special characters that might be found in address data. The Date/Time data type allows you to enter each attendee's registration date appropriately. You use the Yes/No data type to indicate whether an attendee has or has not registered for each workshop.

STEP-BY-STEP 20.2

1. Verify that the new table is open in Design view and that the insertion point is in the first row of the Field Name column. Key **AttendeeID** and press **Tab** to move the insertion point to the Data Type column.

Hot Tip

When you create a table in Design view, you must manually specify the table's primary key field before you save the table.

Warning

Do not use the Number data type for postal codes, phone numbers, Social Security numbers and other numbers that are not used in calculations, as these kinds of numbers contain non-numerical characters such as hyphens and parentheses. Instead, use the Text data type.

STEP-BY-STEP 20.2 Continued

2. Click the **Data Type** list arrow, click **AutoNumber**, and press **Tab** to move the insertion point to the Description column. Key **Unique identifying number** and press **Tab** to move the insertion point to the next field. Your screen should look similar to Figure 20-3.

FIGURE 20-3
AttendeeID field

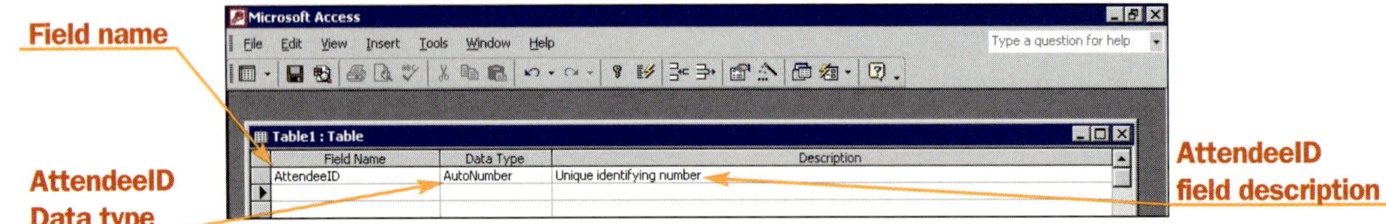

3. Key **Title** and press **Tab**. Observe that the default data type is Text. Press **Tab** and key **Mr., Ms., or Miss**. Press **Tab** to move the insertion point to the next field.

4. Continue to add the remaining fields using Figure 20-2 as your guide. When finished adding all the fields, click in the AttendeeID field to position the insertion point.

5. Click the **Primary Key** button on the Table Design toolbar to specify that the AttendeeID field contains the unique identifier for each attendee. Observe the key icon in the record selector for the AttendeeID field indicating this field is the primary key.

6. Click the **Save** button on the Table Design toolbar to open the Save As dialog box. Key **tblAttendees** in the Table Name text box and click **OK** to save the new table. Your screen should look similar to Figure 20-4.

FIGURE 20-4
tblAttendees in Design view

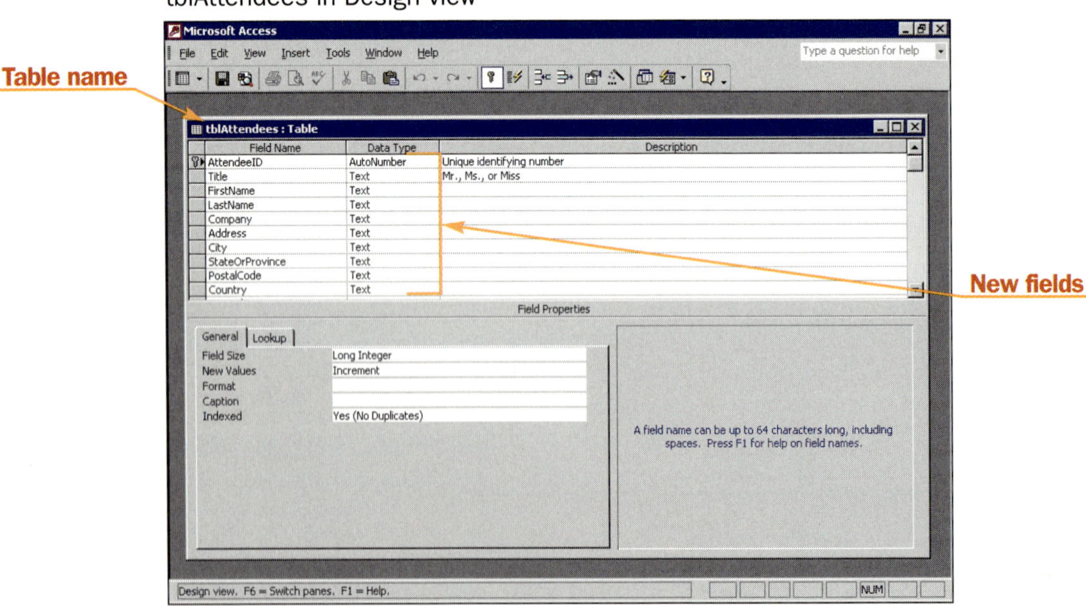

STEP-BY-STEP 20.2 Continued

7. Leave the tblAttendees table open in Design view for the next Step-by-Step.

Modify Field Properties

Field properties are those attributes, such as field length and formatting, which define a field. Setting appropriate field properties ensures that data is entered consistently. When you create a new field, it is created with default properties. You then need to modify those properties to meet your needs. To view a field's properties, you first select the field. The properties for the selected field appear in the Field Properties pane. You press the F6 key to move the insertion point from the Fields pane to the Field Properties pane, make your changes, and press the F6 key to move the insertion point back to the Fields pane. Next, you modify the field properties for the tblAttendees fields.

Did You Know?

The Required property allows you to specify which fields must contain data.

Hot Tip

The Caption property overrides the field name and appears as the column heading in the table datasheet and in any forms or reports based on the table.

STEP-BY-STEP 20.3

1. Verify that the **tblAttendees** table is open in Design view and that the insertion point is in the AttendeeID field name. Press **F6** to move the insertion point to the Field Properties pane.

2. Press the **down arrow** three times to move the insertion point to the Caption property. Observe the description of the Caption property in the Help box. Key **Attendee ID** and press **F6** to move the insertion point back to the Fields pane.

3. Press the **down arrow** to move the insertion point to the Title field and then press **F6** to move the insertion point to the Field Properties pane. Observe the description of the selected Field Size property in the Help box and then key **4**. Press the **down arrow** seven times to move the insertion point to the Required field property and key **Y**. Press **F6** to return to the Fields pane.

STEP-BY-STEP 20.3 Continued

4. Continue to modify the field properties as shown in Figure 20-5. (*Note*: Do not change any field properties other than those noted in Figure 20-5.)

FIGURE 20-5
Field property changes

Field Name	Field Property Changes
FirstName	Field Size=20; Caption=First Name; Required=Yes
LastName	Field Size=20; Caption=Last Name; Required=Yes
Company	Field Size=25
Address	Field Size=25; Required=Yes
City	Field Size=20; Required=Yes
StateOrProvince	Field Size=5; Caption=State or Province
PostalCode	Field Size=10; Caption=Postal Code; Required=Yes
Country	Field Size=20
HomePhone	Field Size=15; Caption=Home Phone
WorkPhone	Field Size=15; Caption=Work Phone
CellPhone	Field Size=15; Caption=Cell Phone
FaxNumber	Field Size=15; Caption=Fax
EmailAddress	Field Size=30; Caption=E-mail Address
RegistrationDate	Caption=Registration Date; Required=Yes
WorkshopA	Caption=Workshop A
WorkshopB	Caption=Workshop B
WorkshopC	Caption=Workshop C
WorkshopD	Caption=Workshop D
WorkshopE	Caption=Workshop E
SpouseName	Field Size=20; Caption=Spouse name
ChildrenNames	Field Size=30; Caption=Children Names

5. Save the table and leave it open in Design view for the next Step-by-Step.

Use the Input Mask Wizard

The Input Mask property controls field formatting and limits the kind of data that can be entered in a field. The **Input Mask Wizard** is a step-by-step process for applying standard formatting, such as the zip + 4 U.S. postal code formatting (xxxxx-xxxx), Social Security number formatting (xxx-xx-xxxx), the U.S. and Canadian phone number formatting ((xxx) xxx-xxxx), and other standard formats. You want to format the RegistrationDate field using the Input Mask Wizard.

STEP-BY-STEP 20.4

1. Verify that **tblAttendees** is open in Design view and then move the insertion point to the Field Properties pane for the RegistrationDate field. Click the **Input Mask** property to position the insertion point.

STEP-BY-STEP 20.4 Continued

2. Click the ellipsis icon that appears to the right of the Input Mask property to start the Input Mask Wizard. Click **Short Date** in the Input Mask list, click the **Try It** text box to position the insertion point, and key **0726XXXX** (XXXX=current year). Your screen should look similar to Figure 20-6.

FIGURE 20-6
Input Mask Wizard, Step 1

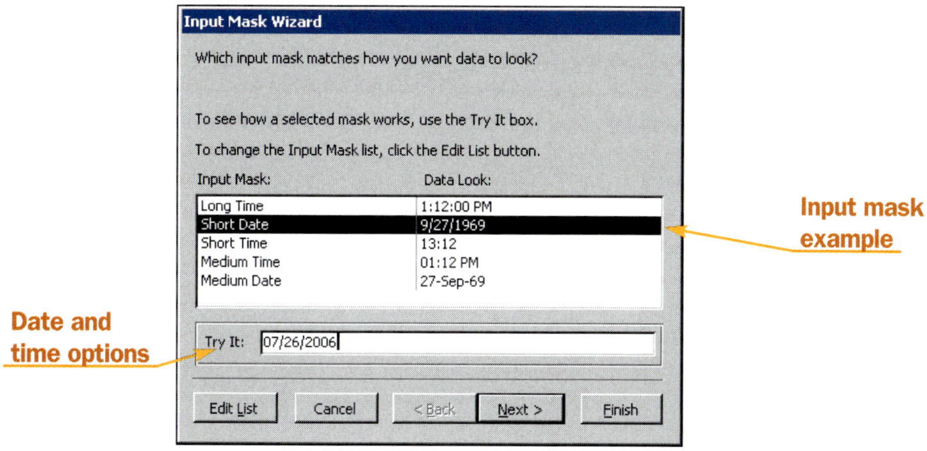

3. Click **Finish**. Then save the table and close it. Leave the database open for the next Step-by-Step.

Insert, Delete, and Reposition Fields

Sometimes you need to update a table by inserting new fields, deleting fields, and repositioning fields in the Fields pane. After reviewing the fields in the new tblAttendees table, you realize that you left out a job title field. After some discussion with Sloane it is determined that you do not need to include the attendees' children names. You open the tblAttendees table in Design view, delete the unwanted field, and insert and reposition the new field.

Warning

Modifying a table in Design view is very easy as long as the table does not contain any data. Once you start entering data, modification becomes more difficult. Therefore, it is a good practice to carefully review table fields and field properties before you begin entering data in the table. Also, be careful before you delete a field. If you delete a field that contains data, the data is lost and you cannot undo the deletion.

STEP-BY-STEP 20.5

1. Verify that the **mdbConferenceJob20** database is open and click the **Tables** button on the Objects bar, if necessary, to view the table objects.

2. Click the **tblAttendees** table in the Database window to select it, if necessary, and click the **Design** button on the Database window toolbar to open the table in Design view.

3. Click the record selector for the **ChildrenNames** field to select the field and press **Delete**.

4. Move the insertion point to the **HomePhone** field and click the **Insert Rows** button on the Table Design toolbar to insert a blank field row above the HomePhone field. Insert a field named **JobTitle** with a **Text** data type on this blank row. Modify the field's properties as follows: Field Size=**25** and Caption=**Job Title**.

5. Click the record selector for the **JobTitle** field to select it and then move the mouse pointer to the record selector until the mouse pointer becomes a left-pointing white arrow. Drag the JobTitle field upward and drop it below the Company field. Your screen should look similar to Figure 20-7.

FIGURE 20-7
Repositioned JobTitle field

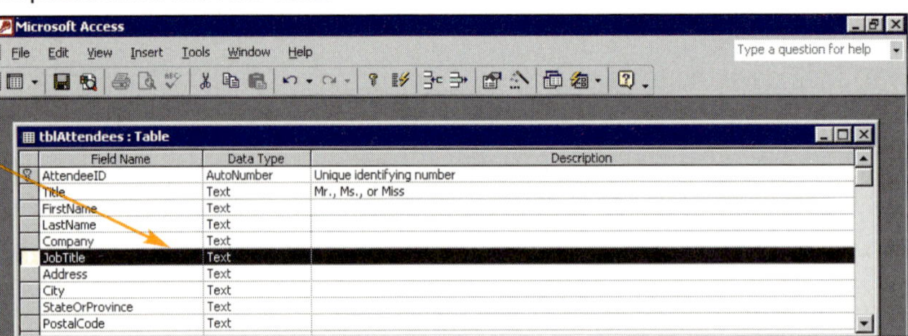

6. Save and close the table, close the database, and close Access.

SUMMARY

In this job, you learned:

- Design view is used to view, add, modify, or delete fields in an existing table.

- You can create a new table in Design view and then manually add the appropriate fields to the table.

- Design view consists of two panes: the Fields pane where you insert, modify, and delete fields and set their data type; and the Field Properties pane where you set the properties for a selected field.

- A field's data type identifies the kind of data a field can contain.

- A field's properties are those attributes that define a field, such as its length or caption.

- The Input Mask property controls field formatting and limits the kind of data that can be entered in a field.

- The Input Mask Wizard is a step-by-step process for applying standard formatting, such as zip + 4 U.S. postal codes and Social Security number formatting.

VOCABULARY *Review*

> **Define the following terms:**
> Data type   Field properties   Input Mask Wizard
> Design view

REVIEW *Questions*

TRUE / FALSE

Circle T if the statement is true or F if the statement is false.

T   F   **1.** You can modify field properties in Design view.

T   F   **2.** The Text data type is used to define fields that contain numbers used in calculations.

T   F   **3.** You should use the Number data type for fields such as postal codes, phone numbers, and Social Security numbers.

T   F   **4.** The Caption property is used to change a field's length.

T   F   **5.** You can insert a new field row in the Fields pane in Datasheet view.

FILL IN THE BLANK

Complete the following sentences by writing the correct word or words in the blanks provided.

1. A field's _________ specifies whether the field can contain text or numbers used in calculations.

2. Field _________ are attributes, such as its length or required status, which define a field.

3. The _________ is a step-by-step process for setting an input mask.

4. Design view consists of two panes: the _________ pane and the Field Properties pane.

5. The _________ data type is used to allow Access to automatically insert a unique identifying number for each record.

PROJECTS

 PROJECT 20-1

1. Open Windows Explorer, switch to the data files, copy the **mdbProject20-1** database and paste it in the folder that contains your solution files. Rename the pasted database **mdbConferenceProject20**. Close Windows Explorer, open Access, and open the **mdbConferenceProject20** database. Click the **Tables** button on the Objects bar, if necessary, to view the table objects.

2. Open the **tblVendors** table in Design view.

3. Insert a new field named **Update** with the **Date/Time** data type below the SupplierID field. Apply the **Short Date** input mask to the field and add **Date Last Updated** as a caption.

4. Switch to Datasheet view and key today's date as the date last updated for all the records.

5. Save the table and close it. Close the database.

 PROJECT 20-2

After discussing the mdbAdventures database with Sloane, you are now ready to add a table that contains a list of tour guides. Copy the **mdbProject20-2** data file and paste it in your solution files folder. Name the pasted database **mdbAdventuresJob20**. Open the **mdbAdventuresJob20** database and display the table objects. Create a new table in Design view. Insert the following fields in the table: **EmployeeID** (Number data type, Caption=Guide ID, Required=Yes), **FirstName** (Text data type, Field Size=20, Caption=First Name, Required=Yes), and **LastName** (Text data type, Field Size=25, Caption=Last Name, Required=Yes). Set the **EmployeeID** field as the primary key. Save the table as **tblGuides**.

  WEB PROJECT

Sloane calls you to ask for a list of Web sites that offer travel news. You also should include in the list any government sites that provide travel warnings. Using your Web browser and a search tool, such as HotBot (*www.hotbot.com*), locate at least five Web sites that meet Sloane's travel news and warnings needs. Print the home page from each site.

  TEAMWORK PROJECT

It is important to understand the different field data types and when you use them. Select a classmate to work with you on this project. Using Access online Help, learn more about the different field data types. Then, create a list of data types containing a brief explanation of when they should be used. Using your list and the database of your choice, create a blank table in Design view containing fields using each data type. Use your list and this table to describe the different data types to your classmates.

CRITICAL*Thinking*

ACTIVITY 20-1

The tblTours table in the mdbAdventures database contains a field named EmployeeID that is used to indicate the Wilderness Treks employee guide for the tour. The employee identification data for this field is already found in the tblGuides table. Instead of manually looking up the employee/guide identification number, you can modify the EmployeeID field to use the Lookup Wizard data type, which allows you to *lookup* the identification number directly from the tblGuides table as you enter data in the tblTours table.

If necessary, use Access online Help to research how to use the Lookup Wizard data type. Then copy the **mdbActivity20-1** data file and paste it in your solutions folder as **mdbAdventures20-1**. Open the **mdbAdventures20-1** database and open the **tblTours** table in Design view. Change the **EmployeeID** data type to **Lookup Wizard** and follow the wizard steps to create a lookup list based on the tblGuides table. The lookup list should show the EmployeeID, FirstName, and LastName fields from the tblGuides table. Save the **tblTours** table and switch to Datasheet view. Using the list arrow added to the EmployeeID field, select the tour guide ID of your choice for each of the tour records. Save and close the table.

CREATING QUERIES

VOCABULARY

Append query

Delete query

Design grid

Expression

Foreign key

Link field

Make-table query

One-to-many relationship

Primary table

Query

Referential integrity

Related table

Select query

Update query

Establish Table Relationships

No single table in the mdbConference database contains all the information that is being gathered about the annual marketing conference. For example, the mdbConference database contains a table with vendor contact information. Another table named tblVendorPayments has recently been added, which contains vendor payment information. To more effectively use the information in the two different vendor tables, you need to establish a linking relationship between them by specifying a link field in each table.

A *link field* is a field in two or more tables that contains a common value. The common value in the two vendor tables is the vendor identification number, which is found in the SupplierID field in the tblVendors table and in the VendorID field in the tblVendorPayments table. In a linking relationship between two tables, the *primary table* is the table in which the link field is the table's primary key. The *related table* is the table in which the link field (called a *foreign key*) is not the table's primary key. In the relationship between the two vendor tables, tblVendors is the primary table because SupplierID field is the primary key. TblVendorPayments is the related table because the VendorID field is not the primary key. This type of relationship is called a *one-to-many relationship*, which means that any one record in the primary table (tblVendors) can have more than one related record in the related table (tblVendorPayments). For example, there can be several payment records for a single vendor.

You begin by opening the database and opening the Relationships window. Then you add the two vendor tables to the window and create the link by dragging the SupplierID field from the tblVendors table to the VendorID field in the tblVendorPayments table.

S TEP-BY-STEP 21.1

1. Open Windows Explorer, switch to the data files, copy the **mdbStep21-1** database, and paste it in the folder that contains your solution files. Rename the pasted database **mdbConferenceJob21**. Close Windows Explorer, open Access, and open the **mdbConferenceJob21** database. Click the **Tables** button on the Objects bar, if necessary, to view the table objects.

2. Click the **Relationships** button on the Database toolbar to open the Relationships window.

3. Click the **Show Table** button on the Relationships toolbar to open the Show Table dialog box and then click the Tables tab, if necessary.

4. Double-click **tblVendors** in the Show Table list; double-click **tblVendorPayments** in the Show Table list; and then close the Show Table dialog box. Your screen should look similar to Figure 21-1.

Hot Tip

It is not necessary for linking fields to have the same name in order to relate tables. However, they must be the same data type and contain the same value, such as employee number, vendor identification number, and so forth.

Did You Know?

It is important to ensure that related tables remain so by preventing the deletion of a record in the primary table when related records exist in the related table. You do this by enforcing referential integrity when you link the tables. *Referential integrity* means you cannot delete a record in a primary table unless you first delete the relationship to the related table.

FIGURE 21-1
Relationships window

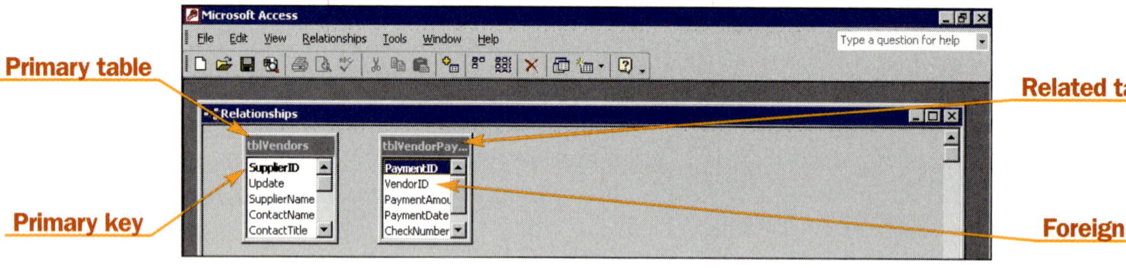

STEP-BY-STEP 21.1 Continued

5. Drag the SupplierID field from the tblVendors table to the VendorID field in the tblVendorPayments table to link the fields and open the Edit Relationships dialog box. Click the Enforce Referential Integrity check box to insert a check mark. Your dialog box should look similar to Figure 21-2.

FIGURE 21-2
Edit Relationships dialog box

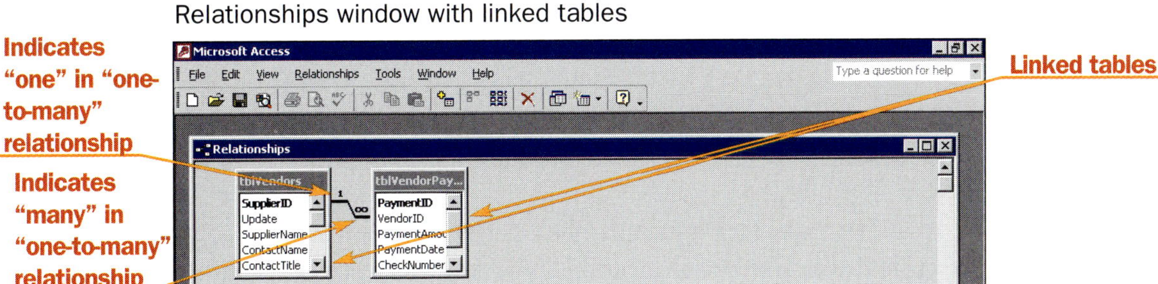

6. Click **Create** to create the link and close the dialog box. Observe the link between the tables. Your screen should look similar to Figure 21-3.

FIGURE 21-3
Relationships window with linked tables

7. Close the Relationships window and click **Yes** to save the layout of the window.

8. Leave the database open for the next Step-by-Step.

Create a Query Using the Simple Query Wizard

When you need to retrieve specific information from a database, you can create a query. A *query* is a request for information based on specific criteria or an action you perform on data. The most common query is a *select query*, which retrieves data from one or more tables using specified criteria and then displays that data in a datasheet. You can also use action queries to change records (*update query*), create a new table from records in an existing table (*make-table query*), add records to the end of a table (*append query*), and delete records from a table (*delete query*).

Sloane drops by your desk and asks you for a list of the payments made to date to conference vendors. You use the Simple Query Wizard, a step-by-step process to create a basic query, to get this information from the tblVendors and tblVendorPayments tables.

STEP-BY-STEP 21.2

1. Verify that the **mdbConferenceJob21** database is open and then click the **Queries** button on the Objects bar to view the query objects.

2. Double-click **Create query by using wizard** to open the Simple Query Wizard dialog box.

3. Click **Table: tblVendors** in the Tables/Queries list and add the **SupplierName** field to the Selected Fields list. Click **Table: tblVendorPayments** in the Tables/Queries list and add the **PaymentAmount**, **PaymentDate**, **CheckNumber**, and **Purpose** fields to the Selected Fields list. Your wizard dialog box should look similar to Figure 21-4.

FIGURE 21-4
Simple Query Wizard, Step 1

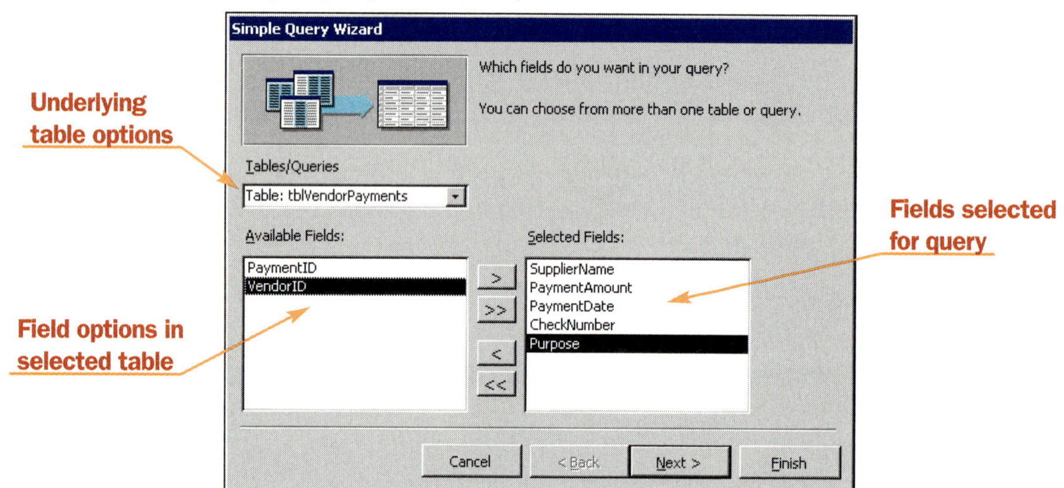

4. Click **Next** twice and key **qryVendorPayments** in the What title do you want for your query? text box. Click the **Open the query to view information** option button, if necessary, and click **Finish**.

5. Select the datasheet column headings and size all the columns for best fit using the mouse pointer. Your query results should look similar to Figure 21-5.

FIGURE 21-5
Query results

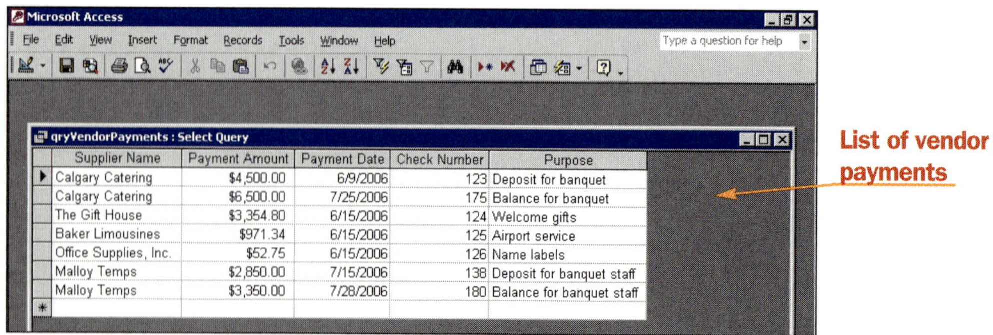

Supplier Name	Payment Amount	Payment Date	Check Number	Purpose
Calgary Catering	$4,500.00	6/9/2006	123	Deposit for banquet
Calgary Catering	$6,500.00	7/25/2006	175	Balance for banquet
The Gift House	$3,354.80	6/15/2006	124	Welcome gifts
Baker Limousines	$971.34	6/15/2006	125	Airport service
Office Supplies, Inc.	$52.75	6/15/2006	126	Name labels
Malloy Temps	$2,850.00	7/15/2006	138	Deposit for banquet staff
Malloy Temps	$3,350.00	7/28/2006	180	Balance for banquet staff

6. Print the query datasheet and then close the query and save the changes to the layout. Leave the database open for the next Step-by-Step.

Create a Query in Design View

You can create a new query or modify an existing query in Design view. Because you did not specify criteria, the qryVendorPayments query retrieves all the records in the underlying tblVendorPayments table. In order to restrict the results of a query, you must set conditions for the fields you include in the query. You set these conditions in the query's design grid in Design view. The *design grid* contains the fields for a query, sorting instructions for the query, and any selection criteria that must be met before a record is included in the query datasheet.

Beverly Harris sends you an e-mail asking for a list of paid invoices for Calgary Catering and Malloy Temps. You create a new query in Design view to get this information for Beverly. First, you create the query, and then you add the two vendor tables. Next, you add the vendor name and payment fields to the query. Finally, you set the criteria to show only those payments made to Calgary Catering.

STEP-BY-STEP 21.3

1. Verify that the **mdbConferenceJob21** database is open and then click the **Queries** button on the Objects bar, if necessary, to view the query objects. 

2. Double-click **Create query in Design view** to view the design grid and open the Show Table dialog box. Double-click **tblVendors** and **tblVendorPayments** to add these tables to the design grid. Then close the Show Table dialog box.

3. Double-click the **SupplierName** field in the tblVendors table to add the field to the grid. Add the **PaymentDate**, **CheckNumber**, and **PaymentAmount** fields *in this order* from the tblVendorPayments table.

4. Click in the **Criteria** row for the **SupplierName** field to position the insertion point. Key **Calgary Catering** and press **Enter** to specify that only records in which the SupplierName field contains *Calgary Catering* be included in the query results. Your screen should look similar to Figure 21-6.

FIGURE 21-6
Query Design view

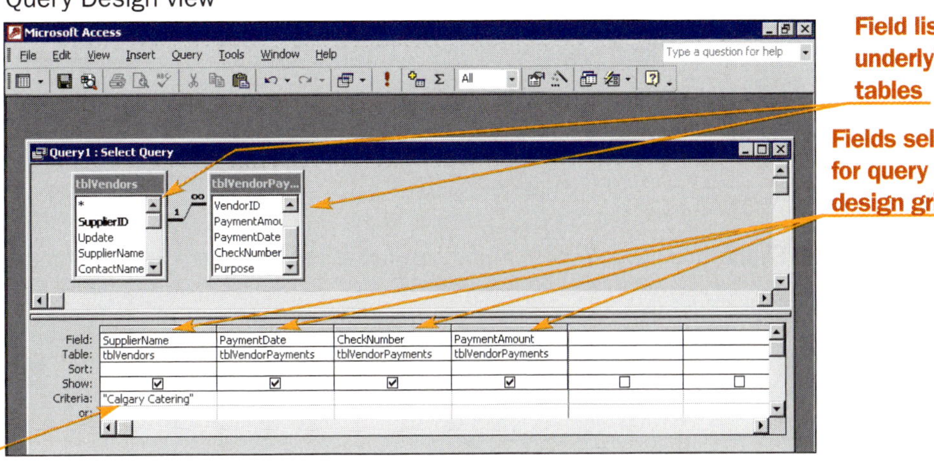

STEP-BY-STEP 21.3 Continued

5. Click the **Run** button on the Query Design toolbar to view the query datasheet. Observe the two paid invoices for Calgary Catering in the query datasheet. Then click the **Design View** button on the Query Datasheet toolbar to switch to Design view.  

6. Change the SupplierName criteria to **Malloy Temps** and run the query.

7. Click the **Save** button on the Query Datasheet toolbar and save the query as **qryPaymentList**. Close the query datasheet and leave the database open for the next Step-by-Step. 

Add a Calculated Field to a Query

An *expression* combines field names, symbols, values, text, and mathematical operators to perform some type of calculation. After reviewing the qryVendorPayments query, Sloane asks you to add the vendors' city and state location to the query results. You can do this by adding an expression to combine the City and StateOrProvince fields into one column on the query datasheet.

You begin by adding the expression, and then you reposition the expression field so that it appears immediately following the SupplierName field in the query datasheet.

> **Hot Tip**
>
> When creating an expression, you surround spaces, commas, and other characters with quotation marks. Access automatically adds a default name, such as Expr1, to the expression. You can select the default name and key a more meaningful name that appears as a column heading in the query datasheet.

STEP-BY-STEP 21.4

1. Verify that the **mdbConferenceJob21** database is open and then click the **Queries** button on the Objects bar, if necessary, to view the query objects. 

2. Click the **qryVendorPayments** query to select it and click the **Design** button on the Database window toolbar to open the query in Design view. 

3. Click the blank **Field** row to the right of the Purpose field and key **City&", "&StateOrProvince** to add the city name, a comma and a space, and the state or province. Press **Enter** to view the expression. (Don't forget to add a space following the comma.)

4. Select the **Expr1** default expression name, key **Location**, and press **Enter** to rename the expression.

STEP-BY-STEP 21.4 Continued

5. Move the mouse pointer over the top of the expression field column until it becomes a black selection arrow. Click to select the expression field column. Move the mouse pointer to the selected column until it becomes a white, left-pointing move pointer. Drag the column to the left and drop it immediately to the right of the SupplierName field column. Click in the SupplierName field to deselect the Location expression field. Your screen should look similar to Figure 21-7.

FIGURE 21-7
Calculated field with expression

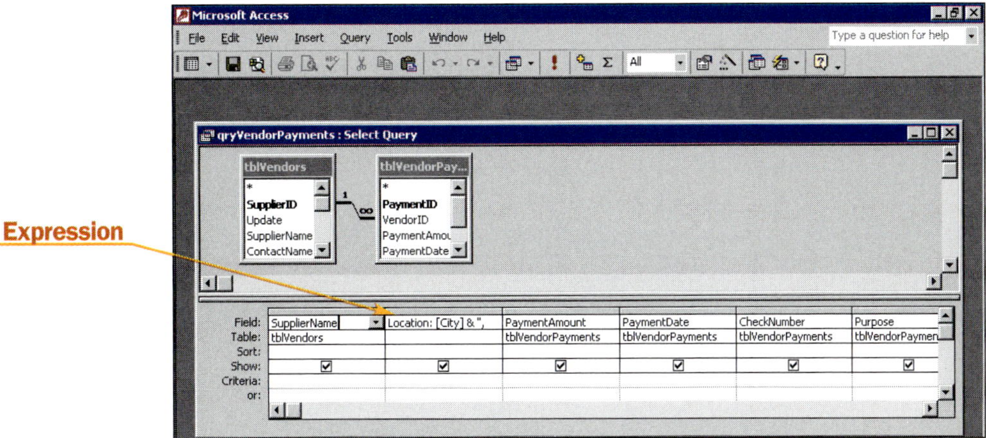

6. Run the query and size all the datasheet columns to their best fit. Your query should look similar to Figure 21-8.

FIGURE 21-8
Query results

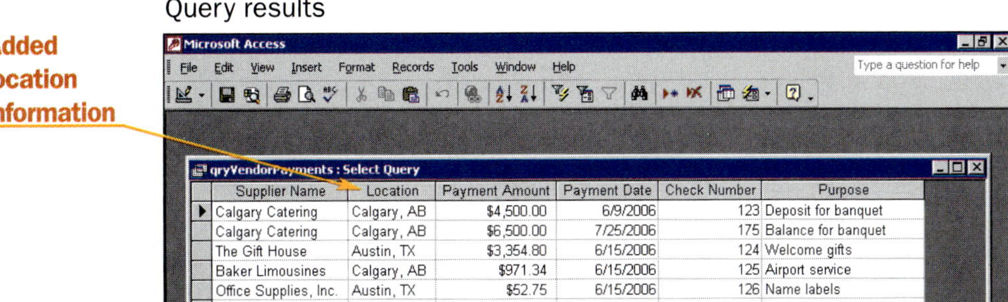

7. Print the query datasheet. Then close and save the query layout. Close the database and close Access.

SUMMARY

In this job, you learned:

- To more effectively use tables with related information, you must link them via a link field, which is a field in the tables that contains a common value.

- In a linking relationship, the primary table is the table whose link field is also its primary key. The table in which the link field is not the primary key is the related table.

- A one-to-many relationship is one in which there is one record in the primary table that links to several records in the related table.

- A query is a request for information from underlying tables based on specific criteria.

- The most common query is a select query that gets data from one or more underlying tables and presents that data in a datasheet.

- You can create a query by using the Simple Query Wizard to select the underlying tables and their fields, or you can create a query from scratch in Design view.

- When you create a query from scratch or modify an existing query in Design view, you work in the design grid, which contains the fields for the query, sorting instructions, and any selection criteria that must be met before a record is included in the query datasheet.

- You can use an expression to combine field names, symbols, values, text, and mathematical operators to create a calculated field in a query.

VOCABULARY *Review*

Define the following terms:

Append query	Link field	Referential integrity
Delete query	Make-table query	Related table
Design grid	One-to-many relationship	Select query
Expression	Primary table	Update query
Foreign key	Query	

REVIEW *Questions*

TRUE / FALSE

Circle T if the statement is true or F if the statement is false.

T   F   **1.** The most common type of query is a make-table query.

T   F   **2.** The link field in both the primary and the related table must have the same field name.

T   F   **3.** In a one-to-many relationship, there is one record in the primary table that can relate to multiple records in the related table.

T   F   **4.** To edit a query's selection criteria, you must view the query in Datasheet view.

T   F   **5.** An expression combines field names with text and other characters to perform some type of calculation in a query.

FILL IN THE BLANK

Complete the following sentences by writing the correct word or words in the blanks provided.

1. The ___________ table is the one in which the link field is also its primary key.

2. The link field in a related table is called a(n) ___________ key.

3. A(n) ___________ is a request for information or an action that you perform on data.

4. The query ___________ grid contains the fields for a query, sorting instructions, and selection criteria.

5. A(n) ___________ query is used to add records to the end of a table.

PROJECTS

PROJECT 21-1

1. Open Windows Explorer, switch to the data files, copy the **mdbProject21-1** database, and paste it in the folder that contains your solution files. Rename the pasted database **mdbConferenceProject21-1**. Close Windows Explorer, open Access, and open the **mdbConferenceProject21-1** database.

2. Using the tblAttendees table, create a query in Design view to list all attendees registered for various workshops. Create an expression in the first field row to show each attendee's first and last name in the same column on the query datasheet. Change the default expression name to *Name*. Add the Company field and the WorkshopA field to the query grid.

3. Change the WorkshopA selection criteria to **"yes"** and run the query. Change the column widths to best fit with the mouse pointer and save the query as **qryWorkshop**.

4. Print the query datasheet and switch to **Design view**. Click the **WorkshopA** field list arrow and click **WorkshopB** to change the field name. Run the query and print the datasheet.

5. Continue to query for attendees registered for WorkshopC through WorkshopE and print each datasheet. Then close the query and save the changes to the layout. Close the database and close Access.

PROJECT 21-2

You want to query the tblTours table to list the tours and their tour guide. Open Windows Explorer, switch to the data files, copy the **mdbProject21-2** database, and paste it in the folder that contains your solution files. Rename the pasted database **mdbAdventuresJob21**. Close Windows Explorer, open Access, and open the **mdbAdventuresJob21** database. Open the Relationships window and double-click the join line between the two tables to open the Edit Relationships window, enforce referential integrity between the two tables, and close the Relationships window. Query the tblTours and the tblGuides tables to list the tour name, location, start date, and tour guide name. Show the tour guide name first in one column in the query datasheet. Save the query as **qryToursbyGuide**, print the datasheet, and close the query. Close the database and close Access.

 ## WEB PROJECT

Melody Stackhouse calls to ask you for help in creating a list of Web sites that contain information useful to the Human Resource (HR) professionals in each of the branches. Using your Web browser and a search tool such as AltaVista (*www.altavista.com*), search for Web sites that might be useful to Melody. Print at least five Web pages.

 ## TEAMWORK PROJECT

There are several different types of action queries you can use to modify data, and it is helpful to be familiar with them. Select a classmate to help you with this project. Then, using Access online Help, research action queries. Finally, describe the four types of action queries and when you might use them to several classmates.

CRITICAL *Thinking*

 ## ACTIVITY 21-1

You often need to calculate totals or perform other calculations in a query. Using Access online Help, research how to total records in a query. Then copy the **mdbActivity21-1** database to your solutions folder and name the pasted database **mdbConferenceActivity21-1**. Open the **mdbConferenceActivity21-1** database and create a new query in Design view that calculates the total of payments made to each vendor. Show the vendor name and the sum of all payments to the vendor. Run the query and print the datasheet. Then save the query as **qryTotalPayments** and close it. Close the database and close Access.

CREATING FORMS

OBJECTIVES

Upon completion of this job, you should be able to:

- Create a simple form with AutoForm.
- Create a form using the Form Wizard.
- Modify a form in Design view.
- Modify control properties.

Estimated Time: 0.5 hour

VOCABULARY

AutoForm

Bound control

Control

Detail section

Field value

Form

Form Footer section

Form Header section

Form Wizard

Labels

Unbound control

Create a Simple Form with AutoForm

A *form* is a guide you can use to quickly enter data in a table instead of entering the data directly into the table's datasheet. Forms are also useful to view data and to modify existing data. Field names on a form are called *labels* and the value entered in each field's text box is called a *field value*. A quick way to create a form is to select a table or query in the Database window and then use the AutoForm. The *AutoForm* process creates a columnar form based on the selected table or query. A form created with AutoForm displays the field names or captions of the underlying table or query as the label for each field, and fields are listed in the same order as they appear in the table or query.

You want to create a simple form you can use to quickly enter vendor payments in the tblVendorPayments table. You begin by opening the conference database, viewing the table objects, and selecting the tblVendorPayments table. Then you use the New Object button on the Database toolbar to create the new form. After you save the form, you use it to enter a new vendor payment record in the tblVendorPayments table.

STEP-BY-STEP 22.1

1. Open Windows Explorer, switch to the data files, copy the **mdbStep22-1** database, and paste it in the folder that contains your solution files. Rename the pasted database **mdbConferenceJob22**. Close Windows Explorer, open Access, and open the **mdbConferenceJob22** database. Click the **Tables** button on the Objects bar, if necessary, to view the table objects, and click the **tblVendorPayments** table to select it, if necessary.

2. Click the **New Object** button list arrow on the Database toolbar to view the new object choices and click **AutoForm** to create the simple form. The form on your screen should look similar to Figure 22-1.

FIGURE 22-1
New form created with AutoForm

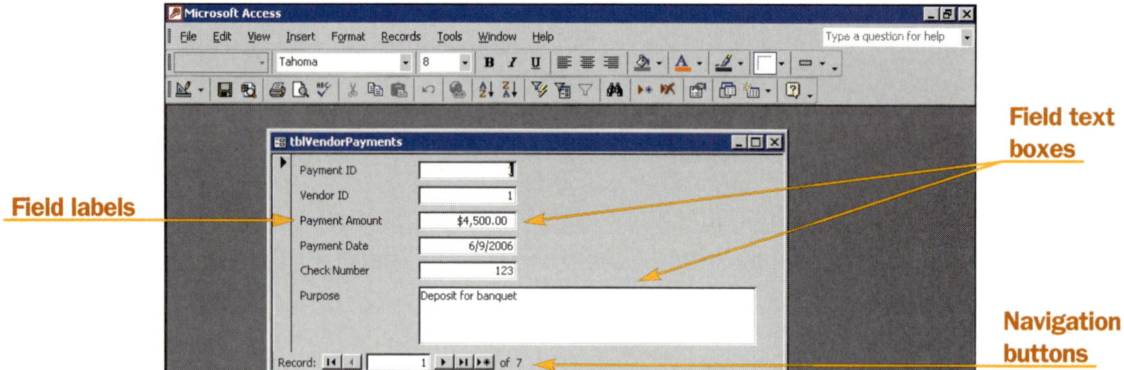

3. Click the **Save** button on the Form View toolbar and save the form as **frmVendorPayments**.

4. Click the **New Record** button on the Form View toolbar to view a blank record in the form. Press **Tab** and key **4** as the Vendor ID field value; press **Tab** and key **75.06** in the Payment Amount field value. Complete the new record using Figure 22-2 as your guide.

FIGURE 22-2
New vendor payment record

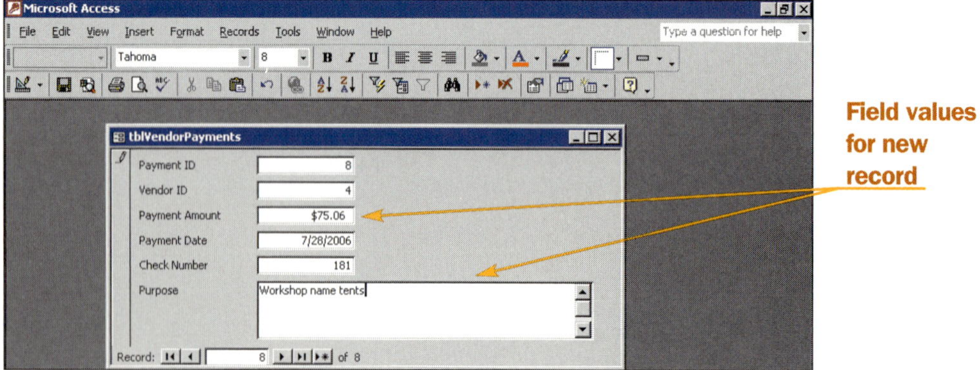

5. Print preview and print the form and then close it. Leave the database open for the next Step-by-Step.

Create a Form Using the Form Wizard

Another way to quickly create a simple form is to use the Form Wizard. The *Form Wizard* is a step-by-step process for identifying the underlying table or query for the form and then specifying which fields to include in the form. You want to create a form to enter attendee information more easily in the tblAttendees table. You do this with the Form Wizard.

STEP-BY-STEP 22.2

1. Verify that the **mdbConferenceJob22** database is open and then click the **Forms** button on the Objects bar, if necessary, to view the form objects. 

2. Double-click **Create form by using wizard** to open the Form Wizard dialog box.

3. Click **Table:tblAttendees** in the Tables/Queries list to select it as the underlying table. Add all the available fields to the Selected Fields list and click **Next**.

4. Click the **Columnar** option button, if necessary, and click **Next**; click the **Standard** style option, if necessary, and click **Next**; key **frmAttendees** in the What title do you want for your form? text box; click the **Open the form to view or enter information.** option button, if necessary, and click **Finish**. Your screen should look similar to Figure 22-3.

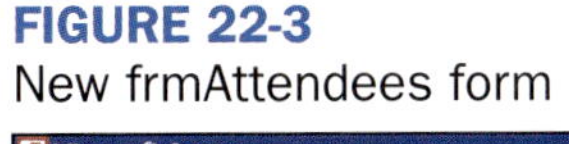
FIGURE 22-3
New frmAttendees form

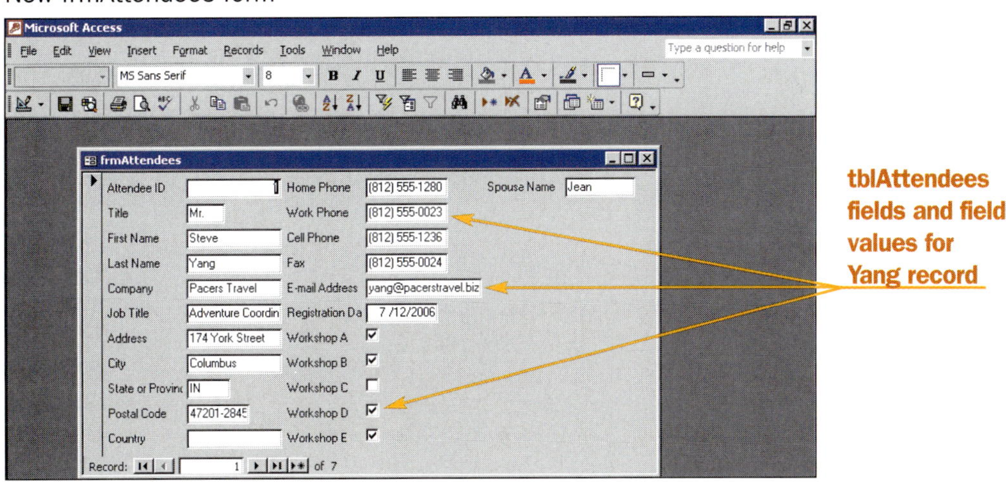

5. Close the form and leave the database open for the next Step-by-Step.

Modify a Form in Design View

A *control* is an object on a form that displays data or performs some action. A *bound control*, such as a field's text box, takes its value from an underlying table or query. An *unbound control*, such as a label, does not take its value from an underlying table or query. Often when you create a basic form using AutoForm or the Form Wizard, you then need to modify the form in Design view to make it easier to read or use. For example, you may need to reposition or resize the label and text box controls in the form.

After reviewing the attendee records in the frmAttendees form in Form view, you realize that several of the text boxes need to be resized to accommodate their field values better. Also, the contents of some of the labels are not completely visible. To fix this, you must resize several of the form's label and text box controls. In order to resize these controls, you must reposition other controls. You open the frmAttendees form in Design view and reposition and resize the appropriate controls.

Hot Tip

In addition to text boxes, controls include option buttons, check boxes, and toggle buttons. You can reposition controls by selecting them and then dragging them with the mouse pointer. If the mouse pointer is a pointing hand, you can drag either the label or text box control by pointing to its move handle. If the mouse pointer is an open hand with all fingers extended, you can move both the label and text box controls at once. You add controls to a form with buttons in the Toolbox.

STEP-BY-STEP 22.3

1. Verify that the **mdbConferenceJob22** database is open and then click the **Forms** button on the Objects bar, if necessary, to view the form objects. 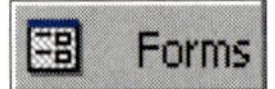

2. Click the **frmAttendees** form to select it and then click the **Design** button on the Database window toolbar to open the form in Design view. 

3. Move the mouse pointer to the right boundary of the form grid until the mouse pointer becomes a sizing pointer. Drag the right boundary of the grid to the right to the 6½-inch position on the horizontal ruler. (*Note*: Resize the Form view window, if necessary, to view the gray area to the right of the grid.)

4. Click the **SpouseName** text box control to select it. Then move the mouse pointer to the SpouseName text box control until it becomes a move pointer with an open hand and all fingers extended. Drag the selected controls to the right until the text box control's right boundary is just to the left of the 6½-inch position on the horizontal ruler. Click in the gray area to the right of the grid to deselect the controls.

STEP-BY-STEP 22.3 Continued

5. Click the **RegistrationDate** text box control to select it. Drag the RegistrationDate controls and drop them below the SpouseName controls. Position the RegistrationDate controls so that the right boundary of the text box control aligns vertically with the SpouseName text box control. Click the **Registration Date** label control to select it. Move the mouse pointer to the Registration Date label control's middle-left sizing handle until it becomes a black sizing pointer, and then drag the control's left boundary to the 4¾-inch position on the horizontal ruler. Deselect the controls. Your screen should look similar to Figure 22-4.

FIGURE 22-4
Resized grid and repositioned controls

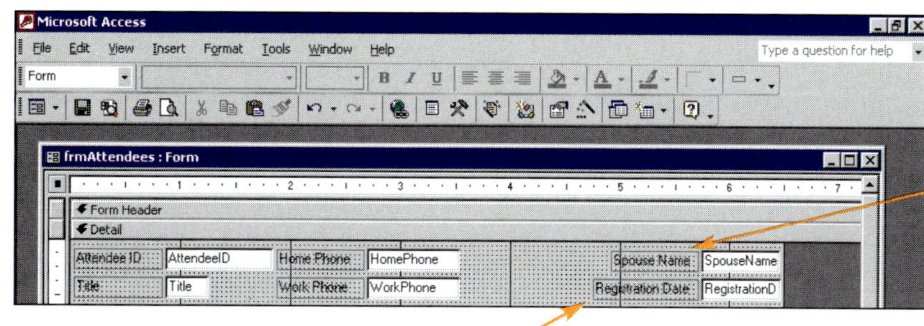

6. Click the **HomePhone** text box control to select it. Press **Shift** and click the **WorkPhone**, **CellPhone**, **FaxNumber**, and **EmailAddress** text box controls to select the multiple controls. Press the **right arrow** several times to reposition all the selected controls until the EmailAddress text box control is aligned at the 4¾-inch position on the horizontal ruler. Deselect the controls. (If you are using Access 2000, drag the selected controls to their new position.)

7. Select **HomePhone**, **WorkPhone**, **CellPhone**, and **FaxNumber** text box controls. Move the mouse pointer to the HomePhone text box control's middle-right sizing handle and drag to the right to the 4½-inch position on the horizontal ruler to resize the selected text box controls. Deselect the controls.

STEP-BY-STEP 22.3 Continued

8. Click the **EmailAddress** text box control to select it. Move the mouse pointer to the control's middle-right sizing handle until it becomes a black sizing pointer and then drag to the right to the 5½-inch position on the horizontal ruler. Deselect the control. Using Figure 22-5 as your guide, continue to reposition and resize the controls as necessary so that the text in each label control is completely visible, the field value for each record is completely visible in Form view, and the controls are attractively spaced on the grid.

FIGURE 22-5
Redesigned form

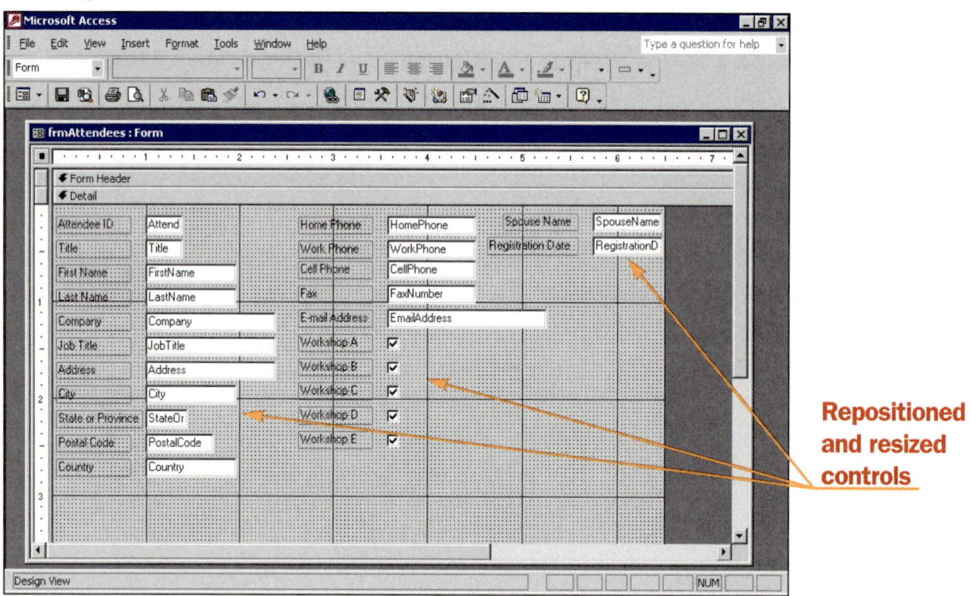

9. Switch to Form view and review all the records to make certain that each label and field value is easy to read. Then switch back to Design view, save the form, and leave it open for the next Step-by-Step.

Modify Control Properties

A form in Design view is divided into three sections: Form Header, Detail, and Form Footer sections. The *Form Header section* at the top of the form contains heading text or images that identify the form; the *Detail section* contains the label and text box controls; and the *Form Footer section* contains text that appears at the bottom of the form.

You want to add some identifying text to the top of the form. To do this, you display the Form Header section, insert a label control, and key and format the label text. Next you format the label text and then add a border to the label control by modifying its properties.

STEP-BY-STEP 22.4

1. Verify that the **frmAttendees** form is open in Design view and then move the mouse pointer to the boundary between the Form Header and Detail sections until it becomes a sizing pointer. Drag the boundary downward approximately ¾ inch.

2. Click the **Toolbox** button on the Form Design toolbar to display the Toolbox, if necessary. Then click the **Label** button in the Toolbox and move the mouse pointer to the left side of the Form Header section. Your screen should look similar to Figure 22-6.  

FIGURE 22-6
Form Header section

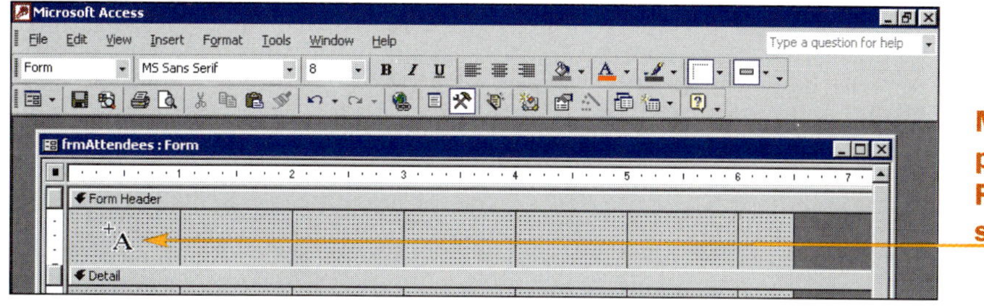

3. Drag to create a label control approximately ¼ inch high and 2 inches wide. Key **Attendee Registration** in the label and press **Enter**. Observe the selected label. Using the appropriate buttons on the Formatting (Form/Report) toolbar, change the text font size to **14 point**, **bold**, and **centered**. Resize the label control as necessary to view the entire reformatted text. Drag the label control to the approximate center of the Form Header section and leave it selected.

4. Click the **Properties** button on the Form Design toolbar to open the Properties sheet for the selected control. Click the **Format** tab, if necessary, and scroll to view the Border Style and Border Width properties. Click the **Border Style** property to select it, click the list arrow, and click **Solid**. Click the **Border Width** property to select it, click the list arrow, and click **2 pt**. Close the **Properties** box and switch to Form view. Your screen should look similar to Figure 22-7. 

STEP-BY-STEP 22.4 Continued

FIGURE 22-7
Completed form

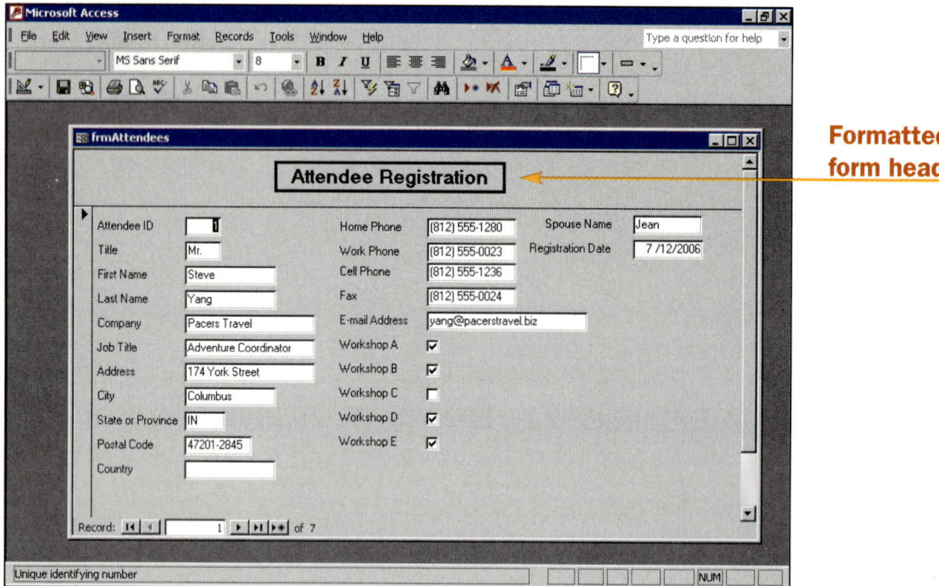

5. Save the form, print preview, and print it. Then close the form, close the database, and close Access.

SUMMARY

In this job, you learned:

■ A form is a guide for quickly viewing records or entering data in a table.

■ Field names on a form are called labels, and field values are viewed or entered in field text boxes.

■ A quick way to create a simple form based on a selected table is AutoForm.

■ You can use the Form Wizard to select the underlying table or query and the fields to include in a form.

■ A form control is an object that displays data or takes some action on a form. In Design view, you see label controls and text box controls. Label controls are unbound controls, meaning they do not get their value from an underlying table or query. Most text box controls are bound controls, meaning they do get their value from an underlying table or query.

■ Sometimes when you create a form using the AutoForm or the Form Wizard, you then need to modify the form in Design view to resize and reposition the form's label and text box controls.

■ In Design view, a form has three sections: the Form Header, Detail, and Form Footer sections.

■ Each form control contains properties or attributes that you can modify.

VOCABULARY *Review*

Define the following terms:

AutoForm	Field value	Form Wizard
Bound control	Form	Labels
Control	Form Footer section	Unbound control
Detail section	Form Header section	

REVIEW *Questions*

TRUE / FALSE

Circle T if the statement is true or F if the statement is false.

T F **1.** The field value is the value entered in a text box on a form.

T F **2.** AutoForm quickly creates a columnar form based on a table you select in the Database window.

T F **3.** Field names on a form are called text boxes.

T F **4.** A control is an object on a form that displays data or performs some action.

T F **5.** You use the Toolbox to insert controls on a form in Design view.

FILL IN THE BLANK

Complete the following sentences by writing the correct word or words in the blanks provided.

1. A label is a(n) ___________ control.

2. A form's label and text box controls are contained in the ___________ section.

3. You can use the ___________ to create a basic form by specifying the underlying table or query and which fields to include in the form.

4. A text box that gets its value from an underlying table or query is a(n) ___________ control.

5. To add identifying text to the top of a form, you can create a new ___________ control in the Form Header section using the Toolbox.

PROJECTS

 PROJECT 22-1

1. Open Windows Explorer, switch to the data files, copy the **mdbProject22-1** database, and paste it in the folder that contains your solution files. Rename the pasted database

mdbConferenceProject22-1. Close Windows Explorer, open Access, and open the **mdbConferenceProject22-1** database. View the Forms objects.

2. Create a new form for the tblVendors table using the Form Wizard. Add all the fields to the form. Use the layout and style of your choice. Name the form **frmVendors**.

3. Modify the form in Design view as desired to ensure that the form is easy to read and use.

4. Add the label **Vendor Data** to the form's Form Header section and then test the form by viewing all the tblVendors records in Form view. Format the label's contents as desired and add a border of your choice to the label.

5. Save the form and then preview and print it. Close the form, close the database, and close Access.

 ## PROJECT 22-2

 You want to quickly create forms to enter the tour guide and tour information in the adventure tours database. Copy the **mdbProject22-2** database to your solutions folder and rename the database **mdbAdventuresJob22.** Use the tblGuides table and AutoForm to create a form containing a subform for entering and viewing data from both the tblGuides and tblTours tables. (*Note:* Because of the relationship between the two tables, Access automatically creates a subform for the tblTours table within the form for the tblGuides table.) Save the form as **frmGuides**. Then preview, print, and close the form. Close the database and close Access.

  ## WEB PROJECT

R. T. Thomas, one of the marketing directors, sends you an e-mail asking for help in finding Web sites that contain information on special Web-based marketing techniques. Using your Web browser and a search tool such as Google (*www.google.com*), locate Web sites that provide information on how to use the Web to market products and services. Print at least five Web pages.

  ## TEAMWORK PROJECT

After taking a look at the frmGuides form that contains a subform, Beverly Harris asks you for more information about subforms and how they are used. Select a classmate to help you with this project. Then, using Access online Help, research subforms. Create a short list of topics you can use to discuss subforms and use the list and the frmGuides form in the mdbAdventuresJob22 database to describe subforms to a classmate. (If you have not yet completed Project 22-2, do so before you begin this project.)

CRITICAL*Thinking*

 ## ACTIVITY 22-1

You recently read an article about creating forms in which the term switchboard was used. You want to know what a switchboard is and how it is used. Using Access online Help, research how to create and use switchboard forms. Then discuss switchboard forms and how they are used with a classmate.

CREATING REPORTS

Create a Simple Report with AutoReport

A *report* is an object that presents information from underlying tables or queries in printed form. You can create many different report types, such as a *columnar report*, in which each record's data is printed in a vertical column, or a *tabular report*, in which each record's data is printed horizontally across the page. You can quickly create a simple columnar report from a single underlying table or query using *AutoReport*.

Sloane is in a hurry to attend a meeting and asks you to quickly print a list of all conference vendor payments for the meeting. You use AutoReport to print the list using the underlying qryVendorPayments query.

STEP-BY-STEP 23.1

1. Open Windows Explorer, switch to the data files, copy the **mdbStep23-1** database, and paste it in the folder that contains your solution files. Rename the pasted database **mdbConferenceJob23**. Close Windows Explorer, open Access, and open the **mdbConferenceJob23** database. Click the **Queries** button on the Objects bar, if necessary, to view the query objects and click **qryVendorPayments** to select it, if necessary.

2. Click the **New Object** button list arrow on the Database toolbar to view the new object choices and click **AutoReport** to create the simple report and view it in Print Preview. The report in Print Preview on your screen should look similar to Figure 23-1.

FIGURE 23-1
New report in Print Preview

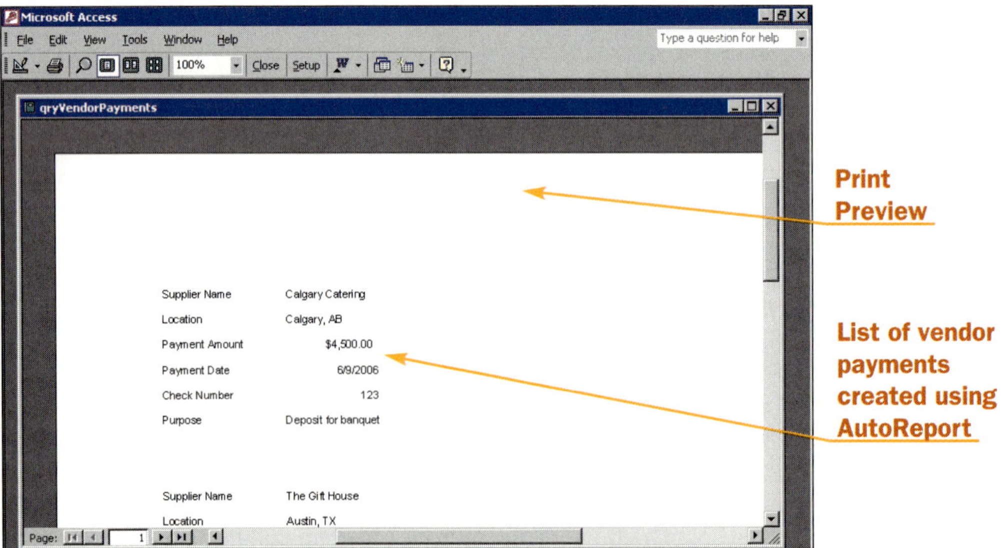

3. Print the report, close Print Preview, and save the report as **rptVendorList**.

4. Leave the database open for the next Step-by-Step.

Create a Report Using the Report Wizard

Another way to quickly create a report is to use the Report Wizard. The **Report Wizard** is a step-by-step process that allows you to select the underlying tables or queries, select the appropriate fields, and group and sort the data for a report. Grouping and sorting options allow you to organize the information in the most useful way. You also select the layout and style of the report when you use the Report Wizard.

Sloane calls you from the meeting and asks you to prepare a report of all conference attendees and the workshops for which they are registered. The report should group attendees by company and should list each attendee in ascending alphabetical order by last name within each company group. Finally, the report should include the total number of attendees registered for each workshop.

S TEP-BY-STEP 23.2

1. Verify that the **mdbConferenceJob23** database is open and then click the **Reports** button on the Objects bar to view the report objects, if necessary. 

2. Double-click **Create report by using wizard** to open the Report Wizard dialog box. Click **tblAttendees** in the Tables/Queries list to select it as an underlying table. Add the FirstName, LastName, Company, WorkshopA, WorkshopB, WorkshopC, WorkshopD, and WorkshopE fields to the Selected Fields list and click **Next**.

3. Double-click **Company** to group records of attendees from the same company and click **Next**. Click the sorting text box list arrow and click **LastName** to sort the records by attendees' last name within each company and then click **Next**. Click the **Stepped** layout option button, if necessary, click the **Landscape** option button, and click **Next**. Click the **Corporate** style, if necessary, and click **Next**.

4. Key **rptAttendeesbyCompany** in the What title do you want for your report? text box, click the **Preview the report.** option button, and click **Finish**. The new report in Print Preview should look similar to Figure 23-2.

FIGURE 23-2
rptAttendeesbyCompany report in Print Preview

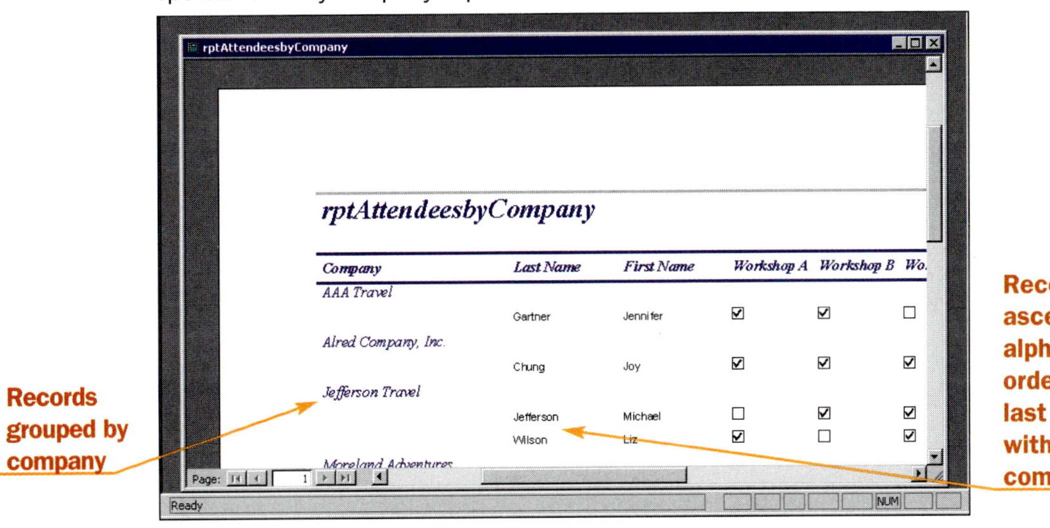

5. Print the report and close Print Preview. Leave the database open for the next Step-by-Step.

Modify a Report in Design View

Y ou may need to modify reports created with the Report Wizard to resize and reposition the report controls, modify the report header text, and so forth to make the report easier to read. Report Design view is divided into several sections. The ***Report Header section*** at the top of the report is used for the report title. The ***Page Header section*** appears at the top of each page of the report and usually includes labels such as *column heading* that appear on each page. The Detail section contains the controls that display data from each of the fields selected for the report. The ***Page Footer section*** appears at the bottom of each page and often contains information such as the page number. The ***Report Footer section*** appears at the end of the report and usually contains report totals.

To make the report more appealing, you need to change the header text to *Attendees by Company* and reposition the workshop check box controls to align them more attractively in the workshop columns. You make these modifications in Design view.

S TEP-BY-STEP 23.3

1. Verify that the **mdbConferenceJob23** database is open and then click the **Reports** button on the Objects bar, if necessary, to view the form objects. 

2. Click the **rptAttendeesbyCompany** report to select it and then click the **Design** button on the Database window toolbar to open the report in Design view. 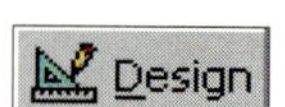

3. Click the label in the Report Header section to select it, select the **rptAttendeesbyCompany** text, key **Attendees by Company**, and press **Enter**. Click in the gray area below the report grid to deselect the label control. Your screen should look similar to Figure 23-3.

FIGURE 23-3
Report Design view

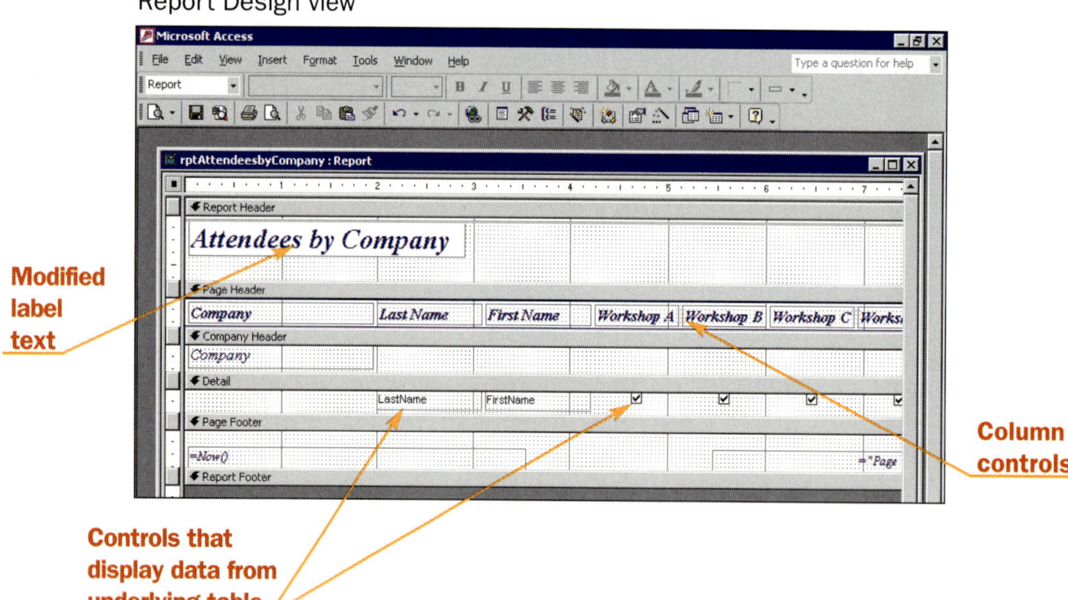

STEP-BY-STEP 23.3 Continued

4. Click the check box control in the Workshop A column and reposition it with the mouse pointer or the right arrow key until the control is aligned below the *sh* in *Workshop*. Deselect the control. Reposition the remaining check box controls in the same manner. Your screen should look similar to Figure 23-4.

FIGURE 23-4
Repositioned controls

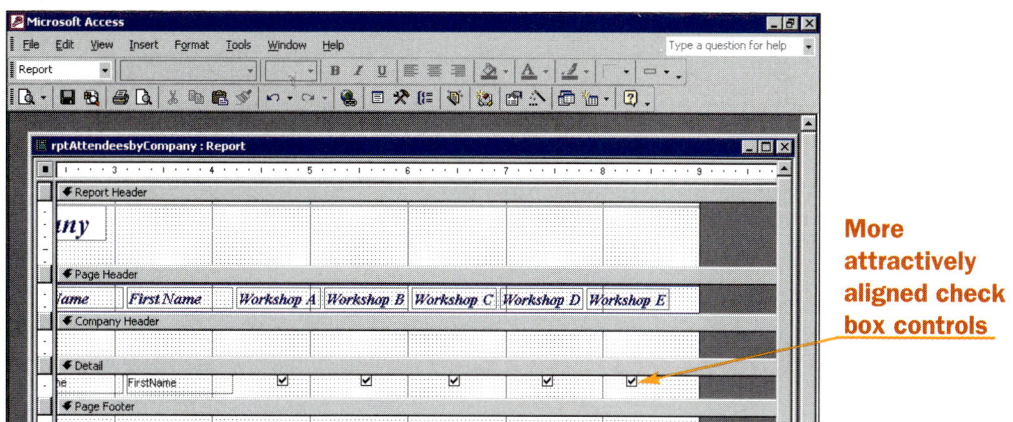

More attractively aligned check box controls

5. Print Preview the report and observe the new header text and repositioned check boxes, and then switch back to Design view.

6. Click the **Save** button on the Report Design toolbar to save the report design changes and leave the report open in Design view for the next Step-by-Step. 

Add a Calculated Control to a Report

A *calculated control* displays the results of a calculation. You create a calculated control by adding an unbound text box control to a report and then keying the expression that performs the calculation in the control. When you insert an unbound text box control in a report, an attached label also is inserted.

To complete the Attendees by Company report, you now need to add the total number of registered attendees for each workshop to the Report Footer section. You do this by inserting text box controls and keying an expression that sums the Yes values for each workshop.

Warning 

Access stores a Yes value as a −1 and a No value as 0; therefore, you can add Yes values, but to show the result as a positive number, you must multiply the total by −1.

Hot Tip 

If you get a blank page at the end of a printed report, you may need to modify the page margins in the Page Setup dialog box, or change the size of the report grid in Design view.

STEP-BY-STEP 23.4

1. Verify that the **rptAttendeesbyCompany** report is open in Design view and then move the mouse pointer to the bottom of the Report Footer boundary until it becomes a sizing pointer. Drag the boundary downward approximately ½ inch to display the Report Footer grid.

2. Click the **Toolbox** button on the Report Design toolbar to display the Toolbox, if necessary. 

3. Click the **Text Box** button in the Toolbox, move the mouse pointer to the Report Footer section below the Workshop A column label, and click to insert an unbound text box control and attached label. Your screen should look similar to Figure 23-5. 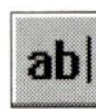

FIGURE 23-5
Unbound text box control and label

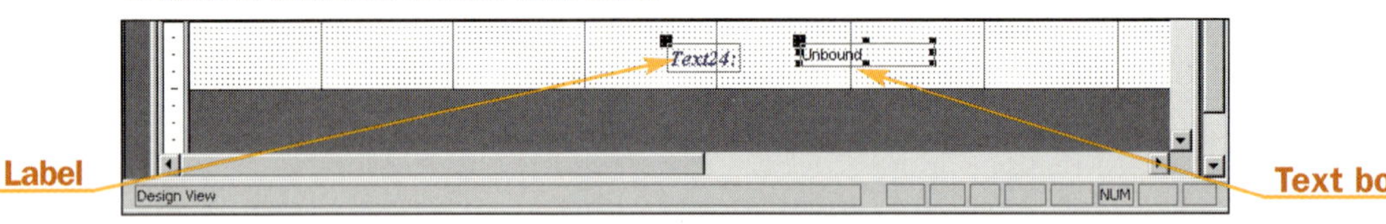

4. Click the label control to select it and drag the middle-left sizing handle to the left approximately 1½ inches. Select the contents of the label control, key **Total Registered Attendees**, and press **Enter**. Then resize the label control to accommodate the text, if necessary.

5. Click the unbound text box control to select it and then click it again to position the insertion point in the control. Key the expression **=Sum([WorkshopA])*-1** and press **Enter** to create a calculated control. Print Preview the report and observe the label and the number 7, which is the total number of attendees registered for Workshop A. Switch back to Design view and size and reposition the calculated control in the Workshop A column using Figure 23-6 as your guide. Deselect the control.

FIGURE 23-6
Resized and repositioned calculated control

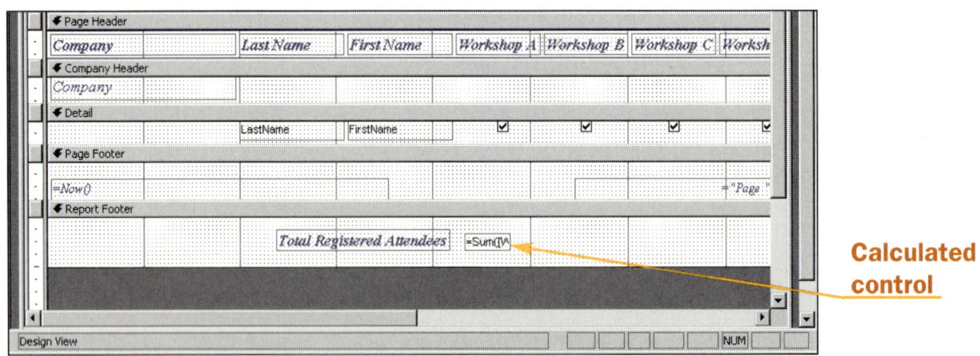

6. Insert an unbound text box control in the Report Footer in the Workshop B column. Select and delete the attached label control. Select the unbound text box control, position the insertion point in the control, key **=Sum([WorkshopB])*-1**, and press **Enter**. Resize and reposition the control in the Workshop B column. Continue to create calculated controls for the remaining Workshops C through E and resize and reposition them appropriately in their columns. (*Note:* You may need to Print Preview the report frequently to see how the totals are aligning in each workshop column.)

STEP-BY-STEP 23.4 Continued

7. Scroll to view the right edge of the report grid and drag it back to the left to the 9-inch position on the horizontal ruler, if necessary, to prevent printing a blank page for this short report.

8. Save the report and then print preview and print it. Close the report, close the database, and close Access.

SUMMARY

In this job, you learned:

- A report is an object that presents information from underlying tables or queries in printed form.

- You can use AutoReport to quickly create a simple columnar report from a single underlying table or query.

- The Report Wizard allows you to select multiple underlying tables or queries, specify the fields to be included on the report, and select the report layout and style.

- When you create a report with AutoReport or the Report Wizard, you may need to modify the report in Design view to change header text, resize and reposition report controls, and add calculated controls.

- A calculated control displays the results of a calculation on a report and is created by keying an expression in an unbound text box control.

VOCABULARY *Review*

Define the following terms:

AutoReport	Page Header section	Report Wizard
Calculated control	Report	Tabular report
Columnar report	Report Footer section	
Page Footer section	Report Header section	

REVIEW *Questions*

TRUE / FALSE

Circle T if the statement is true or F if the statement is false.

T   F   1. A tabular report presents data in a vertical column.

T   F   2. AutoReport is used to create a complex report with multiple underlying tables or queries.

T F **3.** You can change the sort order of records when you use the Report Wizard.

T F **4.** The Page Header section of a report in Design view is used to display labels or data that appears at the top of each page of the report.

T F **5.** You cannot calculate a total of Yes and No values.

FILL IN THE BLANK

Complete the following sentences by writing the correct word or words in the blanks provided.

1. A(n) __________ control displays the results of a calculation in a report.

2. The Report __________ section of a report in Design view is commonly used to display report totals.

3. In a(n) __________ report, data is printed horizontally on the page.

4. The __________ is a step-by-step process for creating a report from one or more underlying tables or queries.

5. You would likely find page number or date controls in the __________ Footer section of a report in Design view.

PROJECTS

 **PROJECT 23-1**

1. Open Windows Explorer, switch to the data files, copy the **mdbProject23-1** database, and paste it in the folder that contains your solution files. Rename the pasted database **mdbConferenceProject23-1**. Close Windows Explorer, open Access, and open the **mdbConferenceProject23-1** database. View the Report objects.

2. Create a simple report listing all vendor information using AutoReport and the underlying tblVendors table.

3. Switch to Design view, display the Toolbox, and add a label control to the Page Header section. Key **Vendor List** in the control and format the text as desired.

4. Save the report as **rptVendors** and then print preview and print the report.

5. Close the report, close the database, and close Access.

 **PROJECT 23-2**

You need to create a report listing each tour guide and their assignments, including the name of the tour, its location, and its start date. Copy the **mdbProject23-2** database from the data files to your solutions folder and rename the database **mdbAdventuresJob23**. Create a report based on all fields in the qryToursbyGuide query using the Report Wizard. Use the layout and style of your choice. Open the report in Design view and make any changes necessary to create an easy-to-read and attractive report. Save the report as **rptGuides** and then Print Preview, print, and close it. Close the database and close Access.

 **WEB PROJECT**

R. T. Thomas sends you an e-mail thanking you for the helpful list of marketing information Web sites. He asks you to suggest some additional Web sites that contain information about the number of Internet users in the United States and globally, and information about which Internet users are shopping online. Use your Web browser and a search tool such as Google (*www.google.com*) to locate Web sites that provide user information about the Internet and the Web. Print at least four Web pages.

  **TEAMWORK PROJECT**

Beverly Harris calls and asks you if it is possible to create a chart in Access. Select a classmate to help you with this project. Then, using Access online Help, research how to use the Chart Wizard. Using the database of your choice, demonstrate to a group of classmates how to use the Chart Wizard.

CRITICAL*Thinking*

 **ACTIVITY 23-1**

You want to print a set of vendor mailing labels from the tblVendors table. Using Access online Help, research how to use the Label Wizard. Then create a copy of **mdbActivity23-1** and paste it into your solutions folder. Rename the database **mdbConferenceActivity23-1**. Create a page of mailing labels for the vendors. Print Preview and print the labels on plain paper. Save the labels as **rptVendorLabels**.

IMPORTING AND EXPORTING DATA

Import Excel Data into a New Access Table

Y ou can import data from other sources, such as another Access database or an Excel worksheet, into a database. You use the Import Wizard to import data into a new table or to add data to an existing table. Tamika Washington is maintaining conference attendee hotel reservation information in an Excel worksheet. You want to import the reservation information into the conference database so that there is one primary source for all the conference information. You open the conference database and import the reservation data into a new table using the Import Wizard. Then you open the new table in Design view and modify the Field Size property for the table's primary key.

Hot Tip

You can use the Link Worksheet Wizard to link Excel worksheet data to an Access database. When you link an Excel worksheet to a database, a small arrow and the Excel icon appear in front of the table object indicating a linked Excel table. Any changes you make to the data in the linked table are reflected in the original Excel worksheet.

S TEP-BY-STEP 24.1

1. Open Windows Explorer, switch to the data files, copy the **mdbStep24-1** database, and paste it in the folder that contains your solution files. Rename the pasted database **mdbConferenceJob24**. Close Windows Explorer, open Access, and open the **mdbConferenceJob24** database. Click the **Tables** button on the Objects bar, if necessary, to view the table objects.

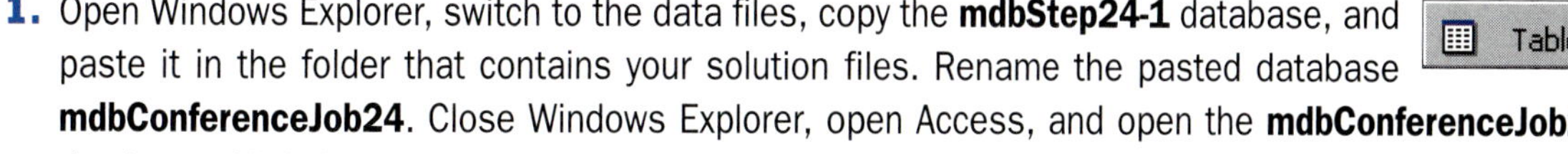
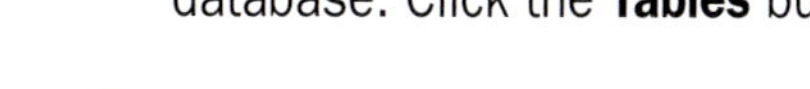

2. Click the **File** menu, point to **Get External Data**, and click **Import** to open the Import dialog box. Switch to the data files, change the file type to Microsoft Excel, and double-click the **Step24-1** Excel workbook to open it in the Import Spreadsheet Wizard.

STEP-BY-STEP 24.1 Continued

3. Click the **Show Worksheets** option button, if necessary, and click **Reservations** in the worksheet list, if necessary. Your dialog box should look similar to Figure 24-1.

FIGURE 24-1
Import Spreadsheet Wizard

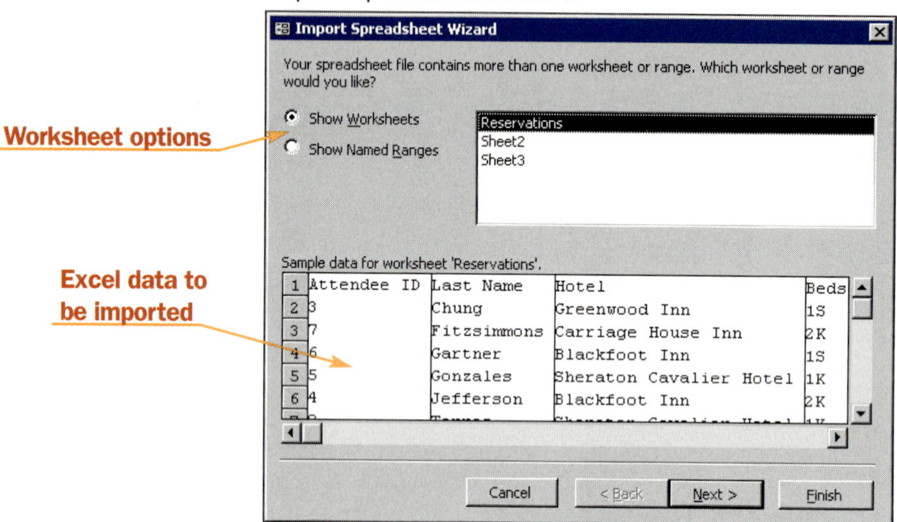

4. Click **Next**, click the **First Row Contains Column Headings** check box, if necessary, and click **Next**.

5. Click the **In a New Table** option button, if necessary, and click **Next**.

6. Click the **Indexed** list arrow, click **Yes (No duplicates)** to specify that the AttendeeID field must contain unique numbers, and click **Next**.

7. Click the **Choose my own primary key.** option button, verify **AttendeeID** is selected in the field list, and click **Next**.

8. Key **tblReservations** in the Import to Table text box, click **Finish**, and click **OK** to complete the Wizard process. Open the new **tblReservations** table in Datasheet view to review the data, and then switch to **Design** view.

9. Change the Field Size property for the AttendeeID field to **Long Integer** and save and close the table. Click **Yes** to close the warning message. Leave the database open for the next Step-by-Step.

Export Data to Word

You can export a table or query results to Word, merge an Access table with a Word document, or export table or query data to an Excel workbook using the OfficeLinks button on the Database toolbar. When you export a table or query results to Word, a Rich Text Format (.rtf) document with the table or query name is created, which automatically opens in Word. When you export a table or query results to Excel, a new workbook with the table or query name is created, which automatically opens in Excel.

Beverly Harris calls to tell you she needs a list of conference attendees' spouses she can use in Word to prepare an invitation to a special breakfast during the conference. You quickly create a query to provide the information and then export the query to Word.

S TEP-BY-STEP 24.2

1. Verify that the **mdbConferenceJob24** database is open and click the **Queries** button on the Objects bar to view the query objects. 

2. Create a query in Design view using the tblAttendees table. Include the Title, FirstName, LastName, and SpouseName fields in the query. Run the query to verify the information, save the query as **qrySpouseName**, and close it.

3. Select the **qrySpouseName** query in the Database window, click the **OfficeLinks** button list  arrow on the Database toolbar, and click **Publish It with Microsoft Word**. A new .rtf document named qrySpouseName opens in Word. (If you are using Word 2000, click **OK** in the Convert Text dialog box to select Rich Text Format (RTF) file type if asked.)

4. Save the new document as **Spouse Name** and then print preview, print, and close it.

5. Leave the database open for the next Step-by-Step.

Create a Simple Data Access Page

A *data access page*, or *DAP*, is an HTML file (Web page) that contains pointers to data in an Access database. When you create a DAP, Access saves the HTML file in the same folder as the database file and adds a shortcut to the HTML file in the Database window. You can create a DAP with AutoPage, with the Page Wizard, or from scratch in Design view. You can edit a DAP in Design view in much the same way as you edit other Access objects.

Sloane wants other employees working on the conference to be able to view the current list of attendees and wants the list grouped by company. You create a DAP based on the underlying tblAttendees table that will be posted to the company intranet. You use the Page Wizard to create the DAP.

> **Warning** 
>
> A DAP contains a connection string that provides the path of the related Access database. A DAP works only if the actual path to the database is the same as the original connection string path. If the actual path is not the same as that in the connection string, you must recreate the connection. To learn more about this issue, see Access online Help. To view a DAP, you must have Internet Explorer Web browser version 5.0 or later installed on your computer.

S TEP-BY-STEP 24.3

1. Verify that the **mdbConferenceJob24** database is open and click the **Pages** button on the Objects Bar to view the Pages objects.

2. Double-click **Create data access page by using wizard** to open the Page Wizard. Select **tblAttendees** in the Tables/Queries list and add all the fields to the Selected Fields list. Then click **Next**.

3. Group the list by company and then click **Next**. Sort the list in ascending order by LastName and click **Next**.

4. Key **dapAttendees** in the What title do you want for your page? text box, click the **Open the page**. option button, and click **Finish**. The DAP window on your screen should look similar to Figure 24-2.

FIGURE 24-2
dapAttendees

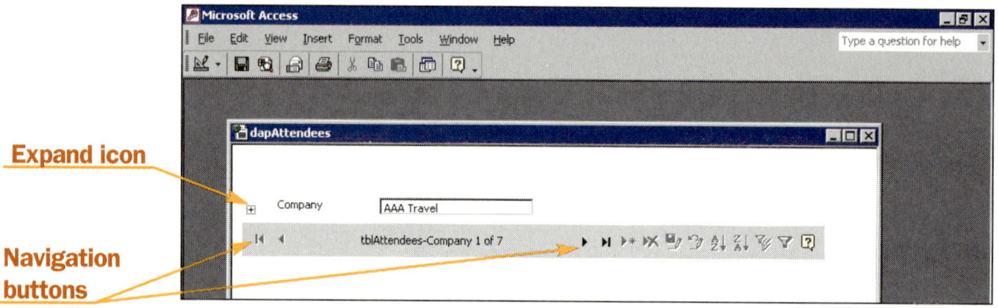

5. Click the expand icon (plus sign) to the left of the Company label to expand the view of the first record. Scroll down to view the record and then scroll up to the top of the page. Click the collapse icon (minus sign) to the left of the Company label to collapse the view of the record. Click the **Next** button (right-pointing arrow) in the navigation toolbar to view the second record. Expand the record, review it, and then collapse the record.

6. Close the DAP window and save the HTML page as **dapAttendees** in the same folder as the mdbConferenceJob24 database. Click **OK** to close the absolute path warning message, if necessary.

7. Right-click **dapAttendees** in the Database window and click **Web Page Preview** to preview the page in the Internet Explorer Web browser. Review several records and then close the browser.

8. Close the database and close Access.

SUMMARY

In this job, you learned:

- You can import data from another Access database or from another application, such as Excel, using the Import Wizard.

- Imported data can be placed in a new table or added to an existing table.

- You can use the OfficeLinks button on the Database toolbar to export a table or query results to Word, to use a table or query results to merge with a Word main document, or to export a table or query results to an Excel workbook.

- When you export or publish a table or query results to Word, a Rich Text Format (.rtf) document is created and automatically opens in Word.

- A data access page, or DAP, is a Web page (HTML file) that contains pointers to data in an Access database.

VOCABULARY *Review*

Define the following terms:
Data access page (DAP)

REVIEW *Questions*

TRUE / FALSE

Circle T if the statement is true or F if the statement is false.

T   F   **1.** A DAP contains a connection string that links it to the original database.

T   F   **2.** You cannot import data from another Access database.

T   F   **3.** You can export a table or query results to Excel with the Export to Excel button on the Table Datasheet toolbar.

T   F   **4.** A DAP is an HTML file or Web page.

T   F   **5.** You can use the Link Worksheet Wizard to link an Excel worksheet to an Access database.

FILL IN THE BLANK

Complete the following sentences by writing the correct word or words in the blanks provided.

1. Access is exported to Word as a(n) __________ document.

2. A DAP contains a(n) __________ string that links it to its database.

3. You can preview a DAP in the Internet Explorer __________ browser.

4. You can import data from an Excel worksheet into a new table using the __________ Wizard.

5. You use the __________ Wizard to create a DAP.

PROJECTS

PROJECT 24-1

1. Open Windows Explorer, switch to the data files, copy the **mdbProject24-1** database, and paste it in the folder that contains your solution files. Rename the pasted database **mdbAdventuresJob24**. Close Windows Explorer, open Access, and open the **mdbAdventuresJob24** database.

2. Use the OfficeLinks button on the Database toolbar to export the tblTours table to an Excel workbook. Save the workbook as **Tours** and print the tblTours worksheet. Then close the workbook and close Excel. Leave the database open for the next project.

PROJECT 24-2

You want to create a Web page containing tour information that can be published to the company intranet. Verify that the **mdbAdventuresJob24** database is open and view the Pages objects. Use all the fields in the Page Wizard to create a data access page (DAP) using tblTours as the underlying table. Title the DAP **dapTours** and save the DAP as **dapTours** in the same folder as the mdbAdventuresJob24 database and preview it in your Web browser. Close the browser, close the database, and close Access.

WEB PROJECT

James Montevo is now in Calgary finalizing the workshop breakout food and beverage service and he calls you with an urgent request. He needs several small flower arrangements for the breakout tables that can be delivered to the conference center no later than tomorrow morning. He asks you to locate several florists in the Calgary area and e-mail him their phone numbers as soon as possible. Using your Web browser or a search tool such as Google (*www.google.com*), locate florists in Calgary and print at least three Web pages.

TEAMWORK PROJECT

You also can export a datasheet or query results using the Export command on the File menu. Select a classmate to assist you with this project. If necessary, use Access online Help to review exporting database objects. Then open the **mdbAdventuresJob24** database and export the **qryToursbyGuide** query to an Excel workbook and retain the formatting. Open the new Excel workbook containing the exported data and print the worksheet containing the data. Close Excel and close Access.

CRITICAL*Thinking*

ACTIVITY 24-1

Melody Stackhouse calls to ask you a question about using Excel data in Access. She wants to know whether it is better to import the Excel data into a new table or to simply link the Excel worksheet to the Access database. You agree to research the question for her. Using Access online Help, look for information that will help you answer Melody's question. Then discuss with a classmate the considerations for determining whether to import or link the data.

BUSINESS WEEK FOUR

COMMAND SUMMARY

ACCESS FEATURE	MENU COMMAND	KEYSTROKE	TOOLBAR BUTTON	JOB
Datasheet view	View, Datasheet View			19
Delete a record	Delete Record	Delete		19
Design view	View, Design View			20
Enter data in a datasheet		Tab, Shift + Tab, Enter, Shift + Enter		19
Export data to Word	Tools, Office Links, Publish It with Microsoft Word			24
Form objects	View, Database Objects, Forms			22
Form Wizard	Create form by using wizard			22
Import data	File, Get External Data, Import			24
Insert Rows	Insert, Rows			20
Label				22
Move between panes		F6		20
New objects	Insert, (new object type)			22
New record	Insert, New Record	Ctrl + +		22
Object properties	View, Properties	F4		22
Pages objects	View, Database Objects, Pages			24
Print a datasheet	File, Print	Ctrl + P		19
Query objects	View, Database Objects, Queries			21
Query Wizard	Create query by using wizard			21
Relationships window	Tools, Relationships			21
Report objects	View, Database Objects, Reports			23
Report Wizard	Create report by using wizard			23
Save an object	File, Save or Save As	Ctrl + S		20
Set the primary key	Edit, Primary Key			20
Show Table	Relationships, Show Table			21
Table objects	View, Database Objects, Tables			19
Table Wizard	Create table by using wizard			19

ACCESS FEATURE	MENU COMMAND	KEYSTROKE	TOOLBAR JOB BUTTON	
Text Box			abl	23
Toolbox	View, Toolbox		⚒	22

REVIEW *Questions*

TRUE/FALSE

Circle T if the statement is true or F if the statement is false.

T F **1.** You can import Excel data into a new or existing table, or you can link an Excel worksheet to a database.

T F **2.** The Form Wizard is a step-by-step process that allows you to select desired fields in underlying tables or queries and print the results.

T F **3.** You can perform calculations on Yes and No values, but you must remember to multiply the result by +1 to get a positive number.

T F **4.** You can add controls to a form or report in Design view using the Toolbox.

T F **5.** When you enforce referential integrity between related tables, you can delete a record from the primary table without breaking the link between the primary and the related table.

T F **6.** A record is an entry in a table that spans a row, while a field is a category of specific information entered in a column for each record.

T F **7.** The AutoNumber data type allows Access to automatically insert a unique identifying number for a record.

T F **8.** A one-to-many relationship between related tables means that there is only one record in the primary table that links to one or more records in the related table.

T F **9.** The OfficeLinks button on the Database toolbar provides options for importing and exporting data.

T F **10.** You should use the Number data type for postal codes, phone numbers, Social Security numbers, and other numbers that are not used in calculations.

MATCHING

Match the correct term in Column 1 to its description in Column 2.

Column 1

____ 1. Report

Column 2

A. An HTML file or Web page that contains pointers to data in an Access database.

____ **2.** Control	**B.** A guide you use to quickly enter data in a table.
____ **3.** Link field	**C.** An object that presents information from an underlying table or query in printed form.
____ **4.** Expression	**D.** Field name controls or unbound controls containing text on a form or report.
____ **5.** AutoReport	**E.** A request for information based on specific criteria or an action you perform on data.
____ **6.** Label	**F.** An object on a form or report that displays data or performs some action.
____ **7.** Query	**G.** Takes its value from an underlying table or query.
____ **8.** Form	**H.** A combination of field names, symbols, values, text, and mathematical operators that perform some type of calculation in a query or report.
____ **9.** DAP	**I.** A field in related tables that contains a common value.
____ **10.** Bound control	**J.** Creates a simple columnar printed report from a single underlying table or query.

CRITICAL *Thinking*

 **PROJECT 1**

The annual marketing conference is now over and it was a great success, thanks in large part to your efforts. Sloane compliments you on your excellent work on the conference and suggests that you create a new résumé that highlights the Office suite skills you perfected while working on the conference project. Use your Web browser and a search engine such as Google (*www.google.com*) to research how to create an effective résumé. Then, create your new résumé in Word using a résumé template or wizard, save it as **Your Name Resume**, preview, print, and close it and then close Word. (*Note:* Depending on your Word security settings, you may see a dialog box warning you that the document contains macros. Continue by enabling macros.) Create four folders on your hard drive and name them **Word Examples**, **Excel Examples**, **PowerPoint Examples**, and **Access Examples**. Copy at least three documents, workbooks, presentations, and database examples to the appropriate folders that you created or modified while working on the conference project.

PROJECT 2

Create a new, blank database for the Human Resources department and name it **mdbGettingHealthy**. Using the Table Wizard and the Personal templates, add a table named **tblExerciseLog** for exercise records and a table named **tblDietLog** for diet records. Modify the tables in Design view to include appropriate field sizes. Then, create a third table in Design view named **tblParticipants** with the following fields: PersonID (primary key, AutoNumber data type, caption=Person ID), FirstName (Text data type, field size=20, caption=First Name), and LastName (Text data type, field size=25, caption=Last Name). Open the Relationships window and create a one-to-many relationship between the primary tblParticipants and the other two related tables. Add three records to the tblParticipants table and then print the datasheet and close the table. Next, add at least one record for each participant in both of the related tables and print the datasheets for both tables. Finally, close the database and close Access.

ADVANCED *Challenge*

To wrap up the conference, Sloane asks you to send a photograph taken at the final awards banquet to all the registered attendees. You plan to mail the photographs in special envelopes that require labels. Using the **mdbConferenceReview** database located in the data files and the Office Links button on the Database toolbar, merge the attendee name and address information to a new Word document to create size 5663 address labels. Save the main document as **Attendee Main Document** and merge to a new label document you save as **Attendee Labels**. Preview, print, and close the label document. Close all Office applications.

3-D references Cell references from one worksheet included in a formula on another worksheet.

A

Absolute cell reference A cell reference that cannot change when a formula is copied.

Administrative assistant A person who generally supports a top-level executive in charge of a major department or business division in an organization.

Animation Special visual and sound effects added to text and other slide objects to add interest and excitement to a presentation.

Animation scheme A pre-defined set of visual effects that can be applied to an entire presentation at one time.

Append query An action query used to add records to the end of an existing table.

Appointment An item entered in the Calendar folder that is less than 24 hours in duration and has a specific starting and ending time.

Attachment A file included with an outgoing e-mail message.

AutoContent Wizard A step-by-step process that creates a formatted new presentation around a common purpose and that contains sample text.

AutoForm A process that creates a columnar form based on a selected table or query.

Automatic page break A page break automatically inserted by Word when a page is filled with text.

AutoReport A process for creating a simple columnar report from a single underlying table or query.

AutoText Keyed and formatted text saved with a unique name that can be inserted in a Word document.

B

Body The main text portion of a letter or other Word document.

Boilerplate text Pre-keyed and pre-formatted text contained in a Word document template.

Bound control A control that takes its value from an underlying database table or query.

Bullet A graphic object added to each line of a list of items in a Word document or PowerPoint slide.

Bulleted list Short text items in a list preceded by small graphic images called bullets.

C

Calculated control A control that contains an expression and displays the results of a calculation.

Calendar folder The Outlook folder in which appointment and event items are stored.

Cell The intersection of a row and column on a worksheet or table.

Center tab stop A text alignment that centers text at the tab stop with the text flowing left and right from the center position.

Character style A style that contains multiple character formatting components such as Bold, Italic, and Underline.

Chart A picture that represents a set of numerical data or the relationship between multiple sets of data.

Clip Organizer An Office XP feature that contains pointers to picture, sound, video, and other media files or clips.

Columnar report A database report in which each record's data is printed in a vertical column.

Columns The vertical organization of a worksheet or table.

Comment A note added to a Word document, Excel worksheet cell, or PowerPoint slide that adds extra information but is not part of the document, worksheet cell, or slide contents.

Complimentary closing A standard letter closing such as *Sincerely Yours*.

Contact An item entered in the Contacts folder that contains the name, addresses, phone numbers, e-mail addresses, and other important data for an individual.

Contacts folder The Outlook folder in which contact items are stored.

Control An object on a database form or report in Design view that displays data or performs some action.

Current document The open Word document in a merge document process.

Custom animation Visual effects applied to individual slide objects.

D

Data access page (DAP) A HTML file or Web page that contains pointers to data in an Access database.

Data type An identifier that specifies the type of data a field can contain such as text, numbers, date and time, and other data types.

Database A collection of related information.

Datasheet A grid of columns and rows used to view a database table contents or query results.

Datasheet view A view of a database table or query in which the table contents or the results of the query are displayed in a datasheet.

Date field A Word field that contains a set of codes used to display the current date in a document.

Decimal tab stop A text alignment that aligns dollar values on their decimal position.

Delete query An action query used to delete records from a table.

Delivery address The envelope recipient's address.

Design grid The grid in query Design view that contains the fields, sorting instructions, and any selection criteria for the query.

Design template A model that controls the overall look of a presentation such as the color scheme, font, font size, background graphics, and text alignment.

Design view A database object view used to view the object's properties or to add, modify, or delete fields or controls.

Destination file The file in which an embedded or linked object is placed.

Detail section The section of a database form in Design view that contains label and text box controls.

Diagram A figure used with or instead of text to help explain complex relationships.

Distribution list A list of multiple TO addressees keyed on the last page of a memo.

Drawing canvas An area in a Word document that surrounds drawing objects to help keep parts of the objects together.

E

Embedded object An object that must be edited with the menus, toolbars, and other features from its source application.

Embedded Word table A table copied from a Word document and pasted in a PowerPoint slide.

Event An item entered in the Calendar folder that lasts 24 hours or longer.

Expression A combination of field names, symbols, values, text, and mathematical operators used to perform a calculation in a database query or report.

F

Field A category of specific information entered in a column for each record.

Field properties Those attributes that define a field such as field length and formatting.

Field value The value entered into a field's text box on a form.

Fill handle The small square at the lower-right corner of the active cell or a selected range of cells.

Footer Information printed at the bottom of a document or worksheet.

Foreign key The link field in a related table.

Form A guide used to quickly enter data in a database table.

Form Footer section The section of a form in Design view that contains the text or data that appears at the bottom of a form.

Form Header section The section at the top of a form in Design view that contains heading text or images that identify the form.

Form Wizard A step-by-step process for identifying the underlying table or query for a form, the fields to be included in the form, and the form's layout and style.

Formula A mathematical calculation.

Function A predefined mathematical calculation used in a worksheet formula.

G

Grouping The process of selecting multiple worksheets for a common action.

H

Handout master The layout used to control the format of presentation audience handout pages.

Header Text that appears at the top of a Word document page or Excel worksheet.

Heading paragraph A short paragraph in a Word document that introduces subsequent paragraphs covering the same topic.

Horizontal line A graphic line inserted in a paragraph from left to right margin of a Word document.

Hyperlink Text or an object that is associated with the path to text or an object or document at another location.

I

Indent Moving text away from the left or right margins in a Word document to draw attention to the text.

Input Mask Wizard A step-by-step process for applying standard formatting such as Zip + 4 postal code, Social Security number, or phone number formatting for a field's contents.

Interoffice memorandum Written communications to someone inside an organization.

Intranet A group of internal Web pages used by employees to view information needed to perform their jobs.

Item Every Outlook appointment or contact created or e-mail message sent or received.

L

Label(s) Small adhesive-backed pieces of paper on which you print text. Also, field names or captions on a database form or report.

Letter address The address of the letter recipient.

Letterhead *See* letterhead paper.

Letterhead paper Special letter paper that contains a preprinted company name, address, and other contact information.

Link field A field in related database tables that contains a common value.

Linked object An object that must be edited in its source application.

Linking formulas Formulas that link worksheets by using 3-D references.

M

Make-table query An action query used to create a new table from records in a existing table.

Manual page break A page break inserted manually to force text to the next page of a Word document.

Memo *See* interoffice memorandum.

Mixed cell reference A worksheet cell reference whose row or column reference does not change when a formula is copied.

N

Navigation buttons First, last, previous, and next buttons used to navigate between database records.

Newspaper-style columns Vertical, side-by-side columns of text in a Word document where the text first fills the left-most column before filling the next column to the right.

Notes master The layout used to control the format of presentation speaker notes pages.

O

Object Information from one file placed in another file.

One-to-many relationship The type of relationship in which there is only one record in the primary database table linking to one or more records in the related database table.

Outline view A Word document view in which heading paragraphs can be promoted or demoted to different outline levels.

Outlook folder A folder in which specific Outlook items are stored.

P

Page break The break between pages in a multi-page Word document caused when the current page is filled with text.

Page Footer section The section of a database report in Design view used for information that appears at the bottom of each page, such as the page number.

Page Header section The section of a database report in Design view used for information that appears at the top of each page, such as column labels.

Paragraph style A Word document style containing multiple paragraph formats such as line spacing, indenting, and alignment.

Picture An image file inserted in a Word document, Excel worksheet, or PowerPoint presentation to add interest and excitement.

Placeholder A container for text and other objects on a slide.

Preparer's initials The initials of a letter's creator.

Primary key A field with unique values that identifies each record in a database table.

Primary table A database table in which the link field is its primary key.

Print area A specified range of worksheet cells to print.

Q

Query A request for information based on specific criteria or an action performed on data in a database.

R

Range A group of worksheet cells identified by their top left and bottom right cell reference.

Record An entry in a database table that spans a row.

Record selector A small button to the left of a specific record in a database table used to select the entire record.

Referential integrity The inability to delete a record in a primary database table without first deleting the relationship to its related database table.

Related table A database table in which the link field is not its primary key.

Relative cell reference A worksheet cell reference that can change when a formula is copied.

Report A database object that presents information from an underlying table or query in printed form.

Report Footer section The section of a database report in Design view that usually contains report totals.

Report Header section The section of a database report in Design view used for the report's title.

Report Wizard A step-by-step process in which the underlying tables or queries, appropriate fields, grouping and sorting criteria, layout, and style criteria for a database report are selected.

Return address The envelope sender's address.

Return address label A mailing label that contains the sender's return address.

Right tab stop A text alignment that aligns numbers or text from the right.

Rows The horizontal organization of a worksheet, datasheet, or table.

S

Salutation Standard letter introduction text such as *Dear*.

Select query The most common type of query, which gets data from one or more underlying database tables using specified criteria and then displays that data in a datasheet.

Slide layout The format of a slide that controls the way text, pictures, charts, and other objects are positioned.

Slide master The layout that can control the formatting of all slides (except the title slide) including font, font size, bullet graphics, headers and footers, and other slide elements.

Small caps A Word document format that places all text in uppercase with the first letter of a word slightly larger than the remaining letters.

Source file An embedded or linked object's original file.

Speaker notes pages Printed pages that contain a picture of a slide, header and footer placeholders, and a text box in which text notes are keyed.

Strikethrough A Word document format that draws a line through text to indicate it should be deleted.

Style A collection of formatting components saved with a Word document or document template using a unique name.

Subscript A Word document format that places text slightly below a line of normal printed text.

Superscript A Word document format that places text slightly above a line of normal printed text.

Synonym A word with the same or similar meaning as another word.

T

Tab formatting mark A nonprinting character inserted in a Word document by pressing the Tab key.

Tab leader line A dashed, dotted, or solid line that fills the space to the left of a tab stop in a Word document.

Tab stops Text alignment icons inserted on the Word horizontal ruler to indicate where text should align.

Table A grid organized into rows and columns. Also, a database object that contains the data.

Table AutoFormat A table style that contains column width, border, shading, font, and other formats that can be applied to a Word table and its contents.

Table Wizard A step-by-step process for creating a database table based on a table template containing predefined fields.

Tabular report A database report in which each record's data is printed horizontally across the page.

Target document The Word document chosen for comparison in a merge document process.

Template A Word model document that already contains formatting and boilerplate text.

Thesaurus A Word feature that enables the replacement of a selected word with another word of similar meaning.

Title slide master The layout that controls the formatting on title slides.

Transition effects Special motion effects used to introduce a slide during a slide show.

U

Unattended mode A slide show in which the slides advance automatically.

Unbound control A control that does not take its value from an underlying database table or query.

Update query An action query used to change records.

V

Views Different ways to display the contents of an Outlook folder.

W

Web page A document that contains text and pictures and is linked to other documents.

WordArt A specially formatted text object you can add to a slide, document, or worksheet to make it more attractive.

Workbook An Excel file that can contain one or more worksheets.

Worksheet A document created in the Excel application used to analyze numerical data.

Writer's name The name of a letter's author.

Writer's title A letter author's title.